PTO x2

Finance for The
Developing Countries

A WILEY SERIES ON
PUBLIC ADMINISTRATION IN DEVELOPING COUNTRIES

FINANCING REGIONAL GOVERNMENT

International Practices and their Relevance to the Third World

By K. J. Davey: University of Birmingham

LOCAL GOVERNMENT STUDIES IN THE THIRD WORLD

The Experience of Tropical Africa

Edited by P. Mawhood: University of Birmingham

MANAGEMENT OF PASTORAL DEVELOPMENT IN THE THIRD WORLD

By Stephen Sandford: Overseas Development Institute

AN INTRODUCTION TO DEVELOPMENT PLANNING IN THE THIRD WORLD

By Diana Conyers: University of Nottingham
and
Peter Hills: University of Hong Kong

QUANTITATIVE METHODS FOR PUBLIC ADMINISTRATION IN DEVELOPING COUNTRIES

By Scott C. Iverson: University of Washington

FINANCE FOR THE DEVELOPING COUNTRIES

By Richard L. Kitchen: University of Bradford

Finance for The Developing Countries

Richard L. Kitchen
*Project Planning Centre
for Developing Countries,
University of Bradford*

Chichester · apore

Library of Congress Cataloging-in-Publication Data:

Kitchen, Richard L.
    Finance for the developing countries.

    Bibliography: p.
    Includes indexes.
    1. Finance—Developing countries. 2. Economic
development—Finance. I. Title.
HG195.K58   1986   332'.09172'4   85–32331

ISBN 0 471 90945 9

British Library Cataloguing in Publication Data:

Kitchen, R. L.
    Finance for the developing countries.
    1. Finance—Developing countries
    I. Title
    332'.09172'4   HG195

 ISBN 0 471 90945 9

Printed and bound in Great Britain

Contents

Introduction

This book is concerned with the financing of development at both the macro- and micro-levels. Given the fungibility of finance the two levels cannot readily be separated, but micro-, or project-level finance generally tends to be subservient to macro-financial considerations. At the macro-level government monetary and fiscal policies generally determine the terms and availability of finance for projects. In addition, savings (or available finance) is given as national income less consumption; any 'gap' between savings and investment is identical to a trade gap between exports and imports. Both need to be financed by capital inflows from abroad. The prevalence of the recipient government guarantee in external financing means that project risk is often subservient to country risk. However good a project looks, it will have difficulty in attracting foreign finance if the country's financial position is not perceived to be sound.[1]

Such a view is certainly not unanimously subscribed to. An oft-repeated remark is that development depends on the identification of 'good' projects, and well-prepared feasibility studies of 'good' projects will enable finance to be found readily. In other words, there is never a shortage of finance for developing countries, only a shortage of well-prepared 'bankable' projects. This view has frequently been aired by diplomats and bankers involved in North–South discussions, but suffers from two other weaknesses as well as the 'country risk' argument. First, it ignores constraints which may impinge on the financing institutions, notably that banks' capital/asset ratios may be low, and that they (and other agencies) may face a constraint in the borrower's debt/equity ratio. Secondly, it ignores the point that the quality of a project depends upon the terms of financing, notably the interest rate and the maturity, and risk. The acceptability of a project depends, therefore, upon the rate of return being above the risk-adjusted discount rate. If the interest rate rises, a project may move from being above the cut-off line to below the cut-off line. Liquidity is a second crucial test for project acceptability. A shortening of maturity may easily turn a 'liquid' project into an 'illiquid' one. There might have been times in the 1970s when the financial markets were extremely liquid that there was more finance available than projects to finance. However, this cannot be said to be generally the case, and the international financial conditions of the early 1980s serve as a sharp reminder that funds are not always available in abundance.

The term 'finance' itself merits some explanation. *The Dictionary of Modern Economics*[2] gives the following definition:

Finance Narrowly interpreted it signifies *capital* in monetary form, that is in the form of funds lent or borrowed, normally for capital purposes, through financial markets or institutions. But in common parlance the term is applied to funds from almost any source, used to undertake any kind of expenditure.

Finance should be distinguished from money. The latter is a particular type of financial asset which is generally accepted in exchange. Other financial assets cannot generally be used in this sense, although many are readily marketable, and can therefore be exchanged for money. The basic definition of money (M1), is currency plus current account bank deposits. These short-term assets form only a part of the financial markets discussed here. With 'finance' we are mainly concerned with longer-term instruments of assets and liabilities, whereas monetary instruments are short-term. This befits one of the preoccupations of the book, the financing of projects, which requires long-term finance. However, as the definition of money is broadened to include time deposits, savings deposits, and other assets, it embraces instruments which increasingly overlap with what is meant here by 'finance'. The book is not only concerned with financial instruments (apart from money M1), but equally with the institutions and markets which mobilize them.

The perception of the need for this book grew from two independent sources.[3] First, my experience of teaching development finance on the M.Sc. course and on post-experience courses at the Project Planning Centre convinced me that there was a need for a single book which covered the ground. Secondly, working on industrial financing with UNIDO has shown me that there is a need to present an overall picture of development finance to civil servants, politicians, and diplomats, and for financial professionals such as development bankers, as well as to students. The book is aimed, therefore, both at students and professional readers. I have attempted to blend together financial theory and knowledge of workings of financial markets and institutions, in order to try to show the relevance of one to the other.

This book does not, generally, attempt to be prescriptive. The wide variations included under the overworked term 'developing countries' prohibit generalized prescriptions. Each government and organization will have its own policy objectives which will largely determine its financial strategy. Therefore prescription, especially by a north European, would be presumptuous. However, I have not let that inhibit me from drawing my own general conclusions from the analysis; a book without some views would be very dull. My conclusions generally lead me to favour the development of money and capital markets, with regulation and supervision but with limited controls. I prefer the use of government revenue and company equity capital, rather than debt, especially foreign debt. I favour the increased securitization of debt, both domestic and foreign. I incline towards a policy of moving towards financial independence rather than dependence on foreign aid and debt. I would tend to support the growth of the private sector (and privatization) rather than government dominance of the economy. However, whether I would keep all my general inclinations when faced with a specific country would depend considerably on the social, economic, and political conditions prevailing in that country.

Although some 80% of investment in developing countries is financed by national savings, domestic financing does not occupy 80% of this book. The financial markets and institutions in developing countries vary considerably from country to country, which limits the extent to which one can discuss them in aggregate, or at a certain level of generalization. However, these countries all face the same international markets and institutions, and therefore they all face broadly similar conditions in external financing. As international financing is therefore a subject which finds a common interest among most developing country readers, and also in non-developing countries, I have given it a prominence beyond its quantitative significance in financing economic development.

The first three chapters of the book are concerned with basic principles and theory. The theory relates largely to domestic capital markets, but some capital market theory relates also to international finance. The two themes of capital market theory and financial repression will recur throughout the book. Chapters 4–6 are concerned with the mobilization of domestic finance, and Chapters 7–9 with external financing. Chapter 10 is concerned specifically with project financing, while Chapter 11 considers a number of the recent proposals to improve development financing. The broad scope of the book inevitably means that some subjects are treated superficially, but I hope that provision of ample references will help the dissatisfied reader to deepen his knowledge elsewhere.

The increasing pace of events in world financial markets means that a few aspects of the book will have already been overtaken by events before it is on the bookshelves. The integration of the major securities markets of the world suggests that the benefits of international diversification may be diminishing. It remains to be seen to what extent third world debt and equity markets become caught up in the present rush for change. Also, the recent sharp decline in oil prices and interest rates up to April 1986, suggests a significant shift in the supply for demand for funds in international financial markets, and changing prospects for several debtor countries and creditor banks. The more optimistic prospects for growth in the North may also help developing country exports, and thereby relieve the strain caused by debt services requirements.

Inevitably in a work such as this I have drawn extensively on the research results of others, and it is to them that I own my main debt. I am also indebted to many people working in the field who over the years have taught me a great deal. Mention of selected individuals tends to be invidious, and I certainly do not wish to embarrass them by association with my errors and naive judgements. However, as a minimum I should mention Vic Richardson of UNIDO, and formerly of Bradford University, who kindled my interest in development finance, and over the years helped it to grow. Dr Nicholas Bruck of EDI, the World Bank, and Professors John Hunter (Michigan State University), Donald Lessard (MIT) and John Samuels (Birmingham University) commented helpfully on my initial outline. Thanks, too, to Professor Samuels for reading and commenting helpfully on a rather scrappy draft. They are not responsible, though, for the errors. I owe a great deal too to the library staff at the Project Planning Centre—Sheila Allcock, Carole Scanlon, and Jill Allsop—who have cheerfully handled my frequent requests for obscure and imprecise references; to the secretarial staff at the Project Planning Centre, notably Jean Hill, Elizabeth Dada, and Sue Mackrill, who with equal cheerfulness typed and reproduced the manuscripts; and to Michael Coombes, Irene Cooper, Wendy Hudlass, John Carden and Jane Miller of John Wiley who have guided this book into its final form. Finally, thanks are due to my wife and children for continued encouragement and curiosity.

NOTES

1. A UNIDO Consultation Meeting on Industrial Financing concluded that 'it is recognised that projects that are entirely viable on their own may be denied financing because they are located in countries with serious balance of payments problems. In such cases the assessment of country risk is at variance with project risk.' (Report on the First Consultation on Industrial Financing, Madrid, Spain, 18–22 October 1982).
2. *The Dictionary of Modern Economics*, ed. D. W. Pearce, Macmillan Reference Books, 1981.
3. Although the book is about finance, profit was not one of these perceived needs. I am reminded of Byron's couplet:
   'Oh Amos Cottle, for a moment think,
   What meagre profits spread from pen and ink'
   (Lord Byron, *English Bards and Scottish Reviewers*).

Abbreviations

AfDB	African Development Bank
AsDB	Asian Development Bank
BIS	Bank for International Settlements.
CAPM	Capital asset pricing model.
CCCE	Caisse Centrale de Coopération Economique.
CDC	Commonwealth Development Corporation.
CMEA	Council for Mutual Economic Assistance.
CMT	Capital market theory.
DAC	Development Assistance Committee.
DFC	Development finance company.
DFI	Direct foreign investment.
EEC	European Economic Community
EIB	European Investment Bank
FAO	Food and Agricultural Organization (of the United Nations).
FIR	Financial interrelation ratio.
GAB	General arrangement to borrow.
GDP	Gross domestic product.
GNP	Gross national product.
IDB	Inter-American Development Bank.
IBRD	International Bank for Reconstruction and Development.
IDA	International Development Agency.
IFAD	International Fund for Agricultural Development.
IFC	International Finance Corporation.
IFS	*International Financial Statistics.*
IMF	International Monetary Fund.
IRR	Internal rate of return.
ITC	International tax comparison.
KfW	Kreditanstalt für Wiederaufbau.
LIBOR	London inter-bank offer rate.
MDI	Multilateral development institution.

MM	Modigliani and Miller.
NIC	Newly industrialized country.
ODA	Official development assistance.
OECD	Organization for Economic Cooperation and Development.
OPEC	Organization of Petroleum Exporting Countries.
RADR	Risk-adjusted discount rate.
SCBA	Social cost–benefit analysis.
SDR	Special drawing right.
SSE	Small-scale enterprise.
TNC	Transnational corporation.
UN	United Nations.
UNCTAD	United Nations Conference on Trade and Development.
UNCTC	United Nations Commission on Transnational Corporations.
UNESCO	United Nations Educational, Scientific, and Cultural Organization.
UNIDO	United Nations Industrial Development Organization.
VAT	Value-added tax.

Chapter 1

The Basic Principles of Development Finance

1. INTRODUCTION

For any appreciation of finance it is important for the reader to have a grasp of the basic principles. These are few in number, but do not always lend themselves to succinct definitions, which perhaps is why the definitions which appear in glossaries and dictionaries of terms do not give a full understanding. Therefore the first chapter is given over to describing these principles. For greater clarity of exposition they are divided into three groups: concepts, financial processes, and the mechanisms which apply the concepts and undertake the processes.

The basic *concepts* of finance to be considered are:

— Risk
— Return
— Security

The basic financial *processes* of importance are:

— Mobilization
— Intermediation
— Maturity transformation
— Risk transfer
— Financial deepening and financial repression

The financial *mechanisms* are:

— Institutions
— Instruments
— Markets

It is immediately clear that there exists some degree of overlap between these three categories, and also some close interrelations between some of

1

the items (for example, between risk and risk transfer). Essentially, the *mechanisms* can be seen as carrying out the *processes*, in accordance with the basic guiding *concepts*.

2. THE BASIC CONCEPTS

(a) Risk

The financial concept of risk does not always coincide with the conventional economic concept. The latter was laid down originally by F.H. Knight (1921), who distinguished between 'risk' and 'uncertainty'. Risk, he stated, is what we have when probability estimates can be attached to the range of possible outcomes. Thus the probability of a certain rainfall can be estimated on the basis of accumulated historical data, and the risk of flood or drought assessed quantitatively. Likewise, in life insurance, actuarial tables can be drawn up, on the basis of historical data, to assess the life expectancy of individuals. On the other hand Knight described uncertainty as a state in which probability estimates cannot be attached to outcomes. This arises when historical data are not available or, if available, bear little relation to future events. If we can make ex-ante measures of risk and extrapolate them reasonably into the future, then we have measurable 'risk'. When we cannot make ex-ante measures, or, more likely, we cannot extrapolate them into the future with any confidence, then we have the unmeasurable 'uncertainty'. In finance, much of the risk really seems to be of the 'uncertainty' type, for although measures (or proxy measures) of ex-ante risk can be derived, their projection into the future appears to be a questionable exercise. On the other hand, even when numerical measures of risk are not available, we can frequently perceive that risk A is greater (or less) than risk B. It may therefore be possible to rank financial risks, even though we cannot realistically attempt to place numerical values on them.

Some numerical indicators of financial risk do exist, though. It is traditional for lending institutions to charge higher interest rates on what they perceive to be higher-risk loans, or to lend for shorter periods. The difference in interest rates between two loans, or the difference in maturities, may be interpreted as measures of the relative riskiness of the two loans. On stock markets, differences in gross yields may sometimes be interpreted as indications of differences in the risk of buying the respective shares; the higher the yield, the higher the risk. The same applies on the international bond markets. In the Eurocurrency markets, with sovereign lending, the higher the perceived risk, the higher the 'spread', i.e. the premium on the interest rate over LIBOR (London inter-bank offer rate) or some other base rate. However, these measures of perceived risk are ex-ante measures, and the ex-post outcome is frequently rather different. The differences between 'high-risk' terms and 'low-risk' terms are often rather small, and in the Eurocurrency market, for example, have sometimes tended to reflect competitive pressures to lend rather than perceived differences in the relative risks of different loans.

For our purpose the most important attempts to measure risk are associated with capital market theory (CMT), also known as modern portfolio theory. The measures are concerned with fluctuations of share prices, which represent the value of capital assets. The first measure used is the average sensitivity of the prices of individual shares to overall stock market fluctuations (market risk). This is the β coefficient. A share with a β coefficient of 1 moves in line with the market index; if $\beta > 1$, then it moves more than the market index; if $\beta < 1$, it moves less than the market index. The higher the β value, the higher the risk associated with the share.

Secondly, an individual share can depart from its average β value from time to time because of company-specific factors. This is known as specific risk, which tells us the change in share price which is not explained by the change in the market index. Both these measures of risk are based on ex-ante historical data, and the confidence with which they can be extrapolated into the future is, of course, variable. CMT uses standard deviation (or variance) as a measure of risk. Although statistically convenient, this is only one possible measure, and perhaps only a proxy measure. We will return to CMT and its relevance to development finance at greater length in Chapter 2.

The principle of risk diversification, or of taking on more than one risk in order to reduce overall risk, will be encountered frequently throughout this book. Although it is derived from CMT, it has widespread applications to a variety of financial institutions, instruments, and markets. As we will show, it applies not only to stock market investment, the immediate application of CMT, but to many types of development finance, and to developing country institutions also.

A further consideration is that a supplier of finance is generally faced with a combination of risks. In some cases the risks may be separable, so, for example, an equity investor may distinguish between specific risk and market risk. Other combinations of risk may be much more difficult to disaggregate. A foreign direct investment, for example, faces business risk, country risk and foreign exchange risk, all of which are closely related. Nonetheless, it is always desirable to try to separate the risks, and to try to obtain at least some sort of ex-ante measures in order to try to assess the future risks. At worst, even a conceptual separation helps to clarify the risks being faced.

(b) Different Types of Risk

So far we have aggregated all the relevant risks with which an actor in a financial system is faced. A useful starting point in the process of disaggregation is Archer and D'Ambrosio (1972, pp. 419–429). They identify a number of different risks faced by capital suppliers (business risk; financial risk; purchasing power risk; money or interest rate risk; market risk). Capi-

4

tal market theory defines market (or systematic) risk, and specific (or unsystematic) risk. To these can be added two further important risks, from our point of view, project risk and country risk. The notion of moral hazard embodies a different, but still important, type of risk. Capital receivers also face risks, in addition to business risk, notably interest rate risk and exchange rate risk. Some of these risks are closely related, and some indeed overlap.[1]

Business Risk

Business risk, whether viewed from the capital supplier (lenders or equity-holders) or capital receivers (a sponsor or business, and its management) embraces all the risks faced in operating a firm or a project and manifests itself in variability in the return received on its assets. Such risks include variability in costs, sales volume, price, competition from other products, technical obsolescence, strikes, disruption of supplies, fire, etc. All these factors can affect the profitability of the business, and therefore represent risks to capital suppliers.

Financial Risk

Financial risk (in a specific sense rather than the general sense in which we used it earlier), relates to the type of financial asset employed in the capital structure of a business. One can draw up hierarchies of financial asset, in order of risk. However, it is necessary to distinguish between the risks faced in operation and the risk faced in the event of failure. In operation, profits can be used to pay, in order of priority:

— interest on secured loans;
— interest on unsecured loans;
— dividends on preference shares;
— dividends on equity.

Thus in terms of return, secured loans are less risky than unsecured loans, which in turn are less risky than equity.

When faced with business failure, what is important is the order in which various claimants, and their claims, are paid out. In general, this is as follows:

— the receiver or liquidator;
— certain preferred creditors (tax authorities, employees);
— secured creditors (secured long-term and trade credits, and debentures which hold a fixed charge over certain assets);
— holders of floating charges over assets (secured loans or debentures);
— unsecured creditors (unsecured loans, trade creditors);
— holders of unsecured preference shares and loan stock, including most convertibles;
— ordinary shareholders (equity).

Thus the hierarchy again is in ascending order of risk. However the order is not the same as for operating risk, in that interest on loans (whether secured or not) in the latter case is paid out before the dividends on (usually secured) debentures. Generally speaking, the hierarchy of risk is the same as the hierarchy of rates of return on the assets—the higher the risk, the higher the rate of return required.

The capital structure of an enterprise determines the degree of financial risk. An enterprise which is highly geared (leveraged is the American term) may find that a fairly small percentage change in its trading profit or in interest rates means that interest charges suddenly absorb all or more of the trading profit. Debt itself becomes a risk. Gearing risk is explored more fully in chapter 10.

Purchasing Power Risk

This refers to the possibility of inflation eroding the purchasing power of the expected return, or of the purchasing power of the assets. The important consideration to the investor is the real rate of return to be obtained, and also the real capital value of the asset (e.g. the real value of a bond or share). A DCF calculation can give us the money value of the expected return, which can then be deflated by the expected rate of inflation, to assess whether or not the asset holder will obtain a positive real rate of return.[2] Of course, estimating purchasing power risk depends upon estimates of future inflation rates, which are very difficult to make accurately.

Money Risk or Interest Rate Risk

This arises from the possiblity that changes in the interest rate will alter the value of an investment. For example, if an investor purchases bonds, and the level of interest rates rises subsequently, then the investor's rate of return will be relatively low, and in addition, the market value of the bond will fall. The reverse is also true. Anyone who borrows at variable interest rates faces the risk that rates will rise, as many developing countries found with Eurocurrency loans in the mid-1970s and early 1980s.

Market Risk

This is a term used in two distinct senses. The first can be called the capital market theory sense, in which the market (or systematic) risk of a security is measured by the sensitivity of the share price to changes in the market index (the β coefficient). The second meaning, and one which may have more applicability in developing countries, relates to the *marketability* of a security. This risk arises when the market in the security is narrow, when the shareholding is large, or when the market is far from perfect. It may then be difficult to sell the security at certain times, or if it is sold, then the seller may be obliged to accept a price which does not fully reflect the value of the underlying assets or their earnings. Most developing countries have underdeveloped capital markets which are far from perfect, and the marketability risk may be common. Development banks, for example, might find their operations constrained because of the difficulty of liquidating shareholdings in client companies if they cannot readily be sold on the market or placed in institutions. (Ironically, development banks are frequently charged with the responsibility of developing the local capital market.)

Specific Risk

Specific risk is the variation which arises in the company's share price as a result of factors specific to that company. Such factors may be changes in its market, its selling price, its raw material cost, a strike, a take-over bid, an improvement in its product, or a host of other factors. These factors, however, do not influence the market generally, but only the individual company. Clearly there is a substantial overlap between the factors which determine business risk and specific risk.

Project Risk

In the pure sense of the term, project risk arises when pure project finance is used. When a lender provides debt or equity finance which can be serviced only out of the project's income, and which is secured only against the assets of the project, then he is entirely dependent upon the success of the project. He has no recourse to any security outside the project. Although pure project finance may be comparatively rare, the notion, and the associated notion of project risk, is an important starting point when arranging the financing of a project. Of course, when any external guarantee or security is provided, the focus of the risk changes to the guarantor or the security. For example, when finance for a project is guaranteed by the government, the lender is faced with country risk rather than project risk.

Country Risk

This lies at the other end of the spectrum from project risk, and arises when finance is supplied to a foreign country. Although the most familiar form of country risk is that faced by international banks lending to states or to state-guaranteed bodies, it also arises with lending to the private sector, and with direct foreign investment. The main risk faced is that of default (or the euphemistic 'rescheduling') by the state, or failure by private sector borrowers, but country risk really reflects the underlying conditions of which default and failure are only the symptoms. These underlying conditions include problems such as economic mismanagement leading to balance of payments or government budget difficulties; world economic recession; deterioration in the terms of trade, the political risk of government expro- priation of assets; repudiation of debt; the imposition of exchange controls; the possibility of natural disaster such as famine, drought, and crop failure and the consequent economic problems; and the man-made disaster of war.

In recent years lending banks have attempted to measure country risk. Generally speaking, this involves identifying a set of country risk factors (e.g. political risk, balance of payments risk as indicated by the debt service ratio or forecasts, vulnerability to natural disaster, and dependence on indi- vidual export commodites. A number of macroeconomic indicators may also be used. These and other indicators may then have weights or probabilities attached to them (often subjective), and an overall figure for country risk is arrived at (Goodman, 1977). To an outsider these attempts at putting numeri- cal values on country risk do not appear to have been very successful, and in numerous cases recently (Poland, Mexico, Brazil) banks have found themselves relying on the beguiling notion that states cannot default, or if they can then western governments and international institutions will not let them. Nonetheless, the belief in country risk assessment persists, and Irving Friedman (1981) wrote 'As banks improve their credit and country risk assessment systems, I believe that they will increasingly learn that loan losses in developing countries are not likely to be higher, and more likely to be lower than in developed countries.' Although one must discount to some extent the optimism of such statements from exposed bankers, it nonetheless indicates a continuing faith in country risk assessments in spite of the dangers evident in 1981, and the subsequent shocks received in 1982 and 1983. As we show in Chapter 9, capital market theory can make a significant con- tribution to a bank's country risk analysis.

The shortcomings of the most popular simple measure, the debt service ratio (annual interest and principal payments to export receipts) have been discussed by Nagy (1976). He concludes that it can be applied only to the middle-income developing countries, can only be used for short-term assessments, and needs great care in interpretation. Goodman (1977) looked at the procedures used by 37 US banks and concluded that 'most of them are unhappy about their risk evaluation methods and seek new ones'. Blask (1978) reviewed seven checklist systems developed by banks and generally found them to be inadequate. On the other hand, banks have tended to shy away from sophisticated quantitative methods, such as econometric models, which are expensive to develop and may be no better anyway. The journal *Euromoney* produces ex-post rankings of country creditworthiness, based on the terms of published loans. Such lists, and the indices derived from the data, are attempts to show how bankers had assessed relative country risks. However, the differences in the terms intuitively appear slight compared to the differences in the risks. Towards the end of 1981, according to *The Economist*, 'bankers . . . were queuing up to lend to third-world Mexico at rates only $\frac{1}{4}$% over their loans to Western Europe' (*The Economist*, 11

December 1982). Such a small difference in spreads can hardly be explained by bankers' perception of the relative risks (unless their perception was rather poor in this case). Rather, it more likely indicates the competitive pressures to lend which the banks found themselves under. As we see in Chapter 8, nineteenth-century developing country bonds carried much greater interest rate differentials.

Exchange Rate Risk

Any party holding a financial asset or liability in a foreign currency potentially faces a foreign exchange risk. The risk is that with a foreign exchange asset, the foreign currency may depreciate relative to the holder's own currency. Conversely, someone with a foreign exchange liability runs the risk that the foreign currency will appreciate relative to his own. In international financing the possibility and extent of exchange rate risk may be very considerable. However, for both borrowers and lenders the possibility usually exists of passing the risk to someone else, often the other party. As an example, the World Bank borrows a variety of currencies on the international markets. It then on-lends these currencies to client states in loans denominated in US dollars. However, the loans may actually be made in a mixture of other currencies and the borrowing country has to repay the loans in the currencies received. In some cases the recipient government passes on the loan together with the attached foreign exchange risks to the country's development bank. The bank, on its larger loans at least, may then pass the exchange rate risk on to its clients, and attempt to use the foreign exchange forward markets to cover any remaining uncovered risks.

Hedging on options and forward currency markets can cover short-term risks. Essentially, someone with a dollar commercial debt to pay in 3 months' time can buy a forward dollar contract to mature in 3 months' time. He is then protected against any foreign exchange fluctuation. If the dollar strengthens he covers his commercial exposure by a gain on the futures contract. If the dollar declines he covers his loss on the futures contract by his gain on the commercial debt. Until recently, forward exchange contracts have been limited to short-term periods. However, the advent of the financial futures markets in Chicago and London has usefully extended the maturities of contracts and the range of currencies. (This paragraph cannot do justice to financial futures markets and options, but their essentially short-term nature places them largely outside the scope of this book. The interested reader is referred to a specialist work, such as Prindl (1976), which incidentally gives a much fuller account of the whole subject of foreign exchange risk, and how to cover it.)

The principle to follow, then, when faced with exchange rate (or any other) risk is to avoid it (risk avoidance) or make someone else bear it (risk transfer). The risk of exchange rate fluctuations can be avoided by lending only the currencies which one holds, as international banks try to do, for example. A borrower (country, firm, or individual) may be able to avoid risk by contracting a loan in the same currency as used on his main export invoices. For example, a country deriving most of its export earnings from crude oil (priced and invoiced in US dollars), avoids exchange rate risk by borrowing (and repaying) US dollars, rather than, say, DM or yen.

Finally, guarantees sometimes absorb the foreign exchange risk in transactions. Such guarantees are generally provided by governments or government agencies, and appear particularly in export credits. Prindl (1976) refers to Switzerland and Japan, which set up exchange risk guarantee schemes in 1974 and 1975 respectively, mainly for export contracts, and for periods of 2 years and over (thereby providing a facility which the shorter-term financial futures and options markets do not provide).

(c) Return

The putative reward or expected return, is one of the two major raisons d'être for financial transactions. The second is the desire to protect one's financial assets from loss, erosion by inflation, tax, exchange controls, or confiscation. The first motive seeks a return in exchange for postponed consumption, and for accepting risk; generally speaking the higher the perceived risk, the higher the return which is sought. However, this simplistic relationship must be expanded to take into account the maturity of the transaction. Again generalizing, the longer the maturity, the higher the risk is thought to be, everything else being equal. Nonetheless the basic relationship generally holds, and we have already seen under the heading financial risk that financial assets in a company can be graded acccording to risk; the riskier the asset, the higher (in principle) will be the expected rate of return. The second motive, that of protecting financial assets, is essentially a low-risk strategy, in which the rate of return is much less important than the security. Such a strategy would give preference to bank time deposits, or domestic government bonds to be held to maturity, rather than equities or foreign bonds.

Capital market theory embodies the notion of the *risk-free rate of return*. This is commonly taken to be the return available on assets, e.g. government securities such as bonds or treasury deposits, or bank deposits where the former are not readily available. However, the extent to which such financial assets are truly risk-free is restricted. Most government securities are exposed to money risk, that is erosion through inflation. As many investors discovered in the 1970s, the real rate of return on many government securities around the world turned out to be substantially negative. The objection can be overcome by buying index-linked government securities, but they are available in only a handful of countries currently (e.g. Brazil, Israel, the United Kingdom). The second objection lies in the maturity of the bonds. The short-term bond (e.g. 30-day Treasury Bill) is often portrayed in the literature as representing the ideal risk-free investment. However, it is exposed to relative risk. An investor might be able to invest in alternative government securities with 30-day maturity and 2-year maturity, but both offer the same redemption yield. If he buys the 30-day bill he might find after 30 days have elapsed that interest rates have fallen, and he regrets not buying the 2-year bond. Conversely, had he bought the 2-year bond he might find that interest rates rise after 30 days, and he cannot move into a higher-yielding asset wihout a capital loss. Moreover, if he is forced by his financial circumstances to sell his 2-year bond before maturity, he might also face a capital loss. Therefore we can only speak of a risk-free rate of return for index-linked investments, and for a specified time period. Once we introduce the notion of flexible time horizons, or multi-period investments, we can no longer be free of risk. Government bonds may, however, be reasonably regarded as low-risk investments in financially stable countries.

(d) Security

The object of security is to transfer some of the risk associated with a financial claim. A typical case is a bank loan to a manufacturing enterprise, which the bank secures against the fixed and current assets of the enterprise. In the event of the failure of the enterprise the bank will be in a position to take over the assets in question to an extent sufficient to retrieve its loan. Thus, in the event of failure it is the shareholders and unsecured creditors who bear the cost, and the taking of security effectively transfers the risk from the bank to them. However, risk transfer may be only partial, as the bank may not be able to recover all its exposure from the assets, and therefore still bears some risk. Claiming of assets is generally a last resort; a lender will usually attempt to overcome his client's difficulties by other means first. Security may take many forms; apart from a claim over a firm's assets it may consist of personal, corporate, or state guarantees; paper securities; or insurance policies. Moreover, it is only one form of risk transfer, although an important one.

In one sense, preoccupation with security can be seen as contrary to the interests of economic development. A lending institution, such as a development bank, needs to be able to take the risk, to some extent at least, of lending to small businesses and businessmen who, by conventional criteria, do not have sufficient equity capital available, nor do they have adequate security to offer against the required loan. It is just these types of enterprises, however, which a country needs to succeed in order to achieve economic growth, and their financing needs to be viewed as venture capital. High risk it may be, but the rewards can also be high, and development finance institutions in developing countries need to have a venture capital portfolio (or subsidiary), composed of mixtures of equity, unsecured convertible loan stock, and secured loans.

Guarantees are rather different in nature from most forms of conventional security, which offer tangible assets against the risk of failure or default.

With a guarantee the risk is covered only by a promise. The guarantee is only as good as the guarantor, and in itself is no assurance of the guarantor's ability, or even willingness to stump up when called upon to do so. An offer of a guarantee usually needs further investigation before it can be accepted with confidence. Of course, security based on tangible assets can also be elusive. Both physical and paper assets can decline in value; movable assets may disappear (e.g. ships), or the assets may not even exist in the first place. A spectacular example of the latter is provided by the Great Salad Oil Swindle (Miller, 1966), in which the tanks of oil offered as security were almost entirely filled with water. Only the top few inches consisted of oil, but that was sufficient to fool the lender's inspectors!

3. FINANCIAL PROCESSES

(a) Mobilization

This is the process of moving savings from savers of funds to users of funds. In a financially underdeveloped society, savers tend to have little inclination to place funds in financial assets, even if they have access to them. Rather currency will be hoarded, or invested in non-productive assets such as gold. The object of mobilization of savings therefore is to persuade such savers to use their savings productively. In financially backward societies this may be done largely by informal mechanisms such as village-level savings and loan associations, or credit unions. Miracle, Miracle, and Cohen (1980) give an account of several such savings methods in Africa. A further example is the early growth of housing finance societies in the UK, many of which terminated when all the members had purchased a house, but some permanent societies persisted and amalgamated to grow into today's large building society movement. The only alternative to informal savings mobilization may be restricted to direct lending to an investor, in the absence of suitable financial intermediaries. At a more advanced state of financial development, mobilization may be achieved through formal financial intermediaries. In rural societies these will typically be savings schemes of post offices and small (sometimes mobile) branch banks. In more financially sophisticated societies, mobilization may be achieved directly, by investing in government bonds, equities, or other capital market instruments. A frequently employed means of direct mobilization of savings is the lottery, used by governments to raise funds, and by individuals as a means of long-odds gambling. (The UK premium bond scheme, though, is a form of government borrowing, as investors may retrieve their capital at any time. However, it is really a low-risk gamble, as no interest is paid, but substantial prizes can be won.)

(b) Intermediation

The process of intermediation is perhaps the most basic and important of the five financial processes discussed. The process consists of an individual, institution, or market which on the one hand takes in funds, and issues claims against itself, these claims becoming its liabilities. On the other hand it supplies these funds to others, against whom it acquires claims, these claims being its assets. Essentially therefore a financial intermediary acts as a middle man between those who have funds which they do not wish to exchange for goods, and those who do not have funds, but do wish to purchase goods. They provide an *indirect* means of transferring funds from savers to borrowers. (In the conventional jargon, *direct* finance is the case whereby a holder of funds supplies them to a user without an intermediary.)

The process of intermediation combines two vital, and more basic, functions. It provides an opportunity for savers to deposit their savings, and earn a return on them, thereby mobilizing funds which otherwise may be dormant (i.e. hoarded). It also provides a focus in the form of an institution, market, or individual for potential borrowers to address themselves to. Secondly, it should transfer risk from the lenders to the intermediary, and/or to the borrower. Individuals with available savings may be reluctant to invest themselves, or to lend directly, or take equity in a borrower's project. They may not want to take the risk; they may not be able to assess the risk; and they may not know how to protect themselves legally and financially if things go wrong. An intermediary, they feel, takes these risks away from them, and in many cases it transfers them to the borrower by taking security. (Of course, some intermediaries prove to be unworthy of the confidence which savers place in them, and fail—the savers thereby losing their funds.) However, the savers must have had confidence in the intermediary, otherwise, presumably, they would not place these funds with it to start with. This function of risk transfer, or perceived risk transfer, is sometimes overlooked in descriptions of intermediation, but it is of course a necessary condition for the first function, that of mobilization. Intermediaries cannot mobilize funds unless savers have confidence in them. The confidence may be misplaced, and savers may greedily ignore warning signs such as the offer of unusually high rates of return; nonetheless it must be there.

The theory of intermediation rests on the relationship between savers and investors. In a completely undeveloped financial sector there will be no transfer of savings from one investor to another. Only savers will be able to invest, and only to the extent that they can save. Effectively this may mean that many who want to make physical investments cannot do so, while many who could invest do not wish to, thus investable resources are not utilized efficiently, and savers who do not wish to invest have no incentive to save.

The theory of intermediation is basic to the theory of financial repression, and is dicussed in more detail in Chapter 3. It also leads to the argument that financial development is a necessary condition for economic growth, which is also examined in Chapter 3.

(c) Maturity Transformation

A further important process performed by financial institutions is the trans-formation of short-term financial instruments into long-term financial instru-ments. This process, known as maturity transformation, is particularly important in the provision of long-term, or project, finance. It can be done by two main methods. The first is quite simply the acceptance of short-term deposits which are used for longer-term lending. The danger of 'borrowing short and lending long' is that depositors are able to draw out their funds at short notice, and may try to do so, while the institution would not be able to recover them at similar short notice from its clients. It relies therefore on the assumption that the proportion of deposits held as short-term funds will be adequate to meet expected withdrawal requirements, assuming that depositors continue to have confidence in the institution. (The holding of insufficient short-term funds will in itself be a reason for lack of confidence.) In general, if depositors feel that they can get their funds back immediately, they will not attempt to do so. This is one secret of the practice of borrowing short and lending long. The other secret lies in the use of the law of large numbers. If an institution has a large number of small depositors it reduces the risk of a sudden upsurge in withdrawals, compared with an institution which has a smaller number of large depositors. In other words it smoothes the fluctuations in withdrawals. Likewise, a large number of small borrowers means that the failure of one or two borrowers will not undermine public confidence in the institution. These two 'secrets' apparently lie behind one of the more striking success stories of borrowing short and lending long, the British building societies (housing finance societies). For many years they have taken deposits withdrawable at 7 days notice (and usually in practice on request), and lent for house purchase, typically repayable over 15–25 years. Cases of failure have been very few, and due usually to corrupt or inefficient management, rather than to the practice of borrowing short and lending long. Occasional crises of confidence have arisen, for example the Derby Building Society experienced a crisis of confidence among depositers following the collapse of Rolls Royce in Derby in 1970. Large numbers of redundancies were expected, to be followed by a call on savings deposited in the building society. Rumour started that the Derby Building Society would be unable to meet a sudden upsurge in withdrawals; investors therefore wanted to withdraw immediately, queues formed at the doors, and the building society was forced to close them. However, it was able to raise short-term funds rapidly from other building societies, announced that it had done so, opened its doors once more, and the queues went away, content that the money was there.

The other striking recent case of successfully borrowing short and lending long is in international banking lending, or the Eurocurrency market. Here the majority of funds are deposited for 6 months or less but most lending is medium term (up to 10, 12, or even 15 years) and individual loans are large. However, in this case banks have relatively small numbers of large depositors, and superficially are much more vulnerable to withdrawals. The stabilization mechanism appears to be the large amount of inter-bank lending, used by banks to balance their books. Moreover, the practice of syndicating loans means that an individual bank usually has a small exposure to any one loan. Although the visible regulatory mechanisms are limited, the visible hiccups have been few.

(d) Risk Transfer

In any investment, whether in financial assets or physical assets, risk is involved. The question of who bears the risk is important, not just in the obvious sense of an individual's or institution's exposure, but in the sense that the apportionment of risk plays an important part in the mobilization of funds and in the provision of funds for investment. In the process of putting together financial packages for a project the division of risks and returns between the parties involved is a delicate and necessary procedure, but one that is not often explicit. The simplest way of passing the risk on to someone else is simply to be in a sufficiently strong position to be able to refuse to accept it. An importer, for example, may be able to insist that the contract is denominated in his own currency. Other types of contract (e.g. Eurocurrency loans) may give the borrower the right to switch the currency of the loan at stated intervals (e.g. every 3 or 6 months), thereby giving him the opportunity to make gains (or inflict losses on himself) from exchange rate fluctuations. However, the risk is still there.

Risk may be transferred or apportioned by two main methods, namely the taking of some form of security or guarantee, or by the choice of financial instrument. The first process has already been adequately described, but the second merits a few words. A financing agency, for example a development bank, may take equity or loan in a project or a combination of the two. Equity cannot be secured, but loan finance usually can. Even if it cannot, it qualifies for payout ahead of equity in the event of project failure. Therefore the higher the proportion of its allocated funds which the development bank puts in as loan, the more it apportions risk to the other shareholders. The process is limited, though, to the extent that the loan is covered by security. Beyond that point any additional loan is at risk.

(e) Financial Deepening and Financial Repression

I am indebted to Shaw (1973) and McKinnon (1973) for these macroeconomic concepts. Financial deepening means 'the accumulation of financial assets at a pace faster than accumulation of non-financial wealth' (Shaw, 1973, p. vii). Shaw's argument is that the development of financial markets and institutions is a necessary condition for economic growth, and that developing countries typically suffer from a condition of financial repression which keeps finance 'shallow' and restricts economic growth. Financial repression is characterized principally by controls on interest rates (either by government or oligopolistic institutions). Private financial savings tend to be invested in non-financial assets such as gold or land; capital movements are controlled and the exchange rate over-valued; there is an insufficient development (or absence) of financial institutions, such as insurance companies and pensions funds, and money and capital markets are restricted. Many of these controls are government-imposed, and effectively limit entry to markets. The theory is essentially monetary, in that it is based on the belief that the money supply, its real value and real cost (i.e. real interest rates) do matter in the process of economic growth. Its policy implications would lead to the *liberalization* of financial markets, particularly the liberalization of interest rates.

In many developing countries interest rates in the formal financial sector are held at artificially low rates, thereby discouraging the growth of financial assets (savings). However, low interest rates also encourage the desire to borrow, and in the formal sector a gap develops between the supply of funds and the demand for funds. Therefore borrowing has to be restricted, and many, especially those without much security, find difficulty in borrowing. Investment may then be made in secure, low-yield projects, and many promising projects in newly developing, high-growth and high-yielding sectors may not have access to investment funds.[3] Therefore new investment in aggregate is restricted; moreover it is not directed effectively (that is allocated to the higher-yielding projects). By way of compensation, informal or kerb markets develop (or expand), but these tend to be short term in nature, and do not make long-term investment funds available. Moreover, informal sector money lenders may find it hard to attract deposits, except at very high interest rates, as they are regarded by savers as risky. They may also suffer from official discouragement or outright prohibition, especially in foreign exchange dealing. The consequence is that their lending rates tend to be very high, and discourage all borrowing except that of desperation.

The argument is that liberalization of the financial sector will remove the controls and constraints associated with financial repression, and thereby encourage saving, investment (and more efficient investment), and economic growth. Interest rates become the principal targets of the proponents of liberalization, and Galbis (1977) has shown theoretically that high real interest rates are growth-promoting because they improve the quality of investment, even if real savings are not sensitive to the interest rate. The theory of financial repression, though, is generally based on the intermediation process described earlier. Since the pioneering works of Shaw and McKinnon, many different formalized models of financially repressed economies have been developed, and are conveniently and clearly summarized in Fry (1982). The subject will be taken up in more detail in Chapter 3, but for the moment it is sufficient to note that in some countries financial repression may well restrict economic growth. (However, it is also relevant to point out that fully developed financial markets may lead to a preference by savers for financial investments rather than physical investments, especially if real interest rates are high, and government borrowing strong. Financial instruments then offer surer, and perhaps higher, rates of return than physical investments. This appears to have been the case in Britain and the United States in the late 1970s and early 1980s, and no doubt in other countries as well.)

4. FINANCIAL MECHANISMS

(a) Financial Institutions

From the point of view of developing countries, institutions can be classified in a number of different ways. Obvious distinctions are between local or foreign institutions, between those which provide only short-term finance; those which are publicly owned and those which are privately owned; those which take deposits and those which obtain funds by offering other types of claims, and formal and informal institutions. However, of the financial institutions which are concerned with providing finance in or to developing countries, many tend not to fit neatly into these categories. Moreover, the character of domestic institutions varies from country to country. However, Table 1.1 sets out the general features of financial institutions.

The table covers the majority of finance provided to developing countries by domestic and foreign financial institutions. In addition, of course, one must bear in mind the government's own revenue-raising bodies, notably the internal revenue, customs and excises, and other tax-gathering organizations which account for the large majority of public sector financing in developing countries, as is shown in Chapter 4.

Informal 'Institutions'

The potential importance of savings and loan associations and mobile bankers may be even greater than their actual importance in developing countries. From these embryo organizations we may see the development of truly indigenous formal sector financial institutions. The moneychangers of Jakarta provide an example, with their elegant premises and terms competitive to the established banks. However, the transition from informal to formal institutions can be difficult. Miracle, Miracle, and Cohen (1980) report the case of an informal association in Cameroun which in 1975 became La Banque Unie de Crédit, Cameroun's sixth-largest bank. It apparently closed in 1979 when the government insisted on appointing the bank's director.

Formal institutions tend to be overwhelmingly urban-based, leaving the rural areas and the poorer urban areas to the moneylenders, mobile bankers, and informal savings and loan associations. However, in some countries even the urban middle classes tend to gravitate to the informal sector. I had reports that this was the case in Tehran before the revolution, where families and smaller businesses tend to stick to their long-established association with their moneylender, whereas the banks tended to be a service for larger business. How widespread this was is difficult to assess, and it is even more difficult to say to what extent it applies in other countries. However, Miracle, Miracle, and Cohen (1980, p. 703) state that (in Africa) 'Many studies, and a number of our informants, suggest vaguely that nearly all adults tend to be members of such [savings and loan] associations where they are found.' My own casual enquiries tend to confirm this. The quantitative importance of the informal sector relative to the formal sector is difficult to assess, though, in any country.

(b) Financial Instruments

While financial institutions establish assets and liabilities these are not generally negotiable instruments in that they cannot be used in exchange. Bank deposits, and loans from banks, for example, cannot be sold to another party. However, the concept of negotiable instruments which can be traded is very old, and in economic history tends in some cases to pre-date non-negotiable claims. Before the days of deposit banking, that is, roughly before 1840 in England and 1860 in the USA, banks tended to issue their loans as notes, which were negotiable instruments. The development of deposit banking meant that such notes were replaced by deposits available to the borrower, and therefore a negotiable instrument was replaced by a non-negotiable one. Bills of exchange, of course, substantially pre-date deposit banking. For the most part, negotiable instruments consist of bills, bonds, and equities. They are usually interest- or dividend-bearing (although recent zero-coupon bonds, offering only capital gain for tax purposes, are an interesting exception), and are, in principle, negotiable. Some are redeemable at a specified time or period in the future, such as treasury bills, most bonds, or certificates of deposit. Others are not (e.g. equities, undated bonds). They represent means by which savings can be invested directly rather than through financial intermediaries, and offer savers incentives in the form of interest or dividends, while their marketability ensures liquidity (although there is always a risk of capital loss unless they are held to maturity). From the point of view of the availability of capital, negotiable instruments are often important suppliers of long-term, or project, finance.

The development of negotiable instruments and their associated markets seems to come at a relatively late stage in the financial growth of developing countries. Certainly in most developing countries financial intermediaries appear to precede negotiable instruments and markets. The reasons for this probably are that the factors for establishing organized capital markets are absent in the poorer developing countries. Such markets require substantial numbers of buyers and sellers, and confidence in the instruments being traded, and those trading them. The ready availability of reliable market information (e.g. about prices) is also necessary, as is the willingness of

Table 1.1 General features of financial institutions

Institution	Types and source of funds	Use of funds
Central banks	Deposits from government, gold and foreign exchange holdings, issuing government bonds.	Lending to government; interventions; money market; loans to domestic finance institutions, overseas investment of reserves.
Commercial banks	Deposit-type claims, mainly local currency for local banks, and foreign currencies for international banks.	*British* type—trade and short-term loans; government securities. *European* type—as above, but long-term loan and equity finance. *International*—short-, medium- and long-term Eurocurrency loans.
Building (housing finance) societies	Deposit-type claims, local currency.	Long-term housing loans.
Credit unions, savings and loan associations	Deposit-type claims, local currency.	Consumer loans, both short- and medium-term.
Development banks	Non-deposit-type claims, local and foreign currency.	Medium- and long-term loans and equity investments. Sometimes working capital finance.
Insurance companies	Non-deposit-type claims, mainly local currency.	Investment in government stock, equities and some long-term loans.

investors to take the risks inherent in any financial markets. Nonetheless, it is interesting to note that markets in negotiable instruments in the now industrialized countries in some cases preceded financial intermediation, and that deposit banking, and non-bank financial intermediaries, appeared relatively late on the scene. The investment of savings in intermediaries, of course, now generally involves a lower level of risk (and lower potential gain) than investment in financial instruments, but this was not always the case. Until relatively recently the history of banking has been dotted with frequent and numerous failures, and it was not until after the Bank Charter Act of 1833 that deposit banking really took off in England (but earlier in Scotland). Deposit banking took off even later in the United States, and Galbraith (1975, p. 99) put it in the decade following the tax on state banknote issues of July 1866. The United States is still notable for frequent bank failures, running at over 50 per year recently.

The developing countries, of course, for the most part inherited the banking systems of their colonial powers, or copied them from the more advanced countries. Therefore formal sector banking tended to start with

Table 1.1 General features of financial institutions

Institution	Types and source of funds	Use of funds
Pensions fund	Non-deposit-type claims, local currency.	As insurance companies, with the emphasis on long-term investments.
Regional and international development banks	Non-deposit-type claims from member governments; foreign and international bonds and loans.	Medium- and long-term loans and equity investments.
Export credit agencies	Government or commercial bank funds, non-deposit.	Short- and medium-term trade credits, insurance, and guarantees.
Merchant banks	Own funds; some deposits and loans from other financial institutions and wholesale depositors.	Accepting trade bills; long-term loans and investments (corporate finance); advice; company flotations and financial packaging.
Non-governmental organizations	Private, often charitable contributors.	Technical assistance, budgetary and project finance. Grants for emergency aid and small 'social' projects.
International Monetary Fund, and certain regional monetary funds.	Member governments; SDRs; non-deposit-taking; possibility to borrow.	Short- and medium-term balance of payments finance.

institutions and practices which had been refined by many years of (sometimes bitter) experience. These banks were established initially for trade purposes, and pre-dated financial markets and instruments, and indeed pre-dated the requirement of the formal sector to provide long-term funds for capital investment, which many negotiable instruments provide. In fact, the difference in financial instruments and markets is one of the more striking differences in financial development between developed and developing countries today. At the level of international finance, too, bonds dominated international capital flows in the nineteenth and early twentieth centuries, and it was not until the development of the Eurocurrency market in the past 25 years that international bank lending became imporant.

(c) Financial Markets

The markets are the arrangements which permit financial claims, or instruments, to be traded. Howver, it is important to distinguish between different kinds of markets.

Primary and Secondary Markets

The primary market constitutes the facilities for the initial sale of financial instruments. For example, bonds may be placed with a number of large institutions, which form the 'primary market'. The secondary market, on the other hand, consists of those involved in the subsequent trade in these bonds, and may comprise brokers, banks, companies, and individuals who from time to time trade in the bonds. Likewise, with equity issues, the issuing houses and underwriters make up the primary market, but the stock market, with its buyers and sellers, and brokers, jobbers, and market makers, comprises the secondary market. The existence of a potentially active secondary market is very important for the issue of securities. If no such market is thought to exist, then the amount of paper which can be issued (and therefore the funds to be raised) is limited to the amount which the much narrower primary market is prepared to hold until maturity. In general, an issue may be much larger if a considerable secondary market exists. It should be noted also that the secondary market is not a fixed quantum. The extend to which it is prepared to take up a particular stock or bond issue depends upon its perception of the quality of the issue. The word 'quality' embraces a number of different characteristics, notably the risk involved (especially the risk of default or failure by the issuer) and the expected return.

Money Markets and Capital Markets

A distinction between the two is often made, but is ambiguous in that different meanings are attributed to the terms.The first definition states that money markets are concerned with short-term instruments (less than 1 year maturity, e.g. certificates of deposit), whereas capital markets are concerned with longer-term (over 1 year) instruments. The alternative is to say that money markets are concerned with non-negotiable obligations (regardless of maturity) whereas capital markets are concerned only with negotiable instruments (again, regardless of maturity). Much of the literature on capital market theory seems to embrace both definitions though.

As with financial instruments, financial markets tend to be underdeveloped in the third world. In Africa the only countries with stock markets are Nigeria, Kenya, Morocco, Zimbabwe, Egypt, Ivory Coast, Tunisia, and South Africa, although some of the countries reject stock markets on political grounds. Even Indonesia, a large, liberal, capitalist country, has a stock market with only some 24 stocks quoted since revitalization in 1977, many of which are foreign. By contrast, the smaller Singapore, Hong Kong, Taiwan, and South Korea have very active stock markets. The difference would appear to lie in the secondary market; in Indonesia it is largely absent, but is very active in the four other countries mentioned. Indonesian companies find the lack of a stock market hinders their ability to raise equity capital, especially given the government regulation requiring that 35% of investments should be provided by equity. Likewise development banks find it difficult to sell off shares even of successful client companies, which inhibits their ability to revolve their funds. The problem of equity shortage, especially for industry, tends to be widespread in the third world, and one which better-developed capital markets could help to solve.

Models of Financial Markets

A number of mathematical models of financial markets have been developed. These models are based on assumptions which tend to approximate much more closely to conditions in advanced rather than developing countries. Essentially they assume freely competitive markets, with unrestricted entry; large numbers of borrowers and lenders, and buyers and sellers; a wide range of financial institutions and markets; and a large number of financial instruments with a range of characteristics such as risk and maturity. They also assume perfect access to information (although not perfect foresight), instantaneous transactions, zero transaction costs, and no taxes. They also make a number of assumptions about investor behaviour, which will be discussed further in Chapter 2. The assumptions are generally known as the efficient market hypothesis.

Even in the more developed money and capital markets, the assumption of efficient markets is open to question, and the mathematical structure of the models, and data requirements leads to abstraction which produces simplification (Samuels, 1981). Moreover, the models are generalized, in that they are not based on the financial structure of any individual country. Therefore even in the West, where individual country differences tend to be less than elsewhere, the models may still lack a sense of realism.

Of course many of the assumptions listed cannot be held to obtain in most developing countries, even with the wildest stretch of the imagination. Institutions are limited in number and type; markets are few, narrow and imperfect; financial instruments are very limited in number and buyers and sellers are few; information is very imperfect, and transaction costs may be considerable. To avoid committing the error of generalization just attributed to models, it must be said that financial markets vary enormously among the developing countries, and really represent a spectrum of markets, from Chad at one end to Korea, Mexico, and Singapore at the other. Therefore no generalized model is applicable. Some countries, for example, Pakistan, are developing markets based on Islamic principles, without interest rates, which have different characteristics to markets with conventional interest rates.

A model of perfect competition is frequently assumed, however, when discussing financial markets, although the assumption may be implicit only. The 'ideal' notion of the market is also sometimes assumed to be the 'ideal' to aim for in practice, and policy prescriptions tend to be along the line of 'market expansion and liberalization'. There is sometimes an implicit assumption made that markets in the West approach the 'ideal' model financial markets, and that developing countries, as a matter of policy, should try to imitate western practice and to develop their own financial markets along the same lines. This assumption is quite clear in Shaw (1973), for example. Such policy prescriptions, of course, have political implications which may not be acceptable to all developing countries, in that it implies a liberal, capitalist form of economic development. The reverse side of the coin, of course, is that such policy prescriptions may be made for political reasons in the first place. Finance is nothing if not a political weapon. On the other hand the argument that financial markets encourage economic development cannot be lightly dismissed, and is examined in Chapter 3.

5. CONCLUDING REMARKS

The above concepts, processes, and mechanisms provide a basis for understanding development finance, and they will be referred to frequently in the rest of the book. They are fundamental, and unchanging, and applied as much 2000 years ago as they do now. Although techniques of finance, and fashions in finance, may change, these principles do not. They can be applied just as much to the developing world as to the industrial world, and they also apply in the centrally planned economies of the world. However, the dominant role of central government in finance in these countries, and the relative absence of borrowing, means that the centrally planned economies tend to be financially underdeveloped, although usually by choice, and the utility of our principles may be restricted.

Two contrasting theoretical themes have emerged from this discussion of financial principles. The first, capital market theory, was designed originally with portfolio investment in mind, on highly developed capital markets such as New York or London. Nonetheless, the principles it incorporates, and some of its results, have wider applications. In Chapter 2 the main results will be discussed, as will their relevance to developing country finance, and the institutions concerned with it. The second theme, financial repression, is of course based on the observed condition of the financial sector in developing countries, notably the market imperfections and controls, and therefore very different in outlook from capital market theory, which is based on an assumption of efficient markets. Financial repression is taken up again in Chapter 3. The two also differ in approaches, in that financial repression models are founded in macroeconomics, but have implications for financial markets and institutions, while capital market theory is founded in microeconomics, but again has implications for the same financial markets and institutions. The two themes are both relevant to our subject, and will recur from time to time throughout the book.

NOTES

1. One example of the relationship between different types of risk is given by Conine (1982). He examined the relationships between business risk and systematic risk,

and found that under certain assumptions the unlevered systematic risk in its most basic form is given by

$$\beta_u = \left(\frac{1 - T}{S_u}\right)\beta \text{ operating income}$$

where $\quad \beta_u$ = unlevered systematic risk
$\quad\quad\quad T$ = tax rate
$\quad\quad\quad S_u$ = market value of unlevered equity
$\quad\quad\quad \beta$ operating income = systematic risk of operating income.

2. The real rate of return is given by

$$\left(\frac{1 + r}{1 + i}\right) - 1$$

where r is the money rate of return and i is the rate of inflation.

3. The problem may not be restricted to developing countries only. In the 1970s the lack of venture capital in the UK led to direct government investments to encourage industries such as microelectronics. However, private sector venture capital funds expanded dramatically in number in the 1980s in the UK.

Chapter 2

Capital Market Theory and the Developing Countries

1. INTRODUCTION

The relationship between expected return and risk is at the heart of capital market theory or modern portfolio theory, as it is also known. The origin of the theory really lies with Markowitz (1952), who demonstrated formally that diversification of security holdings reduces the risk, unless the returns to the securities are perfectly correlated. Subsequent work divided total risk into (a) market or systematic risk, which cannot be reduced by diversification; and (b) non-market, or specific, risk, which can be eliminated by diversification. Therefore the expected return on a diversified portfolio becomes dependent upon the level of market risk which is accepted. A trade-off can then be perceived between the level of market risk and the rate of return expected.

The notion of *risk-free* investment, or returns, now becomes important. Some assets, usually government securities or bank time deposits, can be regarded as being free of risk in that the holder of the securities feels as confident as is possible that the government or bank will not default on its obligation (of course, nothing is risk-free in an absolute sense; Armageddon would produce default in even the soundest government). Moreover, the identification of, and return from, a risk-free investment depends upon the investor's time horizon. Someone looking to invest for 1 month may consider a 30-day treasury bill, or 1-month bank time deposit to be his risk-free investment. Higher returns may be available on longer-dated instruments (e.g. government bond maturing in 5 years' time). However, our short-term investor may be obliged to sell such a bond before maturity, and if interest rates increase in the meantime, he would face a capital loss. Another example is given by the long-term investor. His risk-free rate of return is that available on a bond or time deposit of long-term maturity. Again, taking a higher return on a short-term instrument exposes him to the risk that short-term rates might subsequently fall below that available on the long-term instrument; it would no longer be risk-free.

24

Capital market theory relates an investor's expected return to the risk of the investment. Formally, the trade-off between risk and expected return can be illustrated as shown in Figure 2.1.

At zero risk an investor can obtain the risk free rate of return. As his willingness to take risks increases, so his required rate of return increases. The existence, and shape, of the market line depends upon the efficient market hypothesis. The relationship is known as the capital asset pricing model (CAPM), and is discussed further below.

We referred in Chapter 1 to some of the ambiguity surrounding the term 'capital market'. CMT is mainly concerned with the market in negotiable instruments—that is equities, bonds, and bills, both long-term and short-term, but also appears to embrace non-negotiable instruments such as bank deposits, certainly to the extent that they represent alternative financial investments to shares and bonds. Some writers (e.g. Roll, 1977) have suggested that the theory should be extended to embrace all other risky investment instruments such as gold, land, and other non-financial investments such as stamps, old masters, and fine wines. This suggestion is not without point, as financial institutions such as insurance companies and pension funds tended to invest increasingly in such 'alternative investments' in the 1970s, seeing them mainly as a better hedge against inflation than equities. However, the work involved would be substantial, and little has been done in that direction so far. For the most part, then, CMT is concerned with the market in negotiable instruments, regardless of maturity, and we will refer to the capital market in that sense, at least in this chapter.

As shares represent the underlying assets of a company the share price represents the value that the market places on these assets. Portfolio investment is important because it is always an alternative to physical investments, and secondly, because the issue of stocks and bonds is a means of financing physical investments. Therefore the relationship between portfolio and physi-

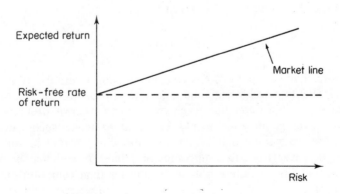

Figure 2.1 Risk and expected return

cal investment is close; the adage 'Investment is the art of buying assets which are worth more than they cost' applies equally to both forms of investment.

Capital market theory has powerful implications, and not only for investment on the stock exchanges of London and New York. It has implications for capital investment decision-taking in both the private and the public sectors, and provides an alternative to what have become traditional methods of taking risk into account, notably sensitivity analysis and Monte-Carlo simulation as described, for example, by Pouliquen (1970). It has implications for development banks' portfolios of projects, and management of export credit agencies and international banks. It also has implications for government fund-raising. However, it was designed with capital markets in the advanced countries in mind, and therefore is not necessarily translatable to the rather different financial market conditions which prevail in developing countries. We shall examine the extent to which it is applicable to developing countries at the end of this chapter.

2.   MEASURES OF RISK

(a)   Definition of Risk

Capital market theory assumes that investors have a notion of 'expected return'. The return, r, over a single period is defined as:

$$r = \frac{D + T - I}{I}$$

where D = dividend;
   T = terminal price of the asset at the end of the period;
   I = initial purchase price of the asset at the beginning of the period.

The theory assumes that the investor uses 'expected values' of D and T, and that the expected value (of T) is given by:

$$\sum_{i=1}^{n} T_i p_i$$

Over more than one period, r is calculated as an internal rate of return. Where T_i is the ith possible outcome, and p_i the probability of that outcome. There are n possible outcomes, each one having its own probability. (Of course, the average investor is not expected to make such calculations explicitly, but we assume that he does so implicitly, in that he knows that there may be several possible outcomes of D and T, and that he attaches intuitive probabilities to these outcomes, and his final valuation of T is his 'best guess'.)

Capital market theory now asumes that the dispe.sion of an asset's return around its expected return is the investor's measure of the asset's riskiness.

The dispersion is measured by the standard deviation (σ) or sometimes by the variance (V, or σ^2) of its return. A further assumption is made that the dispersion of possible returns conforms to the normal distribution. The extent to which an individual investor accepts the standard deviation as a measure of his fear of risk is debatable, and other measures have been proposed. Markowitz (1959, chap. 9) suggested using a semi-variance measure because investors may be more worried about downside movements (loss, or very small gain) than with gain, and that they measure riskiness as the possibility of making a loss. However, the theory continues to use standard deviation as its measure of riskiness, and we will stay with this measure. The assumption of the normal distribution also precludes the possibility of skewed probability distributions. Skewness can be incorporated in models, but again the standard theory does not consider it. On the other hand the use of the standard deviation does enable us to make interpretations of the form 'there is 67% probability that the actual outcome will be within 15% of the expected outcome'.

(b) Variability

The values of shares fluctuate but some fluctuate more than others. The fluctuations are referred to as *variability*, and Figure 2.2 illustrates the movements in price of a high-variability and a low-variability share.

The high-variability share offers prospects of greater gains, and greater losses, than the low-variability share. We can measure the variance or standard deviation of the share price from the mean.[1] Thus high-variability shares will have a greater variance (or standard deviation) than a low-variability share.

The most useful analysis, though, starts when we divide the total variability of share price into two components—market, or systematic risk, and non-market, or specific risk. We owe this distinction to Sharpe (1963) and we will discuss each in turn. However, the basic relationship between them is:

Total risk = Market (systematic) risk + Specific (non-systematic) risk

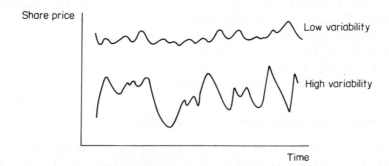

Figure 2.2 High- and low-variability shares

(c) Market (Systematic) Risk

It is generally realized that share prices tend to move in the same direction as overall stock market movements, as measured for example by the Financial Times–Actuaries (FT–A) All Share Index,[2] or the Standard and Poor 500. Thus when the index rises an individual share tends to rise, and when the index falls the individual share tends to fall. However, shares do not usually change by the same percentage as the index; some are more sensitive to market movements than others. To put it another way, the more sensitive shares will change by more than the change in the index, while the less sensitive shares will change by less than the change in the index. Conventionally we use the β (beta) coefficient to measure the sensitivity of the price of an individual share to a change in the overall market as represented by the index. For example, a share with β = 1.3 will on average change by 1.3% for each 1% change in the market. A low-sensitivity share may have a β = 0.8, which means it tends to move 0.8% for every 1% movement in the market. A share with β = 1.0 will generally move in line with the market. High β shares will tend to perform better than average when the market is rising, but worse than average when the market is falling. However, note the phrases 'on average' and 'tend to'. The β measure is not an iron law. Market risk may be seen as a proxy for the risk of fluctuations in the whole economy.

(d) Specific Risk

As we have seen, share prices are affected by overall market factors, and the movement in the index may be taken as a proxy for expectations about the economy. However a company's performance, and its share price, depend on factors specific to the company, as well as on the performance of the economy as a whole. Thus although a share may have a β coefficient of 1 *on average*, it may over certain shorter periods show higher or lower sensitivity to market movements. The explanation is that in these periods it is affected by company-specific factors as well as market factors. Such factors may be an exogenous growth in the company's market, the development of a new product, a cost-reducing innovation, an improvement in management, firing the chairman, or a take-over bid.

Figure 2.3 shows high and low specific risk shares. These show share prices after adjustment for movements in the market portfolio (e.g. FT–Actuaries All Share Index). The variability can be measured in just the same way as a share's total variability, by calculating the variance or standard deviation.

(e) Estimation of Market Risk and Specific Risk

The procedure illustrated in Figure 2.3 is a clumsy way of estimating the specific risk. If we denote specific risk by α, and market risk by β, then we can estimate both simultaneously for a share or portfolio of shares.

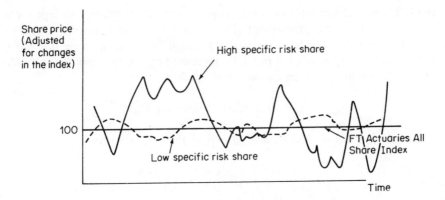

Figure 2.3 High and low specific risk shares

The α and β are estimated by taking data for a share's return, and the return on the market index (or market portfolio) for, say, each month for a 12-month period. Professional investment firms, such as unit trusts and investment trust managers, insurance companies and pension funds, may take returns over a 3-year or 5-year period. The results (for 12 monthly pairs of data) may be plotted on a scatter diagram and a least squares regression line fitted, as shown in Figure 2.4. The least squares regression line is of the form

$$y = \beta x + \alpha$$

where y is the monthly return on an individual share and x is the monthly return on the market portfolio. The β coefficient measures the sensitivity of the returns to overall changes in the market (i.e. the market, or systematic,

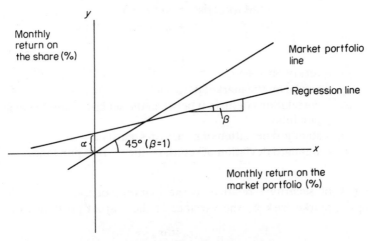

Figure 2.4 Estimation of α and β coefficients

risk). The α coefficient measures the return on the share which is independent of the overall market movement (i.e. the non-market or specific risk).

If, for example, the least squares regression line gives α to be 0.8 and β to be 1.3, then if the market portfolio increased by 3% in a month we would *expect* the monthly return on our share to be:

$$y = (1.3 \times 3) + 0.8 = 4.7\%$$

If the market fell by 3% we would expect the return to be

$$y = -1.3 \times 3 + 0.8 = -3.1\%$$

Note that we would *expect* the above rate of return to be realized. Any form of forecasting, though, is an uncertain occupation, and our expectations may not always be fulfilled.

The correlation coefficient, ρ, which we estimate from the data, indicates the extent to which the individual share price is correlated with the market. (It is the same ρ used in the derivation of the Markowitz mean–variance theorem in Annex 2.1. It is also the same ρ used in the formulae for market risk and β below.) We can also use our data to calculate the standard deviation of the return on the security, and the standard deviation of the return on the market portfolio. Again, both these are used below.

The market portfolio line is the line which passes through the origin at 45°. If our investor held the market portfolio, the return on the vertical axis would be the same as the return on the horizontal axis. Therefore, it is at 45° to the horizontal, and its slope (or β value) is 1. The α value is zero, as there can be no non-market risk (or variance) on the market portfolio.

The market risk of a security may also be expressed as:

$$\text{Market risk} = \text{cov}(r_i, r_m),$$
$$= \rho_{im}\, \sigma_i\, \sigma_m$$

where

r_i = return on asset i,
r_m = return on the market portfolio,
ρ_{im} = correlation coefficient between the security i and the market portfolio,
σ_i = standard deviation of return on security i,
σ_m = standard deviation of return on the market portfolio.

β_i, the risk of security i relative to the market portfolio, is obtained by dividing the market risk by the variance of the market portfolio, or

$$\beta_i = \frac{\rho_{im}\, \sigma_i\, \sigma_m}{\sigma_m^2}$$

(The β value of the market portfolio is:

$$\beta_m = \frac{\rho_{mm}\,\sigma_m\,\sigma_m}{\sigma_m{}^2} = \rho_{mm} = 1)$$

The distinction between market risk and specific risk has important applications, notably when combined with risk diversification, which we will now discuss.

3. RISK DIVERSIFICATION

Modern capital market theory originated with Markowitz (1952). It is concerned with investment portfolio selection, and the systematic diversification of risk. Intuitively it has long been widely accepted that an investor can reduce the risk he is faced with by investing in several securities, rather than just one ('spreading the risk', or 'not putting all the eggs in the same basket'). However, note that diversification must be systematic, and spread across all sectors, rather than random. Markowitz (1952, 1959/1970) provided a proof of this theorem, a version of which is given in Annex 2.1 to this chapter. It is based on the following assumptions:

(a) The return on an investment adequately summarizes the outcome of the investment, and investors visualize a probability distribution of rates of return.
(b) Investors base their decisions on just two parameters of the probability distribution function—the expected return and variance of return. Investors equate risk with variance of return.
(c) The investor exhibits risk aversion, so for a given expected return he prefers minimum risk. Conversely, for a given level of risk he prefers the maximum return.
(d) The returns on all securities are not perfectly positively correlated.

The Markowitz mean–variance theorem can be summarized as follows. Given a choice of two portfolios, A and B, an investor will prefer A to B if:

  (i) $ER(A) > ER(B)$ and $\text{var}(A) \leqslant \text{var}(B)$, or
 (ii) $ER(A) \geqslant ER(B)$ and $\text{var}(A) < \text{var}(B)$

where $ER(A)$, $ER(B)$ are the expected returns on portfolios A and B, and $\text{var}(A)$ and $\text{var}(B)$ are the variances of portfolios A and B.

We can readily substitute 'security' or 'capital investment project' for 'portfolio', as projects have expected returns and variances associated with the returns. The argument for deriving the result is similar.

The principle of diversification enables the investor to minimize the risk of a given expected rate of return, or to maximize the return for accepting a given level of risk. It does, however, imply the acceptance of lower returns for lower risk, or in other words a trade-off between risk and return. Diagrammatically, it can be illustrated as shown in Figure 2.5. The shaded

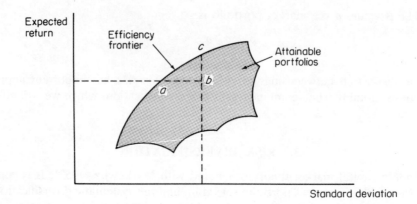

Figure 2.5 The efficiency frontier

area represents all the combinations of risk and return attainable from the available set of securities. Clearly any portfolio on the efficiency frontier is preferable to any other portfolio within the shaded area. For any point (b) within the area, a portfolio (a) exists which has the same expected return, but with lower risk. Likewise, a portfolio (c) also exists which has a higher expected return for accepting the same level of risk.

To be applied practically, the Markowitz model requires an enormous amount of computation. In order to select the efficient portfolios from 100 securities we need data on 100 expected returns; 100 standard deviations, and 5150 pairs of correlation coefficients. However, by using approximations (Sharpe, 1963), the data requirements are reduced from the above figures to 302, which makes it much more manageable. Cohen and Pogue (1967) have shown that Sharpe's approach is reasonably accurate. A number of criticisms have been made, including the use of the standard deviation as the measure of risk, mentioned earlier. Another objection has been raised by Baumol (1963). Assuming that portfolio returns are normally distributed, he showed that some 'Markowitz-efficient' portfolios are in fact inferior to other 'Markowitz-efficient' portfolios, as shown in Table 2.1.[3]

In this case, $ER(B) > ER(A)$, but $var(B) > var(A)$. Therefore according to the Markowitz criterion neither portfolio is strictly preferable, so both

Table 2.1

	Expected return (R)	Standard deviation (σ)	Variance (σ²)
Portfolio A	8%	1%	1%
Portfolio B	15%	2%	4%

would lie on the efficiency frontier. But assuming normal distribution, it is 95% certain that returns will be in the range $R + 2\sigma$. It is therefore 97.5% certain that the return on portfolio A will not exceed 10%, and that the return on portfolio B will not be less than 11%. Therefore an investor would prefer B to A. However, according to the Markowitz criterion, a 'low-risk' investor might prefer A to B. Again the Baumol modification enables us to reduce the number of 'efficient' portfolios.

In spite of such criticisms the Markowitz theorem remains the foundation stone of capital market theory and its basic result, that we can reduce risk by holding a diversified portfolio, is extremely important. It can also tell us what *proportions* to hold each security in, if we know the correlation coefficient between the securities. It is clear that risk can be reduced through diversification without necessarily reducing the expected return. In order to make these calculations we need to know the correlation coefficient of the returns between the two securities. This can be calculated from historical data of share price movements and dividends paid to shareholders, using regression analysis.

If the two securities are perfectly positively correlated (i.e. the returns move exactly together), then there are no gains to be obtained from diversification. The lower the degree of correlation, the greater the extent to which risk can be reduced, and if the securities are perfectly negatively correlated then there exists a combination of holdings which would eliminate risk completely (i.e. the standard deviation = 0). In practice, returns on shares tend to have quite high positive correlations, because they are all exposed to the same macroeconomic risks, or market risks.[4] Therefore risk can be eliminated only to a limited extent by diversification. In fact we cannot eliminate the market risk which affects all shares similarly. We can only eliminate the specific risk by diversification.

So far we have talked in terms of diversification between two securities for ease of exposition, but the principle can readily be extended to portfolios (Markowitz, 1959/1970). However, the fact that we can eliminate only specific risk becomes clear if we consider diversifying to the greatest extent possible, or, in other words, buying every share on the stock market in proportion to each company's market capitalization. We would then in effect have bought the FT–Actuaries All Share Index (or the Standard Poor 500), and the value of our portfolio would always be the same as the index, and would fluctuate in just the same way as the index. We would now be faced entirely with market risk, and all the specific risk attached to individual shares would have been eliminated. In fact we need not go to anything like such lengths before we virtually eliminate specific risk. Portfolio risk can be shown to fall rapidly as the number of securities held increases, and this is illustrated graphically in Figure 2.6. By the time we have about 15 shares in the portfolio we have eliminated over 90% of specific risk, and almost all of the remaining risk is market risk. The curve is asymptotic to a line which represents the market risk, or that portion of the risk which cannot be diversified. The exact

34

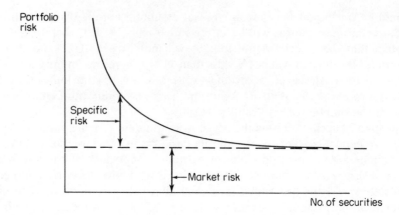

Figure 2.6 The diversification of specific risk

number of shares and the amount of risk remaining depend on the market; in the UK it is possible to diversify away about 65% of total risk, and over 70% in the United States.

The principle of risk diversification has also been extended to the individual company. Should it diversify its activities in order to reduce the risk attached to its earnings? Individual shareholders can easily diversify their risks themselves by holding a portfolio of a number of shares, given that they are faced with a large and efficient capital market. Therefore diversification of activities by the individual firm does not help them. Moreover, the firm will find diversification more difficult than the individual shareholder. It may, however, help the management and employees of the firm to reduce the risks which they face, and to make their jobs more secure, as they face the specific risk of the firm, as well as market risk. (The argument may be rather different, though, in a developing country which does not have a large or efficient stock market, and where the investor may have difficulties in diversifying his holdings, which we will discuss at greater length below.)

The possibility of diversifying market risk by international investment has been extensively studied (e.g. Grubel, 1968; Levy and Sarnat, 1970; Witt, 1978). In spite of difficulties of risk measurement because of exchange rate fluctuations and 'political' risk (is standard deviation of returns what we really mean by risk?), Atherton and Yap (1979), for example, concluded that 'The data studied indicated that a US investor could reduce risk by about a half if the portfolio included investments from several stock markets instead of just one.'[5] The correlations between stock market indices in different countries is less than 1, thereby enabling risk to be diversified to some extent. However, Witt (1978) has shown that even if we have all the historical correlation coefficients, it is impossible to predict an individual correlation coefficient in the future. This problem of prediction, which of course applies also in national markets, restricts the practical application of the model. Nevertheless the general conclusion remains, that if variability between markets continues in the future, and they are not perfectly correlated, then there will be possibilities of risk reduction through international diversification. However, as national markets appear to be becoming increasingly related to each other, the correlation coefficients may tend to increase over time, and risk reduction possibilities may then tend to fall. International diversification is of course practised by certain investment trusts, unit trusts, and other institutional investors.

Although we have discussed international diversification in terms of portfolio investment, the principle can readily be extended to direct investment. As a security represents a claim on the earnings of a company, so it also represents a claim on the projects of the company. Therefore in all our discussions we can once again replace the word 'security' with the word 'project'. In terms of international diversification, then, the implication is that firms (and their shareholders) can benefit from diversifying their physical investments internationally, or by making direct foreign investments. Agmon and Lessard (1977), for example, have shown that international diversification by transnational corporations may reap substantial benefits, if individual shareholders cannot readily diversify their portfolios internationally.

4. PORTFOLIO RISK AND RETURNS, AND THE CAPITAL MARKET LINE

Figure 2.7 shows the efficiency frontier described in the previous section. It represents the set of perfectly diversified portfolios which give the highest expected return for a given level of portfolio risk. An investor will select a

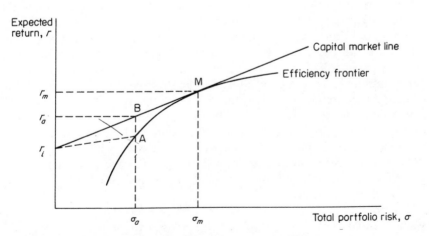

Figure 2.7 The capital market line

portfolio along this line which provides that combination of risk and return which is most to his liking. (Textbooks express this by drawing in the economist's nebulous 'utility functions' for an individual investor, who then selects the point on the efficiency frontier which puts him on his highest 'utility curve', which amounts to the same thing.) We will assume that our investor is risk averse, i.e. for a given level of risk he prefers the portfolio which gives him the highest rate of return, and vice-versa.

We will also give the investor the possibility of investing in risk-free securities, which offer a rate of return, r_i, in addition to the possibility of investing in porfolios composed of risky securities. Short-term government bonds (or bank time deposits) are normally taken as risk-free investments because they offer a known cash return, and are not subject to the risk of default. (Note that we are talking about *money* returns, not *real* returns. Once we introduce inflation we no longer have risk-free investments, unless index-linked government securities are available.)

Given the possibility of risk-free investments and portfolios composed entirely of risky assets, the investor may prefer to combine the two. He may do this by dividing his total portfolio into a risky portion and a risk-free portion. If he puts a proportion x into the risky investment and $(1-x)$ into the risk-free investment, and he expects to earn a return of r_a on the risky investment and r_i on the risk-free investment, then his total expected return, r_t is:

$$r_t = r_a x + r_i (1-x).$$

The investor's portfolio will be located somewhere on the straight line $r_i m$, depending on the value he puts on x. The line is known as the capital market line (CML). That the CML is tangential to the efficiency frontier can be shown as follows. Clearly the CML must intersect the efficiency frontier at some point (the case of $x = 1$). Now the slope of the CML represents the increase in return (δr) which can be obtained from taking on one more unit of risk. Suppose the CML intersects the efficiency frontier at A, then an investor holding a risky portfolio only would find that by taking on one more unit of risk he could increase his return by *more than* δr (the slope of the curve is greater than the slope of the CML at A). He would move up the curve until he reached a point M where the slope of the curve and the slope of the CML were equal. This is the point of tangency. Therefore the CML would be as drawn in Figure 2.7. The only point the investor might choose on the efficiency frontier is the point of tangency, M, known as the market portfolio. He could then locate himself along $r_i M$, according to the value he puts on x. He would not locate himself at a point A, because there exists a point B on the CML which offers him a higher expected return for the same degree of risk as at A.

The point M is the only combination of risky assets that an investor would want to hold, given the possibility of investment in risk-free securities. Therefore, all the different risky investments available must have a price which makes them acceptable to be held in the portfolio M (if they did not, no-one would buy them). Therefore all risky investments must be included in M (again, no-one would hold them otherwise). Thus M represents a combination of all risky investments available on the capital market, which is why it is known as the market portfolio. In practice the nearest thing we have to it is the FT–Actuaries All Share Index, or the Standard and Poor 500 Index in the USA. Thus the nearest we have to an all share index is used as a proxy for the market portfolio.

So far the reader will have got the impression that it is impossible to 'beat' the performance of the market portfolio in an efficient stock market. However, in practice roughly half the shares out-perform the market portfolio, and half under-perform it. Therefore the investor who buys only those shares which out-perform the market will beat the market portfolio. The question is, how to do this? Can it be done consistently? The theory suggests not; the only ways of beating an efficient market are through luck, good forecasting (which anyway contains a large slice of luck), or inside knowledge, use of which is illegal in some countries.

5. BORROWING AND LENDING

In Figure 2.7 we saw the possibility of investing entirely at the risk-free rate of interest. Such investment would be in short-term government securities or a bank deposit, and can therefore be regarded as lending money. The investor also has the possibility of borrowing, and investing his borrowings in risky securities. The lending and borrowing strategies are illustrated in Figure 2.8.

We saw in Figure 2.7 that a lender would take up a position between r_i and M, depending upon his willingness to accept risk. A borrower would be

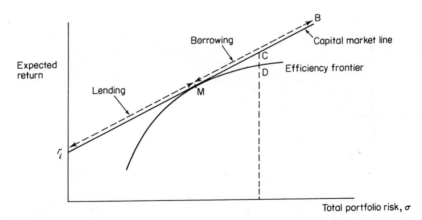

Figure 2.8 Lending, borrowing, and the capital market line

able to increase his risk taking, and his expected returns, beyond M, say to C. Again, he would be above the efficiency frontier, and at C he would get a higher return for the same risk he would face at D, a point on the efficiency frontier.

Figure 2.8, though, assumes that our investor can lend or borrow at the risk free rate of interest, r. In practice that will seldom be the case, the borrowing rate being generally higher than the lending rate. When we introduce differential rates for borrowing (say r_b) and lending (say r_ℓ), then our capital market line is no longer a single straight line (Figure 2.9).

The investor will still be on the section $r_\ell M$ when he can lend. However, he must now borrow at r_b, not r_ℓ. Therefore his capital market line will now be $r_\ell MPQ$.

6. THE CAPITAL ASSET PRICING MODEL

The capital asset pricing model (CAPM) is concerned with the relationship between expected returns and market risk, β. As we are able to estimate β values for portfolios as well as for individual stocks (see below), the CAPM applies to both individual securities and to portfolios. The derivation of the CAPM is attributable to Sharpe (1964), Lintner (1965) and Mossin (1966). It is now central to financial theory and has a number of practical applications. It provides an explanation for the level of individual share prices (asset values), is extendable to all asset valuation, and provides a method for estimating the discount rate for a project. It therefore has considerable implications both for financial investments and physical investments. In its pure form it assumes efficient markets, and we shall discuss the validity of the efficient market hypothesis later. The CAPM has also been subject to

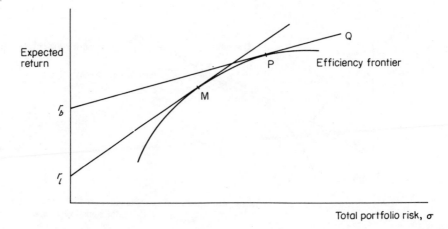

Figure 2.9 Borrowing and lending at different interest rates

extensive empirical testing, and we shall also discuss the results and the acceptability of these tests in the following section.

(a) The CAPM and the Security Market Line

Given an efficient market we have seen that the only efficient way to invest is to divide one's portfolio between the market portfolio and risk-free investments. All other investments, including holdings of individual risky shares, are inefficient. By investing in the market portfolio we diversify all specific risk, and are faced only with market risk. Therefore the returns from individual securities will only compensate an investor for taking on the market risk of that security, as the specific risk can be diversified away. Therefore only a security's market risk (or β value) will explain the expected return on that share.

The expected rate of return on a risky security can be shown[6] to be a straight line with the following equation:

$$r_e = r_i + (r_m - r_i)\,\beta_e,$$

where
r_e = expected return on equity e;
r_i = risk free rate of interest;
r_m = expected return on the market portfolio;
β_e = beta coefficient of equity e.

The straight line is known as the security market line (SML), and can be represented graphically as shown in Figure 2.10. The return on the risk-free investment, r_i, is certain, and therefore has a β value of zero. A security with a β value of 1 will, on average, move in line with the market, and therefore its expected return is equal to the expected return of the market

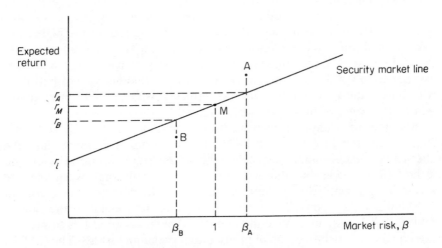

Figure 2.10 The security market line

portfolio r^M. A security with $\beta<1$ will be low risk relative to the market, while a security with $\beta>1$ has high risk relative to the market.

The SML represents the relationship between the expected return and the β value of all the securities on the market; in equilibrium every security will find itself located along the line. In a market with a large number of traded securities, and which is 'efficient', the SML will be a continuous line.

In an efficient market, the SML represents the equilibrium prices of securities in the market. The equilibrium can readily be demonstrated by considering a security which strays from the SML. If a security finds itself above the line, say at point A in Figure 2.10, then it is offering a return which is more than commensurate with that level of risk β^A, and higher than that available on other securities with risk β^A. It will immediately be bought, and its price bid up until the expected return on it has fallen to its equilibrium level r^A. In the same way a point B which is below the SML offers a return which is less than commensurate with its level of risk. In this case the security will be sold, and its price fall, until its expected return rises to r^B, its equilibrium value.

(b) CAPM and the Discount Rate

From our point of view the main result to be derived from the CAPM concerns the criteria for physical capital investment projects. Franks and Broyles (1979) show how the 'traditional' criteria of net present value can be modified to take risk into account using the CAPM. Investment in physical projects to produce a good involves risk taking, just as investment on the capital market involves risk taking. A physical project can be attributed a β value also. For example, one can argue that the β value of a new textile manufacturing project is similar to the β value of the shares of existing textile manufacturing companies. Furthermore, the capital market represents an alternative investment opportunity to a physical investment, but, as we have seen, one that involves a trade-off between risk and return; the higher the risk accepted, the higher the return required. Our physical investment should therefore be seen in the same light as a stock market investment; the return we seek from it will be related to the risk taken. Another way of putting it is to regard the firm as a collection of projects, with its share price representing the value of these projects, weighted by their respective betas.

In appraising a physical investment our decision rule, broadly speaking, is to accept the project if the NPV>0 at our chosen discount rate. An alternative version is that we calculate the internal rate of return (IRR), and if the IRR is greater than our discount rate, then, with some exceptions, we accept the project.[7] Clearly the value placed on the discount rate is crucial. Traditionally the approach has been to say that it is equal to the rate of return available on alternative investments. Another approach is to say that it is equal to the risk-free rate of return plus a premium for risk. The CAPM, however, enables us to be more sophisticated than this. Traditionally an investing organization would use only one rate of discount, but once we acknowledge that it should contain a risk premium the CAPM enables us to estimate the risk premium for *that particular project*. Therefore we use different rates of discount for projects with different levels of riskiness, known as the risk-adjusted discount rate (RADR). Figure 2.11 illustrates the procedure for deriving the rate of discount.

If we have a project A with a fairly low level of risk, say β_A, then the SML tells us that we require an expected rate of return of $ER(A)$ from that project. Therefore if the IRR$>ER(A)$, or the NPV>0 at a discount rate of $ER(A)$, then we can accept the project. $ER(A)$ is our rate of discount for project A. On the other hand a project B, with a higher level of risk, β_B, has a higher rate of discount, $ER(B)$. Therefore no company or government can use a single discount rate, but rather the discount rate used must depend on the perceived riskiness of the project in question. We should speak only of a 'project' discount rate, not a 'company' or 'government' discount rate.

The immediate question which arises is 'how does one determine the level of riskiness of a project, in practice, and hence its discount rate?'. We have already given an indication with reference to the textile manufacturing project; if we have an efficient capital market we can calculate the β value of an existing textile manufacturer, which will give us a measure of the degree of riskiness of textile manufacturing.[8] Once we have an estimate of the β, the SML will then given us the discount rate to use. Alternatively, and more practically, we can use the formula for the CAPM. If we know the risk-free rate of interest, the risk premium, and the β coefficient for the project in question, we can calculate our expected (i.e. desired) rate of return.

For example, if the risk-free rate of interest on government bonds is 8% (in money terms), the risk premium 6% and the β coefficient for the project is 1.2, then

$$E(R) = 8 + (6 \times 1.2) = 15.2\%$$

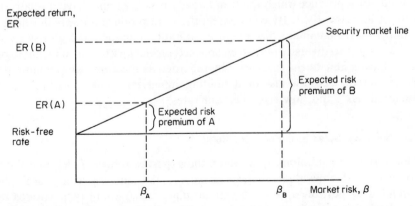

Figure 2.11 The securities market line and risk-adjusted discount rates

Then we would require a rate of return of 15.2% (in money terms), which would be our discount rate (say, 15%).[9] Of course in project appraisal we use a real discount rate, and the above money rates need to be reduced to real terms. For example, the long-run risk-free real rate of return appears to have averaged about 3%.

We have already discussed the estimate of β coefficients. The risk premium is usually taken as the difference between the annual returns on companies quoted on the stock market, and returns on government bonds. For major stock markets, estimates of the risk premium is available. In the case of the USA, Ibbotson and Sinquefield (1982) estimated that the pre-tax risk premium averaged 8.3% (in money terms) between 1926 and 1981; while for the UK, Brealey and Dimson (1976) estimated that the equivalent figure was 9.1% between 1919 and 1975. The average after-tax risk premium to shareholders may have been about 7.5%. DeZoete and Bevan (annually) also provide estimates for the UK. Clearly these figures represent averages over the period, and will be higher at some times and lower at others. Nevertheless it gives a rough indication of the type of risk premium shareholders look for, although they are all in money terms. These figures may not hold for less efficient markets, though.[10]

The 'risk-free' rate of interest used should be the return on a bond which corresponds to the duration of the project. Thus for a project with a life of 10 years the risk-free rate of interest should be the redemption yield available on a government bond maturing in 10 years' time. For a project with a 15-year life it should be the return on a bond maturing in 15 years. (A fuller account of discount rate estimation is given by Dimson and Marsh, 1982.)

In practice a firm planning a physical investment project may find it difficult to attach a precise β value to its project, perhaps because it is a new type of project, or because there is no firm quoted on the stock market which specializes in that type of project alone. (Firms tend to be diversified and involved in several different activities.) Under such circumstances the firm has to fall back on intuitive measures of β. For example, a project to expand capacity of a product which the firm already produces may have a relatively low β value (low risk). By contrast, a project to produce a newly developed product, never commercialized before, would be regarded as high risk (high β). A project to diversify into an established product with known technology, but which is new to the firm, may be regarded as medium risk (medium β). The firm then faces the task of attributing numerical values to its 'high risk', 'medium risk', and 'low risk' discount rates.

(c) Security Betas and Portfolio Betas

The SML is the relationship between the expected return, $E(R)$, and the β coefficient of individual shares. However, the analysis can readily be extended to portfolios, and we can calculate the β value of portfolios by multiplying the β values of the share in the portfolio by the proportion of

Table 2.2

Share	Beta value of share (1)	Proportion of share in portfolio (2)	(1)×(2)
A	0.8	0.5	0.40
B	1.0	0.3	0.30
C	1.1	0.2	0.22
		1.0 Portfolio β =	0.92

the portfolio allocated to each share as follows. The example in Table 2.2 is for a portfolio of three shares.

For a set of diversified portfolios we can now plot $E(R)$ against portfolio β, as shown in Figure 2.12.

As with the SML, the relationship is linear for similar reasons. As investors are efficient only if they hold a diversified portfolio of shares, it is the relationship between the expected return and portfolio β which is of most practical interest, and which has been subject to extensive empirical testing. We will consider the results of some of these tests in the next section. Finally, a note on terminology is needed. We have introduced the capital market line, the security market line, and, initially, the staight-line relationship between expected returns and risk, which we called the market line. In the literature the names used for the different lines do not always follow a strict pattern; some writers use the term 'capital market line' for the SML; others just use the general term 'market line'.

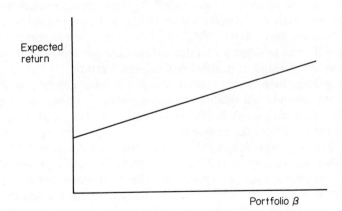

Figure 2.12 Expected return and portfolio β

7. EMPIRICAL TESTING OF THE CAPM

In the early 1970s a large number of empirical tests were conducted to test the validity of the CAPM. Most of these were carried out using New York Stock Exchange or American Stock Exchange data. Among the better-known results were those of Black, Jensen, and Scholes (1972), which found that the relationship between risk (as measured by β) and return can be assumed to be linear for ordinary shares. Blume and Friend (1973), however, conducted tests in different types of market (bull and bear), and their findings were mixed. In a strong market the relationship was strong and positive, and in other markets the relationship tended to be weak or even negative. Fama and MacBeth (1973) found that they could 'not reject the hypothesis (of the two-parameter portfolio model and the models of market equilibrium) that the pricing of common stocks reflects the attempts of risk-averse investors to hold portfolios that are "efficient" in terms of expected value and dispersion of return'.

In all testing there exists a potentially serious methodological problem in that the CAPM incorporates *expected* returns which we cannot measure. We can only measure actual returns and see whether our β values can predict these. However, the relationship between historical β estimates and ex-post returns does not appear to be as strong as the theory suggests it might be. Blume and Friend (1974), for example, found that over 5-year periods, using New York Stock Exchange data, expected returns are positively related to risk, but that they do not appear to increase as fast as they should if the CAPM holds in the short run.[11] Over 40 years, however, returns appear to have a negative, but small, correlation with risk.

R. A. Levy (1974) looked at the ability of β coefficients to predict future performance relative to the market. He found that in certain tests β was a good predictor. In bear markets, high β portfolios performed worse than the market, and low β portfolios beter than the market. On the whole, though, results were mixed. Levitz (1974) found good correlation between risk and return only for extreme values of β (i.e. below 0.8 and above 1.5). Cohen, Zinbarg, and Zeikel (1982, pp. 188–192) review a number of other studies which tend to suggest that the institutional portfolios measured failed to achieve, on average, a positive risk adjusted return.

These findings merely represent a few of the huge numbers of empirical studies undertaken of the validity and applicability of the capital asset pricing model, but they provide sufficient evidence to conclude that the predictive ability of the CAPM is not perhaps as reliable as its proponents would have hoped. That, however, is not sufficient grounds for dismissing it. It merely reflects that forecasting is difficult, and that the future is not merely a repetition of past events. It remains uncertain, and not always predictable by statistical techniques. In this respect, though, capital market theory performs no worse than many other economic models, and perhaps better than some which have not been subject to such rigourous testing.

Roll (1977), however, queried all the previous tests on methodological grounds. He showed that as β is measured against the market portfolio, which is assumed to be efficient, any regression analysis between average returns and betas would, *tautologically*, give a perfectly linear relationship. Moreover, if the market index which is used as a proxy for the market portfolio is not efficient, then the values of betas obtained will be distorted, and the expected return on each share will be only approximately related to the betas as measured on that index. Although Roll's work was thought to have been seriously damaging to the CAPM, it was really a critique only of the tests, rather than of the underlying theory being tested. However, Roll did conclude that there is no possibility of testing satisfactorily the CAPM. Subsequently Cheng and Grauer (1980) claimed to have overcome the problems raised by Roll, and 'provided evidence against the CAPM'. They tested five hypotheses generated by the Invariance Law, and assuming 'stationarity' of returns. This work in turn received some criticisms from Turnbull and Winter (1982) and by Sweeney (1982). There is probably more work to be done on the subject. However, to date the empirical results have not wholly supported the theory of the CAPM.

A further point has been raised by H. Levy (1983), who showed that most efficient portfolios contain short positions. This arises for two reasons. First, for some shares the expected return is lower than the risk-free rate of interest. A portfolio can clearly be improved by selling such shares short. The second reason is one of diversification. If two shares have highly correlated returns it may be efficient to sell one short, even if its expected return is above the risk-free interest rate. The market portfolio, however, contains only long positions, and therefore is most unlikely to be efficient. H. Levy (1978, 1983) proposes a modified CAPM, of which the traditional CAPM is a special case, when transaction costs of zero are assumed. Levy's model would most notably abandon beta as a measure of risk, using variance instead. The advantages claimed for his model are that it takes account of the following:

— Investors hold a limited number of securities, and generally buy long. Therefore short sales play a negligible role.
— As the market portfolio can be both ex-ante and ex-post inefficient, it has no role to play in a reformulated CAPM.
— The reformulated model is consistent with Roll's argument. We no longer expect to find a linear relationship between the sample average return and the sample systematic risk (β) when the latter is estimated on the market portfolio. Therefore all empirical studies which failed to find a linear relationship are consistent with the reformulated CAPM.
— Under the reformulated CAPM the variance of each security is a more suitable measure than beta.

More mundane diffficulties can arise with the CAPM, notably in the empirical measures of betas. By taking different time periods and intervals it is obviously possible for different measures of β and α to be obtained. Cohen, Zinbarg and Zeikel (1982) illustrate this point by comparing differences in β estimates arrived at by four different risk measurement organizations for each of the Dow Jones 30 stocks. General Foods varied between 0.73 and 1.13; International Harvester between 1.14 and 1.51 and US Steel between 0.91 and 1.19. The same source points out considerable instability in β values over time, both in individual stocks and in sectors. Drugs, for example had β values of 0.79 in September 1973 and 1.24 in September 1979.

It has been suggested that some other variable, variable X, also plays a part in determining investor's expected returns, and not just the β coefficient. What variable X might be is uncertain; Kraus and Litzenberger (1976), for example, suggested that it might be the skewness of portfolio returns.

Dissatisfaction with the CAPM has led to the development of an alternative theory to explain asset pricing, the arbitrage pricing theory (APT) (see Ross, 1976a,b). Instead of using the all-embracing β as a measure of a share's market risk, the APT breaks market risk down into a number of common components or factors to which a company's share price might be sensitive (e.g. interest rates, crude oil prices, exchange rate movements, inflation rates, etc.). The sensitivity of a share to changes in each of these components can be measured, and diversified portfolios can be constructed to give desired sensitivities to particular factors. The expected return (ER) on a security or portfolio is then determined by its sensitivities to the factors considered, or

$$ER_i = a + b\beta_{i1} + c\beta_{i2} + \ldots$$

where ER_i = expected return on security or portfolio i;

β_{i1}, β_{i2} = sensitivity of i to factors, 1, 2 respectively.

a, b, c are constants.

The relationship is linear, and is equivalent to the CAPM.

The APT is based on the premise that arbitrage possibilities should not be available in the market. If they are, then investors can make risk-free gains by exploiting them. It does not accord any special role to the market portfolio, and does not assume that expected returns are normally distributed. In effect the CAPM becomes a special case of the more general APT. However, APT has not (yet) proved itself sufficiently attractive to displace the CAPM in the theoretical literature.

Capital market theory, then, is still fertile ground for research, and we can expect further advances and refinements in the theory. Nonetheless the principle of diversification, and the linear relationship between expected return and risk, remain widely accepted, if only in a crude way. However, we know of few tests of the CAPM which have been carried out in developing countries. The presumption has been that if it does not hold in the industrialized countries, then it certainly does not hold in the much less efficient markets in developing countries.

8. THE EFFICIENT MARKET HYPOTHESIS, AND DEVELOPING COUNTRY STOCK MARKETS

Underlying capital market theory is the efficient market hypothesis (EMH). An efficient market is defined as one which fully reflects all available information. For markets to be efficient in a financial sense the following conditions need to be met:

— There are no transaction costs in trading securities.
— All information is freely available to all market participants.
— All participants agree on the implications of current information for current and future security prices, and have the same expectations of the risk and return of each security.
— All investors are 'risk averse', i.e. for a given return they minimize risk, and for a given level of risk they maximize return.
— There is a large number of buyers and sellers in the market.
— A sufficient number of securities is traded to enable participants to acquire a balanced portfolio.

The main implication of the efficient market hypothesis is that share prices reflect all information as soon as it becomes available, and discount future expectations. Therefore it is not possible to make profits by identifying 'undervalued' shares, because they do not exist. It is therefore not possible to beat the market, except by luck, above average forecasting skills or inside information. If a market is efficient, therefore, it renders useless the services provided by investment managers and tip-sheets. An investor might just as well buy the market portfolio, or bet on movements of broad-based indices. It will be apparent, therefore, that in the investment world the efficient market hypothesis is controversial, and belief or non-belief in it can be as intense as religious beliefs.[12] In an efficient capital market all assets are correctly priced, a remark which applies to physical as well as to portfolio assets.

If the efficient market hypothesis were extendable to physical investments, the adage that 'capital budgeting is the art of buying assets which are worth more than they cost' would be useless, as all assets, physical as well as portfolio, would lie on the security market line, and investment would become merely a matter of selecting one's preferred combination of risk and return. This point is important, because both to the firm and government, physical investment and portfolio investment are alternatives. (They are also alternatives to a reduction in borrowing, or for governments, a reduction in taxation.) In the real world, of course, markets are not perfectly efficient, and opportunities for profitable investments which yield excess profits do arise. However the identification of investments, including physical investments, then becomes the art of identifying market imperfections, and taking advantage of them, before others spot them.

Substantial empirical work has been done to test the efficiency of capital markets. The earlier work is summarized by Fama (1970), and the more recent work by Samuels (1981). Samuels concludes that only the New York, London, and Tokyo markets are reasonably efficient, with New York as the most efficient. Of the other markets only Germany could be considered to have some of the characteristics of efficiency, but rather less than the other markets cited. However, no market will ever be perfectly efficient, and one can only rank stock markets by their degree of efficiency. The issues are 'how important is it to be efficient?' and 'to what extent does capital market theory break down under different degrees of inefficiency?'. These questions are particularly important in assessing the relevance and applicability of capital market theory to developing countries, where organized capital markets are limited in number and likely to be much less efficient than London or New York. Annex 6.1 (Chapter 6) lists the developing countries with organized capital markets; obviously a majority of developing countries do not have stock markets. Nevertheless, the countries with stock markets embrace 50% of the population of the developing world, and over 60% of the GNP. If China is excluded from the data, both figures exceed 70%.

Samuels (1981) identifies five types of inefficiency in organized capital markets:

— Inefficiencies due to small size, with an inadequate number of traders to ensure competition, and insufficient securities to enable them to hold a diversified portfolio of their choosing.
— Inefficiencies due to different risk preferences and perceptions of investors. This may be a feature of new markets where participants do not have much experience or understanding of the market.
— Inefficiencies due to inadequate market regulation and standards of disclosure by companies.
— Inefficiencies due to poor communications, so that some investors have an advantage over others. Moreover, the costs of obtaining the information may be significant.
— Inefficiencies due to a lack of competent analysts and professional advisors, resulting in differing expectations about the performance of securities.

To these we can add:

— Inefficiencies due to significant transaction costs, whch may deter small, private investors, thereby limiting the number of market participants, and restricting the market to relatively infrequent, large bargains.

The majority of developing countries do not have organized markets at all, as we have pointed out. Many do have unorganized markets, in that securities are traded, but usually directly between institutions, between institutions and individuals, and between individuals. Stockbrokers and jobbers are absent; in other words there are no market-makers. In this large groups of countries the major inefficiency in the capital market is the lack of information available in an organized market. It is finance in these countries which is the main concern of this book; therefore we shall examine the applicability of capital market theory in the absence of an organized capital market.

Let us start with the organized capital markets in developing countries. What are their characteristics and inefficiencies, and what are the implications for the applicability of capital market theory? First, many tend to be small. Only about half the developing countries with stock exchanges have over 100 companies quoted. Of course substantial industrial and service companies, which make up the bulk of the stock markets in developed countries, are relatively scarce in developing countries. The latter are much more dependent on agriculture, few agricultural enterprises are even incorporated, and those which are tend to be foreign or government-owned. Many of the larger industrial and mining companies fall into the same categories. There is little incentive for foreign companies to obtain a local quotation as few will need to raise capital locally. The main pressure to go public may come from the government, or from a 'diplomatic' urge to encourage a certain degree of local shareholding. As Drake (1980, p. 205) has pointed out, it was transportation and utilities companies which provided the backbone of western stock exchanges in their formative years before 1914. Generally such undertakings are government-owned in developing countries, and so the markets lack this core of infrastructure enterprises.

The volume of transactions also tends to be low. The ratio of stock transactions to GNP in developing countries is usually a fraction of 1%, with the exceptions of Taiwan, Singapore, Korea, and Brazil. The ratio on the larger stock markets in developed countries frequently exceeded 10%, although low values were also recorded on the smaller European markets (Wai and Patrick, 1973, table 11).

A low volume of transactions suggests that the reaction of share prices to new information may not be immediate, and prices therefore may not 'fully reflect' all available information. The consequences will be that a number of share prices may be off the 'perfect' securities market line. However, even if share prices do reflect the available information they may be too few in number to form a continuous SML. Instead, the line will appear as a series of unconnected points. The combination of these two phenomena gives us a scatter diagram of share prices, or a picture of a fragmented capital market. The capital market line may now only be a best-fit least-squares line, and may not be a very good 'fit' (Figure 2.13).

Other forms of inefficiency will tend to reinforce the fragmentation of the capital market. When investors have significantly different perceptions of risk and return the market may have shares demonstrating the characteristics of points A and B in Figure 2.13, where A gives a higher return for less risk than does B. The lack of adequate market regulation and inadequate disclosure standards by companies provides opportunities to rig the market and to make windfall gains because access to information is uneven. Again, some share prices may not truly reflect their risk–return ratio. The fourth

50

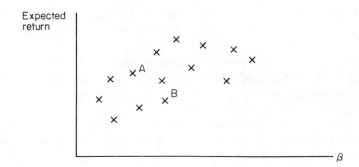

Figure 2.13 Securities market line with a fragmented capital market

inefficiency, poor communications, has a similar effect in that it restricts and slows the spread of information. Some investors who receive information early can then profit at the expense of those who receive it later. In large countries such as Nigeria or Indonesia communications across the country are likely to be slow, and investors outside the capital may receive information much later than those in the capital.

It seems likely that the uneven spread of information among investors, caused by poor communications and uneven disclosure by companies, might result in a lack of confidence in the market by investors. Suggestions of insider dealing, even when it is nothing more than quick reaction to slowly spreading information, may produce cynicism among other investors which leads them to shun the market. Drake (1980) has pointed out the need for official regulation and supervision to ensure full disclosure and wide dissemination of information; to prevent market rigging; and to protect shareholders. Brokers and jobbers need to be seen to be honest. Wai and Patrick (1973) warn of the 'danger of regulatory overkill . . . which may inhibit capital market development'. Alternatively it may drive it underground, as happened in Kuwait. There the well-regulated, official market, with only about 40 quoted securities, did not provide sufficient opportunities for the financial community. This led to the development of the unofficial market (Souq al Manakh), where shares of new companies, and of other companies in the Gulf, were traded. Again, about 40 companies' shares were traded, but payments were made with post-dated cheques (thus creating a forward market in shares), and the bubble burst in September 1982. Authorities responsible for stock market regulation need to tread a narrow path between under-supervision and over-supervision. Investors must have confidence, but should not feel over-protected.

Interestingly, Kuwait is one of the few developing country stock markets which have been tested for efficiency. Gandhi, Saunders, and Woodward (1980) found that the market suffered from 'thinness' (high volatility of share prices, and few quoted companies), and that share prices tended to be serially correlated (a relative absence of random walks). This means that, some investors may be able to predict share prices and thereby to 'beat the market'. In other words there is inefficiency in price determination (although the authors did not identify the reasons for this). On the other hand, the correlation of the different sectors with the all-share market index varied considerably, thereby implying that there is considerable scope for gains by diversification.

Analysts play an important part in identifying the risks and returns associated with individual securities and disseminating their views, thereby helping to ensure that shares take their correct place on the SML. The absence of such analysts will lead to disparate (and often incorrect) views about a share's risk–return ratio, and the absence of expert analysts will tend to prolong irrational behaviour such as a preference for share B over A in Figure 2.13. Relatively high transaction costs, especially high minimum commissions and fixed-rate taxes, will tend to deter small investors, and leave the market in the hands of a relatively small number of large operators who, acting individually, can affect market prices substantially. Numerous small transactions by small investors help to keep markets fluid, and help to maintain equilibrium.

In the developing countries which do not have organized capital markets (the majority), the fragmentation effect is likely to be much greater. In these countries markets will be dominated by a few financial institutions, mainly banks. Central banks will sell government securities to commercial banks and development banks who may in turn sell some to their corporate or individual clients. The market in equities will be dominated by development banks, and other financial institutions, who take equity in companies and then hold it rather than trade it (a process reminiscent of the activities of the universal banks of continental Europe, which have similar relationships with their clients, especially unquoted companies which do not have the possibility of raising funds on the stock market). Under these circumstances trading will be sporadic and 'lumpy' (large parcels of shares will tend to change hands), and the stock market guides to valuation (risk measures, or price-earning ratios) will be absent, as prices will not be available for comparable securities.

In such countries our diagram of a fragmented capital market (Figure 2.13) will have rather fewer points, and they will probably be more widely scattered, with more likelihood of 'irrational' configurations such as the coexistence of points A and B. Moreover, the infrequency of transactions means that points will represent transactions on different dates, thereby possibly reflecting different macroeconomic and political circumstances. It will not be possible to obtain β values for individual shares, as there will be no records of share transactions and no recorded 'market index' with which to compare movements of individual share prices. The notion of a securities market line will be merely intuitive.

9. THE APPLICATION OF CAPITAL MARKET THEORY TO DEVELOPING COUNTRIES

How useful, then, is CMT in developing countries, given that the capital markets will be more or less fragmented, and that they will inevitably fall substantially short of the conditions needed to satisfy the efficient market hypothesis? Two results were obtained from CMT which may be relevant to developing countries:

— The principle of diversification of investments will lead to improved portfolio selection, and improved project selection.
— The discount rate (or cost of equity capital) can be derived from the CAPM.

In addition, the theory has a number of implications for developed country institutions, two of which are:

— Diversification of investment portfolios through international investment can include portfolio investment in developing countries, and direct investment where portfolio investment is restricted.
— International direct investors in developing countries can use the CAPM to estimate their cost of capital.

Two further considerations are:

— The impact of high and unstable inflation and interest rate control on CMT. Volatile inflation and controlled interest rates are not uncommon in developing countries, any may have implications for CMT.
— The relation between efficient capital markets and the economic allocation of investment resources in developing countries. If other markets are badly distorted a perfect capital market may not lead to an improvement in investment allocation.

Little research has been done to try to apply CMT to developing country capital markets, mainly because of the obvious evidence of inefficient markets. Errunza (1977), in a paper presenting the advantages of international diversification of portfolios into developing country stock markets, also commented:

A potential alternative to the use of the M–V (mean–variance) model would be to estimate national and international market factors using the CAPM. Of late, some research has been reported in this area. . . . These works are, however, limited to the developed country markets. Hence, the obvious next step would be to apply the CAPM to LDCs. However, at present, it is doubtful whether substantial insight could be gained from application of CAPM to the developing markets. This is because many of the LDC markets in this study are not very active and available LDC stock market indices are of doubtful quality, consistency or reliability. Also the CAPM assumptions—e.g. homogeneous expectations and risk-free interest rates— may not hold in an international context. Hence the M–V model, which relies primarily on mean and variance of the probability distribution of single-period portfolio returns, is preferred.

(a) The Principle of Diversification

Broadly speaking the principle seems to survive, although not entirely unscathed. The inefficiencies, even in an organized market, mean that the risk is not proportional to the variance of return. Risk estimates may be extremely hazy because of lack of information. Moreover, in small and narrow markets investors may not have available a sufficient range of equities to diversify in the way that they would wish. Countries without organized markets present very limited trading opportunities, and little information, which therefore makes systematic diversification very difficult. An institution will often have little choice in its equity investment opportunities. Nonetheless, holding two equities is likely to present less risk than concentrating resources on only one equity. The danger is that share price movements may be highly correlated, but the Gandhi, Saunders, and Woodward (1980) study of the Kuwait stock market found substantial scope for gains through diversification.

Research into developing country stock market behaviour is limited, though Agmon and Lessard (1977) report a study of some stock markets in Latin America over 1958–68, and found that the risk of a broadly diversified portfolio, compared with the risks of holding an average common stock, were as shown in Table 2.3 (the bulk of the study is reported in Lessard (1975), but these figures are not included in that reference).

Thus diversification in these countries does reduce risk, but not to the same extent as in industrialized countries. In Colombia, for example, only 16% of risk could be diversified away, whereas in the USA about 70% of risk can be diversified away by holding a diversified portfolio.

The question arises 'what characteristics are necessary before one can apply the mean–variance theorem with confidence?' An investor needs to be able to have a considerable choice of stocks in order that he (and all other investors) can construct a portfolio to his liking. What is the minimum number of stocks which would permit this?—50?, 100?, 200? How well correlated are individual securities in developing country markets? Do market inefficiencies tend to produce high correlations in the share prices of

Table 2.3

Country	Portfolio risk as percentage of risk of common stock (standard deviation)
Colombia	84
Argentina	81
Chile	71
Brazil	69

different securities, thereby undermining the arguments for diversification? (i.e. does market risk constitute a high proportion of total risk?) This may arise if developing country markets are subject to investor hysteria, leading to 'bubbles' and subsequent collapses. Such phenomena were characteristic of older stock markets in their formative years, such as the Banque Royale/Mississippi Scheme in France (1719) and the South Sea Bubble in Britain (1720). In recent years Hong Kong and Kuwait have seen similar booms and collapses. How well correlated should be the expected returns and risks on individual stocks? Further research is needed before we can answer the above, and other, questions.

(b) The Discount Rate and the CAPM

We have seen the effect that fragmentation of the capital market has on the SML, and therefore on the CAPM equation. The equation no longer holds exactly, and a share's risk–return ratio may no longer represent its equilibrium value. Moreover, the use of historical share price data to estimate a share's β value will be suspect for the same reason, and the β value obtained may not be reliable; therefore it may be unsound to extrapolate it into the future. For this reason we can no longer estimate a β value for a project, and use the CAPM to estimate the discount rate. The most we can do is to estimate a *range* for the discount rate, say between 10% and 12%. Moreover,the more fragmented a capital market becomes (as we move from larger to smaller markets, and from organized to unorganized markets), the wider the range for the discount rate becomes. As mentioned earlier, in countries without organized capital markets the SML is likely to become merely notional, and the estimate of the risk premium largely intuitive.

So far the discussion has concentrated on the private sector discount rate. But does the CAPM have anything to contribute to the estimation of the social discount rate in developing countries? In countries where prices are substantially distorted, theories of social cost–benefit analysis place substantial importance on shadow pricing of factors, and the use of a social discount rate. It may reasonably be stated that no really satisfactory method has been devised for estimating the social discount rate in the literature of social cost–benefit analysis. Using a CAPM approach, Hirschleifer (1965), Arrow (1966), and Bailey and Jensen (1972) argued that *with perfect and complete capital markets*, government cannot diversify risk any more than the capital market. Both can fully diversify specific risk, but neither can diversify market risk. Therefore the private and social (i.e. government) discount rates will be the same. However, developing countries (and developed, for that matter) do not have perfect and complete capital markets, so the result may no longer be valid. Once we have imperfect capital markets the risk premium becomes impossible to estimate, and the government is faced with the same problem of estimation as the private firm. Moreover, with imperfect capital markets the government may find its borrowing powers to be restricted, and it will then be faced with a capital rationing problem. Further, the two-parameter risk and expected-return model seems very difficult to apply to most public sector projects. If the output is to be sold on the market, and comparable projects exist in the country, then some idea of a risk premium may be obtainable. However, with schools, roads, hospitals, and the large variety of other public sector projects where the output is provided free (or at subsidized prices), how can we estimate a risk premium for these projects? There is no ready answer to this question.

It is easy to identify the shortcomings of the CAPM in estimating the social discount rate for developing countries, but unfortunately the alternative approaches seem little better. To use the rate of return on government bonds ignores the fact that government projects too face systematic risk. Likewise, to use the rate of return on the marginal project ignores risk, and begs the question of 'what is the marginal project?' This seems to be as difficult to identify as the risk premium. The cost of borrowing on the Eurocurrency market, the source of marginal capital for many countries, appears to offer better prospects, but such finance is rarely pure project finance, and therefore will again ignore specific risk. All these methods produce a blanket discount rate for government to use on all projects, and therefore ignore the consideration that different projects face different degrees of riskiness, and that therefore each project should have its own discount rate. Whatever the shortcomings of using the CAPM to estimate the risk-adjusted discount rate (RADR), it may be no worse than the alternatives, and may even be better in countries which do have organized capital markets.

(c) International Portfolio Diversification

Most work on international portfolio diversification has concentrated on markets in industrialized countries, but Lessard (1971) introduced the concept of an investment union among developing countries, and (1975) tested the idea for Argentina, Brazil, Chile, and Columbia. He found that investors in any four of these countries would have benefited from diversification into the others over the period 1958–68, and that investing equally in the four Latin American countries compared favourably with investing in the USA.

Errunza (1977) considered diversification into security markets in developing countries from industrialized countries, and suggested that the empirical evidence supported it. However, he found that there are substantial obstacles to foreign portfolio investment in developing country securities, notably 'portfolio suppression' (political and economic instability, monetary and fiscal policies which result in high and unstable rates of inflation, interest rate controls, lack of capital market institutions, high transaction costs, etc.). He also found that there are problems in obtaining company, industry, market, and country information, that practices of local accounting firms may be different (in some developing countries auditing standards are distinctly lower than in industrialized countries), and that capital controls deterred foreign portfolio investment. In short he found, as we do, that developing country capital markets tend to be fragmented, repressed, and inefficient. Consequently, risk and expected return may no longer be closely correlated. Likewise the market indices used may be of questionable accuracy. All these considerations suggest reservations about Errunza's findings concerning the advantages of portfolio diversification into developing countries.

Nevertheless, funds have been in existence for many years to enable investors to diversify into developing country securities.[13] Some markets, such as Singapore, are readily accessible to unit trusts and investment trusts; in other cases special funds have been set up. The Mexico Fund which invests in the Mexican capital market, for example, is quoted on both the New York and London Stock Exchanges. Sadly its performance has tended to reflect Mexico's national financial difficulties. The market risk in Mexico has therefore been considerable, and for investors in the Mexico Fund, market risk corresponds to the country risk of the international banker. For the foreign investor there may also be substantial foreign exchange risk in international portfolio diversification, which is probably not reflected in market risk estimates based on local currency values. This has to be borne in mind when considering an international portfolio. A few years ago a Swiss investment banker, interviewed in *Euromoney*, said 'the most important thing is to choose the right currency'.

(d) Direct Foreign Investment in Developing Countries

A transnational corporation (TNC) may be interested in two of the results of CMT. First the theory, and existing literature, suggests that international investment diversification, including diversion into developing countries, may improve the risk–return outcome of its investments. In principle a shareholder can diversify his own portfolio internationally, generally more easily than a TNC can make physical investments; therefore there is no need for the TNC to concern itself with diversification in the interests of its shareholders. However, shareholders may be restricted in that they may face exchange controls in their home country and they may face practical difficulties in investing in developing countries, especially in those which do not have organized capital markets.[14] Under these circumstances CMT suggests that TNCs should undertake physical investments in developing countries in order to help their shareholders to diversify internationally. This argument for diversification into developing countries is open to similar objections to the arguments against portfolio investment; namely, that capital markets are imperfect, which may put an outsider at a substantial disadvantage, and thereby lead him to choose the wrong investments or projects. He might choose a share (or project) at point B in Figure 2.13. On the other hand, imperfections in other developing country factor markets—notably in finance, management, marketing skills, and technology—may provide very substantial reasons for TNCs to invest in developing countries, but we will reserve discussion on this point until Chapter 8.

TNCs' second area of interest in the CAPM is the use of the CAPM to estimate the discount rate for their projects in developing countries. The TNC has a number of choices. Should it use the SML of its domestic capital market, which gives the rate of return used by shareholders? Should it use the SML of the country it is investing in, assuming that there is one, or if not, that a rough SML can be estimated? Or, given that it is diversified in a number of countries, should it use a world SML? Further, when investing in developing countries where it perceives the 'political risk' to be high, should the TNC add on an appropriate risk premium to its discount rate? There are no easy answers to these questions. A country operating in one country can, in principle, use the CAPM to estimate its discount rate. However, a TNC can raise capital by borrowing or issuing equity in several different countries, and investing in other countries. If all the world's capital markets were efficient, and there were no exchange controls, exchange rate risks, or transaction costs, the world would have a single unified capital market, and a single securities market line. Our TNC would then be able to read off its discount rate from the world security market line.

However, national capital markets are segmented, rather than integrated into a world capital market; exchange controls, exchange rate risks, and transaction costs *are* important, and a world securities market line can most politely be described as notional. Adler and Dumas (1975) found that 'an MNC's required yield on its domestic projects will generally differ from its required yield on foreign projects and both will differ from the required yield of a foreign firm facing the same foreign projects'. The differences in required yields arose from exchange rate risk, rather than a general ability of TNCs to accept lower returns than local firms. Agmon and Lessard (1975), though, found that TNCs would have substantially lower required rates of return than would a local investor, the TNC's advantage arising from its ability to diversify internationally. Thus the TNC can diversify away much of the market risk of a particular country, which the domestic investor is unable to do. Moreover, what little evidence is available suggests that market risk in developing countries tends to form a higher proportion of total risk than in industrialized countries. However, Agmon and Lessard's approach does require that the CAPM holds in the developing country.

Schapiro (1982, p. 493), reviewing the empirical work done on shareholders' required returns on foreign exchange relative to domestic projects, concludes that the results of the research are unclear. He further concludes that the available evidence suggests that foreign operations tend to reduce a TNC's actual and perceived riskiness, and that the use of a risk premium for political risk ignores the fact that the TNC diversifies political risk by investing in a number of countries. However, there is not yet any general solution to the question of what discount rate a TNC should use for overseas investment, although the indications of CMT are that it may be able to accept a lower rate of return on a project in a developing country than a purely domestic firm could. This conclusion is likely to be of some concern to developing countries, as it implies that TNCs may have some financial advantages over domestic firms as well as advantages arising from imperfections in the markets for finance, management, and technology. However, whether in practice they take advantage of their ability to use a lower discount rate than a local firm is another question. Bavishi (1979), for example, found that 25% of US-based TNCs raised the discount rate when investing overseas, while only 14% made no allowance of any sort in project appraisal. The remainder took the assumed higher risk of foreign investment into account in some other way.

(e) Capital Market Theory and Inflation

In works on CMT it is widely assumed that nominal interest rates (e.g. the risk-free interest rate) fully reflect all the available information on future interest rates. They are seen as consisting of a 'real' component and a 'money' component. This is known as the 'Fisher effect', after Irving Fisher. There is some empirical support for the Fisher effect, but not all studies support it (Roll, 1972). The impact of inflation on returns in the stock market has also been studied, and Jaffe and Mandelker (1976), for example, found 'a negative relationship between the returns and concurrent rates of inflation over the last two decades, while we found a positive relationship between the two variables over a longer period of time'. Bodie (1976) and Nelson (1976) came to similar conclusions. All these studies used New York Stock Exchange prices, but Cohn and Lessard (1981) found that a number of other industrialized countries showed a similar negative relationship. (In other words, stocks do not always provide a hedge against inflation.) However, most studies of inflation and CMT have used data from the more efficient of the world's capital markets, and assume market-determined interest rates. These conditions hold in few developing countries.

Conventionally, CMT is expressed in money rather than real values. Thus the risk-free rate of interest is measured in money terms, as is the risk premium. In countries with low rates of inflation, which do not vary much, this may be acceptable, but in countries with high and fluctuating inflation rates (well into double figures, and sometimes treble figures), money rates of interest may be of little use to investors, especially as they may represent negative real rates of return. If we postulate a negative real risk-free rate of interest,[15] and re-draw the SML in real terms, it would look as shown in Figure 2.14.

Now r represents the risk-free rate of return, and is negative. No investor (at least, no investor who thinks in real terms) will want to earn the risk-free rate of return. Moreover, he may not be interested in the rate of return on the market portfolio either. *A priori* this may also be negative (M_1), or

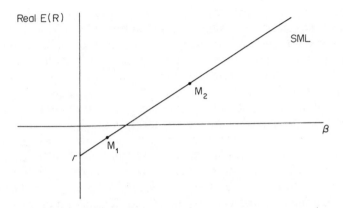

Figure 2.14 The SML with a negative real risk-free rate of interest

positive (M_2). If positive, then investors may be encouraged to invest in the market. However, the encouragement will be rather less if the market is expected to give negative real rates of return. Under these circumstances investors will tend to sell short, or to invest in non-financial assets such as gold, land and property, commodities, coins, stamps or other 'alternative investments' which they expect to give a real (or at least higher) rate of return than they expect from the capital market. The extent to which investors do measure their expected returns in real terms is unclear, but certainly the possibility is there, especially in countries with high rates of inflation, and in the few countries which offer index-linked bonds.

The prevalence of negative real risk-free rates of interest in developing countries led to the development of theories of financial repression which we will examine in the next chapter. Negative real interest rates may be the result of high inflation rates, or government restrictions on interest rates, or often a combination of both. The development of a capital market under such conditions may be different or stunted compared to the industrialized countries; therefore the use of capital market theory in investment decisions may be rather different too. Certainly, it adds credibility to Levy's theory that an efficient portfolio contains a number of short positions.

(f) Financial Efficiency and Economic Efficiency

Financial economists use the term 'efficient' in a sense different from other economists. A 'financially efficient' market is one in which prices fully reflect all available information. An 'economically efficient' market, however, is one which allocates resources in a way which is 'Pareto efficient', i.e. no-one can be made better off without someone else being made worse off. Perfectly competitive markets generate Pareto efficient resource allocations. However, Stiglitz (1981) has shown that financial markets which are efficient, complete, and competitive may not be economically efficient, on two main grounds. First, the transmission of information between shareholders and managers is costly and imperfect: managers may know more about future investment opportunities than do shareholders, but may not transmit this information. Likewise, shareholders may not transmit to management their attitudes to risk, return, and different available projects. Secondly, the objectives of management and shareholders probably will not coincide. The manager is not diversified in the risks he faces, but the (presumably efficient) shareholder is. The two may therefore have different views of what constitutes the right investment for the firm. Because shareholders have limited control (in practice very little) over management, the latter's views will prevail in investment choice. These views may be contrary to those of the efficient shareholder, and contrary to the efficient allocation of resources. Eventually poor investment choice will be reflected in the share price, and may lead to replacement of the management; by then the damage will have been done.

A market which is efficient in a financial sense therefore is not necessarily efficient in an economic sense. A financially efficient market, even in a perfectly competitive economy, may lead to resources not being allocated to those projects or activities which maximize welfare. However, in an economy with market imperfections and distortions, numerous firms would profit from such 'inefficiencies'; indeed they may owe their existence to protection from imports or a government-granted monopoly position. In a country which has a financially efficient capital market but is economically inefficient, many resources will be allocated to those opportunities which arise because of the economic inefficiencies. Thus an efficient capital market may result in a worsening of the use of financial resources, from a national point of view. That, however, is not the fault of the capital market, but rather of the economic arrangements which permit the economic inefficiencies to continue, and thereby to attract finance.

This divergence between financial and economic efficiency may be more widespread in developing than in developed countries (although, as we have seen, the financial markets are probably not very efficient in developing countries). This divergence mirrors the divergence between private and public interests, which is a cornerstone of the large body of work which has been done on social cost–benefit analysis (SCBA). The SCBA literature has been directed particularly at developing countries because market imperfections and distortions are thought to be much greater than in developed countries. If this is true, as seems likely, then the divergence between financial and economic efficiency may also be much greater in the developing countries. Therefore the use of the CAPM to allocate resources to projects may lead to a misallocation of resources. Under such circumstances governments should not repress capital markets, but take steps to reduce the economic distortions.

(g) Other Applications of Capital Market Theory

In this chapter we have discussed only a few of the possible applications of CMT in development finance. We shall look at other possible applications in subsequent chapters, notably the following:

— The use of the mean–variance theorem of portfolio diversification by development banks in the selection of their loans and investments.
— The use of the mean–variance theorem by banks in constructing their international loan portfolios, and the application of risk–expected return analysis to their lending conditions and to 'country risk' analysis.
— The potential use of portfolio diversification and risk–return analysis by export credit agencies.
— A further examination of the application of CMT to direct foreign investment in developing countries.
— Risk diversification applied to Islamic financial principles, under which interest is not permitted, although capital growth is. Banking and investment under Islamic principles is a growing practice in Islamic countries and institutions, and shows a marked preference for the provision of equity rather than debt. In effect savers in Islamic banks therefore may face higher risks than savers in conventional banks.

10. CONCLUDING REMARKS

Capital market theory is essentially a two-parameter model of the financial world, the two parameters being risk and expected return. As such it presents an appealing approach to portfolio management, asset valuation, and investment criteria. However, the results of empirical testing have at best been ambiguous. Nonetheless, CMT probably contributes substantially to explaining the behaviour of relatively efficient markets, and can be a powerful tool of analysis. Its applicability in less efficient capital markets is much less certain, and few empirical tests have been undertaken, especially in developing country capital markets. However, its intuitive appeal still remains, although notions such as the security market line are likely to be crude, and the utility of CMT to analyse and explain financial behaviour in such countries may be limited. Market imperfections are likely to be dominant, especially during the formative years of capital markets, but as markets grow, and understanding and communications improve, CMT may become increasingly relevant. In the next chapter we will examine theories of financial repression, which are explicitly based on market imperfections, and relate their findings to CMT.

Lest any readers from socialist or centrally planned economies should feel that CMT (and this book) are a plea for liberal capitalism, let me add that CMT will, of course, be political anathema to them, and that free capital markets will have no role in their societies. Capital markets, especially inefficient capital markets, can certainly exacerbate inequalities in the distribution of wealth and income in any economy. Developing countries, and their leaders, who already face substantial and growing distribution problems, may well wonder whether the encouragement of a capital market will only aggravate an already pressing problem, and whether any benefits to be gained (which at best are difficult to quantify) would not be more than offset by the costs of increased inequalities of income and wealth. This is a real problem, and one to which theory has little to contribute. A market economist may respond by suggesting that contervailing taxes could be introduced to offset the distributional disadvantages of a capital market, but this in itself assumes that the tax-collection system is efficient, which is seldom the case in developing countries. While we raise the question, we cannot possibly provide an answer as to whether a developing country should encourage a capital market. This is a social and political question for developing country leaders. However, we will examine the possible economic and distributional effects of an organized capital market in Chapter 6.

Finally, nothing has been said about the 'psychology' of capital markets. Market professionals give considerable weight to the importance of market (or crowd) psychology, and consider that it plays a substantial role in explaining market movements. Academic theory does not incorporate such an intangible factor as crowd psychology, preferring to restrict itself to the rational investor, whose behaviour is easier to analyse. We believe that the professionals' experience is not to be ignored, and that theory loses the richness of an added dimension and the virtue of credibility if psychology is omitted from market analysis. Psychology *is* an important factor.

ANNEX 2.1: THE MARKOWITZ MEAN–VARIANCE THEOREM

The Markowitz two-parameter (risk and expected return) mean–variance theorem may be derived as follows.

Consider a portfolio consisting of n securities. Then its expected return, $E(R)$ is given by:

$$E(R) = \sum_{i=1}^{n} x_i u_i \tag{1}$$

where x_i is the proportion of the ith security in the portfolio and u_i is its expected return.

We define the risk of a portfolio as the variance of its return, V. This is determined by:

(a) the variance of the return of each security, and
(b) the covariance of returns between each pair of securities.

$$V = \sum_{i=1}^{n} x_i^2 \sigma_i^2 + 2 \sum_{i=1}^{n-1} \sum_{j=i+1}^{n} x_i x_j \sigma_{ij} \tag{2}$$

Where σ_i is the standard deviation of the ith security (σ_i^2 is therefore its variance), and σ_{ij} is the covariance of returns between two securities i and j.

σ_{ij} is determined by the correlation of the returns of the two securities and the standard deviation of their returns, i.e.

$$\sigma_{ij} = \rho_{ij}\,\sigma_i\,\sigma_j \tag{3}$$

Where ρ_{ij} = correlation coefficient of the returns to i and j, and σ_i, σ_j are the standard deviations of the returns to i and j.

Substituting for σ_{ij} in (2),

$$V = \sum_{i=1}^{n} x_i^2\,\sigma_i^2 + 2\sum_{i=1}^{n-1} b \sum_{j=i+1}^{n} x_i x_j \rho_{ij}\,\sigma_i\sigma_j.$$

To show that diversification reduces the variance (and, by definition, the risk), we will consider a world consisting of two securities 1 and 2. We can invest all in 1, all in 2, or diversify between 1 and 2. (For convenience, we will assume $\sigma_1 = \sigma_2 = \sigma$.)

(i) If we invest all in 1 (i.e. $x_2 = 0$; $n = 1$)
$V = \sigma_1^2 = \sigma^2$.

(ii) If we invest all in 2 (i.e. $x_1 = 0$, $n = 1$)
$V = \sigma_2^2 = \sigma^2$

(iii) If we invest x_1 in security 1 and x_2 in security 2 ($n = 2$; $x_2 = 1 - x_1$).
$V = x_1^2\sigma^2 + (1-x_1)^2\,\sigma^2 + 2x_1\,(1-x_1)\,\rho_{12}\,\sigma^2$
$= \sigma^2\,[x_1^2 + (1-x_1)^2 + 2x_1\,(1-x_1)\,\rho_{12}]$
Now $x_1^2 + (1 - x_1)^2 + 2x_1\,(1-x_1) = [x_1 + (1 -x_1)]^2 = 1.$
or $x_1^2 + (1 - x_1)^2 = 1 - 2x_1\,(1 - x_1)$
$\therefore$ If $\rho_{12} = 1$, then
$V = \sigma^2$ [as in (i) and (ii)]
If $\rho_{12} < 1$, then
$V = \sigma^2[1 - 2x_1\,(1 - x_1) + 2x_1\,(1 - x_1)\,\rho_{12}]$
$= \sigma^2\,[1 - 2x_1\,(1 - x_1)(1 - \rho_{12})]$
If $\rho_{12} < 1$, then $(1 - \rho_{12})$ is positive and $(1 - x_1)$ is positive.
Then $2x_1\,(1 - x_1)(1 - \rho_{12})$ is a positive number, q, and
$V = \sigma^2\,(1 - q) < \sigma^2$
Therefore the variance of return is always reduced by diversification unless $\rho_{12} = 1$ (i.e. unless the securities are perfectly correlated).

NOTES

1. One popular measure of variability is standard deviation/mean.
2. The Financial Times–Actuaries All Share Index, contrary to its title, includes only about 750 out of the 2500 or so stocks listed on the London Stock Exchange.
3. I have taken this example from Witt and Dobbins (1979), p. 15. Incidentally, it has been shown empirically that portfolio returns only approximate to the normal distribution (Mandelbrot, 1963; Fama, 1965).

4. The major exception is provided by gold shares, which tend to move against the market.

5. In part of the paper, Atherton and Yapp (1979) included returns, risk, and correlations in a number of developing country stock markets (India, Mexico, Peru, Philippines, and Venezuela).

6. For proof of the CAPM see, for example, Lumby (1981).

7. It is beyond the scope of this book to discuss the details and shortcomings of discounted cash flow accept/reject rules. There is a large accessible literature on the subject, including Franks and Broyles (1979), chap. 4; Bromwich (1976); Bierman and Schmidt (1975); and Merrett and Sykes (1973).

8. In the United States numerous estimates are available for company betas, and in the UK the Risk Measurement Service of the London Business School performs the same function. The latter gives beta values of the FT–Actuaries industry groupings (one of which is textiles), which enables us to use a sectoral beta rather than an individual company beta. (In the UK the textile group beta is between 0.9 and 1.0.)

9. Franks and Broyles (1979) propose two refinements to this basic model. The first is an adjustment for financial gearing (leverage), the second an adjustment for operational gearing (leverage). Subsequently, Broyles and Cooper (1981) introduce a further adjustment, to take account of the growth opportunities facing the firm. However for present purposes (and most practical purposes), the approach outlined here is adequate.

10. It was suggested to me in Mexico in the mid-1970s that Mexicans looked for real rates of return of the order of 30% on new projects. Given that the risk-free yields at the time were about 15% (in money terms), then this would imply a high general risk premium, or a high value placed on beta coefficients for the new projects in question, many of which were intended to produce goods which had not been manufactured before in Mexico.

11. If, in one short-run period, $E(R) = a + b\beta$, then in n successive periods, $E(R)^n = (a + b\beta)^n$ assuming that returns in each successive period are stochastically independent. If b is positive, then $E(R)^n = (a + b\beta)^n$ is a convex curve, with $E(R)$ increasing faster than β. Therefore although the short-run relationship between $E(R)$ and β is linear, the long-run relationship, theoretically, is not.

12. The story is told of a student walking along with his professor, a believer in the efficient market hypothesis. 'Look', cries the student. 'I have found a $20 note!' 'You can't have', replies the professor. 'If it were a $20 note, someone would have found it already.' Even in the most efficient of markets, someone must be ahead of the game, even if only by a fraction.

13. The Foreign and Colonial Investment Trust was set up in Britain in 1868, to invest in bonds and companies operating in what were then (and sometimes still are) developing countries.

14. The argument for international physical investment may apply more strongly to TNCs from developing countries, as their shareholders may often find it more difficult to diversify internationally than do their equivalents in industrialized countries, where exchange controls are fewer and communications better.

15. In another sense we no longer have a risk-free rate of interest when we introduce inflation, because we are now exposed to money risk (see Chapter 1).

Chapter 3

The Impact of the Domestic Financial System on Economic Development

This chapter is in two parts. The first consists of a discussion of the relationship between financial development and economic development, a subject which has come into prominence over the past 25 years due mainly to the works of Gurley and Shaw (1960) and Goldsmith (1969). The second part is devoted to a discussion of the theory of financial repression, which was developed independently by McKinnon (1973) and Shaw (1973), but whose origins lie in the earlier work on financial and economic development. Repression theory in turn spawned a substantial body of econometric studies on the relationships between saving, investment, and growth on the one hand, and interest rates and inflation rates on the other. The results of the main econometric studies are discussed towards the end of the chapter.

1. THE ROLE OF THE FINANCIAL SYSTEM

(a) Does Finance Matter?

A fully developed financial system consists of a wide range of institutions, instruments, and markets, such as may be seen in the industrialized countries of the West. It is not of course a static system, but one which is changing continuously as new institutions and instruments are developed. The financial system in most developing countries, however, is much less developed, having a much narrower range of institutions and instruments and being smaller relative to the size of the economy. But does this matter? Does the financial system have an important role to play in the economic growth of a country? If so, how and why? What implications does it have for financial policy? It is this type of question which this chapter will address itself to first. Later we will consider the basic macrofinancial relations in an economy, through the theory of financial repression.

The 'development hypothesis' view, often described as the 'neo-liberal' view, ascribes considerable importance to the financial system in economic development. Its supporters maintain that the lack of a developed financial system restricts economic growth and that, therefore, government policy should be directed towards encouraging the growth of the financial system. A contrary, and perhaps extreme, view would be that the financial system has little role to play in the development of the 'real' economy and that it merely provides legitimate opportunities for the private sector to make (and to lose) money. This 'casino hypothesis' of the financial system would imply that government can safely ignore it, or even consider it as being harmful to the growth and distribution of income, and therefore to be suppressed or nationalized, a view generally prevalent in socialist countries.

The development hypothesis view of the financial system sees it as a means to an end, the 'end' being economic development. This, in turn, means achieving a certain combination of growth and distribution of income per head which is regarded as satisfactory. Unless the financial system contributes to this end, the effect of the mobilization of funds will at best be neutral and at worst will result in a squandering of resources leading to inflation and the build-up of debt without producing the means to service the debt, leading to panics, crises, and collapses. This applies with equal force to the use of both domestic and foreign finance. Under such conditions finance effectively becomes a liability which restricts economic growth, or even becomes such a cost that it reduces the level of national income. It is sad, but probably true, to say that a considerable part of the Euromarket borrowing by developing countries in the 1970s was not used effectively, and that in a number of countries the consequent debt service has led to a net loss of resources. As the outcome of the use of finance is necessarily uncertain, there is an inevitable degree of risk to the national economy in its mobilization and use.

Notwithstanding this risk, the development hypothesis sees the financial system as a necessary input into the development process and, therefore, a necessary risk which has to be taken. It took some time before development economists recognized that finance might play an essential role in the development process. Shaw (1973) commented that:

This theme [that the financial sector of an economy does matter in economic development] is excluded from dominant traditions of theory and practice in economic development. Some development theory seems to be designed for a barter world. In other models finance is passively adaptive and its deepening is a by-product of accelerated growth in 'real' things. There is doctrine that ranks financial deepening among obstacles to development and recommends financial repression. That guiding beacon of development practice, the Plan, gives scant heed to finance in the usual case.

Writing from a rather different standpoint, Griffith-Jones (1982) remarked:

The great importance of correct financial policies during attempts at transition to socialism and the fact that it is precisely socialist governments, more than conservative ones, which need most to follow deliberate and often strict financial policies is very rarely recognised by economists and politicians on the Left.

Nonetheless, the availability and efficient use of finance can never be a sufficient condition for economic growth. Rather it should be seen as only one of a number of necessary inputs, alongside natural resources, labour, markets, management, technology, and entrepreneurial ability. Some writers, even fairly recently, have accorded it a subsidiary role (Newlyn, 1977, p. 1). It may be more accurate to suggest that it ranks *pari passu* with the other necessary inputs.

The above conclusion may seem to be in accordance with common sense, but the fact of the matter is that only limited research has been conducted concerning the role of financial institutions and instruments in economic development. On the basis of available research results, one cannot conclusively answer questions such as 'What contribution does the development of the financial sector play in the economic development of a country?' or 'Is economic development impossible without financial development?' or 'Does financial development lead economic development?' or 'What *types* of financial development are conducive to economic development?' Much work has been done on the role of foreign finance in economic development, but even here the findings are not conclusive and conflicting views are held concerning the importance of external finance. This subject is taken up again in Chapter 7.

On the subject of the relationship between financial development and economic development, a consensus appeared to have been reached by the mid-1970s, among the leading writers on the subject, that financial development is important and leads to economic development (Patrick, 1966; Porter, 1966; Gurley and Shaw, 1955, 1960, 1967; Goldsmith, 1969; Hooley, 1963; Khatkhate, 1972, 1982a, b; McKinnon, 1973; Shaw, 1973; Bhatia and Khatkhate, 1975; Galbis, 1977 and Drake, 1980). The findings were supported by a major study by Gupta (1984). However, the reverse direction of causality can be argued on *a priori* grounds, namely that economic growth stimulates the development of the financial sector. A midway position would be to argue for two-day causation (suggested in Gurley and Shaw, 1967).

The contrary position, that financial development follows rather than leads economic development, is taken by some writers, albeit a minority. For example Woolmer (1977, p. 286) concludes in the case of Nigeria:

On the whole the financial system followed rather than led development up to 1971. Political independence and the establishment of a central bank did not fundamentally alter that pattern. The main trends in development were determined by the fortunes of export markets, by foreign capital flows, by fiscal policies and by political events. In the face of such influences the financial system played very much a supporting role.

Among other writers Goldsmith (1973, p. 73) appeared by then to take a neutral position, admitting to a gut feeling that

not only have financial and economic development gone hand in hand. . . . but that the financial super-structure has had considerable influence on the real infrastructure in the direction of accelerating the growth of real national product and wealth, although it may have done so at the price of accentuating social imbalances. . . . A fortiori, there is no proof, or even a clear presumption, of the positive influence of financial development in the process of economic growth at all, or even most, times and places.

(b) The Theoretical Arguments

The core of most of the arguments is the relationship between savers and investors. At the simplest level, in an economy which is completely under-developed financially, there will be no transfer of savings from one individual to another, and the only investment possible will be out of personal savings. Effectively this may mean that many who want to invest cannot do so, while many who could invest do not wish to do so. Thus investable resources are not utilized efficiently, and those who do not wish to invest have no incentive to save.

The transfer of savings from savers to investors may be achieved directly by personal loan, or by taking a share in the investor's undertaking. Alternatively it may be achieved indirectly through a financial intermediary. If intermediaries are to be effective they have to be attractive to both lenders and borrowers. To be effective, they must:

— provide incentives to save;
— increase the volume of investment;
— improve the efficiency of investment.

Savers will now find that they have the possibility of financial investment which offers them a return, which they might prefer to continued high consumption or direct investments. Secondly, putative investors will have access to savings other than their own which increases their funds available for investment. Third, the development of markets in money and financial instruments will tend to channel funds towards the more productive invest-ments. The first and third effects have been described as the division of labour, (a) between savers and investors, and (b) in the process of inter-mediation. They are put forward as explanations of the secularly rising ratios of finance to GNP (Gurley and Shaw, 1967; Goldsmith, 1969). That the development of financial instruments, institutions, and markets provides increased opportunities and incentives for savers to save and for investors to invest is fairly clear. The argument relating to intermediation depends upon a number of specialized financial institutions arising, which in effect form a capital market, and which will recognize the best investment oppor-tunities. (One danger is that the market will recognize only the investors who offer the best security, which might not be the same thing.) It will then allocate funds to the perceived best investments and investors. This function of allocation should then lead to an overall improvement in the efficiency as well as the volume of investment, thereby leading to faster economic growth.[1] Therefore, it is argued, financial development is necessary to promote economic growth. (Note that it is not sufficient, though; a wide variety of other inputs are also needed for investment to be productive.)

Although the above functions of financial instruments and institutions may under certain circumstances be unimportant in stimulating savings, investment, and economic growth, they do not represent a full account of the functions performed. In addition to those discussed, financial instruments and institutions perform the vital functions of maturity transformation and risk transfer.

Maturity transformation permits savers to save short-term, and investors to acquire long-term funds. Savers often prefer short-term to long-term savings, as it represents less risk, and less loss of liquidity. On the other hand, investors in physical assets require longer-term finance, as the returns are generally longer-term, and these returns are needed before the debt can be serviced. By performing the important function of maturity transformation, institutions such as banks can enable the requirements of savers and investors to be met simultaneously.

Risk transfer is an equally important function. Many savers are reluctant to take the risk of undertaking physical investments themselves. They may also be reluctant to lend directly to (or take equity in) those investors who are prepared to take such risks. Quite apart from the loss of liquidity involved in such direct financing, the savers may feel that they do not possess the know-how or the financial and legal muscle necessary to protect their loans or investments. Such savers prefer to use financial intermediaries, in which they have confidence, and which they perceive to be sound. These institutions then provide finance to many investors, thereby diversifying risk. With the use of securities and guarantees the investment risk can be apportioned between intermediary and investor in a variety of different ways, all of which has the effect of reducing the risk faced by individual savers.

By performing the functions of maturity transformation and risk transfer, institutions play a substantial role in increasing the mobilization of savings,and thereby raising the level of investment and hopefully,the rate of economic growth. Organized markets, such as markets in stocks and bonds, can also perform similar, but not identical, functions. Such securities are usually long-term in nature but an organized market generally ensures their marketability and enables savers to regain their liquidity very quickly if need be (although with the possibility of a capital loss). An organized stock market will also to some extent ensure that a company issuing stock is reputably managed, and that those making the market (brokers and jobbers) are also reputable. These factors will increase the confidence of savers, in that the perceived risk of investing in these stocks is reduced.

Stock and bond markets, and other forms of non-bank saving, such as life insurance and pension funds, still play a minor role in most developing countries, and the process of financial intermediation depends crucially on the efficacy of the banking system, and other deposit-taking institutions such as post offices.

(c) The Historical Evidence

The theoretical discussion does not provide a firm conclusion on the relationship between financial and economic development, although the majority of opinion tends to favour the view that financial development leads economic development. Can economic history then provide us with conclusive evidence of the impact of finance on economic growth? Briefly, the answer seems to be no. Goldsmith (1969) has looked at much of the available evidence, and comes to no firm conclusion. In fact it may not be possible on *a priori* grounds to arrive at any firm conclusion. In any period, in any country, economic growth is likely to be influenced by a variety of different factors, of which financial development may be only one. In practice it is likely to be extremely difficult to disentangle the different factors, especially given the patchiness and inaccuracy of much of the economic data. Economists have considerable problems in building econometric models of contemporary economies, and these problems will be magnified if attempts are made to build similar models for economies say 100–150 years ago, when economic relationships were perhaps not the same as they are today.

If one considers some of the major physical investment booms in economic history, such as the canal or railway expansions, it is immediatley clear that any investment required the technology and organization as prior conditions. No amount of financial provision could produce such investments without the technology and organization being available, and without individuals who had the enterprise and the motivation to undertake the projects concerned. Given the idea, the entrepreneur will then look for the finance. Once again we can see that the availability of finance is a necessary ingredient for a project, but by no means a sufficient one. If finance is not available, then enterprises may be stifled. Likewise, if it is available only on unsuitable terms (e.g. interest rates too high, or maturities too short), then again enterprise will be stifled. On the other hand, when finance (or credit) is available on easy terms, but exceeds the requirements of physical investment, then it may be used for speculative purposes, i.e. to purchase existing financial assets or commodities. One ends up with the economists's simplistic notion of a list of projects seeking finance. The projects will be financed to the extent that they appear profitable, given the terms of the available finance.

It is of interest and perhaps instructive to look back over the role played by the financial system in the economic development of Europe in the nineteenth century. The most we can hope to achieve, though, is to see in which direction (if any) the available evidence points and to consider the views of other commentators, for it seems unlikely that any definitive proof can be adduced concerning the direction of causality between financial growth and economic growth. It is worth noting also that the sources of funds for investment were (and still are):

— self-financing from savings and retained profits;
— loan capital from the financial system;

— outside equity capital (usually from the financial system);

— government finance, mobilized through taxation, or government borrowing through the financial system.

Britain was the first European country to industrialize. The pattern of financing was very much dependent, at least in the first half of the nineteenth century, on savings from agriculture, trade, and retained earnings. Banks provided only short-term credit and the mobilization of long-term capital was largely achieved by the flotation and promotion of shares and bonds. By 1850 share ownership, especially of railway shares, was widespread among the middle classes and the petit bourgeois. The established merchant banks such as Rothschilds and Barings were more concerned with foreign than domestic finance, and the role of the commercial banks was passive and largely restricted to accepting and discounting bills. Only in the 1860s did specialized finance companies develop, attempting to imitate France's Crédit Mobilier (see below). Many of these were of doubtful soundness, however, and the financing of investment in Britain continued to depend largely on retained earnings and share and bond issues as a means of mobilizing long-term savings. The stock market in turn provided a market (and therefore liquidity) for these shares and bonds. Government played a largely passive role in economic development.

The story is rather different in continental Europe, where countries were engaged in a catching-up process. Here the gradual accumulation over the years of retained earnings, which had allowed British businesses gradually to expand and to develop new and larger-scale processes, would have been largely inadequate. European enterprises were usually much younger, but were faced with the large, and much more sudden, capital requirements needed to establish, say, a modern iron works or textile mill. Moreover, in the middle part of the century the large capital needed to finance utilities such as railways, could have been raised on the British model only with difficulty, given the absence of a large, prosperous middle class, and less well-developed stock markets. The establishment by the Péreire brothers of the famous finance house, the Crédit Mobilier in France in 1852 is widely taken as being the mainspring of investment finance in continental Europe, which greatly facilitated economic development.

The object of the Crédit Mobilier was to mobilize the substantial savings of the French bourgeois and petit bourgeois, much of which was known to be kept in boxes, or the equivalent. This was done by accepting deposits and selling shares in Crédit Mobilier, the proceeds of which were invested in long-term development projects, both industrial and infrastructural. Shares in these projects would in turn be sold to the investing public. It had the support of the Emperor Napoleon III, and fitted in well with the political philosophy of the Second Empire, born at the same time. That the Crédit Mobilier failed in 1867 is of little relevance to us. What is important is that it is generally thought to have revolutionized banking in continental Europe; indeed, it is seen as the precursor of the modern development bank in developing countries. Jenks (1927/1963) remarked

The banking ideas which thus first achieved institutional form have been of outstanding significance in financial history. For the record it should be stated that the Crédit Mobilier was not the first such institution. The Société Générale in Belgium (founded 1822) and the Banque de Belgique performed similar functions and competed keenly in the field of company promotion and investment. But the notion of the development bank, or industrial bank, really developed from the Crédit Mobilier.

The Crédit Mobilier itself helped to establish foreign subsidiaries or associate companies notably the Darmstädter Bank (Germany) in 1853, and similar institutions in Austria, Spain, Italy, and the Netherlands. These examples, together with developments in company law encouraging joint stock enterprises with limited liability, led to the creation of more joint stock banks. The development of continental investment banking therefore represented a radical departure from the traditional pattern of merchant banking and commercial banking which persisted in Britain. Some commentators attributed to it an important role in economic development. Jenks (1927/1963) speaks of

a type of financial agency which had been developed in France (the Crédit Mobilier) and which was largely responsible for the rapidity with which the capital resources of the continent had been brought to bear upon industry during the fifties (p. 240).

Clapham (1936) states

Everywhere, the new credit institutions gave generous help to industry (p. 385).

Not all commentators are so enthusiastic about the importance of the new banks. Milward and Saul (1973), for example, express the view that

The Péreire's. . . effect on the development of France itself, as also perhaps the effect of banking institutions in general, has been exaggerated (p. 352)

and again

It is an exaggeration to claim that the rapid development of the German economy after 1850 could not have taken place without the growth of joint stock banks (p. 421)

and

Important though their (the banks) role often was, it was less important than in the development of more backward lands, Norway, Russia, or South-eastern Europe, for example, where they sometimes represented the only possible source of capital and entrepreneurial knowledge. Nevertheless, for two decades, there was a very close connection between foreign capital, joint stock investment banks and the industrial sectors, iron manufacture and coal mining, which were growing most rapidly (p. 421).

In France the Crédit Foncier was set up in 1852 as an agricultural and mortgage bank, based on long-term mortgage banks which already existed in Saxony and Prussia, but was not really successful. Clapham (1936) comments that the Crédit Foncier

had not given all the credit which the French cultivator would employ with advantage, so there was room enough for the cooperative credit movement of the late 19th century, and for the official Crédit Agricole initiated in 1900 through which money provided gratis by the Bank of France. . . was to be lent for agricultural development by regional banks (p. 384).

The example of the Crédit Mobilier led to the establishment of Germany's (and Austria's and Italy's) universal banks, which provided equity and loan capital to industry, and which, initially at any rate, dominated the supervisory boards of such enterprises. They nursed their client companies from cradle to grave. By the last quarter of the nineteenth century German banking (and industry) was dominated by the 'four Ds', Darmstädter Bank (1853), Diskontgesellschaft (1865), Deutsche Bank (1870), and Dresdener Bank (1872). Clapham (1936) quotes Schuster of Dresdener Bank in 1908

In Germany our banks are largely responsible for the development of the Empire, having fostered and built up its industries. It is from 1871 that our real development dates, and it is since that year our great banks have been organised. To them, more than to any other agency, may be credited the splendid results thus far realised (p. 390).

Clapham comments

If his historical summary was not literally accurate, it was accurate in substance.

Gerschenkron (1962) attributed considerable importance to the financial system in 'intermediate' countries.

The focal role in capital provision in a country like Germany must be assigned not to any original capital accumulation but to the role of credit creation policies on the part of the banking system.

And on Italy,

But if one were to look for a single important factor that succeeded in offsetting at least some of the great obstacles to the country's industrialisation one could not fail to point to the role performed by the big Italian banks after 1885 (p. 87).

(Italy suffered a number of banking crashes in the early 1890s and the banks were remodelled on the German style, in some cases with German participation.)

On a subject such as this one can never reach definite conclusions. Nevertheless, we tend to think that the weight of evidence and expert opinion comes down in favour of the development of the financial sector contributing substantially to economic development in much of Europe in the nineteenth century. However the effectiveness of the financial sector, and the institutional instruments used, seem to depend both on the level of development and on conditions in individual countries, notably the political system, as we shall argue below. Moreover, the financial sector can also encourage speculation, inflation, and losses, which we will now consider briefly.

The question of the impact of the financial system on economic development comes very close to the hotly contested question of the impact of the expansion of money supply on the economy. The mobilization of savings is one way of effectively increasing the money supply and, although we are primarily interested in the provision of long-term rather than short-term finance, the distinction is often blurred. Indeed Goldsmith (1969) included assets of all financial institutions, which included all the components of money. (It also included substantial double-counting of money.) While this is not the place to become embroiled in the monetarist debate, we have to consider the historical evidence of the impact of increases in total financial assets, including money, on economic growth.

The general historical picture is one of monetary expansion followed by price and output growth, followed by speculation, boom, and bust (Kindleberger, 1978; Galbraith, 1975). Both these authors appear to give considerable importance to the expansion and contraction of credit in the cyclical process, whereas the Monetarists attribute cyclical instability to fluctuations in the money supply, and the Keynesians to changes in investment and consumption, which in turn influences the demand for money and credit and thus the money supply. Kindleberger (1978, p. 72) comments:

The monetarist-Keynesian debate leaves little if any room for instability of credit and fragility of the banking system, or impacts on production and prices when the credit system becomes paralysed through loans rendered bad by falling prices—all of which go far, in my judgement, to explain what happened in the early stages of the 1929 depression.

Galbraith (1975, pp. 124–5) concludes that banks and the money supply played an essential role in panics and crises;

But also essential was the impulse to borrow, invest, risk, speculate. Had this not existed, no bank would have created it. . . . The most that can be said is that the easy provision of money by the banks and the urge to get it for speculative or productive purposes were intimately intertwined. . . . In later years. . . banks would then be ready and anxious to make loans, create deposits and thus enhance the money supply and no-one would come to them for loans.

There appears little doubt, then, that expansion of financial assets has been associated historically with bouts of speculation and with physical investment. Many investment booms have been accompanied by, or followed by, financial expansions which were purely speculative, i.e. buying and pushing up the price of financial assets, or non-productive assets such as gold, without any increase in physical investment.

(d) Foreign Finance

The analysis has so far not referred explicitly to foreign financing. Historically, most flows of foreign finance to developing countries have been long- or medium-term in nature (bonds, aid or Eurocurrency lending). Much of the foreign finance has been used for project purposes and, therefore, with the intention at least of promoting economic growth. (There is an easy tendency to equate investment with economic growth, after the Harrod–Domar model. Of course this is a simplification and economic growth can be achieved without investment, at least for some time, e.g. by more efficient use of labour or existing capacity. Likewise, investment, if made in bad projects or without adequate management, may completely fail to produce economic growth.) For countries with domestic capital or foreign exchange shortages the availability of foreign funds may well relieve bottlenecks and promote economic growth. This subject is discussed theoretically in Chapter 7. The extent to which it has worked in practice is uncertain. In the nineteenth century, and between the wars, the extent of the inability of borrowers to pay interest on bonds and to redeem them on time (see Chapter 8) suggests that the economic results of the borrowing were not all that was hoped for. In recent times the growing need to reschedule Eurocurrency loans again suggests that third world borrowers have not found them to be a panacea for the economic ills of their countries. Ranis (1983) has compared the performance of NICs who have made substantial use of the Eurocurrency market (Argentina, Brazil, and Mexico) with those which have not (Hong Kong, Korea, Singapore, and Taiwan). Growth rates in the two groups have been comparable until recently, but finally the burden of debt service caught up with the first group, to the detriment of their economic performance. (Such comparisons have to be treated with caution, though, because one is comparing small countries with large.)

The overall impact of foreign financing on economic development is, of course, extremely difficult to assess in general. Some statistical evidence of its impact in recent years is mentioned towards the end of this chapter, while Chapter 8 contains a discussion of its impact in the nineteenth century, and in recent times in developing countries.

(e) The Importance of the Political Framework

Commentators have not given much prominence to the impact which the political philosophy of a country has on its financial development and the way in which this influences the relationship between financial and economic development. Yet this seems to be of some importance in explaining at least some of the divergences between countries, and it also has important implications for the degree of reliance which governments place in their financial institutions as agencies of economic development.

The major distinction lies between centrally planned ('socialist') economies and market economies. A pure socialist economy may be perceived as depending on government to mobilize the necessary finance for investment through taxation,[2] retained earnings of state enterprises, and foreign borrowing by government. The savings of individuals are insignificant and the private corporate sector nonexistent. Financial institutions and instruments are in turn severely restricted. Under this scenario the financial sector would have a negligible role to play in economic development and would appear very underdeveloped in comparison with the financial sector in market economies. The low financial ratio achieved by the USSR given on page 78 is a good illustration of this point.

By contrast, picture a pure market economy in which the government's attitude to economic development is passive and whose involvement in the economy is kept to a minimum. The financial sector in this case assumes a much greater importance, as the mobilization of private savings and the function of intermediation and maturity transformation by financial institutions makes available loan funds to investors. In the absence of this financial mechanism those who wish to invest have access to their own savings only, and the level of their investment and therefore total investment and economic growth are likely to be stunted. Certain nineteenth-century European economies—for example Britain, France, and Germany—correspond reasonably to the 'pure market economy' described here, but with important differences between them, some of which were discussed above.

Today's developing country generally fits somewhere in between our pure socialist economy and pure market economy. Clearly those which tend towards the socialist end of the spectrum will have less need of financial instruments and institutions to achieve their development objectives than those which tend towards the pure market economy. However, many developing country governments find themselves pursuing development objectives from a non-socialist standpoint, but without an active private sector or entrepreneurial class to play a substantial role in the development process[3] (nor do they have a developed financial sector which could to some extent substitute for the entrepreneurial class). Such governments find themselves forced into the adoption of state capitalism, in which the government's role in the economy becomes very substantial. Government involvement extends also to the financial sector, where it creates instruments and institutions (e.g.bonds, insurance companies, and development banks) with a view to stimulating private savings and investment. As with more socialist countries, the ratio of financial assets to GNP will appear low, but the important difference is that it persists against the government's will, rather than because of it.

(f) The Different Elements of the Financial System

Writers tend to discuss the financial system and financial development in aggregation, but important insights can be gained by disaggregating it and identifying those elements which might play a substantial role in development and those which do not.

Development and development projects require long-term finance. Non-socialist governments need to be able to raise long-term domestic loans to supplement their revenues from taxation in order to finance the infrastructure and 'social' projects and perhaps agricultural and manufacturing projects and others, depending on the degree of the government's involvement in the economy. The private sector requires to be able to raise medium- and long-term debt and, perhaps more importantly, equity capital. The main domestic mechanisms available to provide them are:

— development banks;
— housing finance corporations;
— bond markets (primary and secondary);
— stock markets (primary and secondary);
— insurance companies and pension funds.

Both development banks and housing finance corporations benefit if they are able to raise funds by selling shares or bonds on stock and bond markets and, in the case of development banks, being able to sell equity stakes in client companies readily. Likewise, insurance companies and pension funds like to hold a substantial proportion of their long-term investments as marketable securities rather than direct investments, which may not be very liquid. Therefore attention becomes concentrated on the development of stock and bond markets. Even in the most financially backward countries, primary markets already exist. Governments can place bonds with whatever financial institutions exist, to a limited extent. There is also likely to be at least a fairly small and narrow institutional market for private sector equity. However, attempts to raise long-term finance through stock and bond issues are likely to be constrained in many countries by the absence of a secondary market for such issues, except in those developing countries which have active stock markets. Here the lack of institutional development is probably not the major bottleneck, because encouragement and promotion by government of new institutions might only spread existing funds more thinly with the overall financial market remaining much the same size. In order to increase the size and liquidity of the stock and bond markets it is necessary to draw in funds from individuals and private sector (non-bank) institutions.

Commercial banking of the conventional British type, with concentration on short-term loans for trade and working capital and lending for consumer expenditure can therefore be seen to contribute little to long-term investment and economic growth. The contribution they do make is mainly through expansion in demand resulting from the provision of credit. By contrast, the universal banking approach of continental Europe which specializes in medium-term loans for investment, taking equity, placing further equity, and assisting with management in client companies can be seen to contribute directly to investment, especially industrial investment. British commercial banking may not be the model which is most conducive to economic growth, a thought which may be borne in mind by development planners and politicians in the third world.

(g) Empirical Studies of Financial Development

It is difficult and, perhaps, impossible to establish the direction of causality between financial and economic development by empirical research, so eventually we have to fall back on non-empirical arguments. However, empirical research can be used to establish whether or not statistical relationships do exist between financial development and economic development and whether the relationship is positive or negative. The major empirical works in the field are those of Goldsmith (1969) and Gupta (1984).

Goldsmith's calculated values of the financial interrelation ratio (FIR)[4] for 1963 put Japan and Great Britain at the top with ratios of 1.75 and 1.71 respectively. Other countries with ratios greater than 1 were Italy (1.37), the USA (1.23), and Canada (1.16). Countries with low ratios were the developing countries Yugoslavia (0.59), Mexico (0.5), Venezuela (0.39), and India (0.35). The USSR, lacking a conventional capitalist financial system, also had a low FIR of 0.36.

Goldsmith also studied the trends over time of the ratio of assets/GNP of financial institutions. For developed countries together the aggregate ratio grew from around 0.4 in 1860 to around 1.5 in 1963. By 1900 the ratio had exceeded 1, but in this year the ratio for the less developed countries was only just over 0.2. By 1963 the ratio for these countries was about 0.7, a considerable increase compared to the 1900 figure, but still a long way behind the ratio for the developed countries.

Goldsmith's own conclusions drawn from the results were not particularly strong:

only a loose association—but a positive and undeniable association, nevertheless—between the Financial Interrelation Ratio (FIR) and real gross national product per head or a similar simple measure of the level of economic development (pp. 376–7).

However, the statistical relationship is weak and supports only

the negative conclusion, namely that real national product per head alone, or any other similarly simple indicator of the level of economic development, is unable to account for the observed values of the FIR except within a rather wide range (Goldsmith, 1969, p. 375).

Gupta (1984), in a substantial but less exhaustive study, used statistical tests to investigate the direction of causality between financial and economic development. For a sample of 14 countries his findings

suggested that the direction of causality ran from financial to real development, thus suggesting an activist role for the financial sector. This finding did not appear to be sensitive to any particular characteristics of the countries included in this sample.

In Chapter 5 we have assembled some further data on the financial structure of different countries. It is evident that compared with industrialized countries the developing countries have a rather higher proportion of their financial assets in the form of money (currency in circulation, bank, and quasi-bank deposits) and a lower proportion in the form of marketable securities.

2. FINANCIAL REPRESSION

(a) The Notion of Repression

Many developing countries do not have free capital markets. Rather they are characterized by what has become known as 'financial repression', which is generally equated with controls on interest rates, and particularly with controls which result in negative real interest rates on deposits. These controls are normally imposed by the government, although they can occasionally arise from agreements between private sector financial institutions to restrict interest rates. The consequence is that actual interest rates are distorted from the equilibrium interest rates which would prevail in a competitive market for money. Repression may also be extended to refer to government restrictions which discourage the development of financial institutions and instruments, leading to incomplete, or fragmented, financial markets. Repression theories originated with McKinnon (1973) and Shaw (1973), following the earlier work of Gurley and Shaw (1960) and Goldsmith (1969). Subsequent theoretical refinements have been conveniently summarized by Fry (1982). Numerous attempts have been made to estimate the impact of financial repression on growth, and the major studies are summarized later in this chapter.

Financial repression restricts the growth of the financial sector. This means that the growth of financial assets and liabilities is restricted, and also that the development of financial institutions and instruments is stunted. This state is described as shallow finance, and can be measured by the ratio of financial assets to macroeconomic variables such as GNP, as in Goldsmith's work, for example. (Perhaps the most convenient measure is M2/GNP.) Shallow finance can be observed in many of the least developed countries, where it arises from the low level of economic development and lack of human and natural resources as much as from actions of the government or private financial institutions. However, we are not primarily concerned with shallow finance in the most underdeveloped of countries where it may be unavoidable, but mainly in those countries which do have considerable natural and human resources, but where the financial sector is suppressed. Nevertheless, as an aside, it may be recalled that it is a small, landlocked, mountainous country with few natural resources which has been one of the world leaders in financial and economic development—Switzerland.

In Chapter 2 we discussed capital market theory, which assumes perfect and efficient capital markets. By contrast, financial repression starts from the position that capital markets are not efficient or in equilibrium. The policy recommendations which spring from an analysis of financial repression are usually concerned with financial liberalization, leading to financial deepening. Liberalization requires that interest rates are freed from government controls, which will encourage the growth of financial assets and liabilities. This in turn is likely to encourage institutional development and to encourage individual borrowers and savers to switch from the informal sector to the formal sector, thereby integrating the two sectors, and from inflation hedges to monetary assets. Eventually the range of financial instruments available would increase, and the overall result would be to transform a narrow, inefficient, and fragmented capital market (in its broadest sense) into a larger, more complete, and more efficient capital market. This in turn, it is argued, will tend to promote economic development.

The banking sector is central to theories of financial repression. In most developing countries bank deposits (or deposits in quasi-banks, such as post office savings banks, savings and loan associations, and credit unions) provide by far the most important vehicle for savings. Other savings instruments, such as marketable securities (shares and bonds), life insurance policies, and pensions schemes, tend to be limited in availability. On the other side of the coin we see that banks and quasi-banks dominate the sources of funds for investment. An investor may save and invest his own funds, but apart from that the main source of capital will be bank loans (from commercial or development banks). He is unlikely to be able to issue equity capital or debentures as the stock market, if there is one, is likely to be narrow. He cannot turn to pension funds, insurance companies, or venture capital companies for loans or equity. Therefore he is dependent on the banking system. In a country with underdeveloped financial institutions and instruments, the willingness of savers to hold money in the form of bank deposits is therefore crucial to the saving–intermediation–investment process (sometimes called debt-intermediation). Repression theories have identified the level of real interest rates as being the crucial determinant of the willingness of savers to hold money in the form of bank deposits.

(b) Instruments of Financial Repression

The main instrument of repression is generally interest rate controls, although exchange rate controls, high reserve requirements of commercial banks and institutional repression can also play a significant role. The literature tends to concentrate on the impact of interest rate controls, often referring to them as a proxy for financial repression.

Interest Rate Controls

Three main forms[5] of administered interest rate control may be identified:

— ceilings on nominal deposit rates;
— ceilings on nominal loan rates;
— ceilings on nominal deposit and loan rates together.

Interest rate floors on deposit and loan rates are also possible, but as they appear to be much less commonly found, we will concentrate on the other controls.

Interest rate controls generally seem to be imposed with the aim of encouraging investment. If interest rates to borrowers are kept low, it is thought this will increase the number of projects which have a positive net present value when discounted at the borrowing rate, and will therefore increase the rate of investment. Ceilings on loan rates will produce this effect directly, it is thought. Ceilings on deposit rates are thought to produce the same effect indirectly, for banks which obtain their funds cheaply will be able to lend them cheaply. Ceilings on both together may eliminate any possibility of anything going wrong with the above analysis.[6]

This line of argument, though, assumes that adequate funds will still be forthcoming from savers to meet the demands of investors, in spite of the ceilings (direct or indirect) on the deposit rate. However, if the supply of savings and the demand for investable funds are both functions of the real rate of interest, the effect may be to raise demand for funds above the equilibrium level, and to depress the supply of funds below the equilibrium level.

Figure 3.1 illustrates the savings (S) and investment (I) functions, both being determined by the real rate of interest (r). For convenience, real interest rates are shown as being positive, but the impact of repression often makes them negative. We will relax the assumption subsequently.

In the absence of interest rate controls, the market is in equilibrium at e, where $I_e = S_e$ and r_e is the equilibrium rate of interest which clears the market. Now if the deposit rate of interest is fixed by government below r_e, say at r_c, then the amount of savings deposited in institutions will fall to S_c.

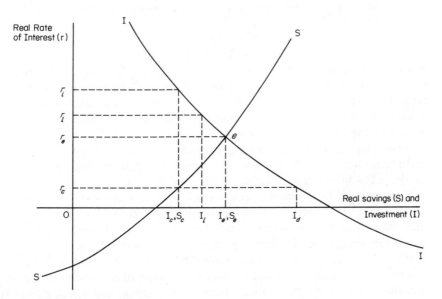

Figure 3.1 Savings and investment under controlled interest rates

Thus the amount available for investment is I_c and the rate of interest charged to borrowers which clears the market is r_i. The effect of the control is to lower both savings and investment by an amount $(I_e - I_c)$. As investment is an important determinant of the rate of growth, the effect of the controlled interest rate is to restrict the rate of growth. The difference between lending and borrowing rates, $r_i - r_c$, will result in higher margins to the financial intermediaries, although the volume of their business will be lower than it would be in equilibrium.

If in addition the lending rate is controlled at a level r_ℓ, below r_i, then the financial intermediaries will have insufficient deposits to meet the borrowing demand at interest rate r_ℓ. Demand for borrowing for investment will be I_ℓ and unsatisfied demand $(I_\ell - I_c)$. The extreme case is that the lending rate should be fixed so that it is equal to the borrowing rate, r_c (or, in practice, slightly above to cover banks' administration costs). Under these circumstances the unsatisfied demand for investable funds would be $I_d - I_c$. With controlled lending rates, financial intermediaries must ration credit by means other than the interest rate. They will therefore tend to favour borrowers with substantial security or an established reputation, which may mean projects with foreign capital, technology, or management. Secondly, they will tend to favour low-risk projects, with relatively low rates of return, as they will not be able to charge a risk premium commensurate with the risk of the project. The consequence is that higher-return, higher-risk projects and projects promoted by younger (and possible more enterprising) entrepreneurs may be starved of capital. In short, the venture capital element of financing may have disappeared and the overall quality of investment may have been reduced, as well as the quantity. Again, the effect may be to restrict the rate of economic growth.

It should be noted that a repressed interest rate system impinges on the current assets of enterprises, as well as on investment in fixed assets. If credit is scarce or rationed, then a firm's capacity utilization may be restricted, because it cannot obtain credit to finance its working capital, which may restrict its output and sales. Liberalization of interest rates, leading to greater availability of short-term credit, may have the effect of increasing the utilization of the existing capital stock.

Figure 3.1 represents a static equilibrium analysis of saving, investment, and the interest rate. If, in period 1, the interest rate on deposits is raised to the equilibrium level, saving and investment will increase. This will increase growth in the next period, which in turn will increase saving and investment in that period. Therefore the implication of repression theory is that liberalizing the interest rate will have the effect of moving a country into a virtuous circle of increasing saving, investment, and growth.

We have assumed so far that, in equilibrium, banks would both borrow and lend at the equilibrium rate of interest, r_e. This, of course, is not correct, and there will always be a spread between borrowing and lending rates to enable banks to cover their operating costs and to make a profit. Therefore the demand for borrowing and supply of savings will never be in exact equilibrium. If the banking sector is competitive, then the disturbance from the equilibrium position caused by differential borrowing and lending rates may be slight. If, however, the banking sector is oligopolistic, there exists the possibility that the spread between borrowing and lending rates may be quite substantial. This would produce an effect similar to the controlled deposit rate r_c in Figure 3.1, and would produce the same pattern of restricted saving and investment.

Oligopolistic tendencies in banking are not restricted to developing countries, but in advanced countries the effects may be less damaging, as alternative channels of savings and borrowing (for example through stock markets, money market funds, building societies, life insurance, and pensions schemes) are more readily available than in less developed countries.

Bank Deposit Requirements

It is normal for central banks to impose reserve requirements on commercial banks. Historically, reserve requirements were intended to provide some stability to the banking system. Typically, in industrialized countries, total reserve requirements may be of the order of 10–15% of bank deposits. However, in several developing countries the figure may become as high as 50%. These reserves are placed with the central bank at low (or even zero) rates of interest, or are invested in low coupon government bonds. Thus the government uses the banking system as a source of finance, and becomes the principal borrower, pre-empting other potential borrowers.

The effect on the banking system is two-fold. First, a substantial amount of the available funds is directed away from potential borrowers. Secondly, the bank's interest rate structure will be distorted. If banks are to make profits they must maintain a wide margin between borrowing and lending rates in order to compensate themselves for the low income they receive on their reserves. This is done by depressing interest on deposits, or by raising the rate charged to borrowers (or both), relative to what would otherwise be the equilibrium rate.

The Direction of Investment

Several governments order their financial institutions to direct a certain proportion of their loans to a specified sector, often agriculture, at low rates of interest. An alternative practice is for governments to set up specialized lending agencies, financed by taxation or cheap government borrowing, to lend to specific sectors. Again, agriculture is often a beneficiary. Such policies may restrict the funds available to the industrial sector, and at the same time raise the cost of those funds which are available.

(c) Financial Repression and the Money Supply

Financial repression is intimately connected with the money supply because total money savings can be roughly equated to bank (and quasi-bank) deposits and notes and coin in circulation, which in turn is the M2 definition of the money supply. Savings can be approximated to M2 because, as we have seen, bank deposits and cash are the dominant forms of saving in developing countries. Financial savings therefore represent the willingness of individuals to hold money balances. Hence saving is equal to the demand for money. An increase in the rate of inflation, whether or not it is caused by an increase in money supply, will, if interest rates remain at the controlled nominal level, have the effect of reducing the real rate of interest. Savers will be discouraged from holding money balances when faced with a low, or often negative, real rate of interest. They will tend to invest in inflation hedges, such as gold, jewellery, real estate, commodities, and the like, which are generally non-productive. This will lead to a decline in money savings in real terms and a decline in funds available for investment, in real terms. This in turn will restrict the rate of economic growth. Therefore control of the money supply under conditions of controlled interest rates is very important. Failure to control it will provoke inflation, reduce real savings, and will therefore be detrimental to investment and economic growth. It should also be noted that the fall in savings is equivalent to a fall in the demand for money, which in itself will have a further inflationary effect, as people are prepared to pay more for inflation hedges. It should also be noted that expectations of higher inflation will be sufficient to have the same results as actual higher inflation. As Shaw (1973, p. vii) wrote: 'money and its relative prices affect real aspects of the development process'.

The combination of inflation and interest controls may produce negative real interest rates, in whch case part of the savings function will be below the horizontal axis in Figure 3.1. At a real interest rate of zero, savings are likely to be positive and will stay so for at least a certain level of negative real interest rates. Many people will want to hold positive money balances, if only for convenience, and others may not realize that real interest rates are negative. Moreover people save for security as well as for gain, and some may not know of any way to save other than through financial institutions. (Inflation itself is a cause of insecurity, as it is perceived to threaten employment. In Britain in the 1970s savings even rose with inflation and negative real interest rates, possibly because saving for security rose.) Eventually, though, as negative real interest rates increase, people tend to look for inflation hedges such as gold, real estate, coins, stamps, and antique furniture, so financial saving falls to zero and may eventually become negative.

(d) An Assessment of Repression Theory

The keystone of the theory is a presentation of the relationship between saving, investment, and real interest rates. However, in any economy this is likely to be a substantial simplification of the determinants of saving and investment. First, the theory starts with the relationships:

Demand for money = private sector financial savings
= bank + quasi-bank deposits
= credit availability + reserve requirements

Private sector financial savings is a function of the real rate of interest. The next step is to equate

Investment = credit availability, which is a function of the real rate of interest.

This, of course, even if correct, explains only private sector investment and only that part which is financed by domestically mobilized resources. Government investment is, in the main in developing countries, financed by taxation, and aid and borrowings from abroad, neither of which is dependent upon the domestic rate of interest. Borrowing by government on the domestic capital market may be a function of the rate of interest, but in many developing countries the issue of government bonds provides only a small proportion of government income.[7] Therefore government investment, which usually provides a substantial proportion of total investment (even in industrialized countries) is not affected by interest rate controls. Government, though, may pre-empt investable funds by imposing high reserve requirements on banks. Evidence discussed in Chapter 10 strongly suggests that much government investment is not very efficient.

Likewise, much private sector investment which is financed from abroad can also be excluded. The availability of direct foreign investment and export credits is not a function of domestic interest rates. On the other hand, shortages of domestic credit may force the local private sector to seek foreign capital. Also the availability of foreign capital, whether to government or the private sector, may discourage the domestic saving effort.[8]

Repression theories tend to assume, at least implicitly, that investment (we are now down to domestically financed private sector investment) is financed entirely by borrowing. This, of course, is a substantial simplification. In any country, however well-developed its financial sector, a substantial proportion of investment is financed by retained earnings, which are not dependent on the intermediation mechanism. In many instances the constraint on new investment may not be the unavailability (or the cost) of credit, but rather the unavailability of equity capital, whether retained earnings or funds raised by issuing new shares. The debt/shareholders' funds ratio and security requirements may in some cases be the restraint on lending, rather than the availability of credit. Therefore financial repression can only restrict that proportion of investment which is financed by borrowing on the domestic market and this, in some countries, may be a fairly small proportion of total investment, even with liberalized interest rates.

Although the impact of financial repression on total investment may be less than indicated by the simplified neo-classical model, it may still reduce the quality of investment. First, financial repression is still likely to encourage self-financed investment at the expense of intermediation and borrowing. Secondly, the credit rationing process will still tend to discriminate against new entrepreneurs, new technologies, and products not previously produced in the country. Lenders will tend to favour borrowers with security and a track record. This may squeeze out some highly profitable, but more risky, ventures. (However, this problem is encountered also in industrialized countries with advanced financial sectors. Most lenders like to have good security.) These arguments have been presented formally by Galbis (1977 and 1982). Repression theories further assume that, given liberalized interest rates, maturity transformation by financial institutions will permit the medium- and long-term borrowing needed for investment purposes. If institutions are reluctant to lend long-term, then an increase in deposits may not have the beneficial effects on investment and growth that are presumed, unless both lenders and borrowers are prepared to use short-term funds to finance long-term assets.

Galbis (1982) has further pointed out that the effects of financial repression on investment may anyway be mitigated by the development of alternative channels of intermediation, at least to some extent. Unorganized money markets will be encouraged, foreign finance may be substituted for domestic finance, and self-financing may substitute for borrowing in enterprises which are squeezed out of financial markets. These mechanisms may be less efficient and more expensive than the alternative of liberalized money markets; nonetheless they may compensate to some extent. The basic theory may exaggerate the impact which repression might have on investment and growth.

Repression theory also places great stress on the banking system as an essential financial intermediary in the saving–investment process. While this may be justified in many countries, others with a wider range of financial instruments and institutions offer investment opportunities in which capital gain, rather than interest on deposits, provides the incentive to save. The theory also appears to assume that if funds are available for investment, then there will be a demand for it, assuming that the price (that is the interest rate) is right. It is likely that investment is determined by a range of factors, of which the interest rate is but one. Other loan conditions, notably the maturity of the loan and the security required, are others. Businessmen, at least in the industrialized countries, would place considerable emphasis on the elusive but nonetheless important 'confidence', which to some extent depends on macro-economic expectations (see also note 6).

A further cause of criticism lies in the assumptions which repression theory makes about the credit allocation procedures of lenders (generally banks). Fry (1978b) stated that under repression, nonprice rationing of investable funds must occur. This typically takes place on the basis of quality of collateral, political pressures, 'name', loan size and covert benefits to responsible loan officers. These criteria can be counted on to discriminate inefficiently between investment opportunities.

Of course all this takes place whether or not interest rates are controlled by government. In countries where no such controls exist, banks still rely heavily on their assessment of the creditworthiness of the borrowers, and the security available, and charging risk premia on higher-risk loans may be a secondary rather than a primary rationing device. Such credit rationing by banks has the effect of restraining the demand for funds, and in itself helps to maintain equilibrium interest rates below what they would otherwise be in the absence of credit rationing. Arndt (1982) has pointed out that credit rationing by banks tends to exclude the less privileged loan applicants, and may justify government-inspired concessional credit schemes, for example for small farmers, for house purchase, for small-scale enterprises, or others who may be identified as priority borrowers. Concessions do not necessarily imply interest rate 'subsidies'; they may come in the form of funds tied to certain specific uses, or in the guarantee or refinancing of commercial bank credit to certain categories of borrowers. A case for government concessional credit schemes is made by Bolnick (1982), in the context of Indonesia's special concessional credit programmes designed to promote the development of indigenous small-scale enterprises.

Finally, repression theory assumes that the level of financial savings is determined largely, if not wholly, by interest rates. We hinted earlier that savings may be determined by a host of non-interest rate factors—notably income, the need for security, social conventions, and others. If in an individual country the interest rates are not an important factor in determining the level of savings, then the theory breaks down, and liberalizing or raising interest rates will not have the desired effect on the level of savings.

This concludes our summary of the theoretical impact of financial repression on saving, investment, and growth. While we find in favour of liberalizing interest rates, it seems that the theoretical argument is not conclusive, nor is interest rate liberalization likely to be a sufficient condition for the development of the financial sector to the extent that it exerts a substantial influence on investment and economic growth. In particular it needs to be accompanied by an institutional development and strengthening so that alternative competitive markets for savings, such as equities, unit trusts, life insurance, and pensions funds, are created. These conclusions, therefore, tend to qualify what is currently regarded as the accepted position, succinctly put by Van Wijnbergen (1982, p. 3):

'Establishing high time deposit rates (high compared to anticipated inflation) has become a standard part of the policy advice given to LDCs by external experts, ranging from the visiting academic economist via the World Bank to emissaries of the IMF.'

However, a further point is that a policy of financial repression which controls interest on deposits at a rate below the equilibrium level implies that savers should subsidize borrowers. *A priori* there seems to be no justification for this, and advocates of interest rate controls need to provide a justification.

(e) Models of Financial Repression

Although the effect of the real rate of interest had dominated the literature on financial repression, it is, of course, by no means the only determinant of saving, investment, and growth. McKinnon (1973) specified that the demand for money in real terms (M/P) is a positive function of GNP(Y) the real deposit rate of interest $(d-p^*)$ and the rate of return on physical capital (r). The investment to GNP ratio (IR) is a function of the rate of return on capital, r, and the real deposit rate of interest $(d-p^*)$. That is

$$M/P = f(\underset{(+)}{Y}, \underset{(+)}{d-p^*}, \underset{(+)}{r})$$
$$IR = f(\underset{(+)}{r}, \underset{(-)}{d-p^*})$$

(d is the deposit rate of interest in nominal terms, p^* is the expected rate of inflation. The signs indicate the expected direction of the effect of the variable. For example, an increase in Y is expected to have a positive effect on M/P.)

McKinnon assumed that the real rate of interest is below the equilibrium level. A rise in the real interest rate will reduce the demand for investable funds, but because it also increases saving it will actually increase the level of investment. McKinnon also assumed that all investment was done by self-financing, rather than borrowing, and that 'a household firm' would consume or save. If it wanted to invest it would have to save until it had sufficient funds to undertake an investment (investment is lumpy). This view is likely to be applicable only in a financially primitive society.

Shaw (1973), by contrast, included 'debt-intermediation' in his model of financial repression, i.e. investors could borrow. Shaw also included opportunity costs (in real terms) of holding money, such as non-monetary financial assets and inflation hedges. However, his model is essentially similar to McKinnon's:

$$M/P = f(Y, v, d-p^*)$$

Where v represents the various opportunity costs (in real terms) of holding money.

Numerous modifications to these basic models have been proposed, notably by Kapur, Mathieson, Galbis, and Fry. They are conveniently summarized in Fry (1982). In the first place, the modifications have involved specifying different savings functions (savings is taken as being equivalent to the demand for money). Secondly, the investment function may be varied.

However, the real rate of interest is always incorporated in one form or another. For example, Galbis (1979b) specifies his demand for money function as

$$M/P = a_0 + \underset{(+)}{a\,Y} + \underset{(\pm)}{a_2 d} + \underset{(-)}{a_3 p^*} + \underset{(+)}{a_4 \mathrm{IR}}$$

Where $a_0 \ldots a_4$ are constants, and d and p^* are included separately for the following theoretical reasons. First, he considers that the nominal interest rate effect can be positive or negative, whereas the inflation ratio effect is unambiguously negative. Second, the effective response of the two components may be different because the interest rate may be known in advance, whereas the expected inflation rate is always a forecast.

Galbis's investment function also contains modifications, for example

$$\mathrm{IR}^p = b_0 + b_1 d + b_2 p^* + b_3 r + b_4 \mathrm{IR}^g$$

Where IR^p and IR^g are the private and government investment to income ratios respectively.

Other writers, e.g. Abe *et al.* (1977), Fry (1980), Leff and Sato (1980), and Fischer (1981) have included foreign savings or investment in their models, some of which we examine empirically below.

(f) Empirical Studies of Financial Repression

Most empirical work has focused on attempts to estimate the impact of interest rate controls on economic growth. Interest rates are generally taken as a proxy for financial repression, and have the virtue, from a research point of view, of being readily measurable. Various models have been tested by their various authors. Work has concentrated on specifying a model in a testable form (data are available for the variables used) and then estimating the values of the coefficients in order to evaluate the impact of the rate of interest on savings, investment, and growth. The method of estimation used is invariably a form of least-squares regression analysis. Tests have been performed on a substantial number of countries over substantial periods of time. The main econometric studies are summarized briefly in Table 3.1. It should be noted that the regressions produce variable results in their correlation coefficient and t-statistics, and in the magnitude of their coefficients. However, it is difficult to do full justice to the studies in the limited space available, and interested readers are referred to the original texts.

In a substantial recent study, Gupta (1984) performed a variety of statistical tests on data for 25 Asian and Latin American Countries. He came to the general conclusion that

In short, the evidence suggested that broad generalisations about the nature and severity of financial repression in the developing countries should be made with extreme caution.

Table 3.1 Summary of some empirical studies

	Author(s)	Date of publication	Test	Period of test data	Implication for repression theory
1.	Christian, J. W., and Pagoulatos, E.	1973	The effect of domestic financial development on the rate of capital formation in 42 developing countries	1962–66	Positive support
2.	Fry, M. J.	1974	Influence of the real rate of interest on growth: Afghanistan		Positive support
3.	Vogel, R.C., and Buser, S. A.	1976	Relationship between capital formation and inflation (a proxy for the real rate of interest) in 16 Latin American countries	1952–71 (for most countries)	Inconclusive/ negative
4.	Abe S. *et al.*	1977	Savings as a function of the real deposit rate for six Asian countries	Early/mid-1950s to early 1970s	Positive support
5.	Fry, M. J.	1978a	Influence of the real rate of interest on growth in 14 developing ESCAP countries	Early 1960s to early 1970s	Positive support
6.	Fry, M. J.	1978b	Ditto 7 Asian countries		Positive support
7.	Galbis, V.	1979a	Relationship between inflation and real interest rates (an index of financial repression) for 19 Latin American countries	1967–76	Inconclusive; data do not permit a true test
8.	Galbis, V.	1979b	Application of the McKinnon model to 19 Latin American countries	1961–73 for most countries	Inconclusive
9.	Hanson,	1980	Impact of change from positive to negative real interest rate in 1967 on saving, investment and growth in Colombia	1967–78	Positive support
10.	Fry, M. J.	1980	(a) Effect of real deposit rate of saving	1964–76	Positive support

Table 3.1 Summary of some empirical studies

Author(s)	Date of publication	Test	Period of test data	Implication for repression theory
		(b) Cost of financial repression in 61 developing countries		Each 1% real deposit rate below equilibrium results in $\frac{1}{2}$% loss in growth of GNP
11. Leff, N. H., and Sato, K. S.	1980	Relationship between availability of credit, level of real investment and growth of GDP in Argentina, Brazil, and Costa Rica	1950–73	Positive support
12. Brodersohn, M. S.	1981	Impact of 'liberalization' on: (a) saving (b) demand for investment in Argentina, Chile, and Uruguay		(a) positive support (b) Inconclusive/ negative
13. Fry, M. J.	1981a	Effect of inflation on real growth in financially repressed economies (12 Asian countries)	1961–77	Positive support
14. Fry, M. J.	1981b	Effect of inflation on real growth in financially repressed economies (7 Pacific Basin countries)	1961–77	Positive support
15. Fischer, B.	1981	Impact of nominal interest rates and inflation rate on investment for 40 developing countries	1960–72	Positive support
16. Leite, S. P.	1982	Survey of interest rates in 10 West African countries	No statistical test	Tentative positive support
17. Gupta, K. L.	1984	Various tests on (a) 12 Asian countries (b) 25 Asian and Latin American countries	1961–77	Limited support

'Positive support' means that the results support the model tested, i.e. that they support repression theory.

Among his detailed conclusions were:

— The growth of the financial sector and increases in real interest rates were both found to have a limited effect on aggregate saving, but both tended to encourage a switch from savings in the form of physical assets to savings in the form of financial assets.
— In the short run demand for financial assets was relatively inelastic with respect to variations in the real rate of interest.
— There was no widespread support for the 'complementarity hypothesis' (that capital formation is a positive function of the real rate of return on cash balances).
— The benefits of financial liberalization were sensitive to the 'inflationary environment' of an economy.
— An increase in the real interest rate brought about by a reduction in inflation was more effective than raising nominal interest rates in achieving a given degree of financial liberalisation.
— The effects of financial reform were concentrated in the initial years, 3 years being the most common period. In the long run the effects of higher real interest rates on real incomes did not appear to be very beneficial.

Gupta concluded that the role of the real interest rate, on its own, in stimulating economic growth may be limited, and should be accompanied by measures to encourage the growth of the financial sector.

Abe *et al.* (1977), in an empirical study of six Asian countries, estimated the following savings ratio:

$$SR^d = \begin{array}{c} -0.636 + \\ (-19.493) \end{array} \begin{array}{c} 0.154y + \\ (25.413) \end{array} \begin{array}{c} 0.112d - \\ (1.832) \end{array} \begin{array}{c} 0.064p^* - \\ (2.077) \end{array} \begin{array}{c} 0.556SR^f - \\ (6.173) \end{array} \begin{array}{c} \text{country} \\ \text{dummy} \\ \text{variables} \end{array}$$

where y = real per capita income;
         SR^f = ratio of foreign exchange savings to GNP
(t-statistics in parentheses).

As can be seen, the deposit rate of interest exerts a positive influence on the domestic savings ratio and the expected rate of inflation has a negative influence. An increase in d of one percentage point raises the savings rate by 0.112 of a percentage point (e.g. from 12.0 to 12.112% of GNP). A decrease in the inflation rate by 10 percentage points increases the savings rate by 0.64 of a percentage point (e.g. from 12 to 12.64% of GNP). However, we see that the foreign savings ratio has a much greater influence on the domestic savings ratio than any of the other variables; a rise in SR^f of one percentage point reduces the domestic savings ratio by 0.556 of a percentage point.

Fischer (1981) in a study of 40 developing countries over 1960–72, found that

domestic savings transferred within the respective country had a greater influence upon capital formation in countries with low and stable inflation rates than in countries where rates of inflation were high and stable.

He went on to estimate the following private sector investment function for the forty countries.

$$IR^p = 10.759 + 0.320d - 0.140p^* - 0.596IR^g + 0.125IR^f + 0.007y$$
$$ (2.640) \quad (2.900) \quad (3.829) \quad (1.398) \quad (4.329)$$

where IR^f = private foreign direct investment ratio
IR^g = public sector investments ratio.

The positive sign of the coefficient of the nominal interest rate and the negative sign for the expected inflation rate confirm repression theories. Fischer estimated that the interest rate and the inflation rate each account for about 20% of the change in the private domestic investment ratio, but the biggest influence is the inverse relationship between public sector investment and private domestic investment. His results support the notion that public sector investment crowds out private sector investment.

Fry (1974) found that in Afghanistan changes in the real rate of interest had a definite impact on growth. Fry (1978a), for 14 developing countries in the ESCAP region, found that increases in the real rate of interest did increase financial savings. The effect may not be to increase *total* savings, rather it may divert savings from inflation hedges to financial savings. The effect, nevertheless, is to increase the availability of loanable funds for investment. Fry (1978b) found that the real interest rate has a positive effect on domestic saving and economic growth in seven Asian LDCs over the period 1962–72.[9] Fry (1980) extended the analysis to cover 61 developing countries and found that saving is affected positively by the real deposit rate of interest, and that credit availability is an important determinant not only of new investment, but also of capacity utilization of the entire capital stock. He further estimated the cost of financial repression to be around $\frac{1}{2}$% in economic growth lost for each 1% by which the real deposit rate of interest is set below its market equilibrium rate. Hanson (1979) studied the impact of the change from positive to negative real interest rates in Colombia in 1967 on saving, investment, and growth and found that they all declined as a result. In a fairly broad study of ten West African countries, Leite (1982) came to the general conclusion that the prevailing policies of low and stable interest rates are inappropriate.

Not all studies have obtained positive results, though. Galbis (1979b), in a study of 19 Latin American countries, obtained inconclusive results. Brodersohn (1981) found a positive relationship between liberalization of interest rates and saving in the Southern Cone countries, but found that the impact on the demand for investment funds was inconclusive or negative. Vogel and Buser (1976) looked at the relationship between real interest rates, saving, and investment in Latin America and the results were again inconclusive.

Few empirical studies have been carried out to estimate the impact of liberalizing interest rates after such a reform has been implemented. Sri

Lanka, where interest rates were raised considerably after the election in 1977, has produced two studies. Roe (1982) found that

a large part of total investment is not governed either as to its total quantity or its allocation by local interest rate conditions. Under present institutional arrangements, the administered interest rates could be set at almost any level without affecting the pattern of investment. Thus so long as these arrangements persist it is impossible to say what is the 'correct' level of these rates, or whether 'high' rates are preferable to 'low' ones (p. 221).

Khatkhate (1982b), although only concerned with the period before the 1977 liberalization in Sri Lanka, was of the opinion that negative real interest rates had resulted in a shrinking of the supply of real loanable funds, leaving the demand for investment finance unsatisfied.

In Latin America, Galbis (1979a) found that liberalizing interest rates in the 1970s had been generally successful in Brazil, Uruguay, and Argentina, but not in Chile.

Korea reformed its interest rates in 1965. This was followed by an enormous increase in time deposits. Van Wijnbergen (1982) has estimated that this growth came from switching money from the kerb, or parallel, market to time deposits, rather than from increased savings or increased mobilization of cash savings. The effect was to tighten credit on the kerb market, which many smaller businesses depend on, and the reform was therefore contractionary in the short run. Van Wijnbergen considered that the contraction would persist if bank lending were restricted by government controls. Tight credit controls, if a permanent feature of bank regulation, would self-evidently restrict investment, and be contrary to the objective of interest rate liberalization.

Japan, perhaps, provides the most discouraging example for the advocates of financial liberalization. In its great growth phase from 1950 to 1970 the Japanese financial sector was notable for its ceilings on deposit rates, which produced real interest rates of zero or fractionally above zero, a household savings ratio which was consistently around 20% of disposable income, a private sector which was very highly geared and heavily dependent on bank loans for new financing, and a banking sector which was obliged to hold artificially low-yielding securities issued by the government and long-term credit banks. Bank reserve requirements, though, were very low, especially when borrowing by banks is consolidated. In other words, Japan managed to experience high growth with a repressed financial sector. The key to the rate of investment was the high savings rate, which reached 40% of GNP in 1972, when households, corporations, and governments are included. It is sometimes suggested that the rapid growth of incomes may have induced a high level of savings, as consumption growth, for various reasons, tended to lag behind income growth. Moreover the facilities for saving, and the social and cultural pressures to save, may have assisted the process, as did the absence of tax on interest on small deposits. For a fuller discussion, see Patrick and Rosovsky (1976). The behaviour of savings in Japan does appear to make it an exceptional case, though, and no other comparable example can be found.

(g) Policy Implications

The theory that financial development leads economic development, coupled with the recognition of a state of financial repression in many developing countries, leads to a policy recommendation of financial liberalization, and, particularly, interest rate liberalization. The most striking example of the implementation of this policy prescription lies in the package of measures which the IMF designs for borrowing countries. Such a package frequently contains a recommendation to raise interest rates, partly to tighten credit and partly to increase savings and thereby increase investable funds and economic growth. However, neither the theory nor the empirical research is unambiguous on the direction of causality between financial and economic development, and some studies have raised doubts about the very existence of such causality. Moreover, it seems quite possible for a country to follow policies of socialist or state capitalist development which may permit economic growth independent of the financial sector.[10] In such countries a prescription of financial liberalism may be largely irrelevant. However, for a country which wishes to encourage private sector investment the theoretical policy advice would seem to be one of removing controls on the capital market. The freeing (not fixing at higher level) of interest rates, reduction of reserve requirements of commercial banks, and the removal of investment direction and interest rate subsidies would appear to form a major part of this package. Other policies, including controls, would be regarded as 'second best'. However, liberalization by itself is unlikely to be sufficient, unless the country has a reasonably well-developed financial sector.

A policy of liberalization based on the belief that financial development leads economic development would be a policy of laissez-faire capitalism, for it assumes that financial markets and institutions are the best judges of the allocation of investment funds. In principle this may be acceptable in some sectors (e.g. services, some agriculture, and most manufacturing industries) but it is doubtful if it would necessarily lead to efficient allocation of resources across a whole economy, especially those with severe price distortions.

The neo-liberal approach implicitly assumes that private profitability and national profitability coincide. However, the widespread distortion between market prices and 'efficiency' prices in developing countries, recognized in the burgeoning literature on social cost–benefit analysis, renders this assumption doubtful. From a national point of view the allocation of investment resources by the financial sector would not, in many countries, lead to an optimum set of development projects. Therefore a policy of financial liberalism may need to be accompanied by a programme of price reform. A further qualification is that the financial sector has an inherent tendency to allocate resources to investors with the best security, rather than those with the best investment schemes. Thus, even within the context of private profitability it is questionable whether the financial sector allocates resources completely efficiently, although it generally does it better than any alternative mechanism.

It is doubtful if a study of financial development can lead to any confident policy prescriptions for economic growth. As Goldsmith wrote (1973, p. 73):

Finally, and this may be the most important point for this discussion, neither our theory nor our empirically founded knowledge is sufficient to appraise the probable effects of a given set of changes in the financial system on economic growth in a concrete situation.

However, it cannot be shown that the alternative of government controls on the financial sector combined with public sector investment leads to faster investment or economic growth. Although the evidence can never be conclusive, the balance of the argument does seem to favour the neo-liberal prescriptions. However, as the case of Japan shows, the difference in circumstances from one country to another means that a 'blanket' policy prescription is probably worthless; individual countries must decide what type of financial sector is likely to be conducive to growth in their own countries. Finally, I would like to emphasise my belief that the financial sector *is* important in economic development, and that a fragmented or inefficient financial sector is just as much a restraint on economic growth as are, say, inefficient transport and power sectors.

NOTES

1. This argument is neo-classical theory, of course, which argues that a marginal unit of capital will be invested where the marginal rate of return is highest. However, the rate of return is based on market prices, rather than on the results of social cost–benefit analysis. Therefore if there are significant divergences between market prices and economic or social prices, the growth of and dependence on the financial system may not lead to an improved allocation of resources, from the point of view of the national economy. (It will, however, enable private investors to make more money.) Significant distortions in markets probably exist in a substantial proportion of the developing world.
2. This point is discussed by Bhatia and Khatkhate (1975). However, their empirical study of eight African countries does not shed any light on it. 'Only if the high government expenditure ratio is associated with both high ratios of tax receipts and of foreign borrowing/government expenditure can it be taken as possible proof of difference in the technology used for savings mobilization and, hence, there need not be a positive relationship between financialization and per capita GDP. As Chart 8 demonstrates, a differentiation of technology is not borne out.' (Bhatia and Khatkhate, 1975, p. 148)
3. Even with a willing private sector, other factors may limit its level of economic activity. For example, Indonesia requires by law that the debt : equity ratio be no higher than 65 : 35 for any new investment, unless approval is obtained from the central bank. Local investors frequently find great difficulty in raising the equity portion of the investment, and the Development Bank of Indonesia (BAPINDO) has identified the shortage of equity (combined with an under-

developed capital market) as being one of the major constraints on economic development. (Private conversations with senior staff of BAPINDO.)

4. The financial interrelation ratio, FIR, $= (F_n + F_x + F_f)/W$, where F_n, F_x, and F_f stand for the market values of domestic non-financial, foreign (net), and financial institutions' instruments outstanding, and W for the market value of national wealth (domestic physical assets plus net foreign balance) (Goldsmith, 1969, p. 283).

5. Interest rate floors on deposit and loan rates are also encountered occasionally, but they have not been taken into account in the analysis here. As an illustration of methods of interest rate controls, Galbis (1979a) found that 17 out of 19 Latin American countries studied had imposed interest rate controls at some time during the period 1967–76. Interest rate ceilings on deposits were encountered in 14 countries, of which five were comprehensive ceilings and nine partial ceilings. Three countries had interest rate floors. In seven countries interest rates were pegged to some form of index, usually as part of a much wider indexation of financial assets and liabilities.

6. The argument assumes that the interest rate is the main determinant of savings and investment rates in a given period. This, of course, is questionable and other important determinants include the expected rates of growth and inflation, the level of excess capacity at the beginning of the period, and all the other factors which make up that elusive concept, business confidence.

7. Nonetheless, government borrowing by offering increasingly higher risk-free rates of return to lenders, may 'crowd out' private sector borrowing. To the extent that crowding out occurs, government borrowing, if used for current expenditure, may be at the expense of private sector investment.

8. The literature on the impact of foreign capital inflows on domestic saving efforts has been summarized recently by Dowling and Hiemenz (1983), for example, and is discussed in detail in Chapter 7.

9. Giovanni (1983) re-estimated Fry's equations for the same countries over a different period (roughly the 1970s) in order to try to test the robustness of Fry's results. He found an insignificant relationship between domestic savings and the real interest rate, concluding, 'Serious doubts are cast on the view that the interest elasticity of savings is significantly positive and easy to detect in developing countries' (Giovanni, 1983, p. 603).

10. However, the discussion in Chapter 10 of the effectiveness of public sector investment does not give us the confidence that it has been generally successful in developing countries.

Chapter 4

Mobilizing Domestic Finance: Government

1. INTRODUCTION

In developing countries, taken together, domestic finance accounts for roughly 80% of total investment, with foreign finance providing the remaining 20%. The volume of literature on the two sources hardly reflects the dominance of domestic finance—perhaps because the literature is dominated by writers from industrialized countries; perhaps, simply, because foreign finance has more financial sex appeal. Research on the development problems of money and capital markets in developing countries is limited. The emphasis given to the development of the financial sector by governments (as reflected, for example, in national plans) is almost non-existent. At the same time, capital markets tend to be dominated by governments through the issue of bonds and direct controls. Government dominance may also prevail in industrialized countries. For example, about 75% of the turnover of the UK Stock Exchange is in government securities. However, in industrialized countries dominance is achieved in markets which are competitive, relatively complete, which are subject to few controls, and where regulation is intended to increase rather than diminish the competitiveness of markets.

Chapters 4–6 will examine the mobilization of domestic funds. This chapter will be concerned with the financing of government, mainly through the instruments of taxation and borrowing. Chapter 5 will examine the role played by the main financial institutions (the central bank; commercial and development banks; merchant banks; post offices, insurance companies and pensions funds; housing finance corporations and savings and loan banks). Chapter 5 will examine also the informal financial sector, and Chapter 6, securities markets. Taken together, these institutions and instruments represent the ingredients for a reasonably complete and integrated financial sector. I have omitted discussion of more sophisticated mechanisms such as futures and options markets, and 'near financial' and hedge markets such as bullion and commodity markets, as they play only a small role in developing countries. However commodity markets may have a significant role in the future in several developing countries, and one can easily envisage commodity markets being established as alternatives to London, New York, and Chicago.

Different institutions and instruments should be seen as competing for funds in the domestic capital market, however fragmented some domestic markets may be. Thus taxation is a means whereby government extracts funds from the market for its own use; government institutions and borrowing instruments compete with private sector institutions and instruments for access to funds, and private sector institutions and instruments compete among themselves. In a competitive market the allocation of funds will be determined by the risk and expected return offered by alternative financial instruments. A structure of interest rates will develop, which will reflect overall market conditions (through the level of the risk-free rate of return) and different degrees of risk. However, as we have seen, the existence of financial repression in many developing countries may severely distort interest rate structures, leading to disequilibrium in the financial markets, distortions to the cost of capital, and distortions in the allocation of resources.

2. AN OVERALL VIEW OF GOVERNMENT FINANCES

Tables 4.1–4.7, derived from the IMF's *Government Finance Statistics Yearbooks*, present an overall view of government revenue, financing (i.e. borrowing), and expenditure for industrial countries, oil-exporting countries and

Table 4.1 General government: total revenue as percentage of GDP

	1975	1977	1979	1981
Industrial countries	36.28	37.07	37.24	39.07
Oil-exporting countries	38.72	34.86	30.81	n.a.
Non-oil developing countries	22.41	24.42	25.07	25.41

n.a. = Not available
Source: Derived from *Government Finance Statistics Yearbook*, vol. VI, 1982, 1984 (IMF).

Table 4.2 General government: tax revenue as percentage of GNP

	1975	1977	1979	1981
Industrial countries	31.58	32.43	32.44	33.65
Oil-exporting countries	17.06	14.29	13.57	n.a.
Non-oil developing countries	18.21	19.94	20.08	20.15

n.a. = Not available
Source: as Table 4.1.

Table 4.3 Central government: source of revenue, 1972 and 1982 (percentage of total current revenue)

		Industrial countries		Oil-exporting countries		Non-oil developing countries	
		1972	1982	1972	1982	1972	1982
1.	Taxes on income and profits	41.43	37.94	35.94	42.40	21.27	20.62
2.	Social security contributions	27.43	32.84	2.28	2.49	12.71	11.15
3.	Domestic taxes on goods and services	18.63	17.27	14.57	4.84	30.48	31.77
4.	Taxes on international trade and transactions	3.43	1.29	13.05	8.22	16.50	17.16
5.	Non-tax revenue	6.41	8.77	31.57	40.63	14.09	17.13
6.	Grants	0.48	0.61	0.48	0.16	2.25[a]	2.39
7.	Other	2.19	1.28	2.11	1.26	2.70	−0.22
	Total	100	100	100	100	100	100

[a] 1973.
Source: as Table 4.1

Table 4.4 Central government: capital expenditure as percentage of total expenditure and lending minus repayments

	1974	1975	1976	1977	1978	1979	1980	1981	1982
Industrial countries	6.66	6.75	6.63	6.77	6.35	6.21	5.93	5.61	5.50
Oil-exporting countries	26.61	29.51	34.29	33.84	35.19	28.99	27.37	30.08	31.55
Non-oil developing countries	16.60	16.28	19.28	17.38	16.81	16.53	16.52	16.79	15.46

Source: as Table 4.1.

Table 4.5 Central government: financing abroad as percentage of total expenditure
and lending minus repayments

	1974	1975	1976	1977	1978	1979	1980
Industrial countries	−0.14	1.23	0.87	2.83	3.24	0.65	0.47
Oil-exporting countries	−2.95	0.52	6.26	3.72	7.81	1.82	n.a.
Non-oil developing countries	5.27	6.49	6.70	4.20	4.20	3.82	3.90

n.a. = Not available.
Source: as Table 4.1.

Table 4.6 Central government: domestic financing as percentage of total expenditure
and lending minus repayments

	1976	1977	1978	1979	1980	1981
Industrial countries	13.69	8.43	8.44	8.66	10.05	9.60
Oil-exporting countries	3.61	8.73	6.45	4.08	9.40	9.67
Non-oil developing countries	15.21	14.18	12.90	12.94	13.45	14.16

Source: as Table 4.1

Table 4.7 Central government: foreign debt as percentage of total expenditure and
lending minus repayments

	1974	1975	1976	1977	1978	1979	1980	1981
Industrial countries	12.91	11.92	11.80	14.58	16.51	15.63	13.73	14.04
Oil-exporting countries	n.a.	n.a.	n.a.	n.a.	n.a.	n.a.	n.a.	n.a.
Non-oil developing countries	49.74	44.71	44.71	46.01	44.60	42.68	42.28	43.38

n.a. = Not available.
Source: as Table 4.1.

non-oil developing countries. General government includes state, provincial, and local government as well as central government. The aggregate figures suffer from the facts that statistical compilation and government financial years vary from country to country, and the availability of data is patchy. Nevertheless, the data do give a good overall impression of government financing. The data in the tables are self-explanatory, but the following main points stand out.

— Government total revenue and tax revenue take a rather lower proportion of GDP in developing countries than in industrial countries (Tables 4.1 and 4.2).
— Governments of non-oil developing countries take much less of their tax revenue from income or profits and much more from indirect taxes on goods and services and international trade and transactions than do other countries (Table 4.3).
— Capital expenditure by governments of non-oil developing countries and oil-exporting countries accounts for a much higher proportion of total government expenditure than in industrial countries. This illustrates the much greater role of government in economic development in the developing and oil-exporting countries (Table 4.4).
— Foreign financing contributes more to government expenditure in non-oil developing countries than in other countries, but is still a small (and declining) proportion of total expenditures (Table 4.5).
— Governments of non-oil exporting developing countries are more dependent on domestic borrowing than the other groups, although the difference is not very great (Table 4.6).
— The ratio of foreign debt to government expenditure is much higher in non-oil exporting developing countries than in industrial countries (Table 4.7). Complete data for oil-exporting countries are not available.

(The definition of oil-exporting countries is given in Note 1 to Chapter 7.)

The aggregate figures in Tables 4.1–4.7 conceal some wide variations from country to country. In Egypt, for example, general government revenue took over 47% of GDP in the early 1980s, whereas in the Dominican Republic and Guatemala the figure was only just over 10%. Taxes on goods and services accounted for over 40% of central government revenue in Zambia, Thailand, Korea, Philippines, Argentina, Bolivia, Nicaragua, Peru, and Uruguay. Taxes on international trade accounted for over 45% of government revenue in Uganda (67% in 1983), Mauritius, Sierra Leone, Sudan, and the Yemen Arab Republic. Capital expenditure accounted for as much as 45% of central government expenditure and lending minus repayments to Sri Lanka in 1982, and 33% in Morocco and Guatemala. Domestic financing (i.e. domestic borrowing) accounts for 45% of central government expenditure in Ghana in 1982, 41% in Mexico, and 36% in Zambia and Sierra Leone. All these figures are well above the aggregates for non-oil developing countries. There are, of course, individual countries with figures well below the aggregate. For example, domestic borrowing as a percentage of central government expenditure was below 5% in Togo, Tunisia, Papua and New Guinea, Chile, Costa Rica, and Paraguay in 1982.

3. TAXATION AND SOCIAL SECURITY CONTRIBUTIONS

Although taxation provides the bulk of government revenue in most countries of the world, the pattern of taxation is markedly different between industrialized and developing countries. The former tend to rely on direct taxation of individuals and companies, with indirect taxation playing a minor role.[1] Developing countries, on the other hand, tend to rely on indirect taxation, notably import duties. The main reasons for the difference lie in the small 'taxable capacity' in developing countries (few people earn amounts which enable them to pay tax readily) and in the lack of an adequate administration to assess and to collect income and company taxes.

The data in Tables 4.8 and 4.9, taken from Goode (1980), show how the composition of tax revenue varies according to the overall tax ratio. In both developing and developed countries the countries with the higher tax ratios tend to rely more heavily on direct taxes for tax revenue, whereas those

Table 4.8   Less developed countries: tax ratios and composition of tax revenue, 1972–76 (unweighted arithmetic means, in percentages)

	Overall tax ratio[a]		
	Highest 15	Middle 32	Lowest 15
Ratio of tax revenue to GNP			
All taxes	25.70	15.39	8.79
Income and profits taxes	9.62	3.76	1.95
Social security contributions[b]	0.87	0.50	0.14
Property taxes	0.33	0.24	0.22
Taxes on goods and services	13.72	9.90	5.76
Other taxes	1.15	0.99	0.73
Composition of tax revenue[c]			
All taxes	100.00	100.00	100.00
Income and profits taxes	37.43	24.43	22.18
Social security contributions[b]	3.39	3.25	1.59
Property taxes	1.28	1.56	2.50
Taxes on goods and services	53.39	64.33	65.53
Other taxes	4.47	6.43	8.30

[a] Sixty-two developing countries, classified by overall tax ratios.
[b] Information on social security contributions may be incomplete; according to the source they 'were included for those countries for which data were available'.
[c] Derived from group averages of ratios to GNP.
Source: Taken from Goode (1980). Goode's tables are in turn based on Tait, Grätz, and Eichengreen (1979).

Table 4.9   OECD countries: tax ratios and composition of tax revenue, 1972–76
(unweighted arithmetic means, in percentages)

	Overall tax ratio[a]		
	Highest 5	Middle 13	Lowest 5
Ratio of tax revenue to GDP			
All taxes	44.46	33.57	22.15
Income and profits taxes	19.99	13.10	6.04
Social security contributions	9.29	7.25	6.12
Property taxes	1.60	2.31	1.56
Taxes on goods and services	12.95	10.30	7.79
Other taxes	0.63	0.62	0.64
Composition of tax revenue			
All taxes	100.00	100.00	100.00
Income and profits taxes	44.93	39.60	27.57
Social security contributions	20.95	21.02	27.96
Property taxes	3.67	7.16	7.05
Taxes on goods and services	29.06	30.48	34.45
Other taxes	1.38	1.74	2.97

[a] Twenty-three countries classified by overall tax ratio; Iceland is not included.
Source: Taken from Goode (1980). Goode's tables are in turn based on OECD (1978)

with low tax ratios tend to rely on the generally more regressive indirect taxes.[2]

Comparison with the OECD countries suggests that if developing countries wish to increase their ratio of tax to GNP over time, then it seems likely to come from increased income and profit tax revenues. Table 4.3 suggests that revenue from these taxes is closely correlated with a country's income level. Conventionally, such direct taxes are progressive, which may make them politically more acceptable than increases in indirect taxation, especially as income rises. Moreover, the heavy reliance of developing country governments on indirect taxation may tend to produce severe distortions in the pricing system (sometimes compounded by a parallel set of subsidies), leading to economic inefficiences and the misallocation of resources.

The 'modern' approach to taxation gives it multiple roles in economic development. It is seen as a major instrument of macroeconomic management, for mobilizing funds for investment, and at the same time it is one of government's main instruments for implementing its income (and wealth) distribution policy. (The 'traditional' approach regarded taxation only as a means of funding government current expenditures plus the costs of defence, maintaining law and order, and the provision of essential social services.) The extent to which taxation increases total savings may be limited, as it may merely tap resources which would have gone into private saving. Its dependence on the formal sector may also mean that it does not even increase the mobilization of saving much. Those who pay taxes would use the formal sector for saving anyway. Indeed, taxation may merely lead to a reduction in national savings and investment, in that to a large extent it finances government current expenditure rather than capital expenditure. However, taxation does play a significant role in the allocation of investments, as it permits government to finance those projects which the private sector would not finance. In addition to obvious areas such as defence and 'social' projects (schools, hospitals, roads, etc.) which may be socially desirable but not commercially profitable, government may also finance large projects which are beyond the scope of the private sector. Such projects, if carried out by the private sector, require substantial equity contributions, which may not be available or forthcoming, and substantial collateral against debt financing. Again, the collateral is frequently not available.

There are clearly limits to the extent to which governments can levy taxation. The limit is embodied in the notions of the tax ratio, i.e. taxes as a percentage of GNP, and in 'taxable capacity', but a precise definition or measure of taxable capacity is elusive (Prest, 1978). There are clearly limits to the extent that taxpayers are willing and able to pay taxes, but again evidence of the relationship between tax rates and tax evasion is difficult to obtain. The 'tax effort' which a government makes (that is, the effort it puts in to raising tax revenues), often attracts attention, especially the attention of external financing agencies in the public sector who may like to see their own contributions supported by tax-raising. Tax effort may be measured against some norm, e.g. Lewis's remark that 'most underdeveloped countries need to raise at least 17% GDP in taxes and other government revenues' (W. Lewis, 1956, p. 129),[3] or, more usually, by comparison with the tax effort of other countries. However, measurement is problematic (R.M. Bird, 1978).

Tait, Grätz, and Eichengreen (1979) provide the main published estimates of tax ratios and tax efforts. They prefer to use the neutral term 'international tax comparison' (ITC) to the more pejorative 'tax effort'. The usual measures of tax effort have been criticized by Newlyn (1985) because they do not adequately reflect government taxation policy, but depend largely on growth in national income. Newlyn distinguishes between two causes for changing tax revenues. The first is the 'built-in' growth element reflecting the growth of the bases of existing taxes as a result of the overall growth of national income, and the second is the 'discretionary change' element resulting from changes the government makes to existing taxes and the introduction or elimination of taxes. Newlyn argues that the discretionary change element can give a unique and unambiguous measure of government tax policy decisions, and therefore of tax effort. In discussions of tax effort there is sometimes an implicit assumption that 'more is better'. This assumption is generally made by proponents of government planning or public sector organizations, notably aid donors, who believe in (or limit their interest to) the importance of the role of government in economic development. Of course, governments as a matter of policy may not *wish* to maximize their tax effort; liberal, laissez-faire governments may even wish to minimize it, leaving development to the private sector as much as possible. Nor may it be desirable that governments should maximize their tax effort. In no country can it be assumed automatically that money in the hands of the government is used more effectively in the national interest than if it were left in the hands of the private sector.

4. THE ECONOMIC IMPACT OF TRADE TAXES

Taxes on imports and, in some countries, exports, tend to provide a relatively high proportion of government revenue in many developing countries. Such taxes have the attraction of being generally easy to collect. They are also used as a tool of economic management in that taxes on imports are seen as a means of keeping down the overall level of imports, thereby helping to maintain the exchange rate, discouraging 'luxury' imports, and also helping to protect local industry. However, there is now widespread concern that the price distortions which are introduced by the general use of high tariffs may mis-direct investment and impede, rather than assist, economic growth. The main adverse effects of high tariffs are as follows.

— High tariffs on imports may be used to maintain an over-valued exchange rate. This may in turn be a serious obstacle to exports, both manufactured exports and agricultural exports.
— Tariffs raise prices of imports and non-traded goods relative to exports whose prices are usually determined by the world market. Again, this will discourage the development of export industries which use imports, unless an efficient (and administratively expensive) import duty rebate system operates. Effectively the burden of the tariff is borne largely by the export sector. (See Clements and Sjaastad, 1985, and *The Economist*, 25 May 1985, 'How protectionists score own goals'.)
— High tariffs on 'luxury' imports tend to encourage the manufacture of such goods behind the protective tariff. At the same time low or non-existing tariffs on more essential items, notably foodstuffs and capital goods, do not encourage their domestic production. The disincentive is increased if such industries have to pay duties on their imported inputs. The effect is to produce an industrial structure which is probably rather different from the one the government would like to see. In economic jargon, effective rates of protection become very unequal from industry to industry, and investment will tend to flow to the highly protected sectors, rather than to sectors where a country has a comparative advantage.
— An over-valued exchange rate, and low or zero tariffs on capital goods, both have the effect of cheapening capital goods relative to other prices

in the economy, especially the wage rate. The effect may well be to encourage the use of capital rather than labour, both by encouraging the choice of capital-intensive industries and by encouraging capital-intensive techniques within an industry.

— A tax structure which is heavily dependent on revenue from import duties will encourage import substitution and a reduction in imports. This in turn will reduce tax revenue from imports, unless the government imposes even higher tariffs on the remaining imports, thereby increasing further the price distortions in the economy.

5. A PROGRAMME OF TAX REFORMS

Current interest in tax reform is mainly concerned with reducing the distortions introduced by taxes on international trade. One reform programme has been presented by S. R. Lewis (1984), the main elements of which are the following:

— The replacement of all existing import tariffs by a uniform tariff on imports, thereby reducing disparities in effective protection.
— The introduction of a more highly differentiated sales tax to discourage consumption of 'luxuries'. In this way the tax will no longer encourage domestic production of such goods.
— The introduction of a uniform export subsidy to correct the bias against exports which is introduced by import tariffs.

This package represents an essential first step for many countries in tax reform. However, it still retains a number of distortions, such as an overvalued exchange rate (and its consequences), and unequal effective protection rates, even though nominal protection is now uniform. (Unequal effective protection arises because some industries will use imported inputs which carry import duty, whereas other industries will use local inputs which carry no import duty.) A second step in tax reforms would be to eliminate these distortions. Such a package might consist of:

— The introduction of a uniform sales tax on domestically produced and imported goods, to replace all import tariffs.
— The imposition of a luxury sales tax on goods whose consumption a government wished to discourage. This may be combined with a reduction in the uniform sales tax on essentials, such as foodstuffs. (In practice, it could be zero or even negative, which would be a subsidy.)
— The introduction of a rebate system for the sales tax on intermediates, so that effective protection becomes uniform and zero for all sectors.

Finally, a country would replace sales tax with a value-added tax (VAT), perhaps using different levels for different categories of goods. A VAT removes all economic distortions. A further reform will see a gradual switch from indirect to direct taxation. Such tax reforms are probably only long-term possibilities for many countries. They all imply a reduction in exchange rates, and possible dislocation of existing industries whose profitability (and existence) is maintained only by high tariffs. Although tax reform will necessarily be gradual, however, it remains desirable for many developing countries.

6. INCOME FROM STATE ENTERPRISES

Aggregated data on income from government-owned enterprises is sparse. What evidence exists, however, suggests that such enterprises act as much as a drain on government revenue as earners of income. Killick (1983), in a study of public sector industrialization in Africa—based on Ghana, Senegal, Tanzania, and Zambia—concluded that 'On our evidence, a large industrial public sector will contribute little to dynamic industrial growth, will tend to become a drain on public finances, will require a net inflow of resources to cover its capital requirements and will discourage the growth of private industry' (p. 57). Gillis, Jenkins, and Lessard (1982) found evidence in both directions. At various periods the public enterprise sector in Brazil and Korea especially, and also Uruguay, India, Taiwan, and Sri Lanka, had generated more than 10% of national savings. In many other countries, though, the state enterprises acted as a drain on public finances. They quote (at various times) Bolivia, Indonesia, Zaire, Zambia, Argentina, Egypt, Guyana, and Panama. In the early 1970s state enterprises made only minimal contributions to national savings in Bangladesh, Thailand, Bolivia, Chile, Uruguay, Somalia, Jamaica, and Colombia. 'In all these nations, the savings of public enterprises accounted for less than 5% of total investment finance over the period 1970–73' (Gillis *et al.*, 1982, p. 266).

The most comprehensive study of the financial performance of public sector corporations, although now somewhat dated, is that of Gantt and Dutto (1968). They looked at the performance of 64 government corporations in 26 developing countries. The overall rate of profit before depreciation was 8% of 'current activity'.[4] Depreciation amounted to 24%, leaving a deficit of 16% on current activity. In other words, the corporations taken together did not generate sufficient surplus to replace their capital, even assuming no inflation. The World Bank (1979) has summarized a number of other studies of the financial profitability of state corporations in individual countries. Overall these tended to give a similar impression of the lack of profitability. Experience varies, of course, and no individual corporation or country will conform exactly to the average. Petroleum industries seem to be the most profitable, and railways the least profitable. Some countries have experienced high profits from state corporations (Korea in 1972, and Uganda in 1971/2, for example) whereas others have experienced high losses (Ghana and Nigeria, in several years). The World Bank (1979) concludes that 'Based on this criterion [financial profitability], the picture of state-owned enterprises is a rather dismal one involving large and mostly continuing financial losses' (p. 12). Although arguments are frequently presented to support state subsidies on the grounds that financial losses may be offset by social benefits, it seems that, taking developing countries as a whole, the diversion of investable funds to finance current losses of state corporations may have a high cost in terms of lost economic growth. One seriously doubts the capacity of governments to operate efficiently, for example, industrial and mining companies. Worldwide experience in market economies suggests that they are better left to the private sector.

Public sector enterprises may receive indirect financial support which is not recorded in their financial reports. Some governments exempt such enterprises from corporation taxes. In other countries dividends are not expected (in other words, the equity is provided free). In yet others the enterprises operate under a regime of government-administered prices, although in some cases the prices will be held below 'market' levels, thereby having a negative impact on the accounts of state enterprises. From time to time government debt is 'written off', thereby releasing the enterprise from the cost of interest payments and the responsibility for debt repayments.

Although generalization across a wide range of countries is difficult, casual observation does suggest that governments have difficulty in ensuring that their enterprises are financially profitable, even though they may in some instances enjoy a monopoly position. The generalization applies just as much to the west as to the third world. The problems of running state enterprises in the third world are well known, but it seems that all the problems of organization, control, finance, personnel, and commercial considerations, which were highlighted by Hanson (1965) some 20 years ago, apply as much today as they did then.

7. GOVERNMENT BORROWING

Deficit financing is commonplace throughout the world's governments. In developing countries governments tend to assume the key role in the process of economic development, financing the major development projects. This may be necessary where private capital and entrepreneurial spirit is lacking (although in some cases the private sector may be exaggeratedly stunted by financial repression). In some cases at least, it may be necessary in order to try to attain the growth and economic distribution aspirations of the country. This deficit financing is met by government borrowing long-term and short-term; domestic and foreign. Here we are concerned mainly with domestic borrowing. Borrowing may be made to finance current expenditure or capital expenditure. Because of the fungibility of finance it is usually impossible to identify the purpose of an individual tranche of borrowing, unless it stated specifically what its use is to be (for example, electricity bonds or road bonds). Even then, it may merely allow funds to be allocated from the specified use to other uses, such as central government current expenditure.

Tables 4.5 and 4.6 show domestic and foreign financing of central governments as percentages of their total expenditure and lending, minus repayments. Essentially Table 4.4 covers domestic borrowing through bonds, bills, notes, and other borrowing, notably from central and deposit banks. Table 4.5 includes foreign loans made by central government and foreign bonds issued by central government; however, it excludes all loans made by non-financial and financial public sector enterprises. Nor does it include those borrowings guaranteed by the state, which can be regarded as contingent liabilities of central government. Therefore the tables cannot be regarded as fully indicative of public sector borrowing, especially foreign borrowing. (The difficulty of obtaining aggregate data for the public sector, let alone private sector, foreign borrowing, was highlighted by the debt crises in Mexico, Argentina, and Brazil in the early 1980s. Even the IMF, and the central governments concerned, did not have overall pictures of the countries' total indebtedness, and debt service liabilities.)

The picture which emerges from Tables 4.5 and 4.6 is that the central governments of non-oil developing countries are rather more dependent on borrowing, both domestic and foreign, than are industrial country governments. To some extent at least this compensates for the limited scope for developing country governments to raise tax revenue. To the extent that government borrowing is inflationary, it suggests that developing country governments may be notable instruments of inflation. A third observation is that government borrowing may be 'crowding out' the private sector. If this is a problem in the industrial countries it is likely to be an even greater problem in developing countries. As we shall see, government borrowing often has a powerful, even a suffocating, impact on developing country capital markets. For purposes of discussion we can divide government borrowing into market borrowing and 'protected' borrowing.

(a) Market Borrowing

In countries with organized capital markets, governments can use these markets as means of issuing bonds. Bonds may be advertised for sale at a fixed price, sold by tender, 'placed' in financial institutions, or even sold by auction. Whatever the method, the government must offer at least the minimum risk-free rate of return which the market will accept. The range of countries with organized securities markets is discussed below. In countries with fragmented, unorganized, securities markets, similar methods of issue may still be used, although the lack of an organized secondary market may restrict interest in bonds, especially from private individuals. The prospect of holding a security which cannot readily be sold until maturity will favour the issue of short- rather than long-term bonds; at the same time it may raise the return which has to be offered. However, market borrowing may encourage the holding of securities, and thereby the growth of the capital market. The risk exists, though, that government exercises its market standing (and ability to offer higher returns) to squeeze out private borrowers.

(b) 'Protected' Borrowing

The term is used to describe borrowing operations in which the government takes advantage of the legal restrictions or requirements which the government itself places on financial institutions. Typical of these requirements are:

— forced borrowing by government from the central bank, either directly or by selling bonds to the central bank;
— high minimum deposit levels which commercial banks must place with central banks;
— legal or moral pressure on commercial banks to hold government bonds;
— legal requirements for post office savings banks to hold government bonds;
— legal requirements for compulsory social security schemes, insurance companies, and pension funds to hold government bonds.

In the many developing countries where commercial bank accounts, post offices savings, and other similar types of deposits account form the vast bulk of savings such requirements as those listed above may give governments very considerable preferential access to the nation's savings (as, indeed, they are intended to). The immediate consequence is that governments are able to offer artificially low returns on savings, as the institutions have no choice but to accept them. This, in turn, has a number of consequences, compared with the situation which would prevail in the absence of such protected borrowing.

(1) The government obtains funds at below the 'free market' rate. This is likely to enable governments to finance projects which they would not undertake if they had to pay a free market rate. Thus investment is biased towards the public sector at the expense of the private sector. This may be appropriate if the social rate of return on government projects is higher than the social rate of return on private sector projects. However, the social discount rate for a country is notoriously difficult to calculate, and there exists a danger that government will undertake projects which ex-ante do not exhibit a social return as high as that of some private sector projects, simply because government can raise funds more readily than the private sector. Moreover, the evident lack of ability of governments to implement and operate projects efficiently means that many projects undertaken may exhibit distinctly low or negative rates of return, ex-post.

(2) The low rates of return discourage private sector saving, and give rise to a state of financial repression, discussed in Chapter 3.

(3) The forced low rate of return which financial institutions receive on government bonds means that they have to charge interest rates on private sector projects which have to be substantially above 'free market' rates, and

substantially above rates paid on deposits. This, in turn, will push up the test discount rate on private sector investments, and cut off a number of projects which would have been undertaken in financial markets less distorted by government intervention.

(4)   Forced investment in government securities limits the ability of financial institutions to invest in other financial instruments, such as equities, and thereby discourages the growth of capital markets. The ability of the private sector to raise fresh capital through stock markets (or even by placing shares directly in financial institutions) is therefore restricted.

The division of domestic credit between the public sector and the private sector is shown in Annex 4.1. For 73 developing countries the public sector took 36% on an unweighted average, which was half as much again as the equivalent figure of 24% for 11 industrialized countries. The average figures, of course, obscure the details, and it is notable that in 29 of the developing countries the public sector accounted for over 50% of domestic credit. In these countries the predominant function of the financial system is to finance government. The dominance of financial markets by government, assisted by controls, at the expense of the private sector, is the process which is known as 'crowding out', and which appears to be fairly widespread in developing countries.

8.   PRIVATIZATION

Privatization is still in its infancy in developing countries, but can be expected to increase significantly as disillusion with state-owned enterprises increases. Although it is often pursued as a way of improving the operating efficiency of enterprises, it also offers governments a means of raising capital by selling shares in state enterprises. As such, raising funds through privatization is no different in principle from selling government bonds. They are merely two types of financial instrument, with the share carrying higher risk and higher expected return than the bonds, and different maturity. The shares are irredeemable (i.e. infinite maturity) whereas the bonds will usually have a specified, finite, maturity date (or period). The government will lose the right to profits attributable to the shares it sells, but will not have to service the debt it would otherwise have issued. Privatization enables the government to cut down on its borrowing and increases equity, rather than debt, instruments in the financial sector. It may also be used as a means of encouraging wider share ownership, if small investors are favoured in share allocations. For further discussion of privatization in developing countries, see Predse (1985) and *The Economist* of 21 December 1985.

9.   PRINTING MONEY

In addition to taxation and borrowing, governments have access to the printing press as a last resort for financing their spending plans. In the normal course of events, and assuming little inflation, governments will allow the amount of notes and coin in circulation to keep pace with, or slightly exceed, the real rate of growth in the economy. However, given a government with ambitious development plans, but whose access to income and borrowing is rather below its desired level of expenditure, the temptation may arise to finance its expenditure by printing more money. This process may work reasonably if the expenditure is made on capital projects for which a demand exists, and which have an acceptable economic rate of return. However, it is likely to be at least partially inflationary in its impact, especially if the projects are in the infrastructure and social fields, and do not realize any revenue. If the printing press is used to meet government current expenditure, such as paying the salaries of civil servants, and the armed forces, and financing deficits of public sector enterprises, it is likely to be rather more inflationary. Although I have devoted little space to discussion of inflation and monetary policy, it is important to make the point that merely increasing the money supply is not a panacea for increasing the government's financial resources. Seers (1981) remarked, in the context of Latin America, that

brutal experience taught the lesson that monetary policy does matter. . . . The military regimes were each preceded by populist governments which paid little attention to monetary or even financial policy (Goulart in Brazil, Allende in Chile, the first phase of the Peronist return to Argentina). They fell into a trap which is easy to understand. In the euphoria of taking office they appeared to have the power to make good shortages of schools, hospitals, etc., and to raise wages and social benefits, thus reducing the acute concentration of income. . . . Arguments that such policies would lead to inflation and/or foreign exchange crises appeared to reflect the monetarist doctrines which the politicians concerned had attacked as socially irresponsible.

The printing press does not offer an easy way out.

However, government is responsible for the money supply. In almost all countries it is responsible for supplying the currency, and maintaining its value, or, in other words, restraining inflation. Monetary policy in developing countries, apart from interest rates, is scarcely discussed in this book, partly because others have discussed it at greater length and better than I could. See, for example, Drake (1980) and Furness (1975). The second reason derives from the uncertainty about the effectiveness of money supply measures and their suitability as measuring rods. It is appropriate to recall Goodhart's Law which, roughly, states that once a particular variable (e.g. M3) becomes a policy target, it consequently starts to behave in such a way as to make it no longer suitable as a target instrument. Monetary control techniques still seem to be very uncertain.

Annex 4.1: Claims of Financial Sector[a] on Government, Public Enterprises and Private Sector, as a Percentage of Domestic Credit, 1982

Developing countries	Central government (net)	Public enterprises	Private sector and other financial institutions
*Afghanistan	58	7	35
Algeria	22	n.s.	78
Argentina (1981)	27	n.s.	73
*Bangladesh	22	34	44
*Bolivia	45	n.s.	55
Brazil (1981)	6	10	84
*Burma	18	67	15
Cameroun	−21	n.s.	121
Central African Republic	33	n.s.	67
Chile	7	n.s.	93
Colombia (1981)	−3	n.s.	103
Congo	13	n.s.	87
*Egypt	56	n.s.	44
El Salvador	39	n.s.	61
*Ethiopia	40	19	41
Gabon	−21	n.s.	121
*The Gambia	16	48	36
*Ghana	58	32	10
Guatemala	40	n.s.	58
*Guyana	75	. .	25
*Haiti	41	21	38
Honduras	29	3	68
India (1981)	43	n.s.	57
Indonesia	−32	10	122
*Iran	36	17	47
Ivory Coast	7	n.s.	93
*Jamaica	55	7	38
Jordan	17	10	73
Kenya	42	2	56
Korea	11	2	87
*Lesotho	55	9	36
*Liberia	67	n.s.	33
Libya	25	n.s.	75
*Malawi	43	13	44
Malaysia	13	n.s.	87
*Mali	44	34	22
Mauritania	23	n.s.	77
*Mauritius	64	n.s.	36
*Mexico	58	6	36
*Morocco	54	n.s.	46
*Nepal	39	21	40
Nicaragua (1981)	18	n.s.	82
Niger	12	n.s.	88
Nigeria	48	n.s.	52
Pakistan	48	n.s.	52
Panama	14	n.s.	86
Papua New Guinea	17	n.s.	82
Paraguay (1981)	−4	8	96
Peru	26	7	67

Philippines	15	7	78
Senegal	23	n.s.	77
*Sierra Leone	84	1	15
Singapore	−35	n.s.	135
*Somalia	42	26	32
Sri Lanka	47	n.s.	53
*Sudan	29	29	42
Swaziland	−20	n.s.	120
*Syria	38	53	9
*Tanzania	65	29	6
Thailand	29	1	70
Togo	16	n.s.	84
Tunisia	12	n.s.	88
Turkey	34	13	53
*Uganda	63	. .	37
UAE	−16	3	113
Upper Volta	1	n.s.	99
Uruguay	14	1	85
Venezuela	−2	1	101
*Yemen AR	72	6	22
*Yemen PDR	68	27	5
*Zaire	78	1	21
*Zambia	68	n.s.	32
*Zimbabwe	29	22	49

Unweighted average, central government plus public enterprises, 73 developing countries, = 36%.

Industrial countries	Central government (net)	Public enterprises	Private sector and other financial institutions
Australia	20	10	70
*Belgium	40	12	48
Canada	9	1	90
France	10	n.s.	90
Germany	16	7	77
Italy	44	n.s.	56
Japan	12	7	81
Netherlands	11	6	83
Switzerland	8	n.s.	92
UK	16	9	75
USA	16	10	74

Unweighted average, central government plus public enterprises, 11 industrialized countries = 24%.

Notes
[a] Monetary authorities and deposit money banks.
* Country in which the public sector accounts for over 50% of domestic credit.
  n.s. = Not specified.
  . . = Negligible.

Source: Derived from International Financial Statistics, 1983 Yearbook (IMF).

NOTES

1. The importance of indirect taxation has probably increased recently in industrialized countries relative to direct taxes. This has come about through the wider incidence and higher rates of value-added taxes in Europe, combined with reductions in personal income taxation.
2. The extent to which indirect taxes are regressive in developing countries is questionable, as many of the poor depend on subsistence rather than on the purchase of goods and services which carry taxes.
3. As Table 4.2 shows, Lewis's target figure of 17% of GDP has been comfortably exceeded in developing countries since 1975.
4. Current activity is the average of current revenues and current costs. This was used as a base rather than the more usual net assets because of the impossibility of valuing assets consistently over the 26 countries.

Chapter 5

Mobilizing Domestic Finance: Formal and Informal Financial Institutions

1. FORMAL FINANCIAL INSTITUTIONS

(a) Overview

This section is mainly concerned with deposit-taking institutions, but also with insurance companies (for life insurance) and pension funds, which receive periodic (weekly or monthly) contributions. The financial sector in developing countries is dominated by deposit-taking institutions (that is, commercial and savings banks, post office savings banks, and housing finance companies), and the use of life insurance, pension funds and direct portfolio investment as vehicles for savings are little developed. Annex 5.1 shows the allocation of financial assets for 45 developing countries and 10 industrialized countries.[1] The 45 developing countries were those which had entries under 'other financial institutions' in the *International Financial Statistics Yearbook*. The data are not complete, as personal holdings of bonds and shares are not included. Data on such holdings are scarce and fragmented, but as we shall see in the following chapter, they are not likely to be significant in many developing countries. The absence of data on 'other financial institutions' does not necessarily mean that they are small or negligible savings vehicles, although they are in many developing countries. For example, the United Kingdom has no entry under these headings in the IFS, and building societies, life insurance, and pension funds are very substantial financial institutions in that country. Life insurance funds mobilized in Indonesia in 1979 amounted to Rps 66 billion, according to the annual report of Bank Indonesia, but they are not included in IFS. Savings bank deposits (Rps 20 billion in 1979) accounts for the entry of the other financial institutions. Nevertheless, both these sums are trivial compared with commercial bank demand deposits (Rps 1674 billion in 1979) and commercial bank time and savings deposits (Rps 1822 billion in 1979). Therefore it is likely that distortions caused by the omission of life insurance and pension funds will be small for most developing countries. Included in Annex 5.1 is a note of the items included under 'other financial institutions' in cases where they were specified in *IFS*.

Data have been derived from the IMF's *International Statistics Yearbooks*. The items included are:

Monetary authorities
Line 14a   Currency outside banks.

Commercial banks
Line 14d   Deposits with the monetary authorities.[2]
Line 24   Demand deposits with commercial banks.
Line 25   Time and savings deposits with commercial banks.

Other financial institutions (savings and mortgage loan institutions; post office savings institutions; development banks; building and loan associations; life insurance associations).

Line 24i   Post office chequeing deposits.
Line 24r   Treasury: private sector deposits.
Section 40: Data on assets and liabilities of other financial institutions.[3]

Total
Line 551   Liquid liabilities.

Total savings is given by currency outside banks + commercial bank deposits + deposits with other financial institutions. In monetary terms, the relationships are

Money (sometimes called M1; line 34 in *IFS*)
$$= \text{The sum of lines } 14a + 14d + 24 + 24i + 24r$$
Quasi-money (line 35) $= $ line 15 + line 25
Money (sometimes called M2) $=$ line 34 + line 35.

The financial survey provides a large measure of liquid liabilities (line 551) similar to what is sometimes called M3. For countries for which there is no financial survey, *IFS* publishes a broader measure of M3, comprising a consolidation of money plus quasi-money and lines 44 (demand deposits) and 45 (time deposits). Therefore total savings in some countries is given by line 551. In others, 551 simply is a sum of lines 34 and 35, and it is necessary to add section 40 to it.

Data are presented for one year only, as in most countries the year-to-year variation in the composition of financial savings is generally small.

A relatively high proportion of savings is held in the form of currency in developing countries (22% as against 8% in industrial countries in our sample). This reflects the lesser importance in developing countries of payments by cheque and credit card, and the greater importance of cash transactions and of the informal sector, financial and non-financial, both of which are characterized by cash transactions. It also reflects the greater use of currency as a form of savings, because people do not have access to financial institutions, or because they do not have confidence in them. Lack of access in turn may be caused by the shortage of branches of banks and post offices, meaning that many people are some distance from the nearest formal institution, or by the feeling prevalent in most countries that banks are for organizations and the middle and upper social classes.

(b) The Central Bank

Traditionally the central bank was the banker for the government. The gradual addition of other responsibilities means that it is now the keystone of the financial sector in most countries. Usually, but not inevitably, government-owned, central banks are the main instrument for the implementation of government financial policies. Central banks are usually associated with maintaining internal and external stability, and with the management and control of the financial sector, but in developing countries they may also be an important instrument for encouraging financial development.

The main functions of the central bank are:

— To act as banker to government, notably maintaining accounts and borrowing for government through the issue of bills and bonds.
— To issue currency.
— To maintain the purchasing power of the currency.
— To hold a country's foreign exchange reserves, and to maintain exchange control regulations.
— To supervise and regulate the commercial banks and other financial institutions.
— To act as lender of last resort to the banking system.
— To perform open market operations, thereby implementing the government's money supply and interest-rate policies.

While these functions are clearly the most important part of the work of a central bank, it is well placed in developing countries to do rather more. It can play a key role in the development of financial institutions and markets, thereby increasing financial savings, intermediation, and maturity transformation. A central bank can encourage the establishment, growth, and geographical spread of institutions, especially development finance institutions, by moral suasion or by the more direct way of providing equity capital. It can act to encourage lending to certain sectors (e.g. small businesses and agriculture) rather than others. By its open market operations it can encourage the growth of the money market, and it can also establish and encourage securities markets by providing the necessary regulatory and supervisory framework. The central bank in Malaysia, for example, performs many of these functions.

The central bank may also play a key role in repressing or liberating financial markets. It is usually the instrument chosen by government to control interest rates, to receive the required reserves from commercial banks and to control the availability of foreign exchange and the exchange rates. Conversely, it may be used as an instrument for financial liberalization, encouraging a flexible interest rate structure, and restricting inflation, thereby maintaining a balance between the supply and demand for funds, and encouraging financial savings. A sensitive approach to monetary policy may do much to encourage financial development. There is no conflict between the central bank's twin functions of maintaining financial stability and encouraging financial and economic development. Indeed, financial stability is likely to be the environment most conducive to development.

The conventional model of a fully fledged central bank may not be appropriate in all countries, and may be an expensive luxury in smaller developing countries. Collyns (1983) has examined some alternative models, ranging from currency boards through 'transitional' central banks to supranational central banks, such as the Banque Centrale des Etats de l'Afrique de l'Ouest and the associated West African Monetary Union. A further question which arises is the relationship between central banks and governments. In principle it is desirable that central banks should enjoy a certain degree of independence, so that they are not completely open to political pressures from government. The balance between independence and subjection to government decree is always delicate, but a degree of independence may be guaranteed if a central bank is at least partially publicly owned (that is, a proportion of its shares are held by the public, and traded on the stock exchange). Nevertheless, it is probably desirable that the government should own 50% of the shares. For fuller accounts of the role of central banks in developing countries, the interested reader is referred to Nevin (1961), Bortolani (1975), and Drake (1980).

(c) Commercial Banks

In spite of their alleged inaccessibility, commercial banks account for 65% of financial savings in developing countries in our sample, compared with 55% in industrialized countries. Moreover, the interest rates offered on time and savings deposits may in many countries be low or negative in real terms, as a result of financial repression. The explanation for their apparent popularity, of course, is that other savings vehicles are very underdeveloped. Commercial banks as a means of savings mobilization have been subject to criticism. UNESCO (1973) commented

Until now it seems that commercial banks—it does not matter if foreign, local, Africanized or nationalized—have not yet taken a positive approach to the problem at hand (i.e. savings mobilization), with very few exceptions.

To be fair, savings mobilization is a prime function of commercial banks only if it can be regarded as profitable business. If governments consider that the banks do not perform the function adequately, they should encourage other forms of institutional saving.

Commercial banks, of course, are financial intermediaries, and therefore they play a large role in the provision of credit and investment funds. Traditionally British-type commercial banks specialize in the provision of short-term business credit, especially trade credit and working capital, and personal credit. They provide little in the way of long-term loans relative to their total assets, and seldom take an equity stake in businesses. European-style universal banks take on the role of investment banks to a much greater extent. The historical background to the development of these different backgrounds is touched upon in Chapter 3. What concerns us here is whether one form of banking will meet the development aspirations of third world countries better than the other.

Given that these countries feel that they need a rapid rate of physical capital formation, it may seem at first sight that universal banks, which performed their function well in Germany in the nineteenth century, would be the more appropriate of the two. The long-term lending, equity investment, and 'cradle-to-grave' paternalistic involvement in all the activities of the client company appears to fulfil functions which are desperately required by private firms in developing countries. Firms often have difficulty raising equity and cannot hire skills in the market because of the shortage of managerial ability. On the other hand, specialized banking functions may lead to greater efficiency. Much depends on the size and state of economic development of the country. However, Khatkhate and Riechel (1980) examined the issue from the points of view of economic efficiency, mobilization of savings, promotion of entrepreneurial skills, financial stability, and conflicts of interest. They found that a universal banking system may be preferable, for many developing countries, to a specialized banking system. A universal system would have advantages in efficiency (notably in economies of scale) and in financial stability. Through the issue of long-term instruments such as bonds, universal banks can mobilize long-term savings. This process, however, generally requires a secondary market in the bonds. Specialized commercial banks, taking short-term deposits, rely on maturity transformation to provide long-term capital, a process which may have some attendant risks of instability. Universal banks can provide (or encourage the development of) managerial and entrepreneurial ability to a greater extent than specialized commercial banks. On the other hand, universal banks do bring with them possible conflicts of interest, such as placing in clients' investment portfolios those equities which the bank wishes to dispose of. In another study, Gill (1983) found that specialized banking systems tended to provide securities market intermediation services more cheaply than universal systems.

Under a specialized banking system commercial banks may set up merchant banking subsidiaries to carry out many of the investment functions of universal banks. They would then be supplemented by specialized development banks, which may be private sector or mixed, but which are mostly government-owned and financed.

(d) Development Finance Companies (DFCs)

A variety of institutions may be included under this heading. The common feature, though, is that they provide long-term finance for development projects. The most frequently encountered DFC is the development bank, some of which specialize in the type of lending they perform, notably industrial lending or agricultural lending. According to Kane (1975, p. 19) 'a basic principle of development banking can be formulated: development banks restrict their financing to bankable development projects'. The definitions of what is a 'bankable project' and what is a 'development project' are too numerous to discuss here, but if we take Kane's notion that other banking and financial institutions would be interested only in the 'bankable' aspect, and other general development agencies would be interested only in the 'development' aspect, we get an idea of what is the essence of the development bank. Identifying or defining projects which are simultaneously 'bankable' and 'developmental' may not be easy in practice. A further aspect of DFCs is that they tend to exist to perform functions which the private sector does not fulfil, so they can be seen as institutions which fill gaps in the capital markets. They will frequently contain an element of government participation, in many developing countries, being wholly owned by government. They also tend to promote and finance enterprises which have at least a substantial element of private ownership.

Although DFCs tend to be associated nowadays with developing countries, this has not always been the case. To start with, they tend to be based, historically speaking, on France's Crédit Mobilier and Crédit Foncier (which still exists), discussed in Chapter 3. Industrialized countries have had their DFCs in this century, notably the Reconstruction Finance Corporation of the USA, established by the Roosevelt government in the early 1930s to counteract the slump, but dissolved at the end of the 1939–45 war. The Industrial Bank of Japan was established in 1902 with private share capital and government promotion and guarantees. The Industrial and Commercial Finance Corporation and the Finance Corporation for Industry were set up in the UK in 1945 by the commercial banks and the Bank of England (which was then also private). Currently it is thriving with the new name of Investors in Industry. Most industrialized countries had similar institutions at some time during this century, and many still exist. One, Germany's Kreditanstalt für Wiederaufbau, has extended its domestic activities to finance third world development. Diamond (1957) contains a list of such institutions. Of course the list has changed since then, with, for example, the establishment of the government-owned National Enterprises Board in the UK, started in the 1960s and wound up in the 1980s.

The present third world can also boast some long-established DFCs.

Mexico's National Financiera was established in 1934 to promote the sale of government securities; it became a fully fledged development bank in 1941. The Land and Agricultural Credit Bank of Kenya was established in 1931 to provide both long-term loans and crop finance. Furness (1975) suggests that the Société Nationale d'Ethiopie pour le Développement de l'Agriculture et du Commerce, established in 1908, might be considered a development bank. However, the vast majority of DFCs have been established since 1945, many following independence in the late 1950s and 1960s of former British and French colonies. Generally speaking, therefore, experience of development banking in the third world is still rather limited. Nonetheless, virtually every developing country has at least one DFC, and some countries have several. The questions arise as to why the third world has adopted DFCs with such apparent enthusiasm, and secondly whether it has been right to do so.

Two different answers can be given to the first question. First, the private sector does not provide adequate institutions or finance to provide long-term capital for investment purposes. The lack of institutions in many countries is aggravated by the lack of a securities market, organized or not, and by the scarcity of retained earnings which, in Britain and the USA at least, provided much of the capital required by the industrial and services sector in the nineteenth century. Secondly, the central role in economic development which governments take on forces them to set up institutions to identify, appraise, promote, finance, and implement investment projects. Such an institution is a development bank. In many countries the dominant role of government in the push for development arises not from a fundamental wish to 'socialize' or 'centralize' the economy, but from a recognition, noted above, of the inadequacy of the private sector to meet any more than a small part of the country's investment needs. Therefore the development bank assumes a wider role than if it were a purely private sector financial institution. It becomes an instrument of government policy, and is generally expected to act in the long-term interest of a country's economic development, a function which may often clash with its criterion as a profit-making institution.

Among the broader aims which governments expect development banks to subscribe to are:

— the creation of employment;
— the saving or earning of foreign exchange;
— the distribution of income (between social classes, regions, different racial or ethnic groups, and even between males and females);
— the diversification of industry;
— the modernization of the agricultural sector;
— the development of small businesses;
— the encouragement of entrepreneurial activity;
— the development of the capital market.

Development finance companies may therefore find themselves obliged to finance projects where:

— The financial structure would not meet normal commercial criteria. Generally this means that the debt/equity ratio is too high, because of the inability of the project sponsors to raise sufficient equity. The DFC may then supplement the equity by taking some itself; this, though, increases its total exposure, perhaps to levels which would not normally be considered prudent.
— The cash flow cannot meet the bank's normal repayment terms. The DFC is then required to extend its grace periods or normal loan maturities. This it may be able to do, but for a DFC which operates on a revolving fund basis the slow repayment circumscribes its ability to finance future (and perhaps more deserving) projects.
— Little or no worthwhile security is available. This applies notably to small businesses (Kitchen, 1978), or businesses which already have a prior charge on their existing assets. In the event of failure of a business, the market for the assets may anyway be very limited, thus ensuring that little will be realized from their sale. The smaller and poorer a country is, the truer this is likely to be.
— The entrepreneur has little track record, either in the line of business being financed, or any other business. These risks apply *a fortiori* if the industry in question, or the technology, is new to a country, which is often the case.

Thus it is apparent that DFCs take high financial and commercial risks, which would normally require high expected returns, according to capital market theory. However, the requirement to meet the government's national objectives implies that from time to time it will be required to finance projects whose financial return is expected to be relatively low, that is below the return which is acceptable on commercial grounds. Moreover, government objectives may lead the DFC to concentrate its lending and investments in few industries, or in one sector (e.g. agriculture), thus depriving it of the possibility of holding a well-diversified portfolio. It seems that the financial and national objectives of DFCs may often be difficult to reconcile. Its financial requirements alone are ambitious; to expect them also to operate as 'social' institutions may be altogether too much. The existence of a sufficient number of projects which are simultaneously financially acceptable and socially desirable would of course remove the dichotomy. However, the distortions prevalent in many developing countries means that DFCs may not be able to meet these conflicting objectives readily. There is a danger, too, that DFCs may become financiers of last resort, lending on projects which are not acceptable to private sector financial institutions.

Capital market theory has considerable relevance to development banks. In what is a high-risk business the search for commensurately high returns is, of course, important. The recognition that some sectors carry more risk than others should enable them to use a higher test discount rate in the higher-risk business. Also, DFCs need a well-diversified portfolio of loans and equity stakes so that they can diversify away specific risk. The principle of diversification is an argument against establishing institutions which are too specialized. Such institutions have limited scope for risk diversification. If DFCs are run along these lines they should be able to achieve consistently improving financial results, which in turn will assist in raising further funds (for example, from the sale of bonds), enable them to increase steadily their lending and investment, and act as an example to the private sector that businesses can be run in a consistently profitable manner. A financially weak DFC is hardly in a strong position to advise its client companies on how to run a business, or to raise its own funds in the market. It should be mentioned, though, that mobilization of funds is, probably rightly, a minor role of DFCs. They can, of course, tap the capital market with bond or equity issues (their own or their clients'), but they are not equipped to mobilize small savings on a national scale. Such functions are best left to post offices or specialized savings and loan banks.

It may be a contentious view, but it seems better to allow DFCs to concentrate on being sound financial institutions rather than social institutions, with governments concentrating on reducing or removing the economic distortions which lead to DFIs facing financial and social objectives which may often conflict. (Governments themselves are responsible for many of the distortions anyway.) The danger of projects which are financially weak is that the returns are small or slow to materialize, or both. By financing such projects, DFCs are immediately restricting their ability to finance future projects, which in turn jeopardize the future economic and financial growth of the country. The experience of the IFC illustrates the weak financial performance of DFCs. The IFC has earned around 15% on its total investment portfolio, but only about 10% on that portion which is invested in DFCs.

The second question posed earlier was whether the policy of establishing DFCs by governments has been sound or not. (The question is not merely academic; it is being asked informally in the World Bank and elsewhere.) The question can be divided into two parts:

1. Is the general concept of the DFC sound?
2. If so, have they been established in the right way?

These questions can only be approached broadly here, as it is beyond the scope of the book to make a detailed assessment of the performance record of DFCs. The raison d'être of a DFC in a market (or mixed) economy is to provide long-term finance (debt or equity) which the capital market cannot, or will not, provide. It is undeniable that such finance is necessary for industry, agriculture, certain services, and infrastructure in cases where it is not financed directly by government, and it is not satisfactory to provide it by rolling over short-term loans, where continued availability is uncertain.

DFCs have provided long-term finance, to the extent that they were able. The question then is whether it could have been provided better by other routes.It is notable, also, that DFCs have often provided finance at interest rates which are below market rates, partly because they are favoured recipients of government funds,and beneficiaries of repressive interest rate policies. They have also acted as a convenient agency for on-lending funds from overseas agencies, notably to small and medium enterprises, which they also receive at concessional rates. In most instances they occupy a favoured and protected niche in financial sectors where institutional competition is often limited anyway.

In countries where financial institutions are limited in number and limited in vision regarding their lending policies, where entrepreneurial activity is largely concentrated on activities which provide quick returns, such as trading, and where security for loans may be limited, then DFCs are probably a necessity. The conditions described prevail in a large number of under-developed countries, of course; but any government which aims to develop an expanding and competitive financial sector should appreciate also that the favoured position of the DFC is, in the long run, incompatible with that aim. Moreover, a protected DFC may even discourage the development of private sector financial institutions, because the latter will clearly be unable to compete with it, and the development of long-term lending by the private sector may be discouraged. Some countries, including Indonesia and the Philippines, do have private sector development banks coexisting alongside government-owned development banks, which shows that they can operate under commercial constraints. The Development Bank of Singapore is a public company, with a stock market quotation. Therefore it seems that the long-term aim of governments in mixed and capitalist economies should reasonably be to privatize their development banks, and encourage them to develop and diversify into activities such as leasing and venture capital funds, and perhaps into other financial services.

A recent World Bank paper (Gordon, 1983) made some interesting comparisons between private sector and government-owned DFCs. Private sector DFCs were found to be generally more vigorous, efficient, and profitable than their government-owned equivalents. They have been more effective in mobilizing domestic resources, and more active in the development of capital market institutions and instruments. Since the late 1960s it appears that private DFCs began to diversify into activities such as merchant banking, brokerage and underwriting, money market activities, and leasing. The result is that the private DFI as originally conceived is now an endangered species. By contrast, government-owned DFCs have stuck much more closely to their original brief.

Had DFCs not been established, would alternative means of providing long-term capital have developed? The most likely alternatives would be for commercial banks to take on increased term financing, and in practice to become universal banks, or for a more substantial capital market to develop, featuring active merchant banks, long-term lending, and equity participation by financial institutions such as life insurance companies and pension funds, together with an active securities' market. In many countries the latter pattern of long-term financing would have been inconceivable in the 1950s and 1960s, and still is for many, as financial institutions and securities markets are very restricted by lack of demand, lack of income, or financial repression. For many countries, then, the alternative to specialized DFCs would have been for the commercial banks to turn themselves into universal banks. This would have required a marked change in practice, which would have been counter to the commercial philosophy of the banks and the training and experience of the senior staff. More simply, foreign-owned banks in many developing countries were probably reluctant to engage themselves in long-term commitments when their future was uncertain. Some host country reluctance to permit foreign-owned banks to become tied in to the country in the long term would merely have reinforced the position. Although commercial banks do nowadays seem more inclined to become involved in long-term financing, it seems unlikely that many would have willingly become universal banks. Therefore it seems reasonable to conclude that in the 1950s and 1960s there was no realistic alternative to the establishment of DFCs. However, many countries and their DFCs are now reaching a level of maturity at which it would be appropriate to examine carefully the future role of their DFCs.

(e) Merchant Banks

Merchant banks are complementary to British-style commercial banks. The US equivalent is the investment bank. With the scrapping of minimum stock exchange commissions in the USA in 1975 the US investment banks transformed themselves into financial conglomerates, and present indications are that the UK merchant banks will follow a similar path in view of the agreement to abolish minimum commissions. Universal banks perform the functions of both commercial banks and merchant banks, broadly speaking. Therefore one tends to find merchant banks only in countries which have UK- or US-type commercial banks.

Merchant banks specialize traditionally in providing trade finance, notably by accepting bills. In the last century they moved to being issuing houses and underwriters, notably for foreign government stocks, and later for corporate stock. They also accept deposits, provide short- and long-term loans, and organize financial packages, all on a wholesale rather than a retail scale. They provide a wide range of corporate services, and act as portfolio managers for corporations and individuals. Unlike investment banks or universal banks, however, they do not deal in securities. That function is (at present) the preserve of stockbrokers and stock jobbers in British-type financial structures. Although merchant banks provide corporate finance, and accept deposits, the volume of the funds they mobilize directly is generally relatively small. Their financial packages will consist substantially of funds from others, notably commercial banks or institutions. From our point of view their main significance lies in the role they play in securities markets, and I will therefore postpone any further discussion until Chapter 6.

(f) Post Office Savings Banks (POSBs)

In many developing countries the post office is the most accessible savings institution for the majority of the population, because it has a large number of widely spread branches, especially in rural areas, and because it is not intimidating to the lower classes, which banks often are. Therefore it mobilizes savings which in many instances would have been hoarded or spent on consumption goods. It is also cheap to administer, as it is only one of a variety of functions conducted by post offices. However, they do not provide credit, so cannot be regarded as financial intermediaries. Instead their funds are usually invested in government bills and bonds, thereby providing a contribution to government finances. To the extent that interest rates are repressed governments will receive funds at low cost through post offices, at the expense of often captive depositors. Moreover, the process tends to draw funds away from the periphery, sometimes impoverished rural areas, to the centre. UNESCO (1973), in the African context, commented that 'with regard to savings mobilization, the POSB is a static and passive institution and a more dynamic effort should be brought to bear on the economy, particularly at local level'. UNESCO (1973) also pointed out that savings deposited in African POSBs had been stagnating, or even decreasing, but (at that time) only two African countries, Algeria and Swaziland, had replaced their POSBs with institutions more suitable for mobilizing household savings, with the Caisse Nationale d'Epargne et du Prévoyance (1966) and the Swaziland Savings and Credit Bank (1965). Certainly, savings banks can offer a wider range of services (notably by providing credit), and can operate as a local or regional institution, thereby encouraging the local economy. They can provide private sector credit as well as government credit.

(g) Insurance Companies and Pension Funds

These institutions provide very important mechanisms for savings in developed countries, and their portfolio investments dominate the stock-markets. By contrast they are of limited importance generally in developing countries. First, their requirements that savers contribute regularly (usually monthly) restricts their use to people with regular wages and salaries, who are relatively less numerous in developing than in developed countries. Secondly, contributions may not be encouraged by the availability of tax concessions. Thirdly, institutions are often obliged to place a substantial proportion, or even all, of their funds in government securities, which in financially repressed economies will offer low or negative real rates of return. Further, such requirements limit the corporate bond and equity investment which insurance companies and pension funds may make, thereby repressing the growth of stock markets and restricting the availability of long-term capital to the private sector.

Although the importance of these institutions in saving and investment may still be small in the third world, there are indications that in some countries they are growing rapidly. UNESCO (1973, p. 43) comments on 'the high growth rate of the life insurance business' in Africa. In Indonesia,funds mobilized by life insurance and social insurance funds grew by 47% and 45% respectively in 1978 to 1979. (The comparable increase in the Consumers Price Index was about 28%.) The comon habit of allowing these savings mechanisms to qualify for tax concessions will tend to encourage their growth, although at the expense of building more distortions into financial markets. Moreover, the institutions are sometimes regarded as being cautious and conservative investors, not given to searching for high returns. In fact, some record depressingly low returns. Under these circumstances the impact of the distortion may be to channel funds into safe but low-yielding investments and away from newer, potentially rewarding, but higher-risk investments.

The growth of life insurance has also suffered from high rates of inflation and repressed financial markets. Emery (1970) considered that 'the insurance industry in most of South East Asia is not an important source of funds'. Only in Malaysia were insurance companies an important source of non-bank funds, and of 'moderate' importance in Singapore, the Philippines, and Burma. Elsewhere the industry was unimportant. Emery considered that the growth of the industry was inhibited because 'only a small proportion of the population . . . is interested in life insurance', and 'severe inflation in Indonesia and Vietnam, to mention only two countries, has discouraged sales of life insurance'. Turning to Latin America, Rietti (1979) noted that the rate of saving through life insurance has been declining in recent years, chiefly because inflationary pressures have discouraged the sale of life insurance policies or contracts with large components of saving.

Data on funds invested in life insurance are scanty in the third world, although the general impression is that the volume is not important. Rietti, (1979) thought that in Latin America only 5% of the economically active population is insured against death, and that for the region as a whole only 25% of national income is covered by life insurance policies, whereas in most developed countries the figure is over 100%.

Pension funds (provident funds) likewise are generally not very important. Emery (1970) reported that only four South East Asian countries (out of 10) had formal funds. These were Malaysia, Philippines, Singapore, and Burma. The funds in Malaysia, Philippines,and Singapore, though, represented important sources of long-term capital, and in Malaysia at the end of 1967 the Employees Provident Fund's investments were about 80% of the total loans and investments of the commercial banks. Since then there has been some expansion in other countries, including Indonesia (mentioned above). Again, investments may be restricted by law or by convention. In Nigeria, for example, the government-owned National Provident Fund invests most of its funds in government securities (Ajayi and Ojo, 1981) as does Kenya's National Social Security Fund (Jetha, 1973). The extent to which compulsory pensions funds increase or mobilize total savings may be questioned. Many of the members of such funds would probably have saved a substantial amount of their contributions in similar funds anyway, and the employer's contribution, in the case of government-run schemes, is little more than an additional payroll tax. What they do appear to do—especially, but not only, in government-owned schemes—is to direct savings into the hands of government. They also perform the function of maturity transformation, as the long term nature of life insurance premiums permits funds to be lent long-term. If alternative savings vehicles were used (e.g. commercial bank deposits), the element of maturity transformation would probably be lacking.

(h) Housing Finance Companies (Building Societies)

These institutions generally accept deposits from members in order to make loans for house purchase to other members. Savers often make deposits with a view to qualifying for a housing loan; indeed in some instances this may be the only good reason for saving in this way, as some housing finance companies do not offer particularly attractive terms to savers. The vast majority of their funds will go to finance house purchase or building, and they represent important means of financing residential building. Only their liquid reserves will be invested in securities, often government bonds. In some countries, though, governments offer tax concessions on deposits and mortgage interest payments, in order to encourage the purchase of houses, owner-occupation, and the general improvement of the quality of the housing stock. While these may be laudable aims, the result is of course a distortion in the financial markets, with more money going into the housing stock than would be the case without the tax concessions. In the UK at least, housing finance has occasionally been criticized for attracting too high a proportion of savings (at the expense of industrial investment), and for encouraging the rise in house prices by providing too much liquidity.

Building societies, of course, borrow short and lend very long. Maturity transformation is one of their important functions. They are, therefore, very vulnerable to a 'run', but they generally seem able to avoid the risk by having large numbers of small savers, most of whom wish to leave their money in the society in order to qualify for housing loans. Stable deposits are essential for their continued operation, as is a dependable stream of repayments. In some countries they are supported by government guarantees (or even government ownership); in others, such as the UK, by a 'lifeboat' agreement between building societies in the event of a run on one of their members, or a failure. They tend to be popular with small savers, and compete with banks and post offices to attract funds. However, it is likely that the promise of a housing loan after a certain level of saving, or a certain period of saving, is reached does act as a real incentive to individuals to save. Because of this, housing finance organizations probaby do encourage a savings effort, and probably do increase savings, rather than merely diverting them from one institution to another.

Interestingly, building societies started as informal savings and loan institutions in the nineteenth century in the north of England. Some were permanent, but many were terminating, being wound up when all their members had purchased a house. Their present size and importance in the British financial sector amply illustrates the potential for informal financial organizations in developing societies to grow into substantial formal organizations.

Building societies tend to have followed the British model in former British colonies, such as Malaysia. In other countries, though, the savings and loan bank and mortgage bank are often the main sources of housing finance.

(i) Savings and Loan Banks

Savings banks (I will use the common abbreviation) are non-profit-making financial intermediaries, whose objectives are:

— To accept household savings, particularly those of lower income groups.
— To grant credit to its savers, and to others, notably small businesses and private individuals, located mainly in their region of operation.

They may be owned by government, regional or local authority, or they may be cooperatives or 'trustee' organizations. They have an extensive history, their origins being traced back to Scotland in 1810. The Trustee Savings Banks started in the UK in 1817, and grew rapidly, reaching 400 savings banks with £14 million deposits for 400,000 depositors. They did not fully achieve their objectives, appealing to the lower middle classes and to the bourgeoisie as well as to the poor, which led to the establishment of the Post Office Savings Bank in 1861. Fishlow (1961) commented that

The Post Office Savings Bank was created in 1861 in dissatisfaction with the performance of the savings banks. It soon surpassed the savings banks in both deposits and depositors. At the same time, it attracted the lower-class saver more effectively, as evidenced by the much smaller average deposit which it held. The Trustee Banks, created with such high hopes, were thus relegated to a secondary role in the cultivation of small savings.

Although the idea of savings banks is very appealing for developing countries, in that they may mobilize savings which may otherwise have been dormant, they cannot automatically be regarded as a panacea for developing the financial sector. Interestingly, UNESCO (1973) reported that the general trend in Africa seemed to be to reorganize the POSBs and convert them into savings banks, or to establish new savings banks. In the late 1960s and 1970s a number of countries followed one or another of these lines, and it would be interesting now to evaluate their performance after 10–15 years of operation.

The lending pattern of savings banks varies considerably. In the United States the savings and loan associations are the largest single source of housing finance, but then the International Savings Bank Institute does not classify them as savings banks. Nor are Britain's building societies so classified. However, it is clear that, generally speaking, one of the main lending functions of savings banks is the provision of housing finance. In Spain they provide 75% of the country's mortgages, and in Italy and Denmark nearly 70%. Loans to the public sector account for about 40% of savings banks' total lending in Argentina, 35% in Australia, and 30% in Thailand. Some lend heavily to small local enterprises (see *The Economist*, 23 May 1981). The triumvirate of building societies, POSBs and savings and loan banks all share the common function of mobilizing small, private savings. In several countries they exist side by side (and, in the UK, coexist with the government's National Savings Bank, which performs similar savings functions) and compete for savings. However, they differ markedly in the provision of credit. It is by no means clear which combination will maximize the mobilization of savings, nor which will be the least-cost solution. Nonetheless, a widespread savings and loan institution with many branches appears attractive for developing countries, in that it can attract small (and especially rural) savings, and provide credit for a wide range of activities. Few developing countries can afford the partial duplication of effort (and costs) if two or more such institutions compete for small savings.

Savings and loan organizations in Latin America tend to be of the USA type, in that they are mainly housing finance societies. The exceptions are in the former British colonies, where building societies have been established. The first savings and loan organization in the region was established in Peru in 1957, but many countries followed suit in the 1960s and early 1970s, with the result that nearly all countries in the region now have them. However, mortgate banks ('Bancos hipotecarios') and capitalization banks had been established in the 1930s, 1940s and 1950s to provide (mainly middle-class) housing finance (Rietta, 1979).

By 1970 the Philippines was the only Asian country to have savings and loan associations. It also had mutual building and loan associations and savings banks. Hong Kong had building and loan agencies (private and public), while Malaysia and Singapore had building societies. Emery (1970) commented 'One of the most successful groups has been the building societies in Malaysia and Singapore . . . their operations could well serve as a prototype for other South East Asian countries.'

2. THE SEMI-FORMAL AND INFORMAL ORGANIZATIONS

(a) Credit Cooperatives and Credit Unions

Cooperative (or mutual) savings and loan schemes are the formal sector equivalent of informal savings and loan schemes (see below). They are formal in that they are registered with the Registrar (or Department) of Cooperatives or the Registrar of Friendly Societies. Both Emery (1970) and Drake (1980) express the view that most successful cooperatives are urban-based, where their membership is mostly white-collar. They tend to provide consumer credit rather than investment funds, though. Agricultural co-operatives, on the other hand, are sometimes used by government and DFIs as means of channelling loans to small farmers for equipment, land improvement, and working capital, and hence are rightly to be considered mechanisms for providing investment finance. Their performance has been marred in some countries by poor repayment records. Although cooperatives can be an important source of finance for small farmers, they are rarely important in volume terms when considered in the framework of total national credit.

Credit Unions are essentially cooperative savings schemes which grant credit to their members. With the encouragement of the World Council of Credit Unions and certain foreign National Associations of Credit Unions, notably in Canada and the USA, they have been established in a large number of developing countries. They tend to be local in membership and activity, typically based on villages, places of work, or even institutions such as churches. In some countries they are very widespread, Emery (1970) recording that the Philippines had over 1000 credit unions by the end of 1967. By the end of 1972, 21 African countries had credit unions. The legal status of credit unions varies from country to country; in some they are legal entities regulated by government; in others they do not have legal status, and really belong to the informal financial sector.

They are generally small, both in membership (the minimum is 25) and volume of funds. They pay interest on deposits, and charge higher (some-times much higher) interest on loans to members. Loans tend to be short or medium term (up to 2 years), and largely for consumption purposes, such as weddings, funerals, purchase of cars, and downpayments on houses. In many cases they provide an access to credit which would not be available from the formal sector (for example, from commercial banks). Supervision and administration is usually performed by elected officers on a voluntary basis, which keeps running costs low, but weak administration is probably their greatest single drawback. They suffer, too, from loan delinquency, especially if supervision is weak, and embezzlement of funds. They do not extend credit facilities to non-members, and with a narrow membership base most have little opportunity for growth. In many cases they offer negative real rates of interest to depositors, which can discourage saving.

Criticism of credit unions and credit cooperatives is easy, and it must be admitted that the author's one contact with credit unions (in Zambia) suggested that they left much to be desired. Therefore it is pleasant to record a recent report of some successful credit cooperatives and credit unions in the provision of agricultural credit and rural finance in Africa (Von Pischke and Rouse, 1983). They found that the Caisse Nationale de Crédit Agricole (Morocco), Kenya's cooperative savings scheme, credit unions in the Cameroun, rural savings clubs in Zimbabwe and credit groups in Malawi had all achieved at least partial, if not total, success. These they contrast with 'the general failure to develop self-sustaining rural lending agencies which mobilise resources internally'.

(b) Informal Savings and Loan Associations

Cooperative credit schemes and credit unions generally are registered with the government or are part of a national movement, and can therefore be considered as formal or, perhaps, semi-formal institutions. Beyond these lie the informal savings and loan associations, which act as savings clubs for members and also provide loans to members. They are used largely by people who do not have access to formal savings and loan associations, and do not have bank accounts, either because such formal institutions are not geographically accessible, or because the individual does not have the right social and financial standing. They are therefore very common in rural areas, where they provide cheaper credit than moneylenders, but are also widespread in urban areas, where they may offer more attractive rates of interest to savers' than are available in the sometimes repressed formal institutions.

Informal savings and loan associations can operate in a number of different ways. They may be fixed fund (like banks), rotating funds, in which the contributions of one month go to specific individuals, in turn, permanent or terminating. They may lend for any purpose, or they may be restricted to lending for specific purposes such as housing and education. They may exist to save for communal expenditure, such as a power-driven village mill. Administration is usually provided free by the members, and is therefore low-cost. While such associations may be important to individual members, it is likely that they take in only a small proportion of total savings in a country. However, Begashaw (1977) has estimated that in Ethiopia informal associations handle savings and loans amounting to 8% or more of the country's national income.

Mobile banks may also operate on an informal basis, providing a service for traders and market places. They may on occasion act as agents for moneylenders or larger businessmen in the informal sector, as suggested in West Africa by Miracle, Miracle, and Cohen (1980). Pawnbrokers the world over provide short-term credit in the informal sector, although in some countries in South East Asia, including Indonesia and Burma, they are owned and operated by government. They can be quite significant, although data on them are limited. In Indonesia in 1979, for example, pawnshop loans totalled 90 billion rupiah, while life insurance contributions amounted to only 66 billion rupiah (Bank Indonesia Annual Report, 1980/81). Emery (1970) reported that in Thailand pawnshops were important sources of funds, ranking fourth after commercial banks, the Govenment Savings Bank and the central bank, in 1968.

(c) Agricultural Credit and Informal Rural Credit Markets

The rural financial sector in many developing countries is itself fragmented, and substantially separated from the urban financial sector. Formal, urban institutions reach the rural areas very patchily. Hence, opportunities for institutional saving and credit in rural areas are limited, and much less than in urban areas, giving rise to 'financial dualism'. In rural areas the informal financial sector becomes much more important than in the urban areas,and 'semi-formal' institutions such as credit cooperatives and credit unions are found, rather than banks and building societies. Many governments (and external donors) have attempted to set up agricultural credit institutions, with the object of channelling credit (often subsidized) to small farmers. Such institutions generally do not accept deposits, and so do not mobilize funds.

The fact that governments consider such efforts necessary strongly suggests that the function of rural credit cannot be performed adequately by the private sector, or at least by the formal private sector. Commercial banks find that the volume of business in rural areas is low. Given the relatively high fixed cost of a branch bank, they may find difficulty in operating profitably in many areas, especially if they are not permitted to adjust the margin between lending and borrowing rates to cover their transaction costs. Even if they try to do this they may succeed only in driving away business. Secondly they usually regard rural and small farm credit as high-risk lending, which will again tend to reduce profitability unless they can push up lending rates without reducing the demand for loans.

Therefore for large areas of the world, rural financial markets are operated by the semi-formal or informal cooperative schemes, and by traditional moneylenders (including merchants, middlemen, and landlords). The latter group have been much criticized for charging usurious interest rates. Bottomley (1963, 1964, 1975) has identified four determinants of interest rates in rural areas.

— the risk-free rate of interest (that is, the opportunity cost of funds);
plus — a premium for risk;
plus — a premium to cover transaction costs;
plus — an element of monopoly profit.

It is difficult in practice to divide rural interest rates into these four components. What is generally accepted, though, is the result that commercial interest rates in rural areas are well above rates charged by formal agricultural credit institutions. The World Bank (1975) lists nominal and real interest rates to farmers, by source of loan. In every country listed the rate charged by commercial lenders was well above the rate charged by institutions. Real interest rates were presented for both institutional and commercial lenders for 23 countries. As a rough summary the real interest rates charged, averaged over 23 countries, were 3.6% by institutional lenders and 54% by commercial lenders. The difference is staggering.

Of course most institutional credit is subsidized, but one is bound to reflect on other reasons for the high real rates charged by commercial lenders. Of Bottomley's four determinants, three are entirely acceptable charges to make. In any financial market, interest rates consisting of the risk-free rate plus a risk premium plus transaction costs is normal. In fact, money markets could not exist without such a basis for interest rates. What is not acceptable (except, no doubt, to the moneylender) is the element of monopoly profit, which I will examine in greater detail below. A further possible explanation for the very high interest rates is that moneylenders universally overestimate the risk of rural credit, and therefore charge an unduly high risk premium. We are inclined to discount this explanation on the grounds that money-lenders are experienced and know their business. The risk premium element may be high, but if so it is probably justified. Yet another possible explanation is not included in Bottomley's determinants of rural interest rates is that of the ignorance of the borrowers. Quite simply they may not realize the true rate of interest they are paying, especially on short-term credit. Further, they may not know about alternative sources of finance, whether formal or informal, which may be cheaper. Quite recently the UK government made a requirement that all lenders should quote the true annual rate of interest, as this was felt to be necessary to protect borrowers, who never realized the true rates they were being charged. The problem may be considerably greater in rural areas in developing countries, where the diffusion of education and pocket calculators is much less widespread than in the UK. However, the evidence on this point tends to be anecdotal rather than systematic.

Other writers have stressed other factors, which are in the main market imperfections. Long (1973) included

— the scarcity of capital;
— high administrative costs;
— high default rate;
— the seasonal character of demand for credit,

as explanations of the difference between interest rates in formal and informal markets. High administrative costs and high default rates have their parallels in Bottomley's work, but the scarcity of capital and the seasonal nature of demand emphasize the differences in underlying supply and demand between formal and informal markets. Wai (1957, 1977) mentions too the supply side (shortage of capital, monopoly profit, inadequate collateral, high default rates) and the demand side (the low level of agricultural incomes and savings; borrowing for the basic necessities of food, clothing and shelter; seasonal demand; and the low level of education and literacy of farmers) in explaining interest rates in informal markets.

Monopoly profit is the element of rural credit which has raised the ire of academics and become the target of government administrators, who have attempted to reduce its impact by providing alternative, cheap, institutional credit. But how widespread, and how big, is the monopoly profit? Unfortunately the evidence is limited. To quote the World Bank (1975)

Only a few studies throw light on the question of informal market interest rates. The studies indicate that in Ecuador, India, Indonesia, Thailand and the Republic of Vietnam, average interest rates on commercial loans are not out of line with competitive rates. But in Malaysia and Chile, the high rates are to a substantial extent due to the monopoly held by moneylenders (p. 29).

Wai (1977) made a rough attempt to account for the difference between interest rates in unorganized and organized money markets, based on data for institutional loans to farmers which fall overdue. He concluded that risk factors and monopoly profits each account for about one-sixth of the difference, urgency of demand for one-third, with the remainder being due to other factors, notably shortage of capital and inadequate collateral.

The high cost and scarcity of credit in the informal sector has prompted many developing country governments to set up specialized rural or agricultural credit institutions. Foreign aid donors have encouraged the process with technical assistance, and by using the institutions to implement rural development programmes. The object of such institutions has generally been to provide more credit to farmers at interest rates well below those prevalent in the informal credit markets. Wai (1977) found that in 13 countries both these aims had been achieved to some extent if one compares the period 1948–51 with 1968–71. The gap between informal and institutional interest rates had narrowed from 34% in the early period to 19% in the later period, on average, indicating that the two markets had become closer. On the other hand, he reported, laws to reduce informal interest rates had generally not succeeded.

Many schemes have been established, owned, financed, and subsidized by governments. However, in a few countries, notably India and Brazil, the private sector has taken a leading part, albeit with government encouragement or pressure. Commercial banks have generally played a small role. An exception is the attempt by the Nigerian government in 1977 to order the commercial banks to open branches in rural areas. For the period 1977–80, 200 rural branches were allocated, followed by a second phase of another 266 branches. Although this has led to an increase in rural credit, and provided much greater opportunities for rural savings, the scheme appears to be generally unprofitable for the banks. Notable problems of accessibility, staffing, bank accommodation, low business volume, and security persist (Osuntogun and Adewunmi, 1983). Rapid increases in rural branches of commercial banks have taken place also in India, Indonesia, Philippines, and Sri Lanka. In the long run one hopes and expects that the rural credit system will become integrated into the rest of the national money market via the commercial banking system. However, the process is not going to be easy, and Wilson (1980) has emphasized the need for close cooperation between government and commercial banks if rural banking is to be established successfully.

The provision by government of cheap credit through rural credit institutions appears at first sight to be an ideal solution. The attempt to eliminate monopoly profit in the informal market is worthy, and one is sympathetic with attempts to make life less difficult for the rural poor. However, such programmes seem to suffer often from high default rates, poor and expensive loan administration, misallocation of loans so that they go mainly to the wealthier farmers or are used for consumer credit, and the failure of the institutions to encourage local financial savings. Many do not even take deposits, and even if they do, interest rates are often repressed. Perhaps more important, though, is that they distort financial markets, leading to misallocation of resources, and in my view the case has not been adequately made for the heavy subsidization of rural credit at the expense of other sectors of the economy. It seems to me that interest rates charged by moneylenders may to a large extent reflect the true risks and costs of providing rural credit, apart from the element of monopoly profit, which according to Wai (1977) may not be all that great anyway. The fact is that the fragmented, small peasant farm business is very high-risk. This is not the fault of the credit market, but rather the fault of the agricultural structure. It is likely that if serious economic development is to take place in the rural areas, agricultural prices will have to be increased in many countries, and land holdings will have to be consolidated considerably, so that reasonably sized, soundly run, and soundly capitalized farms become established, which will be much better credit risks than many of the existing borrowers. Competition to lend money would then increase, and interest rates come down. This, of course, would be an uncomfortable process, and the problem of absorbing the new landless classes would be very difficult. However, the same process happened earlier in many of the present industrialized countries, and anyone who thinks that economic development can be achieved without such growing pains is deluding himself. The provision of cheap credit merely prolongs the present unsatisfactory agricultural structures, and if governments want to help the rural poor, they can do it better by giving direct subsidies (in cash or in kind) and by offering higher prices for agricultural products. Adams (1980) comments that 'Too many of the current rural financial market policies are received wisdom on this topic and are medieval in character, and I feel that it is time to drag rural financial market policies into the twentieth century', a view with which we have much sympathy.

(d) Informal Urban Credit

While a reasonable amount of research has been done on rural credit markets because of their importance to agriculture, the information available on urban credit markets is very limited. A study by Timberg and Aiyar (1984), in India, concluded that informal urban credit markets play an important role in the financing of trade and industry in urban areas, and account for as much as 20% of commercial credit outstanding in the markets studied. Small industrial units use them significantly. Rao (1981) reports a Reserve Bank of India survey which found that 'non-institutional' sources of credit provided the following proportions of borrowings:

— 39% of borrowings of small industrial units with investment in plant and equipment up to 1000 rupees;
— 25% of borrowing of all small industrial units;
— 3.5% of borrowing of partnerships owning small industrial units;
— 26.5% of borrowing of private limited companies owning small industrial units;
— 21.4% for proprietary concerns in the small industry sector.

Interest rates generally in the informal markets seemed to be 2–4% above bank lending rates, although they may be as much as 10% higher. Interestingly, Timberg and Aiyar found that transactions costs were lower, and bad debt experience probably better, in the informal market than with bank loans. Compared with commercial banks, informal lenders have the following advantages.

— They do not have the cost of idle funds demanded by reserve requirement regulations.
— They have continuous intimate contact with their clients and the local business community generally, which helps them to lend without security.
— They have fewer costs of paperwork and bureaucratic procedures.

These advantages, and Indian experience, suggest that the informal sector may play a significant part in financing businesses in urban areas in developing countries. Anecdotal evidence[4] supports this conclusion, although systematic evidence is scarce.

3. CONCLUDING REMARKS

In many developing countries formal financial institutions are still underdeveloped and not competitive. Institutions are often few in number, and access to them is not easy for a substantial proportion of the population. The consequence is that savings vehicles are limited, and therefore savings mobilization is limited too. As a consequence, informal financial organizations flourish, and fill the gap which the formal institutions have not yet filled. However, informal financial markets suffer from many weaknesses and imperfections which restrict their usefulness. Although several governments make efforts to remedy the institutional deficiencies by establishing financial institutions, these in turn have their deficiencies. Private sector financial institutions often need encouragement to spread and grow, and government efforts should be directed at removing restrictions and perhaps providing incentives to private sector financial institutions.

Annex 5.1: Financial Assets held with various Financial Institutions (%) (1982, unless otherwise stated)

	Central bank	Commercial banks		Other financial institutions	Total
	Currency outside banks (*IFS* line 14a)	Demand deposits (*IFS* lines 14d and 24)	Time, saving and foreign currency deposits (*IFS* lines 15 and 25)	(*IFS* lines 24i, 24r, section 40)	
Developing countries					
Algeria (1981)	40	32	9	19	100
Argentina	18	13	61	5	97
Barbados	12	15	63	10	100
Benin	36	41	19	4	100
Bolivia (1981)	36	22	40	2	100
Brazil (1981)	8	25	8	55	96
Burundi	44	32	10	14	100
Cameroun	22	39	38	1	100
Colombia	16	23	25	33	97
Dominican Republic	18	18	40	24	100
Ecuador (1981)	23	57	18	2	100
Egypt	31	13	51	5	100
Ethiopia	39	26	27	8	100
The Gambia	44	24	31	1	100
Guatemala	18	17	61	4	100
Guyana (1981)	16	13	51	20	100
Honduras	19	25	46	8	98
Indonesia	24	33	42	1	100
Iran (1980)	26	28	42	4	100
Jamaica	10	19	63	8	100

Jordan	33	23	43	1	100
Kenya	13	33	28	25	99
Korea	10	13	60	17	100
Lesotho	20	28	51	1	100
Malawi	14	23	42	20	100
Malaysia (1981)	10	11	41	38	100
Mauritius	17	17	63	3	100
Mexico	14	13	62	8	97
Morocco (1981)	27	38	14	21	100
Nigeria (1981)	24	30	35	3	92
Pakistan	31	35	33	1	100
Panama	–	20	69	11	100
Philippines	13	11	59	17	100
Singapore	12	13	45	30	100
Sri Lanka	16	15	49	20	100
Tanzania (1981)	32	42	25	1	100
Thailand	13	6	72	9	100
Togo (1981)	49	27	20	4	100
Trinidad and Tobago	9	20	59	10	98
Tunisia	19	37	28	13	97
Upper Volta	36	34	22	8	100
Venezuela	8	21	34	32	95
Zaire (1980)	36	45	14	2	97
Zambia (1980)	14	34	37	11	96
Zimbabwe	8	21	32	39	100
Unweighted average, 45 developing countries	22	25	40	13	100
		65			

Annex 5.1 (Cont'd)

	Central bank	Commercial banks		Other financial institutions	Total
	Currency outside banks (*IFS* line 14a)	Demand deposits (*IFS* line 24)	Time, saving and foreign currency deposits (*IFS* line 25)	(*IFS* lines 24i, 24r, section 40)	
Industrialized countries					
Belgium (1980)	18	15	38	29	100
Canada	4	10	44	42	100
France	7	22	33	36	98
Germany, Fed. Rep.	7	13	51	29	100
Italy (1979)	8	42	35	15	100
Japan	4	13	36	47	100
Netherlands	5	10	30	55	100
Switzerland (1980)	11	12	48	29	100
Sweden	5	7	37	51	100
USA	7	19	33	41	100
Unweighted average, 10 industrialized countries	8	16 ⎱_55_	39	37	100

Notes

(i) Lines 14d and 15 are deposits with the central bank, not commercial banks. However, the entries are few, and the amounts small.

(ii) In some cases the percentages do not total 100, which can only be explained by errors and omissions in the data.

Source: Derived from *International Financial Statistics*, 1983 Yearbook (IMF).

Other financial institutions: details (where available)

Algeria	Post office cheque deposits; treasury private sector demand deposits; savings bank.
Benin	Post office cheque deposits and savings bank.
Bolivia	Development banks.
Burundi	Savings bank.
Cameroun	PO and treasury cheque accounts savings bank.
Egypt	Specialized banks; PO savings bank deposits.
Guatemala	Development bank.
Guyana	Building society and life insurance.
Indonesia	Savings banks.
Iran	Specialized banks.
Korea	Trust accounts; postal savings deposits; life insurance.
Malawi	PO savings bank; building society; life insurance.
Malaysia	Savings institutions.
Morocco	PO demand deposits; treasury demand deposits; other financial institutions.
Pakistan	PO savings deposits.
Panama	Savings bank.
Philippines	Development and savings banks.
Singapore	Finance companies; PO savings deposits; life insurance.
Sri Lanka	National Savings Bank deposits
Thailand	Development institutions; government savings bank.
Togo	PO cheque accounts; savings bank deposits.
Upper Volta	PO cheque accounts; savings bank deposits.

Industrialized countries

Belgium	General savings fund deposits; life insurance.
Canada	Savings institutions; life insurance.
Germany	Building societies; life insurance and pension funds.
Italy	PO savings and chequeing deposits; special credit institutions; insurance companies; treasury private sector deposits.
Japan	Specialized credit institutions; insurance institutions.
Netherlands	Savings banks; life insurance and pension funds.
Switzerland	PO cheque accounts; life insurance; trustee accounts (domestic liabilities).
Sweden	Mortgage and credit institutions; insurance companies.
USA	Other bank-like institutions.

ANNEX 5.2: A NOTE ON ISLAMIC BANKING

The steady spread of both national and international Islamic financial institutions in parts of the third world calls for a mention of the principles of Islamic banking. The main tenet, of course, is that interest should not be paid on deposits, nor charged on loans. This has led to deposits being treated as a form of equity in the bank, and rewarded with a dividend or a share of the profits. Likewise, traditional loans are replaced by a form of equity investment in the borrower's activity.

In many Islamic countries conventional financial institutions coexist with Islamic institutions. However, even the conventional institution may be caught up in Islamic principles. For example, banks may not be able effectively to proceed against defaulting borrowers for interest not paid, if the courts do not recognize interest as a proper payment. Likewise, courts may not recognize mortgages on property, so the traditional form of security is effectively not available to lenders. These conditions appear to apply to conventional banks in Saudi Arabia, for example.

Among the devices used by Islamic banks to avoid interest charges on loans are:

— Taking an equity stake in a client's enterprises.
— Purchasing capital equipment or buildings for a client, and then leasing the asset to the client, often on a rental-purchase or hire-purchase basis.
— Buying stocks of materials which a client needs, and selling them to the client at a price which yields a profit to the bank, payment being made at a future date. In this way working capital may be provided.
— Making a 'service charge' to cover the cost involved in providing a loan. The charge is based on actual costs, rather than a percentage of the loan.

The equity character of much Islamic financing means that risk, and risk diversification, should play a much more important part than they do in conventional bank lending with traditional security. Moreover, there is considerable scope for secondary market activity in the investments of Islamic financial institutions, and stock markets may therefore have an increasingly important role to play in Islamic countries. For further information the reader is referred to a specialist work such as Ahmed, Aqbal, and Khan (1983).

NOTES

1. Wai (1972) conducted a comparable exercise, in more detail. Wai included lines 27a, 47a, and 45c (capital accounts and shares of banks and other financial institutions), lines 26a and 46a (bonds and certificates of banks and other financial institutions), and lines 88ae and 88af or 88bc (government debt held by non-financial private sector). I have omitted these because capital accounts are in part equity and in part cash reserves. The reserves will be placed in other institutions (often the central bank), and equity, like government debt, represents negotiable financial instruments held by the private sector. Few data are available in *IFS* on this subject, so I have preferred to discuss the subject under securities markets. Bonds and certificates of banks likewise may be held by the non-financial private sector in part. They may or may not be negotiable. However, part may also be held by the financial sector, and to include these claims as well as the deposits of the financial sector would be double-counting. Wai consulted national sources for

19 developing countries to obtain data for life insurance payments and government debt held by the non-financial private sector. The additional data from national sources amounted to 14% of the financial savings data presented in IFS, for the 19 countries concerned (which were mostly middle- or high-income developing countries). It is probable, though, that inclusion of data from national sources from the developed countries would add more than 14% to the financial savings of developed countries.

2. Line 14d appears in country data where the monetary authority (usually the central bank) also acts as a commercial bank and accepts deposits. There line 14d is included under commercial bank deposits.

3. The presentation of data in section 40 is complex. For some countries it is conveniently summarized in line 45, time and savings deposits, but for other countries it is not, and other items have to be summed to arrive at a figure for total deposits with other financial institutions. In some cases it is necessary to sum the assets of the institutions to arrive at figures which are then used as a proxy for their liabilities.

4. One piece of ancedotal evidence was the widespread use of informal sector moneylenders in Tehran by small and medium-size businesses before the revolution. I do not know whether this practice still continues.

Chapter 6
Mobilizing Domestic Finance: Securities Markets

1. INTRODUCTION

Chapter 2 considered the applicability of capital market theory to developing countries, and reviewed the evidence on the efficiency of developing country stock markets, which was rather scarce. This section will consider the contribution which securities markets[1] can make to financial development, whether they should be encouraged in developing countries, and if so, how.

At various times arrangements for share trading have been set up in 48 developing countries, listed in Annex 6.1. Currently, about 35 of these could be described as being at least moderately active. The majority of the world's securities markets are therefore now in developing countries. These markets vary greatly in size, activity, and efficiency, and some have had a chequered history. At one extreme Singapore is one of the larger and more active markets in the world. At the other extreme the markets of Indonesia and Egypt have both experienced effective closure in recent years, and are struggling to grow once again, but both have only a handful of stocks quoted, and very limited activity. The Istanbul Stock Exchange is being revived, after many years of inactivity. Activity in Paraguay, Peru, Bolivia, and Trinidad is very limited. Extensive detail on many markets is given by van Agtmael (1984).

2. ADVANTAGES OF SECURITIES MARKETS

What, then, are the advantages and disadvantages of having a securities market? The following appear to be the principal advantages. They are not listed in any particular order, because the ranking will depend on the reader's viewpoint, whether that of an investor, a government official, or a firm.

— A stock market enables companies to raise fresh capital both initially, by going public (primary issues), and subsequently through secondary issues (rights issues or placements of stock). Thus a stock exchange can provide

146

additional capital for industrial, service and utility companies, which might otherwise find it difficult to raise fresh equity. Companies may then be able to expand more readily.[2] It is well known that the ratio of debt to shareholders' funds tends to be high in developing countries. An ability to raise new equity capital may then enable a company to overcome a gearing constraint when it wishes to expand. Moreover, a 'sound' gearing ratio is in itself desirable. A company can stand a high proportion of debt when profits are high. However, when profits turn down, as they are liable to do from time to time, a highly geared company can be forced into liquidation.

— A stock market provides governments with an alternative means of selling bonds and raising capital. The virtue of this depends on the ability of the government to use the funds efficiently for the benefit of the national economy. A drawback is that the government may be able to 'crowd out' the private sector and starve it of fresh capital, either by offering more competitive terms or by rigging the new issues queue in its own favour. Governments can usually service high-yielding paper by printing money or by issuing more high-yielding paper. Of course this may be inflationary, but the private sector is constrained by its ability to pay interest and dividends, and to repay debt, out of its profits.

— A stock market provides savers and financial institutions with a further outlet for their funds. Investment in equities (and government stock, unless held to maturity) is, of course, investment in risky instruments. However, investors have different risk-taking capacities, and like to be offered a range of risks, and a corresponding range of expected returns. A stock market enables investors to select the portfolio which gives the risk–return combination which is to their liking. Moreover it enables them to diversify their investments and reduce risk. A stock market, by offering various returns, may be particularly important to investors whose only alternative is to place deposits and receive low, repressed, rates of interest. It can therefore encourage saving, and the mobilization of funds. If the secondary market is reasonably active, investors have a market which may be much more liquid than some alternatives, such as gold or real estate.

— A stock market provides a hierarchy of rates of return (and therefore of the cost of capital) between equities, corporate bonds, and government stock. Therefore firms and government raising new capital have to pay a rate of return which reflects both the rate of return on alternative investments and the risk associated with the undertaking. Therefore the allocation of capital is improved, ex-ante, at least. This is important in a capital market which is otherwise repressed, and where the cost of borrowing is not related either to the demand for capital or to the riskiness of the investment it will be used for.

— In some countries, for example Nigeria, a stock market has provided an important mechanism for the indigenization of the ownership of foreign firms. A firm required by law to be, say, 60% Nigerian-owned was able, through an offer for sale, to offer 60% of its shares to the public. This ensured a reasonably wide ownership which otherwise would have been rather difficult to secure. In much the same way, stock markets can provide a vehicle for government corporations to go public. Dickie (1981) describes the Indonesian government's attempts to diversify and indigenize ownership of shares.

— A stock market can bring foreign capital into a country from foreign portfolio investors wishing to diversify internationally.

3. DISADVANTAGES OF SECURITIES MARKETS

The criticisms of stock markets are essentially the following.

— They encourage unequal distribution of wealth, by enabling those who are sufficiently wealthy to invest with a view to increasing their wealth, without ostensibly working for it. Such 'speculators' and 'capitalists' are, of course, the bane of the left, and governments which are concerned to demonstrate a commitment to a more egalitarian distribution of wealth and income may well find the existence of a stock market an anathema. Of course, as most investors know very well, it is possible to lose as well as to make money on stock markets. Other governments may regard stock markets as a form of gambling, and ban them as they ban casinos and horse racing.

— Stock markets can encourage rash speculation both by individuals and institutions which, followed by collapse, can lead to the ruin of both, with consequent destabilizing effects on the national economy. Wall Street in the late 1920s, Hong Kong in 1973, and the unofficial market in Kuwait (Souq Al Manaqh) in 1982 are but three striking examples. Kindleberger (1978) provides many others.

— Stock markets can provide an opportunity for dishonest activity, such as conflict of interest, market-rigging, insider dealing, issuing false or misleading prospectuses, pushing and selling over-priced or worthless stock, etc. Such practices, of course, are as old as Law's Mississippi Scheme, the South Sea Bubble, and the flotation of Poyais bonds.

— Although stock markets may allocate funds to the activities which are expected to show the greatest financial profit, these may well not be the most profitable from a national point of view, because markets and prices are seriously distorted in many developing countries. Therefore the development of stock markets may lead to a deterioration in the allocation of resources, not an improvement.

The first objection is essentially political rather than financial or economic. However, simply to refuse to have a stock market may be throwing out the baby with the bathwater, and governments should consider other means of encouraging the redistribution of income, such as more effective taxation.

(We suspect anyway that those inclined to make money will find ways of doing so, whatever the political colour or distribution policy of the government.) The second objection has considerable substance, as does the third, even for governments which are inclined to encourage stock markets. Careful regulation (of which we say more below) can help to reduce these problems. The fourth objection, too, is one of substance, but many governments retain the authority to prohibit private sector investments if it believes they are not in the national interest. Governments also need to correct price distortions if they are not happy about them.

On balance we are substantially in favour of encouraging stock markets in developing countries. Encouragement from other writers is limited (academic writing generally on the subject is limited, though). Wai and Patrick (1973) in perhaps the best-known paper on stock markets in developing countries, give rather muted support. Lloyd (1976, 1977) is in favour, but pessimistic. Drake (1980, 1977, and earlier writing) is consistently in favour, and Dickie (1981) also appears supportive. Samuels (1981) and Samuels and Yacout (1981) appear to want to support stock markets, but draw back on the grounds that they are inefficient, which may well lead to increasing inequality in the distribution of wealth, and that they may therefore do considerable harm in the time which elapses before they become substantial and well-regulated. Consistent practical support, though, has come from the Capital Markets Department of the IFC, which has provided assistance in capital market (a broader term than securities market) development in a total of 66 countries since 1971.

As mentioned above, some 36 developing countries now have stock markets, and the potential for creating stock exchanges in other countries may be limited in the near future. Therefore we will concentrate our attention on the difficulties which securities markets encounter, and what can be done to make them rather more effective, rather than the steps to be taken in establishing new markets. However, it may be useful first to describe some of the preconditions which are needed for a securities market to be successful.

4. THE SUPPLY OF SECURITIES

Investors need a reasonable choice of both government securities and company stock so that they can set up the type of portfolio they wish, and change it readily. This implies that there must be a reasonable number of fairly large companies willing to make their shares available to the public. Van Agtmael (1981) suggests at least 20 initially. Many of the smaller and poorer countries do not have a sufficient number of suitable companies, as their enterprises are mainly unincorporated firms and government-owned utilities and industries with few suitable private sector manufacturing and service enterprises. Some of those which exist may enjoy a protected monopoly, which does not make them ideal candidates for ownership by the public. Government enterprises which might in principle lend themselves to sale to the public in many cases make losses. Of the companies which are suitable, some may be subsidiaries of foreign firms which do not need to raise capital on the local market, and will only go public for reasons of goodwill or in response to government pressure. Family-owned firms may also be reluctant to dilute their ownership and control. Few firms may be willing to meet the standards of disclosure which are required of public companies. (By public company I mean a company owned by the public, not a company owned by the government.) Privately owned companies may find ample opportunity for tax evasion, which may not be available to them if they go public. Recognition of this problem has led numerous commentators to suggest a concessionary tax regime for companies which are willing to go public. However, in Iran tax concessions led to listings of family-controlled companies which were largely cosmetic, with few shares available to the public, and negligible trading (Rischer, 1975). Finally, repressed interest rates in a country may mean that the more creditworthy firms have ready access to bank loans at low, tax-deductible interest, especially in countries where high ratios of debt to equity or of debt to shareholders' funds are accepted. Why should they then go to the trouble of raising what may be more expensive capital on the stock market? Drake (1983) has identified this as a major obstacle to new share issues in Indonesia, where dividends (not tax-deductible) of 15% at least are expected.

5. THE DEMAND FOR SECURITIES

A well-functioning market requires a mix of long-term investors (such as insurance companies, pension funds, investment trusts, and unit trusts), and short-term investors (often individuals) which keep the market fluid. There must therefore be a substantial number of institutions which hold the savings of individuals, and individual investors. This in turn implies a reasonably widespread distribution of wealth and income within a country, and a sizeable middle class. Countries which have highly skewed income and wealth distributions are unlikely to have the right mix of investors to keep the market active and fluid. The success of the Malaysian and Singapore stock exchanges may be attributable partly to the large numbers of middle- and lower-middle-class shareholders (Drake, 1980).

In addition to having an adequate level and distribution of wealth a country must possess individuals willing to buy shares. Investors need to be made aware of the functioning of the stock exchange, and of the possible risks, as well as of the possible returns. This requires active, but responsible, promotion on the part of stock exchange authorities, investment trust and unit trust associations, and shareholders' representative bodies. A speaker at a 1983 conference in Cairo on capital market development remarked that 'shares are sold—not bought'.

At the same time financial institutions need to be willing and able to buy shares. As Drake (1980) has pointed out, the conventional view that institutions are scarce and small in developing countries no longer accords with the facts. Nonetheless, in some cases institutions may need to be persuaded of the desirability of equity investments; they may also need to be freed from requirements to invest very heavily (or even entirely) in government stocks.

Undoubtedly the most important factor determining the willingness to buy and to hold securities is the elusive 'investor confidence'. Investors need to have confidence in the macroeconomic performance of the economy (market risk). Doubtful growth prospects and fears of inflation are bad for stock markets, which perform badly under either worry. Investors need also to have confidence in the firm whose shares they buy (specific risk). They need confidence in the firm's products and markets, its management, and in its integrity in disclosing information. Finally, they need to have confidence in the integrity of operation of the stock market, and of its members. Suggestions of malpractice, not unknown in even the best-regulated stock markets, deter investors. They also need confidence in the standards of accounting required of firms and in the auditing of the accountancy profession.

6. CAPITAL MARKET SERVICES

A stock market needs the support of firms to issue shares to the primary market, and to make a secondary market in shares. There are a number of different ways of providing such services, and which one is selected will depend largely on the size of the market and the nature of a country's existing financial sector. One system is the traditional British one of merchant banks (or, sometimes, stockbrokers) acting as issuing houses, that is selling new shares to the public or placing them in institutions. Stockbrokers then act as agents for those wanting to buy or sell existing shares, or place orders with stock jobbers, who buy and sell shares on their own account. Together they make the secondary market. (This division of functions between brokers and jobbers, known as 'single capacity', is disappearing in the UK following the agreement to scrap brokers' minimum commissions, and a restructuring of financial service firms taking place.) Under European systems, universal commercial banks act as issuing houses, and also make markets in existing shares, whereas in the USA the functions of issuing houses, broker, and jobber is also performed simultaneously by investment banking firms. The argument in favour of single capacity is that it avoids conflict of interest, which is a risk with other systems. Other systems are likely to be cheaper, though, but they probably entail more watchful supervision and regulation. In small markets it may well be the case that the level of activity will be insufficient to support both competitive broking and jobbing services, and some form of dual capacity may be necessary. In developing countries, development banks may make both primary and secondary markets.

Underwriting arrangements form an important part of the issuing procedure, both for primary and secondary issues. The issuing house (merchant bank, stockbroker, or development bank) will usually act as the main underwriter and will, in turn, arrange for other institutions to sub-underwrite the issue (unless small). Sub-underwriters may be other merchant banks, financial institutions, investment banks, stockbrokers, or development banks. In exceptional cases directors of the firm or outside individuals willing to secure a stake will agree to underwrite all or part of an issue. The underwriting procedure is very important because it gives the company issuing the stock a guarantee that it will receive all the funds it expects from the issue. Underwriting involves taking a risk of being left with shares which, demonstrably, are difficult to sell, except at a loss. For accepting this risk, underwriting fees are charged, which will vary according to the perceived risk. These fees often form a substantial part of the total costs of an issue. The latter may generally be of the order of 5–10% of the total funds raised, although exceptionally they may be more. Clearly, the existence of firms and institutions willing to underwrite issues is an important condition for the operation of a securities market, and is one of the more important functions of merchant banks, investment banks, or universal banks.

While issuing houses create the primary market for shares, a secondary market is equally important (investors need to feel that they can sell their shares when they wish). In some countries this has led to governments supporting stock exchange prices from time to time. *The Financial Times* reported on 18 November 1983 that

The South Korean Finance Ministry has ordered the Korean Securities Finance Corporation (KSFC) to provide 20 bn. won (US$25.3 mn.) in soft loans to securities firms to support the flagging stock market.

Such government intervention is, of course, contrary to the spirit of a free market, but may be necessary in countries where the market is still thin and confidence fragile. Nonetheless, investors should not be able to count on being baled out when the market falls.

Finally, it is worth reminding readers that much financial malpractice arises from the existence of conflict of interest. In countries where the level of financial probity may be less than the highest, it is probably worth trying to avoid any financial arrangement which could give rise to conflict of interest.

7. THE LEGISLATIVE AND REGULATORY FRAMEWORK

Any country with a stock market needs comprehensive company law which includes the conduct of public companies, disclosure requirements, shareholders' rights, etc. Beyond this a framework for market regulation is needed. The regulatory authority may be statutory, the model being the United States' Securities and Exchange Commission, or it may be done on a self-regulatory basis, such as by London's Council of the Stock Exchange. The latter has evolved in a rather peculiar way over a long period based on the desire for self-regulation, combined with a reluctance by successive governments to involve themselves in the running of the stock market. In developing countries, the function is performed sometimes by the central bank, as in Brazil, sometimes by statutory bodies such as Egypt's Capital Market Authority. Generally speaking, we take the view that the fragile stock markets of developing countries cannot afford scandals, so the tougher is the regulatory authority, the better. Indeed, it remains to be seen whether Britain's self-regulating system can survive the changes which now appear likely in market trading.

Although firm authority is desirable, this should not be confused with excessive regulation. Indeed, regulation requires a delicate and subtle hand of authority, sufficient to maintain investor confidence, but not so forceful that it strangles the child. Codes of conduct for brokers, jobbers, and other securities' firms; procedures for recording deals; capital requirements for securities' firms and disclosure requirements of firms; new issues regulations, among other things, are all matters with which regulatory authorities should concern themselves. However, the rules need to be suited to local conditions (it is no use insisting on a minimum size of primary issue of $20 million if it means that only 10 firms in the country qualify to go public), and the regulatory authority must be prepared to change them swiftly if experience shows that they are not suitable. The regulators have to tread carefully.

8. MEASURES TO ENCOURAGE MARKET DEVELOPMENT

Once a government has decided to allow an official stock exchange, or it has one which operates perfunctorily, it may feel that some measures of encouragement are desirable. In fact Brazil, in the 1960s, pursued a policy of financial reform and capital market expansion as a development strategy. Ness (1974, 1983) chronicles the incentives introduced by the Brazilian government, which are probably wider-ranging than those introduced by any other country. The first main measures taken in Brazil to stimulate the stock market were embodied in the Capital Markets Law of 1965, which first of all introduced reforms of company disclosure, stock trading regulations, issue regulations, and the protection of minority shareholders. Investment banks were authorized which would perform underwriting functions, the number of seats on the stock exchanges were substantially increased, and a training programme for stock exchange personnel initiated. Beyond these general measures, specific measures were introduced to increase both the demand for, and the supply of, stocks. On the demand side, the Capital Markets Law provided for:

— a substantial reduction in the withholding tax on dividends, and exemption of capital gains from income tax;
— personal income tax exemption of about $400 in dividends;
— the offsetting of shares and bonds purchased against gross income for tax purposes—smaller allowances were given for investments in unit trusts

and savings deposits—qualifying investments had to be held for 2 years;
— lower tax rates for firms which go public;
— 10% of individual and 5% of corporate tax liabilities could be placed
  in special unit trusts, which would largely invest in the new issues of
  companies.

Investments could be withdrawn gradually after 2 years. According to Ness, the last was the most effective incentive, and fuelled the stock market boom of 1970–73.

Subsequently, conditions placed on share purchases by commercial banks and insurance companies were liberalized, and permission was given for the creation of private pension funds and offshore unit trusts and investment trusts which would channel foreign portfolio investment into the Brazilian market.

The stock exchange boom up to mid-1971, when the average price earnings ratio exceeded 30, and the subsequent collapse, probably indicates that the incentive package was overdone. Nevertheless it did give rise to an enormous increase in the level of stock market investment and activity, in the number of quoted companies, and in the new funds raised on the market. The boom conditions have never really returned, and the market has been dominated increasingly by institutions and government securities. Ness clearly has mixed feelings about the reforms. He comments (1974)

Politically, it is doubtful that a broadly representative government could implement a series of measures as all-encompassing as the Brazilian financial markets reform programme which contains many measures which at first primarily benefit the upper classes and business.

And in 1983:

Undoubtedly the Brazilian financial system is today more diversified, more soph-isticated and more responsive to economic conditions than prior to its reform. Whether this is the result of conscious government policy directed to the development of these markets or primarily of experiencing a period of exceptional economic growth in the period 1967–1980 is a matter for serious questioning.

Other countries have introduced a variety of incentives. Korea, Venezuela, Indonesia, and Iran introduced special tax concessions for firms going public. In France investors are allowed to offset share purchases against income for tax purposes. By contrast Hong Kong, Malaysia, and Singapore have been at some pains to curb, rather than encourage share speculation. The Indonesian government has set up a National Investment Trust (P. T. Danareksa) as an investor, underwriter, and stabilizer of share prices. Drake (1983) sum-marizes the incentives (and some disincentives) available in various South and South East Asian markets. He notes that Korea's Securities and Exchange Commission requires that all equity be issued at par, which is a disincentive to firms to issue new stock when their share price stands above par. The UK government, which until recently levied 2% tax on purchases of stock, and capital gains tax, appeared to discourage the direct purchase of equities by individuals, who by contrast received tax concessions if they invested through the intermediaries of life insurance or pension funds. The 1984 budget went some way to removing these distortions, though.

9. THE EFFECTIVENESS OF SECURITIES MARKETS

A major criterion for judging the effectiveness of stock markets is to measure the new capital which they raise for firms and government. The information which is available is limited, and not particularly encouraging. The only comprehensive survey of developing country securities markets (Wai and Patrick, 1973, p. 300), concluded that:

In the aggregate, public issues, by underwriting or other means, through the capital market simply are not quantitatively important; only the government and a few large companies benefit.

The main exception to the general rule was Brazil. Wai and Patrick produced the results shown in Table 6.1 for the late 1960s and early 1970s. The table indicates that between 23% and 32% of new investment was obtained through the issue of shares and bonds, and that some 5% of GNP was mobilized in this way, which would be one-third of total savings if the savings ratio were 15%. The figure of 5% was similar to that obtained in developed countries. Of course these issues include private placements as well as public issues. There is no evidence, though, that stock markets increase savings and their mobilization, rather than merely diverting savings from one vehicle to another.

Table 6.1   New issues of securities—selected ratios (%)

	$\dfrac{\Delta M_g}{\Delta M}$	$\dfrac{\Delta M}{I}$	$\dfrac{\Delta M}{Y}$
All LDCs	44	27	5
Africa	86	32	5
Asia	48	23	5
Latin America	26	29	6

ΔM_g = new issues of government securities;
ΔM = total new issues of securities;
I = gross domestic investment;
Y = gross national product.

Countries included
Africa: Kenya and Nigeria.
Asia: Taiwan, India, Korea, Malaysia, and
                 Thailand.
Latin America: Argentina, Brazil, Chile, Colombia, Mexico,
                 and Venezuela.

More recently, Samuels and Yacout (1981) concluded for Nigeria that 'Despite a reasonably active secondary market, the primary market has not made a major contribution as a provider of funds. The new funds raised on the market for the private sector, as a proportion of GDP, are low, being in each year less than 1%.'[3]

Calamanti, in three recent studies of stock exchanges in Tunisia (1979), Ivory Coast (1980a) and Morocco (1980b), found that in general the Abidjan Stock Exchange (formed 1976) had achieved a certain measure of success by 1979, in savings mobilization, spread and indigenization of ownership, but that the stock exchanges in Tunisia (created 1969) and Morocco (created 1967) had suffered from stock shortages, although in Morocco 'There is good reason to think that the establishment of the stock exchange did a good deal to stimulate the supply of new share issues, especially from 1973 on.' Over 1971–77 new issues on the Moroccan stock exchange increased fivefold, while new issues to GDP rose from 2% to 4.5%, and new issues to gross domestic capital formation remained constant at 14%. In Tunisia, Calamanti (1979) found that after 8 years of operation, 'the new issue market still contributes little to the mobilisation of savings and to the financing of investment, and has proved unable so far to broaden stock exchange business'.

The Malaysian Stock Exchange, widely regarded as one of the more successful in the third world, has, like Nigeria, been used as a means of indigenization of foreign companies. In 1981 net new issues accounted for 25% of gross fixed capital formation, and amounted to over 8% of GNP. Of the 4.7 billion Ringgit raised in 1981, only 900 million, or 25% went to the private sector, the remainder going to the government sector.

Stock shortages appear to be a factor restricting investment on the Nairobi Stock Exchange. Parkinson (1984) studied the response to new issues on the exchange over 1974–78, and found that in almost every case they had been fully subscribed. However, their total value was trivial in relation to the investment needs of the country. Moreover it appears that Kenya has a significant supply of savers willing to investment in corporate securities, but who through frustration are encouraged to invest in non-productive areas. By contrast, the author's observation of the Jamaican Stock Exchange does not suggest a shortage of stock, even though the market index has risen some eight times over the period 1980–84, and new stock issued has been minimal. In both these countries, companies appear unwilling to issue new securities, and the feeling concerning Jamaica is that founder families wish to maintain their dominant control of the public companies.

Of course there are other yardsticks with which to measure the 'success' of stock markets. Efficiency, in the sense of modern capital market theory, was discussed in Chapter 2. Another would be the distribution of shares among the population. A measure of activity, such as the value of transactions to market value, GNP, or bank debits would be another useful indicator (Wai and Patrick, 1973, calculated all of these). It is clear, however, that most developing country stock markets still have major deficiencies of one form or another, and that the day is some way off when they will become like Singapore or Hong Kong, or even Malaysia, let alone Tokyo, London, or New York. However, it should be borne in mind that significant share dealing has been taking place in London for well over 250 years, and that for most of the time the market has slowly developed and improved. Developing country markets too will take time to develop, and many are still in their infancy.

10. OVER-THE-COUNTER (OTC) STOCK MARKETS

This type of market can be a forerunner, an alternative, or a parallel market to an organized stock market. The minimum requirement is a single 'market maker', who acts as a combined broker–jobber. The market maker buys and sells shares for others, acting as principal, and matching bargains between buyers and sellers. The firm acting as market maker obviously needs sufficient capital to hold substantial amounts of stock on its own account. It is obviously preferable to have more than one market maker to provide some competition, but for the smaller, least developed countries a start can be made with one. For countries with an existing stock market, an OTC market can permit dealings in shares of companies who, for one reason or another— usually small size or a short trading record—do not qualify for admission to the stock exchange. An OTC market can act as a stepping stone to a full market quotation.[4] Alternatively, it can operate as an alternative market in its own right, as with the NASDAQ (National Association of Security Dealers' Automated Quotations) market in the USA, which rivals the New York Stock Exchange in terms of number of companies quoted, and turnover.

Superficially, a development bank seems ideally placed to act as a market maker. DFCs are often charged with responsibility of encouraging stock markets, and they often hold a substantial portfolio of shares in their client companies. An ability to sell these shares helps them to revolve their capital, and to make fresh investments. The danger, though, is that they push their weak shares on to clients. Safeguards may be needed to protect clients from this possible conflict of interest, and any share dealing operation of a developing bank should be established as a separate company with independent trustees. Alternative market makers may be commercial banks or merchant banks. A universal type of commercial bank would normally fulfil the role of market maker, although again the same moral hazard may exist as with development banks.

An active OTC market can provide a valuable source of capital for small companies wishing to grow. However, it should be emphasized that these markets tend to be unregulated in many countries, which leads to some sharp practices. A minimum of regulation at least is needed.

11. STOCK MARKETS AS A VEHICLE FOR FOREIGN INVESTMENT

As direct foreign investment has attracted a certain amount of approbrium in a number of developing countries, it is worth considering whether portfolio investment on developing country securities' markets would be a more attractive method of attracting foreign equity capital. Alternatively, securities' markets may be viewed as a means of attracting foreign equity capital from non-bank investors rather than debt from the overstretched commercial banks. Certain equity is currently more attractive than debt for many developing countries, and inflows of foreign portfolio investment may enable local firms to increase their capital, and to reduce their debt equity ratios. Limitations on the proportion of a firm's equity which may be foreign-owned would prevent control passing into foreign hands. However, although portfolio investment would avoid the objectionable aspects of direct foreign investment, it would be far easier to withdraw, making it a much more volatile source of capital. One possible way around this problem is to insert a minimum period of foreign investment, as is done, for example, by Argentina and Chile, which both have a minimum period of 3 years for foreign investment. Such a rule, though, may deter some investors.

A recent IFC survey, reported by van Agtmael and Errunza (1982) collected data on the 11 largest third-world stock markets to assess the potential for foreign investment. From the point of view of the investors these markets offer further possibilities of diversification if they are not well-correlated with industrial markets, and they may offer higher returns. On the other hand the markets are widely thought of as being small, with small companies, limited turnover, limited information, beset by political and currency risks, restrictive controls and inefficient (although inefficiency may offer scope for abnormal returns). The IMF survey produced the data shown in Table 6.2. Many of these markets appear to offer favourable opportunities. They compare reasonably in capitalization with countries such as Spain ($16 billion) and Sweden ($12 billion) which have received substantial foreign investment recently. The trading volume is not unfavourable (Germany, Belgium, Netherlands, and UK were all between 19% and 21% in 1980), and returns in most countries were attractive, and apparently sufficient to offset the higher risk (as measured by variance) compared with the US market. Over 1975–80 the return on the Capital International World Index was 10.3%, and on the Standard and Poor 500 (New York) 9.7%. The weighted average annual return on nine developing country markets (excluding Singapore and the Philippines) was 46.3%. Most markets have their idiosyncrasies and rules (notably on capital gains and withholding taxes), but nonetheless they may offer some attractive opportunities for high returns and diversification. Funds have been established to enable US investors to invest in Mexico (by Merrill Lynch) and Korea (by the IFC).

Smaller developing country markets may need to expand before significant foreign portfolio investment can be attracted. Markets such as Indonesia (24

Table 6.2   Results of IFC study of 11 developing country stock markets (data relates to 1980, unless otherwise stated)

Market	Market capital-ization (billion US$)	Number of companies listed	Annual trading volume as percentage of market capital-ization	Average annual rate of return 1975–80 (%)[a]	Correlation coefficient with US market (CIP index)[b]
Singapore	27	263	14	30	0.42
Mexico	18	271	18	47	0.22
Brazil	13	614	21	5	−0.03
Chile	9	263	16	123	−0.18
Argentina	4	277	29	97	−0.02
Korea	4	344	49	30	0.23
Greece	3	110	3	3	−0.01
Philippines	2	195	31	n.a.	n.a.
Jordan	1.6	65	9	40	0.34
Zimbabwe	1.6	62	11	30	0.00
Thailand	1.2	77	26	22	−0.36

[a] Based on 25 most active stock (10 in the smaller markets). Returns are apparently calculated in domestic currencies.
[b] Including currency changes.
Source: Derived from van Agtmael and Errunza (1982).

quoted companies in 1984), Ivory Coast (26 companies in 1983), Morocco (62 companies in 1983), Jamaica (32 companies in 1984), and Kenya (55 companies in 1983) probably have longer-term rather than immediate potential.

12.   CONCLUDING REMARKS

The spread of stock markets in the third world has been quite rapid in recent years, and the scope for new markets may now be limited.[5] However, on the basis of the few systematic studies which have been done, it is unlikely that they are going to be a panacea for solving the problem of savings mobilization, investment, and growth which developing countries face. In some countries, in fact, their contribution may be negligible, while in others it could have harmful effects on the distribution of income and wealth, although no firm evidence of such an occurrence has come to light. However, it seems that their most favourable impact may be in the liberalization of capital markets, in that they present alternative choices for institutions, savers, and firms faced with repressed interest rates or banking cartels, although such an effect, of course, is difficult to measure. But in most countries any addition to the supply of scarce, long-term capital, especially equity, is most welcome. It must be remembered, though, that many developing country stock markets are still at an early stage of development, and it would be unreasonable to expect economic miracles to spring from them overnight.

An interesting current trend is the growing internationalization of stock exchange business, with (mainly institutional) investors seeking to diversify internationally, and looking for stock which is cheaper than in their own domestic market. In the past Latin American stock exchanges particularly have been recipients of portfolio investment, and there are prospects for other stock markets to receive similar investment, once they reach a certain size and efficiency. Such investment can only increase the level of activity of markets, and increase the financial resources available to domestic firms. Conversely, successful domestic third world firms may be able to seek foreign listings. For most developing countries, though, such moves will only occur in the medium to long term.

Annex 6.1 Third World Stock Exchanges

Area and country	Name of exchange	Date of establishment	Reorganized/revitalized	No. of companies listed (1983)	Market capitalization (1981) (US$ million)	Trading volume (1981) (US$ million)
Africa						
Egypt	Alexandria Stock Exchange / Bourse des Valeurs Du Caire	1883/96	1981	160	n.a.	30[g]
Ivory Coast	La Bourse des Valeurs d'Abidjan	1976		26	235[e]	44[e]
Kenya	Nairobi Stock Exchange	1954		55	200	n.a.
Morocco	Bourse de Casablanca	1929/48	1967	62	460[a]	10
Nigeria	The Nigerian Stock Exchange (Trading at Lagos, Port Harcourt and Kaduna)	1961		93[h] (Plus 1 equity in the second tier market)	6,000[h]	10
Tunisia	Bourse des Valeurs Mobilière de Tunis	1937	1969	48[b]	n.a.	41[c]
Zimbabwe	Zimbabwe Stock Exchange	1896	1951	62	356[e]	71[e]
Latin America and Caribbean						
Argentina	Bolsa de Comercio de Buenos Aires	1854				
	Bolsa de Rosario					
	Bolsa de Cordoba	1929	1929	238	1,398	442
	Bolsa de Mendoza					
	Bolsa de La Plata					
Brazil	Bolsa de Valores do Rio de Janeiro	1876		593	n.a.	n.a.
	Bolsa Oficial de Valores de Sao Paulo (Also eight other trading centres)	1876		506	12,577	6,169

Annex 6.1   Third World Stock Exchanges

Area and country	Name of exchange	Date of establishment	Reorganized/revitalized	No. of companies listed (1983)	Market capitalization (1981) (US$ million)	Trading volume (1981) (US$ million)
Bolivia	Being established					
Chile	Bolsa de Comercio de Santiago	1892		212	n.a.	n.a.
Colombia	Bolsa de Bogota	1928	} 193	} 1,398	7,050	360
	Bolsa de Medellin	1961			} 220	
Costa Rica		1945	1976	n.a.	n.a.	n.a.
Ecuador	Quito	1969		} 29	184	n.a.
	Guayaquil	1969			168	n.a.
Jamaica	Jamaica Stock Exchange	1969		32[g]	n.a.	6.5[g]
Mexico	Bolsa de Valores de Mexico	1894		215	10,100	4,184
	Bolsa de Valores de Monterrey	1950				
	Bolsa de Valores de Guadalajara	1960		n.a.	n.a.	n.a.
Paraguay	Camera y Bolsa de Comercio de Paraguay	1978		n.a.	n.a.	n.a.
Peru	Bolsa de Comercio de Lima	1860	1970	n.a.	n.a.	n.a.
Trinidad and Tobago		1981		n.a.	n.a.	208[f]
Uruguay	Bolsa de Valores	1864		58[b]	156	17
Venezuela	Bolsa de Comercio de Caracas	1947		73	2,656	47
	Bolsa de Comercio del Estado Miranda	1958		n.a.	n.a.	n.a.

Asia

Country	Exchange	Established	Year			
Bangladesh			1954 (then East Pakistan)	49^g	n.a.	n.a.
Hong Kong	Hong Kong Stock Exchange	1891	1976	219	40,700	18,900
India	Ahmedabad	1894				
	Bangalore Stock Exchange Ltd	1963				
	Bombay	1875				
	Calcutta Stock Exchange Association Ltd	1908		3,358^e	8,400	
	Delhi Stock Exchange Association Ltd	1947				2,500
	Hyderabad Stock Exchange Ltd					
	Indore Stock Exchange	1943				
	Madras Stock Exchange Ltd	1930				
	(Exchanges also at Cochin, Kanpur, and Pune)	1957				
	(Estimated at about 5000 in 1986)					
Indonesia	Jakarta Stock Exchange	1952	1977	24^g	72	7
Iran	Teheran Stock Exchange	1968		n.a.	n.a.	n.a.
Korea	Korea Stock Exchange	1920	1956	336^g	6,100	3,869
	Pusan Stock Exchange	1969		n.a.	n.a.	n.a.
Malaysia	Stock Exchange of Malaysia	1937	1960	278^g	29,200^g	2,430^g
Pakistan	The Karachi Stock Exchange Ltd	1948	1960	n.a.	n.a.	n.a.
Philippines	Manila Stock Exchange	1927		326	705	n.a.
Singapore	Stock Exchange of Singapore	1930	1960	149^g	600^g	125^g
Sri Lanka	Colombo Brokers Association	1889	1975	About 35 / 118	34,807	6,376
Taiwan	Taiwan Stock Exchange	1962	1975	121^g	8,790^f	8,300^g
Thailand	Bangkok Stock Exchange (1963) Ltd	1962	1975	95^g	1,700^g	448^g

Annex 6.1   Third World Stock Exchanges

Area and country	Name of exchange	Date of establishment	Reorganized/revitalized	No. of companies listed (1983)	Market capitalization (1981) (US$ million)	Trading volume (1981) (US$ million)
Middle East						
Bahrain		1983		n.a.	n.a.	n.a.
Israel	The Tel-Aviv Stock Exchange Ltd	(Then Palestine) 1935	(Palestine Exchange established in 1953)	n.a.	6,300[g]	1,550[g]
Jordan	Amman Financial Market	1978		109	2,500	225
Kuwait	Kuwait Stock Exchange	1977		46[d]	25,000	6,700
Lebanon	Bourse de Beyrouth	1920		n.a.	n.a.	n.a.
Turkey	Istanbul Stock Exchange	1873	1985	341	800	n.a.

Notes to Table

(i) Dates of establishment vary according to source. Some take the date of formation of a brokers' association, others the date of an over-the-counter market, others the date of establishment of a formal trading exchange.

(ii) Other countries which have attempted to establish share trading in the past are:

Syria (over-the-counter market, until nationalization in 1965).

South Vietnam (law published in 1972).

Tanzania and Uganda (operated with Kenya as a regional market in Nairobi, but their companies are no longer traded).

Mauritius (has had a daily call-over conducted by the Mauritius Chamber of Brokers since 1804, but is largely inactive).

Nicaragua (a small experimental exchange was set up in 1973, but never became active).

El Salvador (securities market legislation adopted in the early 1970s, but a market was never established).

Ethiopia (the central bank sponsored the Addis Ababa Share Exchange until the revolution in 1974).

[a] 1977; [b] 1978; [c] 1980; [d] 1981; [e] 1982; [f] 1983; [g] 1984; [h] 1985; n.a. = not available.

Sources: Wai and Patrick (1973); van Agtmael (1984); *The Economist*, 19 October 1985; various national sources.

NOTES

1. I use the term 'securities market' to mean markets in government bonds, and company equity and loan stock, and the wider term 'capital market' to embrace both securities markets and money markets.
2. A company near its borrowing limits has only two means of raising fresh capital: from retained earnings or equity issue; the latter is much quicker. For example, a company issuing shares at a price/earnings ratio of 10 is effectively obtaining 10 times its current annual earnings immediately. If earnings remained constant it would take 10 years to raise the equivalent funds through retentions, assuming no distribution of dividends in the meantime.
3. The gearing effect of new equity should not be forgotten when considering its contribution to investment. If the ratio of debt to shareholders' funds is 3 to 1, then every $1000 raised in new equity permits further borrowing of $3000, or total new investment of $4000.
4. In the UK, the Unlisted Securities Market acts as a further stepping stone to a full stock market quotation, as does the Second Marché in France.
5. An interesting exception is the possibility of a Gulf Stock Exchange emerging. Kuwait already has a stock exchange and a volatile unofficial trade, Bahrain has recently set one up, and has a substantial over-the-counter market in stocks of its own and of Saudi Arabian companies. The United Arab Emirates is currently considering a draft law to establish a stock exchange. In Saudi Arabia there is considerable opposition to the establishment of a stock market, but there is an active unofficial market and, of course, substantial sums available for investment purposes. Further, an opportunity exists to create an offshore international capital market in the Gulf with trading in US, European, and Japanese securities (see *Investors Chronicle*, 9 December 1983—Gulf Banking and Finance Survey). There is also a rumour that China is considering the establishment of a securities market. As a first step a small over-the-counter market has started in Shanghai.

Chapter 7

Foreign Capital for Developing Countries: Background and Public Sector Flows

1. INTRODUCTION

Chapters 7 and 8 will look at trends in foreign capital flows to developing countries in recent years, the advantages and disadvantages of different forms of foreign finance, and the impact of foreign finance on the recipient countries. For the most part, I shall be examining the non-oil-exporting developing countries, which are the countries which generally need foreign finance, although some oil-exporters[1] are recipients from time to time, particularly of DFI. It is convenient at this point to note that the statistics I shall use are from the OECD, the IMF, the World Bank, the United Nations, and the BIS. Each uses different definitions of country groups, and hence the statistics are not strictly comparable, although the differences which arise are generally slight. This chapter looks first at the role of foreign capital inflows in the development process, followed by an analysis of public sector flows. Chapter 8 will be concerned with private sector flows, in which we include export credits as well as commercial bank credits and direct foreign investment. Export credits frequently lie across both the public and private sectors, in that in some countries the finance is provided by commercial banks, but guarantees, insurance and any subsidies are provided by the public sector. However, for convenience I will discuss export credits in Chapter 8.

2. THE SAVINGS GAP, THE TRADE GAP, AND CAPITAL INFLOWS

In an economy in equilibrium savings are equal to investment. In an optimally planned economy the actual level of investment is equal to the desired level of investment, and therefore savings equal the desired level of investment. However, economies are seldom in equilibrium, and in a developing economy a shortfall usually exists between savings and the desired level of investment, which countries seek to fill by capital inflows. Another view of the same problem is to note a shortfall between export earnings and imports, which again is filled by capital inflows. That these two gaps are equivalent can be demonstrated using national income identities.

$$Y = C + I + X - M$$
$$Y = S + C$$
$$\therefore S + C = C + I + X - M$$
$$\text{or } S - I = X - M$$

(Y = GDP, C = consumption, I = investment, X = exports, M = imports, S = savings). ($S-I$) represents the savings gap, and ($X-M$) the trade gap.

Therefore, given a shortage of finance for investment, a government can pursue a combination of the following three policy measures in order to close the gap.

(i) increase savings;
(ii) increase the trade surplus, or reduce the deficit;
(iii) resort to foreign capital inflows.

(Note that increasing the trade surplus has the effect of increasing savings, by increasing foreign exchange reserves. Savings consist of net foreign currency earnings plus domestic currency savings.)

The two gaps, the trade and savings gaps, may be projected as unequal ex-ante, but by definition they will be equal ex-post. Therefore some economists have taken the higher of the two projections as the foreign exchange gap for a country. A notable early work of this type was Chenery and Strout (1966). McDonald (1982) reviews more recent works. This method has been used by international agencies such as UNIDO and UNCTAD to project the aggregate external financial requirements of the third world (or the non-oil-exporting developing countries). The Harrod–Domar model is usually used to make the projections, the relationships being

$$I = g \times \text{ICOR}$$

where I = investment required, g = projected growth rate, and ICOR = incremental capital output ratio.

Domestic savings (S) is then projected, usually on the basis of historical savings ratios, and the foreign capital inflows (F) then needed are given by

$$F = I - S + D,$$

where D is the sum required to service the accumulated foreign debt.

The model can also be used to project the foreign debt of the country, and to shed light on its debt servicing capacity.

The model is essentially very crude, and its practical usefulness can only be to indicate orders of magnitude. Both the definition and measurement of ICORs present considerable difficulties, and the future values of ICORs and savings ratios are difficult to project. A common assumption is to hold them constant, which of course is unlikely to be realistic. Nonetheless, for our purposes it serves to illustrate the role of foreign finance in the two gap models, and the subsequent build-up of debt that arises as a consequence. Once a country wishes (or has) to reduce its external debt, the identities clearly show that to do this it must implement policies which are aimed at reducing the savings gap or reducing the trade gap. Ex-post, of course, reducing the two gaps amounts to the same thing.

3. THE RELATIONSHIP BETWEEN FOREIGN CAPITAL INFLOWS AND ECONOMIC GROWTH

It is easy to fall into the assumption that an increase in foreign capital inflows will lead to an increase in a country's economic growth. Indeed this assumption lies behind the widespread clamour for increased financial flows to developing countries. However, it is an assumption which should be examined closely, not only for aid flows but for all capital flows. In order for foreign capital inflows to be 'productive' they must be invested in projects which produce returns greater than the cost of the capital. Secondly, there must not be any secondary effects of the foreign capital inflows which have the effect of reducing the rate of return on investment so that it falls below the cost of capital. The arguments for increased foreign capital flows (including aid) often make a number of *ceteris paribus* assumptions, which are not stated explicitly. As we shall see, foreign capital inflows may have a number of secondary effects which it is dangerous to ignore.

The first such assumption is that all the other necessary inputs for projects can be made available readily, simply by buying them abroad if they cannot be found locally. Such inputs include management, technology, skilled labour, communications, repair and maintenance, and other services, all of which tend to be in short supply in many developing countries. The solution to buy them abroad tends to be expensive, and may lead to undesirable and costly irregularities in supply. Still at the level of project financing, it seems to be widely assumed that foreign finance is risk-free for the host country. This is far from the case, as recent experience with interest rates and exchange rates moving against borrowing countries has amply illustrated. But even if we abstract from such risks, there are still the internal country risks of market risk and specific risk which could lead to the rate of return on the investment being lower than the cost of borrowing. To the extent that the interest and repayment of foreign finance is guaranteed by the government, the whole of the risk is carried by the host country. This applies to most borrowing (aid, development bank and commercial bank loans, export credits, and foreign bonds). Only with direct foreign investment is the supplier of foreign finance faced with project risk. Lessard (1982) has explored some possible means of shifting part of the risk from the host country to the supplier of finance, which will be discussed in more detail in Chapter 11.

There has been much academic discussion on the relationship between foreign finance (especially aid) and domestic savings in developing countries. Advocates of increased financial flows to developing countries frequently made the (implicit) assumption that such flows will provide finance which is entirely additional to domestic savings. However, there may be *a priori* reasons for thinking that foreign finance may displace domestic savings, at least to some extent, in which case the additional investment which it provides may not be as great as suggested by the face value of the foreign finance. The availability of foreign finance may permit governments to reduce (or at least, not to increase) taxation; to increase government current expenditure, or to divert government funds from development projects to military expenditure or prestige projects such as airlines or steel mills which give low or negative social returns. On the other hand the provision of foreign finance for development projects in the state sector may often bring with it a requirement that government meets part of the cost. Government may then need to increase its resources, either through higher taxation or higher borrowing to meet its increased commitments. The effects may be to increase government saving at the expense of private saving, or to 'crowd out' the private sector from the country's capital markets, neither of which may be desirable. Alternatively, a government may not increase its resources, but may meet its required contribution by diverting funds from other uses.

Numerous statistical studies of the relationship between economic growth and capital inflows have been undertaken. Most of these have concentrated on aid inflows rather than commercial capital flows. Really these studies represent a special case of the study of relationships between savings (or financial repression) and economic growth discussed in Chapter 3, and first introduced by Goldsmith with his discussion of financial development and economic growth. Moreover, the tool of regression analysis is used in the studies reported here as it was in the studies reported in Chapter 3, and the methodological problems associated with regression analysis remain the same. The main problem is that the economic growth of a country depends upon a large number of factors other than capital inflows (or, more narrowly, aid). Indeed, in many countries the role of capital inflows is likely to be minor, at best. Secondly, aid inflows may be determined by the rate of growth (least developed countries attract most aid), which means that the direction of causation in the relationship is unclear, and, moreover, cross-country regression analysis would tend to suggest that aid produced low growth rates! Thirdly, there will be time lags between the disbursement of aid and a recorded impact on growth. The time lag will depend on the type of aid (i.e. programme or project), and if project aid, will probably depend upon the types of project selected. Finally, there is always the problem of guessing what might have happened to growth rates in the absence of aid.

In the light of these difficulties a positive correlation between growth and capital inflows can only lead to the weak conclusion that capital inflows do not appear to reduce growth. Likewise a negative correlation can only be taken to suggest that capital inflows do not appear to encourage growth. In view of these difficulties I will do no more than present a brief outline of the studies.

A major recent statistical study was undertaken by Gupta and Islam (1983). Using data from 52 countries, they looked at three relationships.

— Single-equation relationships between foreign capital and growth.
— Single-equation relationships between foreign capital and domestic savings.
— Simultaneous-equation relationships between foreign capital, domestic savings, and growth.

The authors found that domestic saving was much more important than foreign capital, both quantitatively and statistically, in determining growth. Considering different forms of foreign capital, they found that both foreign aid and DFI in general made a positive contribution to growth, but that it was impossible to say which of aid and DFI made the greater contribution. However, all types of foreign capital, but especially aid, tended to have a negative effect on domestic savings, thereby reducing their net effect on growth. But the effects on savings were more ambiguous than the effects on growth. The authors, though, were generally inclined to suggest that foreign aid is more useful than foreign private investment. Turning to other forms of capital inflow, these were generally found to have a significant positive impact on growth as well as a significant negative impact on savings, but the results were not unambiguous, and should be treated with caution.

The other studies can be divided into two groups:

— Studies which investigate the relationship between foreign aid and the domestic savings ratio. Rahman (1968), Landau (1971), Weisskopf (1972), and Papenek (1973) all found negative relationships, and only Begley (1978) found a positive relationship, but only for some Latin American countries.
— Studies which investigate the relationship between the rate of growth and the inflow of foreign aid. Two early studies, World Bank (1968) and OECD (1969) found that foreign aid did not lead to higher growth rates, although Papanek (1973) was neutral. Positive relationships were found by Brecher and Abbas (1972) and Islam (1972) for Pakistan, and Jacoby (1966) for Taiwan. Gulati (1978) and Mosley (1980) both obtained mixed results, suggesting a positive relationship for poor countries and negative or insignificant relationships in some advanced countries. These results are conveniently summarized by Dowling and Hiemenz (1983), who conclude that 'Irrespective of these methodological difficulties, the available empirical evidence suggests that financial aid does not necessarily accelerate economic growth. And there is no *a priori* reason why such an outcome should be taken for granted.' Notwithstanding their appreciation of the difficulties, Dowing and Hiemenz proceed to apply regression

analysis to a pooled sample of time-series and cross-country data for Asian countries in the 1970s. They conclude that:

these results strongly support the hypothesis that foreign aid contributes to economic growth and . . . are also supportive of the hypothesis that the rapidly growing economies of Asia are able to utilise aid effectively.

However, it seems unlikely that the debate can ever be conclusively resolved by the use of regression analysis.

Fewer studies are available on the relationship between growth or saving and private capital inflows. Again, the regression analysis used is subject to the reservations of interpretation mentioned above. Papanek (1973) found an insignificant correlation between domestic savings and private capital inflows, and between aid and foreign private inflows. However, in all cases foreign private inflows appeared to make a positive contribution to growth, but only in the Asian group of countries was the contribution substantial.

4. RECENT TRENDS IN EXTERNAL FINANCIAL FLOWS

Annex 7.1 to this Chapter shows the current account deficit of non-oil developing countries from 1973 to 1984, and how it was financed. The deficit rose sharply in 1974 and 1975 following the first round of OPEC price increases, and again from 1978 to 1981 following the second round of oil price increases. However, the growing current account deficit was accompanied in most years by increases in the financial reserves of non-oil developing countries, made possible by their evident ability to borrow more than enough to meet their current account deficits. Only in 1975 and in 1982 did they, in aggregate, need to draw down their official reserves in order to finance the current account deficit.

Annex 7.1 shows the financial flows received by non-oil developing countries to meet the current account deficit and changes in reserves. The table is structured so that:

| Current = account deficit | Use of reserves | + | Capital outflows | + | Non-debt creating flows | + Net external borrowing |

so that, for example, in 1983
$$59 = -10 \quad -20 \quad + 23 \quad + 66$$

In money terms the current account deficit rose by 10 times between 1973 and 1981, although in real terms the increase was only five times over that period. This, though, is still substantial. Of the main financial inflows, non-debt creating flows rose 2.8 times in money terms, whereas net external borrowing rose by over 10 times. Thus it is clear that the non-oil-exporting developing countries became much more dependent on debt finance over the decade to 1981. This became the source of the debt service problem facing many of countries (and their creditors) subsequently. Annex 7.1 also highlights the magnitude of the current account deficits to be financed. The oil-exporting countries have generally shown a surplus on current account in the period under consideration, although they too experienced deficits in 1982 and 1983, and were no longer able to make funds available (either directly, or through western institutions) to finance the deficits of non-oil developing countries. Rather, the western countries and institutions financed the deficits of oil-exporting countries, leaving fewer resources to finance the deficits of non-oil-exporting countries, which were generally considered less creditworthy. At the same time tight monetary policies in the West restricted the growth of funds. Non-oil exporters therefore had to cut their current account deficits after 1981 to the level of the funds available, whereas in previous years the available funds had generally been sufficient to meet the deficits which the borrowing countries wanted to incur. Indeed, before 1981 the liquidity of the international financial system at times was such that potential borrowers had funds pushed towards them by eager (even over-eager) lenders. After reaching a peak of $120 billion in 1981, net new external borrowing fell to only $47 billion in 1984 (Annex 7.1).

One useful indicator of the magnitude of the current account deficit is to compare it with exports. In 1982 the current account deficit of non-oil developing countries amounted to 35% of their exports. By contrast it had been a mere 13% in 1973, before the first round of oil price increases pushed the figure up to 29% in 1974. By 1977 the ratio was down to 17%, but rose steadily thereafter, reaching a peak in 1982. By 1984 the figure had fallen to around 12%, following a fall in imports in 1983 and a strong rise in exports in 1984.

While Annex 7.1 is useful in that it focuses attention on the current account deficit of non-oil-exporting developing countries, and its financing, it does not give a complete picture of the flow of financial resources to all developing countries, and it gives no information about the sources of finance. Annexes 7.2 and 7.3, from the OECD, go some way to filling these gaps in information. Annex 7.2a presents total net resource receipts of all developing countries at current prices from 1970 to 1984, while Annex 7.2b presents the same information in real terms (1983 prices and exchange rates). Annexes 7.2a and 7.2b include all financial flows to all developing countries, net of repayment of principal but excluding interest and military financing. They do not allow for unrequited financial flows from developing countries, such as deposits of reserves and oil surpluses on the Eurocurrency market, direct investment (for example, in property) or portfolio investment. Annex 7.3 summarizes the main changes which have taken place in financial flows to developing countries since 1960.

The statistical changes are self-evident from the tables. The major items of note are the relative decline in importance of ODA (until 1982) and the compensating relative increase of non-concessional flows. Within ODA, DAC bilateral aid increased by 35% between 1970 and 1984, but more substantial increases came from OPEC bilateral aid and multilateral aid, the latter reflecting the policy of governments of directing more aid through these channels. Of the non-concessional flows, the largest increase came from capital market finance, mainly in the form of Eurocurrency loans. The relative importance of both direct investment and export credits declined, the former quite markedly. In total, resource transfers increased in real terms by 74%, or an average rate of growth of 4% per year over 1970–1984. This is faster than the rate of growth in GDP in the industrial countries, which averaged a little over 3% during the same period. The growth rate obtained would be higher, but 1984 saw a sharp fall in real resource transfers compared with 1983.

Annexes 7.2a and 7.2b are concerned mainly with long-term capital flows, that is flows which are not repayable within 1 year. Data collection on short-term flows has only started fairly recently, and is probably still not very accurate. However, in some years it has provided perhaps 20–25% of total lending, and has increased rapidly in importance. Short-term lending is usually bank lending, and in debt crises it has largely replaced longer-term lending. It therefore has replaced finance which can be used for capital investment. Short-term lending plays a prominent role in debt rescheduling, which is discussed in Chapter 9. It has been widely used to permit debtor countries to meet interest payments on time.

5. PUBLIC SECTOR FINANCIAL FLOWS

The vast majority of public sector financial flows to developing countries is accounted for by official development assistance (ODA). In all recent years bilateral aid and multilateral aid has substantially exceeded non-concessional flows. In 1984 officially supported export credits amounted to $7.5 billion, and I discuss these in the next chapter as they have more the character of private flows than public flows. Of the remaining $12.5 billion of non-concessional flows, multilateral agencies (mainly the IBRD) accounted for $7.5 billion, and bilateral agencies for $5.0 billion. Most multilateral agencies have soft-loan windows, but provide only small amounts of concessional finance, with the IDA, EEC/EIB and United Nations grants providing over 80% of multilateral concessional finance in 1984. Loans and grant disbursements by multilateral agencies are summarized in Annex 7.6.

6. OFFICIAL DEVELOPMENT ASSISTANCE (ODA)

The flow of aid from governments of developed countries to governments of developing countries is really a phenomenon of the period since 1945.

Previously, colonial powers had provided budgetary support to colonial governments, but the intention had been to pay for the costs of government, defence, and the maintenance of law and order rather than economic development. The roots of development aid lie in the Bretton Woods agreement, establishing the IBRD, and the US's Marshall Plan, for the reconstruction and development of Europe after the 1939–45 war. Bilateral aid grew steadily, as is shown in Table 7.1.

Before we look at recent developments in aid, it is worth reminding readers that ODA comes in three main forms: project aid, programme aid, and technical cooperation programmes. It is the first two which interest us in this book, although the costs of technical cooperation are included under

Table 7.1 Flows of financial resources to developing countries and multilateral agencies, 1956–65 (billion dollars)

	1956	1960	1965
Official flows	3.3	5.0	6.3
Of which, from			
USA	2.0	2.8	3.7
France	0.6	0.8	0.8
UK	0.2	0.4	0.5
Germany	0.2	0.3	0.5
(Private flows)	2.9	3.0	3.9)

Source:– Development Assistance. Efforts and Policies (OECD, 1966).
Note: The table covers flows from DAC countries only, and the official flows may include non-concessional flows as well as aid. Data for later years are given in Annex 7.2.

ODA in Annexes 7.2a and 7.2b. Typically, technical cooperation has accounted for about 30% of bilateral ODA from DAC countries in recent years (OECD, 1985a, p. 111). A breakdown cannot readily be made between programme aid and project aid, although an analysis of data in OECD (1984a) suggests that about 40% of bilateral aid from DAC members, excluding the USA, was project aid. A further distinction to be made is that between bilateral and multilateral aid. The former is from one government to another; the latter is from one of the multilateral development agencies (World Bank, UN agencies, EEC agencies; regional development banks; OPEC multilateral agencies) to governments, and usually originates from aid provided by individual governments and channelled through the multilateral agencies. In order to qualify as ODA, financial transfers must contain a grant element[2] of at least 25%.

(a) Evaluating Aid

The grant element measure of aid used by the OECD has a number of unsatisfactory features. First, it equates aid which is 100% grant with aid which may have substantial repayment costs, the extreme being the aid with exactly 25% grant element. Secondly, it takes no account of the quality of the aid. Quality can be taken to embrace considerations such as the extent to which aid is tied, and the real value of aid when tendering is restricted to one country (which might even mean one firm), rather than internationl competitive bidding. The higher capital costs associated with tied aid may be accompanied by higher operating costs of equipment, in that the equipment may be inefficient in its use of materials, power, and labour, relative to competing equipment. The costs of management contracts, spare parts, and consumables may also be higher. The increasing use by industrialized countries of mixed credits (aid plus export credits or other commercial credit) for projects is a more subtle form of tying, used notably by France and Japan, and increasingly by the UK. The tying of aid to specific sectors (such as agriculture or infrastructure) which may give lower returns than other sectors (e.g. industry) may further reduce its quality. The process of fungibility may offset the tying effect if it releases recipient government funds for other investments. However, it may also have the effect of tying in recipient government funds if they have to be used to match the aid in some way, such as paying the domestic costs of the project. Thus aid may be used as a means of discouraging industrialization, which might be convenient for those donors who do not want to see more countries developing into new Taiwans and South Koreas, which compete effectively in world markets for industrial products. Mosley (1982) has attempted to combine some of these elements in indices of aid quality. Harvey (1983) indicates how alternative aid offers may be evaluated. Leipziger (1983) has raised an objection to the grant equivalent which is grounded in the discount rate of 10% used to calculate it. In practice, donor and recipient may face different opportunity costs of capital, in which case the costs of a loan or grant to a donor will be different from the benefits of a loan or grant to a recipient. The consequence is that there may be possibilities for shifts in terms which will make one party better off without making the other worse off, thereby increasing the global welfare arising from aid. Alternative formulae[3] have been proposed to take the above considerations into account. However,the formulae are rarely of practical use to recipients, as a straight choice on loan terms rarely arises.

(b) Aid Policies and Trends

There can be little doubt left that there are some differences between the publicly stated reasons and policies for aid-giving and the true motivations of donor governments. There is no reason to be surprised at this; indeed it would be surprising if donors did not pursue their own selfish interest, at least to some extent. In addition to the public commitment to 'assist development', donors will generally pursue their own commercial and political interests. The balance between altruistic and selfish motives varies from donor to donor, some being nearer the altruistic end of the scale, others nearer the selfish end. Observers of aid policies place their own interpretation on the available evidence, the titles of books such as *Aid and Imperialism* (Hayter, 1971), *The Politics of Foreign Aid* (White, 1974), and *Aid and Influence* (Faaland, ed., 1981) being indicative of the lines of argument followed. An up-to-date survey of Western European aid policies is given in Stokke (ed., 1984), and donor interests are discussed in detail in Cassen *et al.* (1982).

The theoretical basis for foreign aid nowadays appears to be based on a combination of theories which have developed at various times in the past. First the Harrod–Domar model explained the relationship between capital investment and growth, through the incremental capital–output ratio (ICOR). The Cobb–Douglas function permitted more determinants of growth, such as labour and technical progress, to be included, and this has subsequently been extended by various writers to include such determinants as natural resource endowment, managerial skills, the level of education, entrepreneurial ability, and other socio-political factors. A further development was that of the two-gap model, which argued that a given target rate of growth would imply an estimated savings gap and an estimated foreign exchange gap. Foreign capital inflows of an amount equal to the larger of the two estimated gaps would then be needed. Balanced growth associated with Nurske, and 'big-push' theories, associated with Rosenstein-Rodan, were popular in the 1950s and early 1960s. Big-push theories emphasized the importance of a very large amount of investment in a country in a short time, and have parallels with the successful Marshall Plan in Europe. However, big-push theories have since fallen out of favour since the other necessary inputs, notably skilled labour, technology, and management, which were available in Europe after the war, remain in short supply in many developing countries. Rostow's stages of growth theory, with its critical rate of investment required for take-off into self-sustained growth, has elements in common with the 'big-push' theory. In the past 15–20 years heavy emphasis has been placed on the project-by-project approach to development, on the basis that a plan is really a coordinated series of investment projects, and that what is needed is adequate project finance, combined with techniques of project identification, formulation, appraisal, and implementation. These theories have been described more fully by Mikesell (1968).

Project aid clearly has its roots in the latter approach. Programme aid appears to rest on the two-gap model, although early models, such as Harrod–Domar, Cobb–Douglas with extensions, and big-push theories all called for substantial capital sums in the days before the distinction between programme aid and project aid was so marked. The third element of aid, technical assistance, is aimed at increasing the level of education and skills, thereby augmenting the supply of those inputs which are complementary to finance, but generally in short supply. It derives from emphasis on the importance of human capital in the development process.

Recently there has been a renewed emphasis on the importance of programme aid, some of which is now described as structural adjustment aid. This is essentially balance of payments support (closing the foreign exchange gap), and is intended to enable countries to adjust the structure of their economies while still continuing to grow, rather than having to use the weapon of restricting aggregate demand to close the balance of payments gap. The adjustment process is described further in Chapter 9. There has been a strong demand from developing countries for more programme aid so that the slow-down in growth which arises from conventional balance of payments policies can be avoided. This requirement coincides with a wish of many developing countries to have more say in how aid is allocated, which leads them to prefer programme aid to project aid. With the latter the projects tend to be selected, it is alleged, by the aid agencies rather than the recipient government, and tend to satisfy the criteria of the donor rather than those of the recipient. One step which has been taken towards programme aid is that since 1980 the World Bank has been permitted to allocate up to 10% of its resources as structural adjustment loans, which is programme rather than project aid. With programme aid the recipient can receive the funds quickly, whereas project aid may take two or more years to disburse, because of the procedures to be gone through to plan and to approve the project.

Through the 1970s and early 1980s the stated aid policies of the industrialized countries shifted gradually towards assisting the poorer countries, and the poorer people within these countries. The same trends in emphasis emanated too from multilateral agencies such as the World Bank and the United Nations agencies. The poverty orientation of aid emphasized basic needs, rural development, and urban infrastructure development. These were areas where it was felt that projects could directly benefit the poor. Trickle-down theories were perceived to have failed, and donors emphasized the importance of reaching the poor directly. Eventually even wider criteria in aid allocation were proclaimed. Some donors emphasize human rights (Netherlands, Norway, Sweden, USA), democratic development (Sweden, USA) and free market economies (USA). The extent to which these stated policies, especially those related to sectoral allocation, have changed the allocation of aid, appears limited, as Table 7.2 illustrates.

Least developed countries do not appear to have received an increase in share of ODA since the mid-1970s, their percentage of total bilateral and multilateral aid remaining constant at a little over 20% (OECD, 1984a). Some donors (e.g. Norway, Sweden, Denmark, UK, and Switzerland), have evidently attempted to increase the proportion of their aid to least developed countries, but their efforts have been outweighed by the absence of significant

Table 7.2 Sector shares of allocatable bilateral ODA commitments (percentages)

		1975/76	1982/3
1.	Development of public utilities	22	30
2.	Agriculture	14	16
3.	Education	18	16
4.	Health, social infrastructure, and welfare	13	13
5.	Industry, mining, and construction	11	8
6.	Others	22	17
	Total	100	100

Source: OECD (1984a), p. 92

proportional increases from such large donors as the USA, Japan, and France, all of whom continue to allocate well under 20% of their aid to least developed countries.

A more systematic study of aid allocation to 90 countries over 1970–72 and 1976–78 has been undertaken by Dowling and Hiemenz (1985). Their statistical analysis found a bias in per capita aid flows against large, populous countries, but it did not confirm that there has been any bias in aid allocation towards middle-income countries. However, they found that there appeared to be a bias over 1976–78 against a sub-group of the least developed countries, which received less aid than other lower-income countries. The countries concerned were Burundi, Chad, Ethiopia, Malawi, Mali, Rwanda, Somalia, Upper Volta, Bangladesh, Burma, India, and Nepal. An earlier study by Croswell (1981) of 101 countries over 1976–78, reported by Dowling and Hiemenz (1985), confirmed a bias against large population countries in the allocation of per capita aid, also found previously by Edelman and Chenery (1977) and Isenman (1976). However, evidence in these studies of a bias towards middle-income countries was conflicting.

On the basis of the above analysis it is not obvious that there has been any significant shift in aid towards the poorer people in the poorer countries over the past 10 years. To some extent this is because some donors' stated intentions are merely cosmetic, and political and commercial advantage have remained the main criteria for aid allocation. However, anecdotal evidence does suggest that some donors have had genuine difficulty in finding suitable projects to benefit the poor, getting the agreement of the recipient government to those projects, and then implementing the projects. In some cases the poor may be hard to reach, as difficulties in distributing disaster relief show.

The motivations for aid allocation by donors have been the subjects of a number of statistical studies, the most recent by Maizels and Nissanke

(1984). They developed a model based on three donor interests (political and security, investment, and trade interests), and contrasted it with a model based on recipient need, defined by the variables GNP per capita, the physical quality of life index, GNP growth rate, balance of payments current account : GNP ratio, and population. The donor interest model gave good explanations of the allocation of bilateral aid, but a poor explanation of multilateral aid. Conversely the recipient interest model gave a good explanation of the allocation of multilateral aid, but not of bilateral aid. Over the 1970s there had been a notable switch among bilateral aid agencies away from donor interests and towards recipient interests but, as the authors comment, there seems to have been a switch back to donor interests in the 1980s, with the United States transparently using aid as an instrument of foreign policy and investment interests, and several other donors using aid in mixed credits to subsidize capital goods exporters. Moral and humanitarian motivations for aid seemed to have been pushed aside by the mid-1980s.

A number of studies by McKinlay and Little of aid allocation in the 1960s by four major aid donors (United States, France, Germany, and the United Kingdom) reported by Maizels and Nissanke (1984), came to much the same conclusions. For all four donors the donor interest model provided a good explanation of aid allocation, but the recipient need model did not produce statistically significant results. The theme of donor interests, which in fact vary considerably from donor to donor, is taken up more extensively in Cassen *et al.* (1982). Statistical analysis can only present a simplified model of donor interest, which for most countries is complex and, at times, beset by conflicting interests.

(c) Issues in Development Aid

The three main issues which have received attention in recent years are:

— Is aid effective?
— Who should determine aid priorities and policies?
— Should aid be increased?

Is Aid Effective?

There has for many years been almost an uncritical consensus (in public) in the 'development business' that aid is a good thing, and the more aid that is provided, the better. Many doubters have suppressed their true views on the subject, and donors too have at least paid lip service to the desirability of aid, in spite of the private reservations of some politicians and officials. Few writers have risked public opprobrium by breaking ranks, but among those who have are Professors Bauer and Yamey and, more recently, Jackson and Eade on the impact of food aid.

Two major dissenting works are by Bauer (1976 and 1981). In a restatement of their case, Bauer and Yamey (1981) make the valid point that little effort has been made to examine critically the effects of aid on recipient countries. At best, they argue, the *maximum* contribution of foreign aid is the grant equivalent it contains. If recipient governments were able to use the money effectively, they would be able to borrow it on commercial terms anyway. However, they maintain, the costs of aid to developing countries are likely to be greater than the benefit they receive from the concessional terms. Aid, because it is supplied to governments, 'reinforces the disastrous politicization of life in the Third World', in that it increases the economic and political power of governments and increases their scope for patronage. Many governments, they believe, are not fit to hold this elevated position, in that they are limited in capability and integrity, and, contrary to their public pronouncements, do not put the people they represent first. Aid, they claim, helps to maintain overvalued exchange rates, 'and since most aid is free and need not be repaid, there is little pressure on governments to use the resources productively'. Furthermore, 'It is a mistake to suppose that aid goes to the poor. It is given to their governments.' Even if it did get to the poor, they argue, it would remove the incentive for the poor to improve their skills and better themselves. In short, it would be debilitating. Nor is aid even beneficial to the donors, in that it fails to win political friends. Bauer and Yamey point out that in international forums it is the aid-giving West which receives the criticism of the developing countries whereas the Soviet bloc, which gives much less by any criterion, receives little criticism from the South. Other than for the relief of disaster, they conclude, official aid should be terminated. Failing that, they add, aid to the poorest should be left to non-political charities; it should be bilateral not multilateral, so as to retain some measure of political control; it should not be tied, as tying merely converts it into a subsidy to the country's exporters; it should be 100% grant; and it 'should not go to the governments which pursue policies which patently undermine economic advance and the living standards of the people at large'.

The argument against food aid provides a specific instance of aid diminishing local effort. Food aid superficially appears to be a humanitarian way of feeding the hungry South with the food surpluses of the North. However, its long-term effect is to discourage the development of local agriculture by reducing the demand for its products, and the prices. Moreover food aid helps to develop tastes for imported, rather than indigenous, foodstuffs. It also pre-empts the scarce resources in the local distribution system. These objections, and others, have been chronicled by Jackson and Eade (1982), who recommend substantial reductions in food aid in all cases except emergencies such as famines and disaster relief.

Two staff members of Britain's Overseas Development Administration, writing in their personal capacity, have attempted to refute Bauer's arguments (Healey and Clift, 1980). They make the valid point that aid goes largely to the least developed countries which do not have access to the international private capital markets, and which find it difficult to attract private foreign investment, primarily because of their low level of economic development, but in some cases because of the policies followed by their governments. Moreover, they argue, medium-term commercial credits are of too short maturity to finance long-term physical investments. Concessionality is defended first on the rather weaker grounds that developing countries are less advanced that developed countries and therefore more prone to investment errors. Secondly, concessional terms are justified as compensation for the loss incurred by tying aid—which amounts to saying that the concession is no more than a grant for the donor country's capital equipment manufacturers.

Healey and Clift argue that aid-financed projects are more carefully scrutinized and monitored than projects financed by foreign bank credits or export credits, which is undoubtedly true. Little systematic and impartial evidence is available on the success of individual aid projects. However, the authors point to a number of country studies of the impact of aid, and conclude that it has generally been favourable (the countries concerned are Malawi, Kenya, Botswana, Lesotho, Swaziland, Taiwan, and Korea). They admit that the evidence concerning the impact of aid on growth and saving (such as the regression-based studies described above) is difficult to interpret, and generally inconclusive. Finally, they conclude that moral and humanitarian grounds for providing aid are valid.

It seems, though, that many of the Bauer arguments survive, and, in this writer's view, have not been adequately refuted by the proponents of aid. Moreover, the 'moral' argument in favour of aid becomes diluted in the light of the often cynical attitudes of some donor governments described above, which leaves the aid lobby on rather shaky ground. Indeed, it does seem that the basis of official aid, that it is made from one government to another government (bilateral) or that it is made from multilateral agencies (government-owned) to governments needs examining. If instead aid were to be chanelled through non-governmental organizations, in both donor and recipient countries, then perhaps it would avoid being sullied by the hands of government. Private aid contributions could be allowed against income in assessing tax, if necessary, to encourage people to give directly. An alternative for project aid is for it to be chanelled through development banks in the donor country. These development banks need not be wholly (or even partly) government-owned. Nor need financing necessarily be provided to governments in developing countries. The development banks would be free to invest in, and lend to, whatever projects or organizations they choose, although, of course, they would be subject to the investment laws of the recipient country.

Who Should Determine Aid Priorities and Policies?

Third world governments all have their own development strategies and policies. There is a risk, therefore, that the sectors and projects which aid donors wish to assist may not be those which recipient governments wish them to assist. Differences may arise because the two parties have different ideas about development policies, or because the project selection criteria of the two are different. There is therefore scope for conflict. To some extent conflict may be avoided by the effect of the fungibility of finance. However, in the countries which are heavily dependent on aid, where governments have little of their own money, a government's flexibility in shifting finance from one project to another may be severely limited. Under these circumstances a country may end up with a portfolio of projects which are selected more by foreign aid agencies than by its own government. While in some countries this may not necessarily be harmful, and may even be beneficial, it does seem to have provoked demands in international forums in recent years for developing country governments to have more say in the use of foreign aid. Consequently, there has been a persistent demand for a switch from project aid towards programme aid.

Edgren (1984) has distinguished between five levels of conditionality, as shown in Table 7.3. The recipient countries feel vulnerable to pressures, particularly at the policy level and also at the project/programmes level. The IMF (although it is not an aid agency) and the World Bank, through its structural adjustment loans, apply particular pressure at the policy level. The conditions of bilateral donors may be felt mainly at the level of choice and design of project, although there is a growing view among bilateral agencies that policy reform should be a condition for aid. A possible quid pro quo would be for donor agencies to reduce the tying of aid or provide more programme aid in exchange for policy reforms. Conditions at the fourth and fifth level, such as the tying of aid, and instances of condescending residual imperialism, may irritate recipients rather than raising fundamental questions of principle. However, procurement tying can influence the choice and design of projects, which in turn can influence policy matters. Fairly low-level conditionality may be felt higher up the scale.

Table 7.3

	Level	Criteria
1.	General political compatibility	The government's general political and economic strategy
2.	Policy level	Specific economic and social policy measures (monetary policy, pricing policy, taxes, nationalization measures, etc.)
3.	Project/programme level	Institutional reform, financial or staff contributions, official regulations, etc.
4.	Financing conditions	Recipient's ability to pay; potential as a market for donor's export industry
5.	Administrative conditions	Procedures for resource transfer, reporting arrangements

At the project/programme level, the extent to which a donor government can relinquish control of the choice of sector, and project, and can hand over the implementation to the recipient government, is likely to be restricted by its domestic political constituency. Bilateral aid agencies appear to feel the need to satisfy the probings of the anti-aid lobby, which in some countries may have the support of the majority of the electorate. This lobby will with some justification seize upon any cases of ill-conceived or badly implemented aid-financed projects which come to light, whether the responsibility lies with the donor or recipient.[4] Clearly, therefore, aid agencies need to think carefully before handing over responsibilities for aid priorities or projects to the recipients.

Should Aid be Increased?

The 'aid lobby' has, since the Pearson Report (1969) called for the indus-rialized countries to give a higher proportion of their GNP as development aid. The Pearson Report set a target at 0.35% of GNP to be provided as aid. The figure was subsequently revised upwards to 0.7% GNP. A further target was 1% of GNP, if commercial flows are included. The pressure for increased aid has been maintained through the work of the international agencies (notably the United Nations) and independent reports such as those of the Brandt Commission (1980 and 1983). Annex 7.5 shows the proportion of GNP donated as aid by the major donors. OPEC members have been easily the most generous, the CMEA countries strikingly ungenerous. What is more, the OPEC surpluses have effectively supplied substantial bank lending to developing countries through the intermediation of the western commercial banks. The CMEA, of course, provides no commercial finance.

Within the OECD members one can draw a rough distinction between the 'like-minded' countries (represented by, for example, Norway, Sweden, Denmark, and the Netherlands) and the 'hard-line' countries such as the USA and Japan. The former typically give over 0.7% of GNP as aid, the latter under 0.35%. The attitudes of the latter are conditioned by ideology as much as by meanness. The present government of the USA, in particular, appears to believe that aid is inherently inefficient and wasteful, and explicitly believes that commercial finance, particularly direct foreign investment, is preferable to aid.[5] Other hard-line countries, though, appear to use aid, and to restrict aid, for selfish reasons rather than for ideological reasons.

The desirability of increasing aid depends upon one's view of the effectiveness of aid, as opposed to other forms of financial flows. Political opinion in the industrialized countries generally appears to be against substantial increases in aid, and there is a body of opinion in developing countries which supports this position, largely because the effects of tying, and 'political interference', mean that the costs outweigh the benefits. However, a number of schemes have been put forward with the intention of increasing aid flows, and I will examine some in Chapter 11.

7. OTHER SOURCES OF PUBLIC SECTOR FINANCE

(a) Aid from OPEC

The main sources of public sector finance shown in Annex 7.2 have already been discussed. One omission is flows from OPEC, which grew rapidly after the first oil price increases in 1973/74. Much of OPEC finance is supplied on highly concessional terms, both from bilateral and multilateral agencies. It is rarely tied, as OPEC members do not have significant capital goods industries to which aid may be tied. The only real possibility is to tie aid to oil and gas purchases, but this is rarely done. However, a substantial amount of OPEC aid is restricted to Arab or Islamic countries. For example, membership of the Islamic Development Bank is restricted to countries with a substantial Islamic population. The terms of OPEC aid usually tend to be generous, though. A number of the agencies have had difficulty in finding sufficient projects to enable them to disburse their available funds. OPEC have been relatively generous donors; aid as a percentage of GNP has been consistently above 1% since 1970 (Annex 7.5), until it fell below in 1984.

(b) Aid from the CMEA

Ad from the CMEA (Council for Mutual Economic Assistance) countries has been very limited in quantity, and represents a minute proportion of their GNP, 0.21% in 1984, compared with 0.36% of GNP from OECD members (Annex 7.5). Around 70% of this small amount of aid goes to countries with which the CMEA has close political relations, notably Vietnam, Mongolia, Cuba, and Afghanistan (OECD, 1984a). The CMEA argues that the economic backwardness of the third world is the direct result of colonial exploitation by the western nations, and that the provision of compensating aid is the responsibility of the west, not the CMEA. This extremely dubious historical argument, in the author's view, is no excuse for the abdication of what is a moral responsibility. However, the argument appears to be meekly accepted by much of the third world; at North–South official meetings it is usually the OECD whose aid record is criticized by the developing countries, not the CMEA's record.

8. A NOTE ON 'AID VERSUS TRADE'

Attempts have been made, notably by Johnson (1967) and Thirlwall (1976, 1983) to compare the value of $1 of additional exports with $1 of 'pure' aid. At a practical level, developing country pressure groups, such as UNCTAD, have argued against protectionism in the industrial countries, believing that increases in third world exports will act as a significant stimulus to growth. The theoretical discussions have generally considered only the direct effects of aid or trade, but Yassin (1982) has argued that the indirect effects may be more important than direct effects. Although the argument is unproven,

I tend to agree with this view, hence the prominence given in this chapter to the effects of aid on savings and growth. Moreover, I tend to believe that an economy dependent on its own efforts in trade is likely to prove more dynamic and robust than one which is dependent on government to government aid; but obviously this is also an unprovable assertion. However, the discussion is not of practical consequence as developing countries, individually or collectively, are not offered a choice of trade or aid. Moreover, the development lobby calls for increased aid and increased trade in parallel, rather than arguing that one should be increased at the expense of the other. In general we believe that the case against protectionism stands on its own grounds, and that in the medium and long term all parties will reap benefits from increases in competitive trade. The provision of aid is not adequate compensation for restricting imports from the third world.

Annex 7.1 Non-oil Developing Countries[a]: Current Accounting Financing, 1973–84 (billion US dollars)

	1973	1974	1975	1976	1977	1978	1979	1980	1981	1982	1983	1984
Current account deficit[b]	11	37	47	33	30	57	62	77	113	103	59	38
Use of reserves	–10	–3	2	–13	–12	–14	–22	–18	2	14	–10	–22
Capital outflows[c]	n.a.	n.a.	n.a.	n.a.	n.a.	–10	–11	–27	–37	–38	–20	–9
Non-debt-creating flows, net[d]	10	15	12	13	14	18	25	24	28	29	23	23
Net external borrowing	11	25	33	33	28	63	70	98	120	98	66	47
Memo item												
Current account surplus of 12 oil-exporting developing countries	7	68	35	40	29	6	63	111	53	–12	–16	n.a.

[a] Excludes China prior to 1977. Prior to 1878, 12 oil-exporters are excluded. Since 1978, eight major oil exporters in the Middle East are excluded. See Note 1 to this chapter.
[b] Net total of balances on goods, services, and private transfers as defined in the IMF's Balance of Payments Statistics (with sign reversed).
[c] For 1973–78, included under other items.
[d] Mainly official transfers and direct investment flows (net).
Source: Derived from IMF Annual Reports 1983, 1984, and 1985.

Annex 7.2: Net Flows of Funds to Developing Countries, 1970–84

Annex 7.2(a): Total Net Resource Receipts of Developing Countries from all Sources, 1970–84 (current prices and exchange rates)
$ billion

	1970	1975	1976	1977	1978	1979	1980	1981	1982	1983	1984[d]
I. Official development assistance	8.08	20.07	19.99	20.72	27.71	31.67	37.50	37.28	34.74	33.65	36.60
1. Bilateral	7.01	16.23	16.12	15.89	21.70	25.43	29.71	29.35	27.23	26.12	n.a.
2. Multilateral agencies	1.07	3.84	3.87	4.83	6.01	6.24	7.79	7.93	7.51	7.50	n.a.
II. Grants by private voluntary agencies	0.86	1.34	1.35	1.49	1.65	1.95	2.31	2.02	2.31	2.20	n.a.
III. Non-concessional flows	10.95	34.31	37.85	44.23	57.15	52.16	59.34	70.46	60.36	63.90	64.12
1. Official or officially supported	3.96	10.53	13.32	15.71	18.78	18.39	24.42	22.15	21.99	19.60	20.75
(a) Private export credits (DAC)	2.09	4.42	6.74	8.84	9.70	8.85	11.12	11.30	7.09	5.50	n.a.
(b) Official export credits (DAC)	0.59	1.20	1.39	1.44	2.22	1.73	2.46	2.01	2.66	2.10	n.a.
(c) Multilateral	0.71	2.53	2.54	2.69	3.09	4.16	4.85	5.72	6.61	7.00	n.a.
(d) Other official and private flows (DAC)	0.25	0.75	0.80	0.63	1.36	1.14	2.24	1.96	2.63	(3.00)	n.a.
(e) Other donors[a]	0.32	1.63	1.85	2.11	2.41	2.51	3.75	1.16	3.00	(2.00)	n.a.
2. Private	6.99	23.78	24.53	28.52	38.37	33.77	34.92	48.32	38.37	44.30	43.37
(a) Direct investment	3.69	11.36	8.31	9.82	11.59	13.42	10.54	17.24	11.86	7.80	12.0
(b) Bank sector[b]	3.00	12.00	15.00	15.50	22.87	19.67	23.00	30.00	26.00	36.00	} 31.37
(c) Bond lending	0.30	0.42	1.22	3.20	3.91	0.68	1.38	1.08	0.51	0.50	
Total receipts (I + II + III)	9.89	55.72	59.19	66.44	86.51	85.78	99.15	109.76	97.41	99.75	100.72

Annex 7.2(a): _(continued)_

	1970	1975	1976	1977	1978	1979	1980	1981	1982	1983	1984[d]
For information:											
ODA to developing countries and multilateral agencies, total	8.35	22.08	22.01	23.84	30.04	32.12	39.95	37.54	36.95	36.18	36.60
DAC countries	6.95	13.85	13.95	15.73	19.99	22.82	27.26	25.54	27.73	27.56	28.64
OPEC countries	0.40	6.24	6.10	6.07	8.13	7.65	9.59	8.53	5.89	5.48	4.54
CMEA and other countries	1.00	1.99	1.96	2.04	2.28	2.65	3.10	3.47	3.33	3.24	3.42
Short-term bank lending	..	..	..	16.00	17.00	16.00	26.00	22.00	15.00	−2.00	n.a.
IMF purchases, net[c]	0.34	3.24	2.98	−0.43	−0.85	0.52	2.61	6.18	6.41	12.43	3.56

[a] Other official flows from OPEC countries, Luxembourg (up to and including 1981), Spain, and Yugoslavia.

[b] Excluding (i) bond lending and (ii) export credits extended by banks which are included under private export credits. Including loans by branches of OECD banks located in offshore centres, and for 1980, 1981 and 1982 participations of non-OECD banks in international syndicates.

[c] All purchases minus repayments including reserve tranches but excluding loans by the IMF Trust Fund included under multilateral ODA above.

[d] Provisional. Data on ODA from _OECD Observer_, July 1985; data on non-concessional flows derived from Colaço, F. X., 'international capital flows and economic development' _(Finance and Development_, September 1985.

Note: Figures concerning non-DAC member countries are based as far as possible on information released by donor countries and international organizations, and completed by OECD Secretariat estimates based on other published and unpublished sources. They may therefore not comply in all respects with the norms and criteria used by DAC members in their statistical reports made directly to the OECD Secretariat.

Reproduced with permission from OECD (1984a)

Annex 7.2(b): Total Net Resource Receipts of Developing Countries from all Sources, 1970–84

	1976	1977	1978	1979	1980	1981	1982	1983	1984
I. Official Development Assistance	29.50	27.98	32.06	32.93	36.05	36.23	33.69	33.80	35.75
1. Flows from bilateral sources	23.92	21.59	25.25	26.53	28.75	28.52	26.21	26.23	27.35
(a) DAC countries	13.70	13.34	14.87	16.74	16.99	17.71	18.35	18.53	20.10
(b) OPEC countries	7.46	5.66	7.82	7.13	8.19	7.46	4.56	4.33	3.79
(c) CMEA countries	2.07	2.01	1.87	2.20	2.48	2.88	2.86	2.94	2.95
(d) Non-DAC/OECD	0.05	0.11	0.16	0.14	0.81	0.21	0.18	0.07	0.10
(e) LDC donors	0.64	0.47	0.53	0.32	0.28	0.26	0.26	0.26	0.41
2. Flows from multilateral agencies	5.58	6.39	6.81	6.40	7.30	7.71	7.48	7.57	8.40
II. Grants by private voluntary agencies	1.94	1.97	1.87	2.00	2.17	1.97	2.30	2.34	2.50
III. Non-concessional flows	54.59	58.53	64.59	53.45	55.66	68.56	60.10	82.12	54.00
1. Official or officially supported	19.21	20.79	21.29	18.84	22.91	21.55	21.90	19.82	20.00
(a) Private export credits (DAC)	9.72	11.70	11.00	9.07	10.43	10.99	7.06	5.50	5.00
(b) Official export credits (DAC)	2.00	1.91	2.52	1.77	2.31	1.95	2.65	2.10	2.50
(c) Multilateral	3.66	3.56	3.50	4.26	4.55	5.57	6.58	7.22	7.50
(d) Other off. & private flows (DAC)	0.83	1.54	1.17	2.10	1.91	2.62	3.00	3.00	3.00
(e) Other donors	2.67	2.79	2.73	2.57	3.52	1.13	2.99	2.00	2.00
2. Private	35.38	37.74	43.50	34.61	32.75	47.01	38.21	62.30	34.00
(a) Direct investment	11.98	12.99	13.14	13.75	9.89	16.77	11.81	7.80	9.50
(b) Bank sector[a]	21.63	20.51	25.93	20.16	21.57	29.19	25.89	54.00[a]	24.00[a]
(c) Bond lending	1.76	4.23	4.43	0.70	1.29	1.05	0.51	0.50	0.50
Memo: Official development finance[a]	33.16	31.54	35.56	37.19	40.60	41.80	40.27	40.92	43.25
Total resource flows (I + II + III)	86.03	88.48	98.72	88.38	93.88	106.76	96.09	118.26	92.25

Annex 7.2(b): (continued)

For information:

ODA to developing countries and multilateral agencies, total	31.75	31.54	34.53	33.88	37.60	36.37	36.88	36.39	37.40
DAC countries	20.12	20.82	22.66	23.38	25.57	24.85	27.61	27.54	29.30
OPEC countries	8.80	8.03	9.23	7.84	9.06	8.14	5.80	5.43	4.60
CMEA countries	2.08	2.03	1.88	2.22	2.50	2.84	2.92	3.04	3.00
Non-DAC/OECD	0.10	0.17	0.21	0.20	0.19	0.27	0.27	0.12	0.20
LDC donors	0.65	0.49	0.55	0.24	0.28	0.27	0.28	0.26	0.30
Total bank lending	..	41.68	45.20	36.56	45.96	50.59	40.83	35.00	18.00
of which: Short term	..	21.17	19.27	16.40	24.39	21.40	14.94	−19.00	−6.00
IMF purchases, etc.	4.30	−0.57	−0.96	0.53	2.45	6.01	6.38	12.48	5.50

(a) Bank Sector includes, for 1983 and 1984, significant amounts of rescheduled short-term debt. The real evolution of bank lending is best reflected in the line showing "Total bank lending" at the bottom of the table above. The evolution of total resource flows needs to be adjusted accordingly.

(b) Bilateral and multilateral ODA plus multilateral non-concessional flows.

.. = negligible.

Reproduced with permission from OECD (1985a).

Annex 7.3 Total Resource Flows to Developing Countries by Major Types of Flow, 1960–1984 (percentage shares of long-term total flows)

	1960–61	1970	1975	1980	1981	1982	1983[a]	1984[a]
I. Official Development Assistance	55.9	41.8	37.3	38.4	33.9	35.1	35.9	41.9
1. Flows from bilateral sources	53.6	36.5	30.5	30.6	26.7	27.3	27.8	32.0
(a) DAC countries	47.7	27.9	17.2	18.1	16.6	19.1	19.7	23.6
(b) OPEC countries	—	1.9	10.0	2.6	2.7	3.0	4.6	4.4
(c) CMEA countries	5.2	4.9	2.6	2.6	2.7	3.0	3.1	3.5
(d) Non-DAC/OECD	0.1	—	—	0.9	0.2	0.2	0.1	0.1
(e) LDC donors	2.6	1.8	0.7	0.3	0.2	0.3	0.3	0.5
2. Flows from multilateral agencies	2.3	5.3	6.8	7.8	7.2	7.8	8.0	9.9
II. Grants by private voluntary agencies	..	4.2	2.4	2.3	1.8	2.4	2.5	2.9
III. Non-concessional flows	44.1	54.0	60.3	59.3	64.2	62.5	61.6	55.2
1. Official or officially supported	18.9	19.5	18.5	24.4	20.2	22.8	21.0	23.5
(a) Private export credits (DAC)	5.9	10.3	7.8	11.1	10.3	7.3	5.8	5.9
(b) Official export credits (DAC)	8.1	2.9	2.3	2.5	1.8	2.8	2.2	2.9
(c) Multilateral	2.3	3.5	4.4	4.8	5.2	6.8	7.7	8.8
(d) Other off. and private flows (DAC)	2.7	1.2	1.3	2.2	1.8	2.7	3.2	3.5
(e) Other donors		1.6	2.9	3.7	1.1	3.1	2.1	2.3

Annex 7.3: (*continued*)

	1960–61	1970	1975	1980	1981	1982	1983[a]	1984[a]
2. Private	25.1	34.5	41.8	34.9	44.0	39.8	40.6	31.7
(a) Direct investment	18.8	18.2	20.0	10.5	15.7	12.3	8.3	11.2
(b) Bank sector	6.3	14.8	21.1	23.0	27.3	26.9	31.8	20.0
(c) Bond lending	..	1.5	0.7	1.4	1.0	0.5	0.5	0.6
Total resource flows (I + II + III)	100.0	100.0	100.0	100.0	100.0	100.0	100.0	100.0
Memo: Official development finance[b]	58.2	45.3	41.8	43.2	39.2	41.9	43.4	50.7

[a] 1983 and 1984 percentages have been calculated using a baseline figure for ordinary long-term bank sector lending business, i.e., $30 billion instead of the $34 billion shown in Table 7.2(b) and $17 billion instead of $24 billion after excluding from long-term flows estimated amounts rescheduled from short-term in those years (see footnote to previous table).

[b] Bilateral and multilateral ODA plus multilateral non-concessional flows.

— negligible .. not available.

Reproduced with permission from OECD (1985a)

Annex 7.4: The 'Financing Mix' of Developing Countries (and territories) (1980–81 annual averages)

	Percentage of total ODA	Percentage of total non-concessional flows	Percentage of total receipts	Percentage of total debt	Memo items		
					No. of countries	Percentage of total GNP	Percentage of population
ODA reliant countries							
(i) Completely reliant (over 90% ODA)	23	1	8	3	41	2	8
(ii) Highly reliant (66–90% ODA) excluding India (see below)	25	4	11	8	28	5	7
Sub-totals	48	5	19	11	69	7	15
Middle position countries (33–66% ODA)	26	13	17	16	33	7	7
'Market terms' countries							
(i) ODA significant (10–33% ODA) excluding China (see below)	12	22	19	21	20	16	12
(ii) ODA not significant (less than 10% ODA)	4	57	40	48	26	51	14
Sub-totals	16	79	59	69	46	67	26
India and China							
India (81% ODA)	9	1	3	4	1	7	21
China (11% ODA)	1	3	2	1	1	12	30
Totals	100	100	100	100	149	100	100

Reproduced with permission from OECD (1983a).

Annex 7.5: ODA as a percentage of GNP, 1970, 1975, 1980–84 (Net disbursements)

	1970	1975	1980	1981	1982	1983	1984
DAC countries							
Netherlands	0.61	0.75	1.03	1.08	1.08	0.91	1.02
Norway	0.32	0.66	0.85	0.82	0.99	1.06	0.99
Sweden	0.38	0.82	0.79	0.83	1.02	0.85	0.80
Denmark	0.38	0.58	0.74	0.73	0.76	0.73	0.85
France							
(incl. DOM/TOM)	0.66	0.62	0.64	0.73	0.75	0.74	0.77
(excl. DOM/TOM)	0.42	0.38	0.38	0.45	0.49	0.47	0.52
Belgium	0.46	0.59	0.50	0.59	0.59	0.69	0.56
Germany	0.33	0.40	0.44	0.47	0.48	0.49	0.45
Australia	0.62	0.65	0.48	0.41	0.56	0.49	0.46
Canada	0.41	0.54	0.43	0.43	0.41	0.45	0.50
United Kingdom	0.39	0.39	0.35	0.43	0.37	0.35	0.33
Finland	0.06	0.18	0.22	0.28	0.30	0.33	0.36
Japan	0.23	0.23	0.32	0.28	0.28	0.33	0.35
Austria	0.07	0.21	0.23	0.33	0.35	0.23	0.28
New Zealand	0.23	0.52	0.33	0.29	0.28	0.28	0.27
Switzerland	0.15	0.19	0.24	0.24	0.25	0.32	0.30

United States	0.32	0.27	0.27	0.20	0.27	0.24	0.24
Italy	0.16	0.11	0.17	0.19	0.24	0.24	0.32
Total DAC	0.34	0.36	0.38	0.35	0.38	0.36	0.36
Other OECD countries	—	(0.03)	0.09	0.13	0.14	0.06	n.a.
OPEC countries							
Saudi Arabia	5.59	7.50	4.95	3.49	2.54	3.29	3.29
Kuwait	6.19	7.26	3.52	3.63	4.60	3.86	3.81
UAE	0.00	11.68	3.82	2.60	1.34	1.44	0.17
Qatar	n.a.	14.59	4.28	3.74	1.66	0.13	0.16
Iraq	0.13	1.95	2.35	0.92	0.19	−0.11	−0.14
Other	0.28	0.66	0.18	0.16	0.08	0.14	n.a.
Total OPEC	0.80	2.92	1.84	1.51	1.02	1.03	0.86
CMEA countries[a]	0.16	0.14	0.17	0.21	0.21	0.21	0.21

Notes: 1970 and 1975 data exclude administrative costs for all countries with the exception of the United States. DAC countries are ranked according to their performance vis-à-vis the GNP target in recent years.

DOM = Départments d'Outremer

TOM = Territoires d'Outremer

[a] These estimates are uncertain and contentious

Reproduced with permission from: OECD (1984a, 1985a)

Annex 7.6 Net Disbursements of Concessional and Non-Concessional Flows by Multilateral Agencies, 1960–1984
At 1983 prices and exchange rates

$ million

Agency	1960–61[a]	1965–66[a]	1970–71	1975–76	1978	1979	1980	1981	1982	1983	1984
					Concessional flows						
Major Financial Institutions											
IDA	-122	824	567	1754	1142	1310	1447	1866	2353	2336	2492
IBRD	—	—	—	19	86	110	100	86	58	48	41
IDB	-318	-23	552	438	376	343	306	426	364	365	438
AfDB and Fund	—	-58	—	10	44	56	90	88	121	158	111
AsDB and Fund	—	-47	8	105	183	119	140	142	176	223	304
IFAD	—	—	—	—	—	3	51	73	104	144	170
Sub-total	-440	696	1127	2326	1831	1941	2134	2681	3176	3274	3556
United Nations											
WFP	..	..	315	512	466	539	506	527	592	630	..
UNDP	..	..	552	553	475	533	619	769	711	617	..
UNHCR	..	..	20	119	139	256	435	425	364	356	..
UNWRA	..	..	113	145	125	139	147	165	234	211	..
UNICEF	..	..	118	167	190	215	232	208	203	246	..
UNTA	..	..	121	107	129	119	33	204	195	253	..
UNFPA	—	—	..	..	..	153	141	126	112	122	..
Other UN	..	..	91	381	436	314	220	346	331	304	..
Sub-total	463	666	1330	1984	1961	2268	2333	2771	2743	2739	(2739)
Others institutions	—	—	8	13	1002	724	1577	462	39	33	16

Total above	23	1362	2464	4324	4794	4933	6044	5914	5958	6046	(6311)
EEC	37	390	524	895	913	1194	995	1401	1138	1215	1287
Arab OPEC Funds	—	—	—	422	1103	272	268	396	396	314	149
Total concessional	60	1762	2988	5640	6810	6399	7307	7711	7493	7575	(7747)

Non-concessional flows

Major Financial Institutions											
IBRD	832	884	1474	2589	2385	2919	2970	3505	4515	5117	5268
IFC	36	55	156	264	66	111	277	496	290	166	127
IDB	..	..	262	362	425	458	532	626	828	957	1551
AfDB	—	—	10	64	94	94	91	68	114	145	470
AsDB	—	..	73	359	260	285	307	379	471	550	513
Others	—	—	3	12	1	7	10	16	13	9	14
Sub-total	868	939	1978	3649	3231	3874	4187	5090	6231	6944	7943
EEC	—	—	86	61	88	166	241	234	319	202	84
Arab OPEC Funds	—	—	—	100	178	224	120	236	48	80	191
Total non-concessional	868	939	2064	3810	3497	4264	4548	5561	6598	7226	8218

[a] The data for this period are shown after deduction of capital subscription payments by developing countries; — nil or negligible; .. not available. Figures in brackets are provisional

Reproduced with permission from OECD (1985a)

NOTES

1. Prior to 1985 the IMF/World Bank group of oil-exporting developing countries consisted of Algeria, Indonesia, Iran, Iraq, Kuwait, Libya, Nigeria, Oman, Qatar, Saudi Arabia, United Arab Emirates, and Venezuela. Some of these countries, notably Nigeria, Venezuela, and Iraq, have been substantial borrowers, and Indonesia and Algeria have also borrowed, but to a more limited extent. The utility of the classification for the purpose of analysing financial flows may therefore be limited. Since 1985 some IMF data have been restated, excluding eight Middle East oil-exporters (Iran, Iraq, Kuwait, Libya, Oman, Qatar, Saudi Arabia, and the United Arab Emirates). See for example Annex 7.1. Unless otherwise stated, I use the old classification.

   A further IMF reclassification of countries in 1985 involves the distinction between 'fuel-exporters' and 'non-fuel-exporters'. The fuel-exporters are Algeria, Bahrain, Congo, Ecuador, Gabon, Indonesia, Iran, Iraq, Kuwait, Libya, Mexico, Nigeria, Oman, Qatar, Saudi Arabia, Syria, Trinidad and Tobago, Tunisia, United Arab Emirates, and Venezuela. The remaining developing countries are the non-fuel-exporters. For further details of country classifications, see IMF Annual Report 1985, Annex IX.

2. The grant element is a measure of the concessionality of a loan. Concessions may be given through low interest rates, grace periods, and extended maturities. The definition of grant element adopted by the OECD is

$$\text{Grant element} = \frac{\text{Face value of loan} - \text{Present value of repayments}}{\text{Face value of loan}} \times 100.$$

   The present value of repayments is to be calculated at the market rate of interest, which is conventionally taken to be 10% for these purposes. Therefore a loan made at 10% interest will have a grant element of zero. Conversely, a loan which does not have to be repaid (i.e. a grant) has a grant element of 100%. A number of criticisms have been made of the grant element as a measure of concessionality (see text).

3. One such formula for calculating grant equivalents which takes into account the cost to the recipient of tied aid, delay and the extra cost of imported goods is

$$\text{Value of aid} = \frac{\text{Procurement value}}{\text{Face value} \times \text{donor price index}} - \text{Payment equivalent}$$
$$- \text{Cost of delay} - \text{Extra cost of imports}$$

   all in present values.

   Procurement value   = the cost from the cheapest source.
   Face value   = amount of loan.
   Payment equivalent   = Present value of the cost of repayment at the borrowing country's discount rate.

   Cost of delay $= \text{Original NPV} \left(1 \, \frac{1}{(1 + r)^n}\right)$

   where r = borrowers' discount rate and n = delay in years.
   Extra cost of imports = extra cost of materials and spare parts as a result of tied procurement sources.

4. A quotation from the *Yorkshire Post* of 21 January 1985 illustrates the point. 'Tanzania received more aid per head that any other country. Seventy per cent

of the state's budget comes from foreign aid. What has happened to these billions? They have been used to set up a monstrous bureaucracy and to cripple the country's once flourishing agriculture with a system of enforced collectivisation. At the same time as farmers have been driven to despair by being paid too little for their produce, Nyerere has augmented his army of officials and time servers. Industrial output has fallen again, as in the previous three years. Having squandered its foreign aid, Tanzania has no money left to buy raw materials. Food is short and severly rationed. People fight over kerosene supplies in the shops.'

On the other hand a survey in the UK (Bowles, 1978) found that 46% of the sample were in favour of British overseas aid, and 39% against. As many as 79% were in favour of richer countries giving help to poorer countries.

5. A notable consequence of the disillusionment has been the refusal of the USA to meet in full the 6th replenishment of the IDA. Many other donors have followed the USA's example, albeit with reluctance. They have followed because they do not wish to increase their share of total IDA contributions, but have largely compensated by contributing the shortfall to a special FY 84 account, or to the Special Fund. The overall effect has been to stretch out IDA-6 for an additional year.

Chapter 8

Foreign Capital for Developing Countries: Export Credits and Private Sector Flows

1. HISTORICAL BACKGROUND

There have been four major waves of financial flows from more developed to less developed countries, all of which ended in considerable financial distress. The first started in 1822, and mainly involved flows from Britain to Latin America.

(a) The First Wave, 1820–40

Between 1822 and 1825 bonds were issued in London by Prussia, Spain, Naples, Russia, Denmark, Colombia, Chile, 'Poyais',[1] Peru, Portugal, Austria, Greece, Buenos Ayres (*sic*), Brazil, Mexico, Guatemala, Guadalajara and the Central American Confederation. Some borrowers appeared more than once. The largest amounts raised were £4.2 million, then a sizeable sum, by Colombia (1824) and Denmark (1825). Although the total nominal value of all these bonds issued during this period was about £73.7 million, the actual amount raised was only about £46 million; but the amount due to be repaid was the nominal figure.

The first of today's developing countries to borrow was Colombia, in 1822. The nominal amount of capital issued was £2 million, but as the issue price was 84%, only £1.68 million was actually raised. The nominal coupon was 6%, but the discount meant the effective interest rate was 7.1%, compared with yields on British Government Consolidated Stock (Consols), the risk-free rate of interest, of between 3.6% and 4.0% during 1822. Moreover, it is not certain that Colombia would receive even £1.68 million, for it was sometimes the practice of agents to retain some of the proceeds to make interest payments in the first year or two. At times, also, agents would use the proceeds of the issue to buy the stock on the market, in order to maintain its price, which, it was thought, would help to sell the remaining stock. (Stock issues, in those days, were sold gradually over a period of time.)

Thus the recipient might receive much less than even the amount paid, pushing up the effective interest costs to even higher levels than the estimated 'spread' over the yield on Consols. In many cases the true interest rate on bonds was well over 10%, and the redemption yields even higher. Such yields naturally attracted greedy investors.

The most quoted and spectacular case is the second Greek loan of £2 million nominal in 1825. Here the agents used much of the proceeds to buy the stock so as to maintain the price in the market, before sale of the stock was completed. They retained a further £200,000 to meet interest payments. All the Greeks received was £200,000 in cash, plus two small warships in 1828. Yet they had to pay £100,000 annual interest (5% on £2 million), which must have meant an effective rate of interest of 20–25%, at least.

Even assuming that the country received all the proceeds of the loan, the true borrowing rate was often more than double the yields on Consols. The spreads of today's Eurocurrency loans looks charitable by comparison with the spreads of the 1820s. Even given good management of the funds, it is hardly surprising that borrowing countries were unable to repay. While the London capital market became rapidly disillusioned with foreign lending, one would be surprised if the feeling was not reciprocated by the foreign borrowers.

Holders of South American government bonds were soon to know their fate. By 1827 all were in default, as were the Spanish and Greek governments. Brazil did resume debt payments in 1829, and Buenos Ayres paid up all arrears after 30 years of default on the interest. In fact, few genuine interest payments were ever made, although some were made by the agents retaining 1 or 2 years' interest before handing over the proceeds of the loans. In most cases the defaults continued for many years. From time to time, countries issued new bonds to meet the interest arrears on old bonds. Such earlier attempts at debt rescheduling were made by Mexico (1831, 1837, *et seq.* to 1864), Venezuela (part of old Colombia) (1841), Colombia (1845 and 1861), Ecuador (1855), Chile (1842), Peru (1842), and Buenos Ayres (1857). In many cases, default occurred on the new bonds, which were subsequently honoured by a further issue to clear the arrears. A full account of debt rescheduling attempts is given by Rippy (1959).

The experience of the first substantial wave of foreign lending and direct foreign investment in developing countries was nothing short of a disaster. Those who put up the money generally lost their principal, and received little interest on it. Nor were the proceeds put to good use by the borrowers. They were substantially used for armaments (uniforms for the navy and a ship for the admiral), and often fuelled wars against neighbouring countries. No doubt much went into private pockets. Jenks (1927, p. 63) comments

'The violence, the corruption, the instability, the financial recklessness which characterized most of the South American republics during a large part of the century are in no small way attributable to the early laxity of the London money market.'

Moreover, defaulters lost their creditworthiness, and were unable to borrow again for many years. However, they did borrow again, with results which were not altogether dissimilar, as we shall see.

(b) The United States Boom

Naturally, these disappointments discouraged investors from lending to Latin America, at least for a time. The next major wave of developing country lending was to North America, during the 1830s. (The frontier nature of the United States at this time fully qualifies it for the title of developing country.) Loans were raised in London by the federal government and by many state governments. Most of the borrowing was for infrastructure, notably railways. Cottrell (1975) says that by 1838 a quarter of American state borrowing of £172.3 million had been for canal and railway development. Some of this had been in the form of paper accepted in payment for capital goods (e.g. rails and rolling stock) from Britain, an early form of export credit. The peak lending period was 1834–38, and long-term development finance was augmented by a flood of American short-term bills of exchange and bank notes, especially from the recently created Bank of the United States, which hit the London market.

The crash can be traced to the financial crisis in Europe of 1837–38, the collapse of the cotton price (on which America largely depended), the consequent inability to redeem notes and bills of exchange secured on cotton, and the general collapse of credit. In spite of attempts by European investors to support the paper of the Bank of the United States (they were tied in, and had to put in more to attempt to protect their existing exposure) the collapse surely came. Unfortunately, much of the longer-term lending was also insecurely based, as progress with canal and railway projects was slower than expected. The projects had generally been expected to generate sufficient revenue to service the debts, but increasingly interest payments on old debt had to be met by taking on additional debt. The first sign of approaching difficulties was the delay of Pennsylvania in paying a dividend due in February 1840. A year later the Bank of the United States failed, the last nail in the coffin of American creditworthiness in Europe. This failure created a further collapse of credit, and individual states were unable to borrow to meet interest payments due. In 1841–42 nine states stopped payment (Arkansas, Florida, Illinois, Indiana, Louisiana, Maryland, Michigan, Mississippi, and Pennsylvania). Michigan (in part) and Mississippi repudiated their debts on the grounds that they had been contracted unconstitutionally, and that the contracts had been broken by the unwarranted conduct of agents. Florida claimed that it was only a territory of the federal government when the debt was floated and therefore unable constitutionally to incur any obligation. The repudiation was incorporated in the Constitution of the State of Mississippi in 1875, and the bonds remain in default, in spite of sporadic attempts to have them redeemed (Annual Report of the Council of Foreign Bondholders, London, 1980). The nominal value amounts to about $7 million. Thus from the point of view of the lenders, experience in North America largely repeated that in South America 15 years earlier. Jenks (1927, p. 104) puts the value of the defaulted securities at $100 million. However, all but those of Mississippi were redeemed sooner or later.

(c) Private Foreign Investment

The law permitting the establishment of joint stock companies in Britain in 1825 led to a substantial increase in company funds in Britain, imitation abroad, and substantial private foreign investment. A large number of mining and foreign trading joint stock companies were established to operate mainly in Latin America. Hobson (1914) speaks of 74 mining companies formed between 1820 and 1825. The Statistical Society, quoted by Hobson, indicates that 41 foreign mining and foreign trading companies set up in 1820–25 had collapsed by 1827. Rippy (1959) speaks of 46 joint stock companies (28 in mining) with a nominal capital of £35 million, established to operate in the new Latin American republics. A few survived, but not with any lasting impact. As indicated, most investments were lost, and Jenks (1927, p. 56) states that 'Up to the middle of the century only the Anglo-Mexican, the Real del Monte and the Imperial Brazilian are known to have returned anything like their original capital to the participants in the form of dividends'. Randall (1972) thinks that there may have been some benefit in the form of transfer of mining technology to Mexico, but generally it seems that the benefits derived by the participants were slight. The 1840s, however, saw very substantial expansion in investment in joint stock companies in Britain, largely in railways, and subsequently in Europe and the United States, a large part of which came from Britain. Both direct and portfolio investments were undertaken, and were generally accompanied by British management and workers. However, private foreign investment at that time does not seem to have gathered the widespread opprobrium with which it is regarded in the developing countries of today, and developed in the United States and Europe seemed to benefit as a result. The same may not be true for eighteenth- and nineteenth-century colonial investments, however, where the policy of the colonial power was to obtain commodities cheaply, and secure a market for exports of manufacturers, which was enforced effectively by restrictions on trade and shipping between the colony and the metropolitan power.

(d) The Second Wave, 1860–75

British foreign investment continued steadily during the 1840s and 1850s, notably in railway ventures in the United States and in continental Europe. By 1860, though, England was experiencing a further boom in the floating of foreign government bonds, which persisted with some ups and downs until 1876. Jenks (1927) chronicled foreign government bonds issued in

London over this period. Bonds of developing country governments totalled £505.9 million. By contrast bonds issued by developed country governments amounted to less than half of this amount, at £218.4 million. The United States accounted for £150 million of the latter figure, in three 'jumbo' loans. The coupon rate of interest divided by the issue price gives the true rate of interest, in most cases between 7% and 10%, well above the rate of return on Consols, which lay between 3.1% and 3.5% throughout the period 1860–76. Moreover, the true rate of interest is likely to be well below the real cost paid by borrowers. The issue price is the price to the public, generally rather more than the price received by borrower. Moreover the bonds were to be redeemed at par, that is 100. Therefore the redemption yield would be somewhat higher.

Once again, default was widespread. Latin American defaults were again frequent, but by no means the only ones, with Turkey and Egypt notable defaulters, too (Table 8.1). The total outstanding British investment in Latin American government bonds at the end of 1880 was £123 million at par value. Venezuela's sterling bonds had been in default most of the time since 1867, but an adjustment had been effected in 1880. Rippy (1959) concludes

On the whole, Latin America government securities had been a decidedly poor investment for nearly 60 years. British bankers and not a few Latin American governments alike had been scandalously dishonest. English bankers, brokers, and exporters, and grafting Latin American bureaucrats, had profited at the expense of British investors.

During the period 1870–1914 substantial direct foreign investment also took place. It is difficult statistically to separate portfolio and direct investment,

Table 8.1 UK loans to Latin America in default, end of 1980

Defaulting country	Amount of default (£)	Date default began
Bolivia	1,654,000	1875
Costa Rica	3,304,000	1874
Dominican Republic	714,300	1872
Ecuador	1,824,000	1868
Colombia	2,100,000	1879
Guatemala	544,200	1876
Honduras	3,222,000	1872
Mexico	23,540,800	1866
Peru	32,688,320	1876
Paraguay	1,505,400	1874
Total	71,097,020	

Source: Rippy (1959)

and difficult to estimate even the total, but the United Nations (1949) gives the tentative estimates of total foreign long-term investment outstanding at 1914 (Table 8.2).

Table 8.2   Foreign long term investment outstanding, 1914

Investing countries	Million US dollars
United Kingdom	18,000
France	9,000
Germany	5,800
United States	3,500
Belgium, Netherlands, Switzerland	5,500
Other countries[a]	2,200
Total	44,000
Distribution of investments	
Africa	4,700
Asia	6,000
Europe	12,000
North America (North of Mexico)	10,500[b]
Latin America	8,500
Oceania	2,300
Total	44,000

[a] Rough estimate: includes the investments of Japan and Russia (e.g. in China), of Portugal (e.g. in Brazil), and of Sweden (e.g. in Russia).
[b] Of which the USA received $6800 million, making it a net debtor country.

(e)   The Third Wave, 1918–30

The 1920s saw a third wave of bond lending to developing countries. By now the USA had replaced Britain and France as the major supplier of foreign capital. By the early 1930s many of the bonds were in default, partly as a result of the depression and protectionism in the North, which meant that the borrowers were unable to earn sufficient foreign exchange to service their debts. Once again, though, incompetence and dishonesty played its part. Winkler (1933) recorded the story, and produced a list of loans in default (Table 8.3). Direct foreign investment, which after 1914 was dominated by US companies, expanded rapidly in the 1920s, as did foreign portfolio investment, but the financial crisis at the end of the decade brought it to a halt, and the 1930s saw a period of disinvestment. By 1929 the value of US direct investments abroad was approaching $8 billion, of which about half was invested in Latin America (Lewis, 1938). Although it is difficult to

Table 8.3   Government, state, and city bonds in default (direct and contingent) 31 December 1933 (thousand $US)

Country	Original amount	Amount outstanding	Interest in default
Argentina	130,331	113,863	8,724
Austria	61,000	53,415	4,806
Bolivia	70,400	61,348	9,649
Brazil	1,445,045	1,169,433	198,693
Bulgaria	164,901	108,905	6,381
Chile	590,783	451,060	53,476
China	368,244	346,378	228,686
Colombia	189,173	163,906	12,912
Costa Rica	27,591	18,690	1,116
Ecuador	20,046	17,475	14,395
Germany	603,158	524,364	16,667
Greece	168,222	161,238	16,011
Guatemala	10,331	6,890	614
Hungary	86,650	80,519	7,350
Jugoslavia	325,558	279,004	23,362
Latvia	7,413	7,303	5,962
Mexico	750,319	621,800	554,706
Panama	16,500	14,912	550
Peru	119,350	114,141	20,439
Rumania	347,680	325,244	5,458
Russia	17,679,645	17,053,494	10,940,125
Salvador	21,750	17,200	1,797
Turkey	424,500	370,147	31,224
United States	85,038	83,038	249,810
Uruguay	237,437	170,540	5,523
Total	$23,951,065	$22,334,307	$12,418,436

Source: Derived from Winkler (1933).

assess the value of, and the returns to, direct foreign investment, Lewis concluded 'On the whole it seems likely, though not proved, that the direct investments have resulted in financial gains for the nation (i.e. USA) as a whole considerably in excess of losses.' The opposite was the case with portfolio investment. The value of direct foreign investment to the host countries, especially the developing countries, is of course much more questionable, and difficult to generalize about.

(f)   1945–70: An Absence of Private Lending

After the 1939–45 war the United States for a time represented the only substantial source of private foreign capital. Portfolio investment remained at a low ebb and bank lending was not substantial, which left direct foreign investment as the major source of private foreign capital, with some private export credits. The United Nations (1956) wrote:

'In less developed countries in particular, the function formerly performed by foreign private portfolio investment has been taken over to a large extent by public capital in the form of loans or grants channelled through national agencies and the IBRD.'

It was during this period that development aid appeared, to some extent replacing budgetary support which had previously been allocated to colonies by their metropolitan governments.

Private and official capital flows to developing countries from 1956 to 1970 were as shown in Table 8.4.

Table 8.4 Private and official capital flows, 1956–70 (million $US)

	1956	1960	1965	1970
Direct investment	n.a.	1767	2468	3408
Bilateral portfolio	n.a.	633	655	809
Multilateral portfolio	n.a.	204	247	343
Export credits	n.a.	546	751	2174
Total Private Flows	2881	3150	4121	7574
Official Flows	3312	4965	6199	7967

n.a. = not available.
Sources: *Development Assistance Efforts and Policies, 1966 Review* (OECD); *Development Assistance Annual Review, 1971* (OECD).

(g) The Fourth Wave, after 1970

The fourth wave of lending came in the 1970s, mainly through the form of bank loans rather than bonds. (Perhaps by then developed country bond holders had learnt their lesson.) Again, financial distress was the consequence, but I will postpone a detailed analysis until Chapter 9. In the remainder of this chapter I will examine private financial flows to developing countries since 1970 in some detail.

2. FOREIGN FINANCIAL FLOWS SINCE 1970

Annex 7.2 indicates that in recent years about 40% of total net financial flows to developing countries have been private. In most years bank lending has contributed the bulk of private flows, with export credits (private and official) and direct investment each contributing similar but smaller amounts. Portfolio investment contributes a negligible amount. The three major items therefore are export credits, direct investment, and bank lending, and I shall examine each of these in turn. Finally, I will examine briefly the subject of portfolio investment.

(a) Export Credits

Official export credits date from the 1920s, with Britain being the first country to set up an agency (the Export Credit Guarantee Department, ECGD) to administer them. Other industrialized countries soon followed with their own schemes. Although the details of their operations vary (OECD, 1982) they all help exporters to offer fixed-interest medium-term credit to customers, thereby assisting exports. Essentially they were established to provide financial services which the market did not provide, either by supplying finance, or insurance, or both. They have also been used to provide export subsidies, usually through concessional interest rates, with the subsidy being met by the exporting company's government.

In practice export credits had been developed much earlier. In the nineteenth century British companies exported considerable amounts of capital goods, notably railway lines and rolling stock to foreign (largely American) railway companies. These were paid for by bonds issued by the railway companies, which the British exporters would help to place with a merchant bank, who would then market them further. The bonds were sometimes secured against the land or future earnings of the railway company, and were sometimes in convertible form. Lewis (1938) and Jenks (1927) give details of this type of issue. Such railway bonds were not without their problems, and provided several cases of fraud, such as the Interoceanic Railway in Honduras and the Transcontinental Memphis–Pacific Railway Company. The latter was a fictitious company which raised over £800,000 on the Paris market and never laid down a single rail. Indeed, the fictional and fraudulent Great South Central Pacific and Mexican Railway in Trollope's novel *The Way We Live Now* is no more a flight of fancy that some of the non-fictional fraudulent schemes foisted on a gullible investing public.

Export credit arrangements soon became a means of competition between exporting nations to assist their exporters. Therefore in 1934 the International Union of Credit and Investment Insurers (known as the Berne Union) was established, and effectively operated as a cartel to standardize the terms of export credits. It has been replaced since 1976 by the establishment by OECD member governments of the International Arrangement on Officially Supported Export Credits, commonly known as the 'consensus'. The main role of the consensus has been to fix minimum rates of interest for fixed-interest export credits with a repayment period of at least 2 years. In addition it sets ceilings on repayment periods for credits for different types of goods (credits on ships and aircraft, for example, are generally granted longer repayment periods than plant and machinery). Consensus terms have been negotiated annually between member governments, and have led to substantial differences of opinion between members, particularly over the issue of subsidies.

Medium-term export credits are available on capital goods rather than consumer goods, and the vast majority of trade in these items has traditionally been between industrialized countries, although credits have always been made available to developing countries too. Until recently they have been on the same terms as those available to industrialized countries. However, the consensus arrangement produced a structure of different interest rates based on the GNP per head of borrowing countries, which generally means that developing countries pay lower rates of interest on export credits than do industrialized country borrowers. In 1983 the rates established were as shown in Table 8.5.

The rates have varied from year to year, but the figures in Table 8.5 give an indication of the differences charged to countries of different income levels. Category 1 includes the OECD members and most Eastern European countries; category 2 includes mainly the newly industrialized countries such as Algeria, Brazil, South Korea, Malaysia, Mexico, Nigeria, and Taiwan, while category 3 contains the rest of the developing world.

The above rates, established for 1983/84, were generally rather higher than they had been in earlier years of the consensus, and represent a closing of the gap between consensus interest rates and market interest rates. In 1981, for example, consensus rates were 7–8¾%, while long-term market rates (in sterling and dollars at least) were around 15%. The IMF has estimated the cost of the interest rate subsidy by OECD member country governments at $2 billion in 1978, rising to $7 billion in 1981. The same source estimates that 18% of all US exports, 34% of French, 35% of British, and 39% of Japanese exports have received official financial support (IMF survey, 13 December 1982). These considerable subsidies gave rise to strains between OECD member countries. In one camp was the United States, which wished to eliminate subsidies (the US Eximbank does not receive any subsidy), while the French (and others) have wished to maintain or even increase the subsidies. At the same time the divergence of international interest rates led to further strains, as domestic market rates on yen, Deutschmark and Swiss

Table 8.5 Consensus interest rates on export credits, 1983/84

Borrowing country	Criteria (GNP/head)	Length of loan (Years)		Maximum credit term (years)	Minimum cash payment (%)
		2–5	Over 5		
Category 1 (relatively rich)	Over $4000 (1979)	12.15	12.4	5[a]	15
Category 2 (middle-income)	Not in categories 1 and 3	10.35	10.7	8.5	15
Category 3 (relatively poor)	Under $624 (1978)	9.5	9.5	10	15

[a] Exceptionally 8.5 years.

francs were somewhat below the consensus rates. Since 1981 Japan has been permitted to charge a fixed margin over its agreed domestic interest rate. These considerations, together with the increasing weariness with protracted annual negotiations, led to a new system being introduced from 1984.

A scheme has now been developed whereby consensus rates are pegged automatically to the average of five countries' domestic long-term government bond yields, and adjusted by the OECD every 6 months. Any increase in the average of the five long-term government bond yields will be added to the base rates in Table 8.6 ('the matrix'), but if interest rates fall, only half the fall will be subtracted. In May 1983 the average of the five long-term government bond yields was 10.1%. Commercial export credits usually cost about 1.25% above the long-term government bond yields, which reflects the risk premium. Therefore at that time, on average, unsubsidized export credit would have cost about 11.35%, which coincided with the rate then being charged to middle-income countries for credits in excess of 5 years. Finally it has been agreed that other low-interest rate countries may, if they wish, use the system which has been agreed for Japan since 1981. It remains to be seen how the new arrangement works, but it still appears to be somewhat cumbersome.

The matrix rates for the first half of 1986 are shown in Table 8.6, and in fact have fallen steadily from the 1983/4 rates. A further bone of contention is the use of mixed credits, which is a package consisting of an export credit softened by a dose of concessional aid. Obviously these credits are made available to developing countries and, equally clearly, they provide project finance. Mixed credits were initially devised by the French, but have since been used by several other countries. The effect of a mixed credit package is to enable an exporting country to offer 100% financing (rather than 85% maximum under an export credit), longer maturities (up to 20 or 25 years), grace periods, and interest rates several percentage points below the consensus rates. Several countries, notably the UK and the USA, have opposed mixed credits on the grounds that they merely use aid as a form of export promotion, and therefore as a subsidy to capital goods producers, which is counter to the spirit of aid-giving, and also counter to the principle of not subsidizing exports. Nonetheless the UK and the USA are among the countries which have established mixed credit funds, as have Canada, Japan, and

Table 8.6   Matrix rates (percentages), Jan.–June 1986

	To 5 years	Over 5 years
Relatively rich	10.95	11.20
Intermediate	9.65	10.85
Relatively poor	8.80	8.80

Italy. Developing countries, in their role of receiving mixed credits, have little to fear apart, perhaps, from increased tying of aid. However, those developing countries which are trying to export capital goods, often in competition with western suppliers, find it hard to compete with conventional export credits, and almost impossible to compete with mixed credits.

A form of export credit provided by European banks, and which is now spreading to UK and US banks, is 'à forfait' finance. This is commercial credit whereby a bank, at an exporter's request, agrees to buy the debt the exporter has arranged for his foreign customer. The bank buys a debt at a discount, and will usually require it to be guaranteed by the importer's bank, unless the importer is a state corporation or large TNC. The paper thus acquired is a fixed-term, fixed-interest note, and is negotiable. From the point of view of the buyer it unties the source of finance from the source of equipment as, for example, a French exporter can arrange for a British bank to accept the debt. Traditionally, à forfait finance has been used for exports to Eastern Europe, although it has spread to exports to developing countries, mainly the Middle East and Asia. However, the exposure of western banks in many third world countries is restricting their willingness to buy such risky debt. It does, though, provide an interesting example of risk-sharing in international financing.

So far, I have discussed export credits which are provided by developed countries, and guaranteed and subsidized by their governments. As credit terms undoubtedly form a constituent of an export promotion package, and a significant element in obtaining orders, any developing country which wants to export capital goods, whether to industrialized countries or to other third world countries, must be able to offer terms similar to those offered by Western exporters. They therefore need a fund to finance export credits, and an agency to offer insurance or guarantees against commercial and political risks. Developing countries which are short of capital, and often substantial borrowers on world markets, may find it difficult to offer medium-term credits to support their exports. However, a number of countries have set up export credit schemes, including Argentina, Mexico, Hong Kong, Malaysia, Venezuela, India, Pakistan, and Sri Lanka. Nevertheless the problem of providing finance remains, and several schemes have been proposed to assist developing countries to raise finance, most of which have involved the acceptance (and discounting) of developing countries' export credit paper by foreign banks or international agencies. Some of these schemes are discussed further in Chapter 11.

(b)   An Alternative to Export Credits: Countertrade

In the event, the trend in some developing countries has been to retreat from assisting exports through better export credits, and to shift to various forms of countertrade. The terminology and arrangements in this type of trading can be a little confusing.[2] The main terms are:

— *Barter*, the direct exchange of goods between the importer and exporter without any exchange of money.

— *Compensation agreements*, which allow the full or partial payment for goods to be made in other goods. Unlike straight barter, compensation payment is usually staggered over an agreed period of time. The agreement is specified in a single contract.

— *Counter-purchase, or parallel trade* involves two separate contracts, one for delivery by the exporter, the other for repurchase of the goods by the exporter. Such arrangements are sometimes made on a government-to-government basis, and the repurchase may in fact be made by a third party, or even a third country.

— *Buy-back agreements* (known also as industrial cooperation), whereby the exporter of machinery or a turn-key factory agrees to be paid, in whole or in part, in the goods produced by the factory. The plant exporter will usually arrange his own long-term financing for the plant in his own country.

— *Offset arrangements*. An exporter of goods agrees to make an offsetting investment in the importing country, to help increase financial flows of equity and to create employment. Offset is used between developing country importers of aircraft and defence hardware, and exporting countries. Governments are generally involved in the agreement.

— *Evidence accounts* are an extension of counter-purchase, whereby the exporter and importer maintain accounts of goods traded over a period of time, rather than entering into separate counter-purchase agreements for each transaction. The agreement, for example, may aim to maintain a balance in trade on a year-by-year basis.

— *Switch trading* is a triangular compensation arrangement between three countries, which is used to correct imbalances in bilateral trading arrangements between two of the countries. If country A has a trade surplus with country B, which is disrupting a bilateral agreement to achieve a trade balance, then A may purchase balancing goods from a third country C, which would buy goods to the same value from country B. When non-convertible currencies are involved the deals become complex, and usually involve a trade broker or agent.

Eastern European countries have traditionally been the main parties involved in countertrade. It arises when the initial importer is short of foreign exchange to pay for the goods, but has a surplus (or surplus capacity) of another good which it wishes to sell on the international market. In many cases the second good may be in excess supply on the world market, so that it is difficult to get sales, or good prices. Countertrade may offer opportunities to sell at better than world prices. Barter is of course the oldest method of trade, and has recently produced examples such as the exchange of Russian machinery for Algerian wine and other goods in the 1960s. Buy-back deals sprang into prominence in the 1970s, particularly between the West and Eastern Europe. The West's process plant producers sold numerous chemical and petrochemical plants to Eastern Europe and arranged to be paid in the products of these plants (see *The Economist*, 10 February 1979). They then had to dispose of the products on the world markets, at a time when those markets were already suffering from excess supply. Consequently they received lower prices than anticipated, and also angered western-based chemical producers. Therefore buy-back deals can be high risk for the plant exporters. In addition to price problems there may be difficulties arising from poor-quality goods and low production levels, although management contracts may help to overcome these difficulties. Other examples of buy-back agreements in recent years have been the supply of a jeans factory to Hungary and a tractor factory to Poland. In 1984 Russia agreed to provide about one-third of the financing for an alumina plant in Greece, and to buy back two-thirds of the annual output for the first 10 years (*The Economist*, 14 July 1984). Bulgaria is supplying a tomato concentrate plant to India, with a guarantee to buy back 50% of the output.

The dividing line between different forms of countertrade is often hazy, but all developed rapidly during the recessions of the late 1970s and early 1980s, encouraged by the shortage of foreign exchange in developing countries and slack world markets both for their commodities and consumer goods, and for the capital goods of the industrialized countries. The governments of several countries such as Indonesia and Pakistan insisted on countertrade deals to pay for large import contracts (Walsh, 1983).[3] Indonesia has exchanged rubber, coffee, cocoa, and cement for fertilizer products; Iran has exchanged crude oil for New Zealand lamb and wool, and Angola has arranged to use oil to pay Portugal for a hydroelectric project. There are many other examples to be found. However, government insistence on countertrade arrangements has perhaps been less successful than intended, because of the difficulties in making trade arrangements, and the bureaucratic delays involved. Exchanging goods for money is much more straightforward.

Although barter, countertrade, and buy-back arrangements are essentially matters of international trade, they are of interest to us because they represent substitutes for financial flows. Buy-back or compensation agreements involve the supply of capital goods which are 'paid for' over time, as with an export credit. However, they are not included in the international statistics of the provision of export credits. (They also tend to cut out the banks, who normally provide the finance for export credits, which has led banks to set up subsidiaries to handle barter, countertrade and buy-back arrangements.) What is more, these trading arrangements enable developing countries to maintain their investment programmes at times when finance is scarce, and to do so without increasing their financial indebtedness. Also, the division of risk is different. With, say, a buy-back deal, much of the risk is borne by the plant supplier, in that he is responsible for marketing part of the output, and also faces some of the risk of poor plant performance and management. The buyer, on the other hand, has an assured market for part of his output.

(c) Export Credits and Capital Market Theory

Finally, to return to flows of traditional export credits, it is of interest to consider the extent to which they conform to the flows which would be predicted by modern capital market theory. If export credits were allocated according to theoretical considerations, suppliers of credit would rank countries and borrowers according to risk, and charge higher interest rates or higher insurance premiums (or both) to the higher-risk borrowers. They would also build up a diversified loan portfolio in order to reduce specific risk. In fact, interest rates are seldom raised in proportion to risk; it may be said that the contrary is the case, with third world borrowers, who are granted preferential interest rates by the consensus arrangement, probably representing, on balance, higher risks than borrowers in OECD countries. Insurance premiums are more likely to reflect relative risks, especially in cases where the export credit insurance agency is private or run on private lines. Britain's Export Credit Guarantee Department, for example, has four categories of country risk, and the insurance premiums take these into account. In Germany, though, there is no ranking of premiums according to country risk. However, the premium charged to private buyers is generally higher than the rate charged to public sector buyers, and premiums vary according to the size of the contract and the length of the repayment period. Insurers may also from time to time suspend cover for certain countries where they think the risk merits it.

As export credits follow orders for capital goods the export credit and insurance agencies are restricted in their discretion in building up a diversified portfolio of export credits. Therefore they may not be able to diversify as they would wish. However, in countries where the finance is provided by commercial banks they may be able to combine their export credit exposure with their other loan exposure in a loan portfolio which is to their liking. For example, a bank which has a high level of loan exposure to one country may decide to decline export credit to that country, so that its total exposure is not too great. However, the process of diversifying risk may be distorted by financial guarantees from an export insurance agency, which in effect is then picking up the risk of an inefficiently diversified lending portfolio. The export insurance agency is then in danger of finding itself with an inefficiently diversified portfolio of insurance risks. The only remedy available to it is to decline further insurance and guarantees to individual countries, which the agencies do from time to time. Where a government-backed insurance and guarantee agency operates alongside commercial insurance companies, there is a risk that the commercial agencies accept only the lower risks, and the government agency is left to pick up the higher-risk business.

(d) Direct Foreign Investment (DFI)

Annex 7.2 indicated the level of net direct foreign investment going to developing countries over 1970–84. The flows have fluctuated somewhat, a

downturn in 1974 being due to disinvestment caused largely by nation-
alizations in the Middle East of foreign oil company assets. Further down-
turns occurred in both 1980 and 1983, reflecting both recession and an
increasing reluctance of western and Japanese companies to invest in the
third world. The distribution of DFI by group of country, and its importance
to the different groups is shown in Table 8.7.

Although the distribution of DFI is not complete in Table 8.7, it is clear
that least developed countries receive very little, and that almost 50% of
DFI goes to UMICs. Moreover, the LLDCs receive a very small proportion
of their external finance from DFI, but, surprisingly perhaps, the LICs were
more dependent on DFI than their wealthier relatives, the LMICs and the
UMICs. It may be misleading, though, to place much reliance on 2 years'
figures; for 1976 the author estimated the following proportion of DFI to
total financial flows:

LLDCs	LIC	LMIC	UMIC	Higher income
1	9	9	21	19

Source: Kitchen (1979a), based on OECD data.

The financial cost of DFI to developing countries is difficult to ascertain.
One tentative estimate (Kitchen, 1979a) suggests that dividend payments on
capital employed rose from about 12.5% in 1967 to over 25% in 1974. On
this basis DFI was a relatively expensive source of finance, compared with
Eurocurrency borrowing. Moreover, there are often other financial outflows
not related to profit, such as management fees and technology fees, although
these payments in principle reflect the value of services provided rather than
the cost of capital. However, it must be remembered that DFI is risk-free
investment from the point of view of the host country; that it does not entail
the debt service payments associated with debt; and that dividends are only
paid once the investment is profitable, which is at least a crude indication
of a successful investment.

Theories of Direct Foreign Investment

The traditional theory to account for international capital movements,
whether direct investment or portfolio investment, is that capital will flow
to the places where its marginal productivity (or rate of return) is highest,
assuming freedom of capital movements. The well-known diagram (Figure
8.1) illustrates that under such conditions, global output will be maximized.
The model assumes a world consisting of two countries, X and Y. The
distance O_xO_y represents the world's total capital stock, and MPK_x and MPK_y
represent the marginal productivity of capital in X and Y respectively. Under
conditions of no capital movements, assume an amount O_xQ_1 is invested in
X, and Q_1O_y is invested in Y. Total output in X is O_xABQ_1, and in Y is

Table 8.7 Distribution of DFI by type and income group of country, 1981–82 average

	All LDCs		LLDCs		China and India		Other LICs		LMICs		UMICs		Unallocated
	$bn	%	$bn	%	$bn	%	$bn	%	$bn	%	$bn	%	
Direct foreign investment	14.54	100	0.12	0.8	0.10	0.7	2.31	15.9	1.67	11.5	6.76	46.5	3.58 24.6
Percentage of total flows to country groups	14.5		1.7		3.0		15.2		11.6		16.9		17.9

Source: Derived from OECD (1984a), Table II.A.3.
Definitions: LDCs = developing countries; LLDCs = least developed countries; LICs = low-income countries; LMICs = lower middle-income countries; UMICs = upper middle-income countries; (OECD definitions).

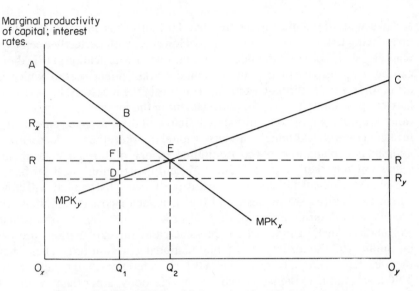

Figure 8.1 The theory of international capital movements

O_yCDQ_1. If capital movements are now permitted, capital will move until $MPK_x = MPK_y$. This occurs at E, with capital of O_xQ_2 in X and Q_2O_y in Y. (The movement may represent changes in either portfolio or physical investment or both.) Total world output is now O_xAEQ_2 (in X) plus O_yCEQ_2 (in Y). Y has lost Q_1DEQ_2, while X has gained Q_1BEQ_2. World output has increased by an amount of BED.

If the capital movement takes place in the form of DFI, the entire gain, BED, would accrue entirely to capital owners in country Y. If the capital movement takes the form of portfolio investment, say in country X bonds, then the yield on X bonds will gradually fall from R_x% to R%. Holders of the bonds in country Y then receive Q_1BEQ_2 in interest payments, leaving the same net gain as before. So far country X has received no *direct* benefit from the capital flow, although the economy may benefit from lower interest rates, increased employment, and the possible retention of earnings attributable to foreign capital. However, we have so far assumed no taxation and, typically, taxes will be levied both on bond interest and profits on DFI, ensuring that some of the net gain will be retained by the government of country X. The extent of the gain will depend on the level of tax, but investors in country Y may be able to offset the tax through double taxation agreements. The initial statement of this theory is due to McDougall (1960).

Readers of Chapter 2, which dealt with modern capital market theory, will probably by now have noted that the traditional theory outlined above is a one-parameter model of investment (the rate of return), rather than a two-parameter model (the rate of return and risk). We saw in Chapter 2 how portfolio investors can diversify risk through international investment, and we considered the argument that DFI by firms may be a means of diversifying risk for their shareholders. However, with perfectly open capital markets, shareholders can undertake their own diversification. DFI, though, can be a means of circumventing capital market imperfections which may arise, for example, through exchange controls in the investors' home country, lack of opportunity for portfolio investment in the foreign country, or restrictions on foreign portfolio investment imposed by the government of the foreign country. Although modern capital market theory does offer an additional explanation to the traditional theory of foreign investment, it seems unlikely that by itself it is a sufficient explanation of all DFI.

Since McDougall (1960) put forward the theory that capital will flow to where the returns are highest, and that it is factor cost differentials which are likely to determine the location of production, a variety of alternative explanations of DFI have arisen. In some cases the explanations are based on studies of the behaviour of multinational corporations. These newer theories have generally explained DFI by reference to the behaviour of TNCs, and to the existence of market imperfections rather than by reference to investment theory and international trade theory. Hymer (1976) and Kindleberger (1969) emphasised the TNC's control of proprietary technology among other possible monopolistic advantages. Vernon (1966) introduced the influence of considerations such as communications costs and transport costs on the location of production, and identified product standardization and the diffusion of knowledge among the monopolistic advantages of TNCs. Rugman (1979) introduced capital market theory into the subject, emphasizing (as outlined above) the TNC as a vehicle for equity diversification where international capital market imperfections and transaction costs presented barriers to direct equity investment. Rugman also discussed the gains to the TNC of transfer pricing, a topic which has been given considerable prominence in discussions of the operations of TNCs in developing countries. Buckley and Casson (1976) introduced the concept of advantages to TNCs which arise from multiplant economies and specialization, as, for example, in the motor industry. They saw the international spread of manufacturing as the least-cost solution for a vertically integrated TNC. This would not generally involve the internalization of a monopolistic advantage, which they saw as a special case, albeit an important one. Current theories of direct foreign investment may incorporate all the above explanations, but emphasis is on the transfer of non-financial and proprietary intangible assets (especially technology) by the TNC, which needs to appropriate and control the rate of use of its internalized advantages. See, for example, Black and Dunning (1982) and Casson (1983).

The authors cited have been writing primarily about DFI in industrialized countries (where most of it is located) rather than developing countries, but it is more appropriate to concentrate here on explanations of DFI in developing countries. A description of the historical growth in DFI will be a useful starting point, and the following four stages are set out in rough chronological order.

In most developing countries the initial form of DFI was in trading, followed in some by mining, especially for precious metals such as gold and silver, and precious stones. In others, investment in food and tobacco crops for export to the North also took place at the secondary stage. Examples are provided by the development of sugar estates in the Caribbean and tobacco growing in Virginia. The third stage followed from the demand in the industrialized countries for industrial minerals such as copper, and agricultural crops such as cotton or palm oil. Subsequently investments were made to permit a degree of processing of such goods prior to export. The fourth stage saw the arrival of investment to satisfy growing markets in the host country, notably the production of industrial goods as import substitution. Also in the fourth stage we can include investment in industry for export, especially in export processing zones. The process is summarized in Table 8.8. Apart from a quest for profits, which can be taken for granted, the development of trade is the dominant explanation for all the stages except 4(a). Even this form of DFI can be explained in some cases as arising from trade if the investment was made to protect an established market which was threatened by import restrictions and the possibility of an investment by a competitor. Stages 1, 2, and 3 can all be explained by the location of raw materials or factor cost differentials in production. DFI has been made with the intention of obtaining supplies of materials at lower cost than similar materials in industrialized countries, or with the aim of obtaining materials which were not available at all elsewhere. The foreign companies concerned have invested, in many cases, because of the absence of domestic investment, for whatever reason. Only in a few cases can DFI be explained by a wish to diversify and reduce risk, or by multiplant economies and gains from transfer pricing, although the latter may be a consequence, rather than an explanation, of DFI.

Table 8.8 The development of direct foreign investment in developing countries

Stage	Nature of investment
1	Trading facilities
2	(a) Mining of precious metals and stones
	(b) Food and tobacco crops
3	(a) Industrial minerals and oil
	(b) Industrial crops
4	(a) Industrial investment for the host country market
	(b) Industrial investment for export

The Pattern of Direct Foreign Investment

DFI is dominated by companies from the United States, which own nearly 50% of the $131 billion of foreign-owned assets which the OECD estimates to be located in third world countries. Other important sources of DFI are the United Kingdom, the Federal Republic of Germany, and Japan. Together these four countries supply over 75% of direct investment in developing countries. The dominance of the four leading countries as sources of DFI has tended to increase since 1970, as Table 8.9 shows, although it is now said to be declining (World Bank, 1985). There is also a small but growing contribution of DFI from third world transnationals—see Lal (1983) and Wells (1983).

There are some strong regional patterns discernible in the direction of DFI. United States companies tend to invest in Latin America, Japanese companies in the Far East and Australia. French and British companies tend to invest in their former colonies, largely in Africa, and other European companies from the Federal Republic of Germany, Holland, Spain, and Italy are also investing in Africa. DFI goes predominantly to the newly industrialized countries (NICs), which tend to receive about 50% of the total, whereas the low-income countries (LICs) receive well under 10%.

Advantages and Disadvantages of Direct Foreign Investment

From the point of view of the recipient developing country, DFI provides scarce resources of finance, technology, marketing, and management, resources which are largely lacking in many developing countries. In other

Table 8.9   Net direct investment flows from DAC countries to developing countries 1970–81: individual countries' shares (percentages)

	Shares in investment flow	
	1970–72	1979–81
United States	47.3	48.2
Germany	11.4	10.1
United Kingdom	8.6	8.9
Japan	6.1	10.9
France	5.7	7.3
Netherlands	5.6	1.8
Other	15.3	12.8
	100	100

Source: Derived from OECD (1983b).

words, DFI in many cases permits developments in industry, agriculture, and even infrastructure which the country's own resources would not permit. However, *a priori*, it is not always clear that the economic benefits outweigh the economic costs. In addition, DFI may bring with it political and social consequences which the host country government considers undesirable. It is beyond the scope of this book to discuss more than the financial questions involved, and for a wider discussion the reader is referred to detailed studies such as UNCTC (1983a,b).

From a financial point of view DFI provides an inflow of (often scarce) foreign exchange in the form of equity investment in an enterprise, and sometimes supporting loans. To the extent that indigenous equity capital is in very limited supply, foreign equity may ease investment bottlenecks in projects, especially larger projects. It is also a non-debt-creating flow, as dividends are only paid from the profits of the enterprise, and the principal can only be repatriated following the sale of the equity (or assets). If the enterprise is not profitable, then no financial outflows arise. This is in marked contrast to projects which are financed substantially by foreign loans, which have to be serviced regardless of the success of the project, and which, generally, are exposed to the risks of exchange rate and interest rate fluctuations. The debt crises of the early 1980s led to a degree of reassessment of the widely held belief that DFI was a dubious benefit to developing countries; at least it appeared in a more favourable light compared with commercial debt. Equity carries less risk than debt, from the point of view of the host country. The risk is borne by the foreign company, or its government, to the extent that the investment is insured by the foreign government.

A further advantage of foreign equity over foreign debt lies in its maturity. Commercial debt, especially, is usually medium-term, say 5–8 years, or perhaps up to 10 years. The debt service burden implied by such maturities may be too short for some projects. Equity, which does not have to be repaid in a fixed period, offers much more stable financing. A related point concerns the general desirability of the ratio of equity to debt in periods of recession; declining profits combined with high gearing (and hence high debt service) can readily lead to insolvency and bankruptcy, while a less highly geared company could survive a profits fall. The availability of equity capital, even if foreign equity, is not to be dismissed lightly. To the extent that finance is a constraint on development, it seems that the shortage of equity capital may be a greater impediment than the shortage of debt capital, a subject I return to in Chapter 10.

(e) Bank Lending

As we saw in the previous chapter, international bank lending has been a relatively recent phenomenon in developing country financing. Its rapid growth since 1970 has been funded by the Eurocurrency market, either in the form of loans by an individual bank for small sums, or in the form of syndicated credits for larger sums. The increases in the oil price in the early 1970s stimulated demand, in that oil-importing developing countries were faced with a sharp increase in their import bill, which generally they were unwilling to reduce. At the same time western banks were receiving large deposits from oil-exporting countries, which had become substantial savers. The oil price increase deepened the recession in the West, with the result that the banks' traditional borrowers were unwilling to borrow substantially. Developing country borrowers and lending banks from the West therefore naturally came together: they needed each other.

Although Annexes 7.2a and 7.2b show significant dips in bank lending in 1979, 1982 and 1984, the share of net receipts of developing countries from bank lending increased from 15% in 1970 to over 30% in 1983. Since the debt crisis first emerged in 1982, however, the pattern of bank lending has been confused. First, banks tended to cut back on new long-term lending, replacing it with short-term lending of less than 1 year maturity. The inability of many borrowers, though, to repay maturing loans and, in some cases, even to meet the interest payments, led to the rescheduling of many debts. This meant that short-term debt (that is, maturing within 1 year) was converted into longer-term debt. Thus Annex 7.2b shows $54 billion of net long-term lending in 1983, but the reality was lending of $35 billion, with a fall in short-term lending of $19 billion, as these loans were rescheduled as long-term debt.

By 1984, however, banks had become much more reluctant to lend to developing countries, and total long-term lending fell to $24 billion at 1983 prices and exchange rates. Of this, some $6 billion was accounted for rescheduled short-term debt. Although figures are not yet available, the impression is that new lending continued to be restricted during 1985. It should be noted, though, that figures for bank lending for 1983 and 1984 are more uncertain than usual, because of the statistical problems created by short-term flows and rescheduling. Indeed, there appears to be some conflict in the 1984 data between Annexes 7.2a and 7.2b.

The Impact of Bank Lending

As commercial bank finance is the most expensive source of debt capital for developing countries, the obvious effect of the change in structure of external financial flows has been to increase the overall cost of external financing. The second, less obvious, impact has been to shorten the overall maturity of external financing, as bank borrowing has generally substantially shorter maturities than development aid. The increased costs and shorter maturities resulting from commercial bank borrowings have been two factors contributing to the repayment problems experienced by several developing countries in the early 1980s, problems which in aggregate are referred to as the 'world debt crisis'. A third problem arose from the practice that bank borrowings carry variable interest rates rather than the fixed interest rates normally associated with ODA. The risk (and, indeed, the fact) of exposure to interest rate increases on existing debt meant that borrowers were from time to time faced with higher debt service costs than they might have anticipated, which again contributed to the world debt crisis. (A fourth technical factor of the crisis, the exchange rate risk, arose equally with aid, export credits, and bank borrowing.)

In spite of the problems outlined above, bank borrowing has at times appeared very attractive to developing countries, relative to other sources of funds. For project financing it has generally been possible to mobilize syndicated credits relatively quickly; the negotiating period may be 6 months or less, compared with perhaps 2 years or more for bilateral or multilateral project aid. Aid agencies usually require detailed feasibility studies, conducted according to their specific, and sometimes demanding, standards, whereas commercial banks generally pay little attention to the proposed use of credits, but look instead to guarantees, preferably from the government. Moreover bank credits, unlike much aid finance, are not tied to purchases from the country of origin, and in that sense provide better quality finance. For general balance of payments financing, developing country governments may prefer to turn to commercial banks rather than to the IMF. Again, the banks have generally been satisfied with a government guarantee, whereas the IMF attaches its well-known 'conditionality' to loans, which is often not to the taste of borrowing governments, and which might lead to considerable internal unpopularity and even civil unrest. Annex 7.2 shows that the IMF even became a net recipient of funds from developing countries in 1977 and 1978. The tightening-up by the banks on their third world funding from 1982 onwards meant that government had to turn increasingly to the IMF (and to World Bank structural adjustment loans) for balance of payments financing.

The relatively easy availability of commercial bank loans probably gave rise to considerable bad lending and bad borrowing. The easy pledging of government guarantees, and their easy acceptance, was at the root of the problem. Borrowing governments in several cases paid inadequate attention to the use of the funds, and to planning their future foreign exchange income and commitments.[4] Their problems were enhanced by declining export earnings when the recession came, and also in some cases by reported 'leakages' of foreign exchange. At the same time the much-vaunted country risk assessments of the commercial banks failed to identify countries which may run into difficulties; either that, or by the time they did identify potential difficulties the banks felt themselves so tied in that they feared a reduction in lending would imperil existing credits, and, ultimately, their own balance sheets.

Risks of Bank Loans

The risks which a national economy faces through borrowing foreign currency at variable interests have exact parallels in the risk faced by a company with similar borrowing. A deterioration in a country's balance of payments makes it more difficult to service debt. The higher the proportion of debt to exports, the higher is the economy-wide gearing. This gearing has a similar effect to high gearing in a company's balance sheet, except in this case the relevant ratios are one of debt : shareholders funds, and number of times interest is covered. Traditionally, a country's debt service : exports ratio has been regarded as safe if it is below 25%. However, sudden shifts in exports, imports, interest rates, and exchange rates can rapidly alter a country's debt service capability, even though the level of debt remains unchanged. The debt service ratio may turn out to be a false indicator, and the debt/output ratio is useful as a second indicator of indebtness. However, any debt ratio will be useless if debt estimates are substantially inaccurate, which has often been the case in recent years.

The practice of charging different interest rates to different borrowers allows the banks, in principle, to charge an interest rate adjusted for their perceptions of the risk of the loan. The usual mechanism is to charge LIBOR (London Inter-Bank Offer Rate) plus a spread. The higher the risk, the higher the spread would be. Financial journals such as *Euromoney* and the *Institutional Investor* produce league tables from time to time, ranking sovereign borrowers in order of spreads with the lowest spread at the top. Is the spread really a true indication of the perceived riskiness of the loan? It is sometimes argued that perceptions of risk may be distorted by a bank's eagerness to compete for a loan. Feder and Ross (1982) compared a subjective listing (by bankers) of countries' chances of default compiled by the *Institutional Investor* with spreads charged on 78 loan transactions to 34 countries. They found ' a systematic relation between bankers' subjective probabilities and credit terms in the Euromarket', taking into account not only the spread but also the length of maturity and the grace period. Nonetheless, the feeling remains that although spreads may explain bankers' perceptions of the *relative* risks of default, the apparently small difference in spreads between low-risk and higher-risk borrowers may not compensate for the absolute difference in the risk of default.

Patterns of Bank Borrowing

Developing country borrowing on the Eurocurrency market has been dominated by a handful of countries. According to the OECD (1983a), at the end of 1982, 20 developing countries accounted for 87% of the debt disbursed by banks to all developing countries. More striking still is the fact that the top four borrowers (Brazil, Mexico, Argentina, and Venezuela) accounted for 67% of bank debt to developing countries. The top six (adding the Republic of Korea and Chile) accounted for as much as 77%, while Brazil and Mexico together accounted for 50% of disbursed bank debt. Thus the distribution of borrowing has been highly skewed. The dominance of the large borrowers tends to obscure the fact that many smaller countries make more modest use of the Eurocurrency market. At the end of June 1982 some

58 developing countries were net debtors to the Eurocurrency market. This figure does not include a substantial number of countries who borrowed from the market, but whose deposits on the market exceeded their borrowing. These countries included India, Indonesia, and China, the three largest developing countries in terms of population. Therefore the Eurocurrency market has supplied funds to a large number of developing countries, most of whom have borrowed on a relatively modest scale.

In contrast to the heavier borrowers, who at times have found access to the market to be perhaps too easy, with banks competing strongly for loan business, the least developed countries have found access difficult or impossible. OECD (1983a, p. 61) has a list of 31 countries who obtain over 90% of their external financing in the form of ODA. These countries have virtually no access to commercial credit markets. A further 29 countries obtain over 66% of their external financing in the form of ODA. With a few exceptions (India, Jordan, and Bahrein, for example), these countries also have little access to commercial bank borrowing.

While it can generally be said that some developing countries have taken whatever opportunities were available to them to borrow on the Eurocurrency market, some have generally resisted the temptation, and others have borrowed with some reluctance. Wellons (1977) chronicled The Philippines, Indonesia, Colombia, India, Kenya, and Nigeria (at the time of writing) as 'ambivalent borrowers'. India, for example, has always had ample offers of project aid, and the government considered that Eurocredits competed with, rather than supplemented, official aid, and that commercial borrowing might merely displace the cheaper, longer-maturing official aid. China and Indonesia since 1975, also, have consistently borrowed rather less than they could have done. In both cases reluctance to borrow appears to have arisen from a fear and distrust of foreign indebtedness. This reluctance has had the beneficial effect of keeping their credit rating high, which has meant lower spreads and longer maturities when they have turned to the market.

What makes a country (or strictly speaking, a state) creditworthy in the eyes of the Eurocurrency market? The question can only be answered in the generality of indicators such as 'ability to repay' (as measured, perhaps, by the debt service ratio), growth prospects, financial stability (as indicated perhaps, by the rate of inflation), and military and political stability. Banks are generally coy about their assessments of country risk; clearly they would not want to risk offending governments by being too frank about their perception of a country's creditworthiness. The uncharitable might also suggest that in view of the perilous state of their external loans, some banks also have good reason to be coy about their methods of assessing creditworthiness, as these have obviously failed in some instances.

The developing countries, in aggregate, have played an important part in the rapid expansion of the Eurocurrency market since 1970. By mid-1984 the external positions of the BIS's 'reporting banks' were as shown in Table

8.10. The 'Total' figures include assets and liabilities *vis-à-vis* other groups of countries, and, importantly, inter-bank lending, most of which is conducted within and between the major financial centres of the world. Assets and liabilities *vis-à-vis* the developing countries are mainly with non-banks. Thus at the end of June 1984 the non-OPEC developing countries accounted for 48% of total loans to non-banks by the 'reporting banks', if we assume that all the loans to these countries were to non-banks. If loans to OPEC are included the figure rises to 64%. On the liabilities side, OPEC provided 31% of the deposits by non-banks, while total developing country deposits accounted for 61% of non-bank external deposits. These deposits are frequently the reserves of the central banks of the countries concerned.[5]

Loan Agreements: Negative Pledge and Cross-default Clauses

Discussion of the mechanics of the Eurocurrency market, and the complex legal and financial loan agreements which frequently run to 60 pages or more, are beyond the scope of this book. Interested readers are referred to Wellons (1977) , Johnston (1983), and UNCTC (1983b). It is sufficient to say that a putative borrower needs a good knowledge of these subjects, or good advice from someone who has the knowledge. There are, though, the important negative pledge and cross-default clauses which generally appear in these agreements, and which merit some explanation, if only because they will crop up again in the following chapters. The clauses have some applications in corporate financing, but are mainly associated with sovereign lending.

The negative pledge means that the borrower undertakes not to enter into any future loan agreements which give the future lender a prior claim over existing lenders. In terms of sovereign borrowing this means that a state (or state corporation) cannot, for example, enter into an agreement which gives the lenders specific security, such as the proceeds from the export of a given commodity, which can be used to repay that specific loan. Nor could the

Table 8.10 External assets and liabilities, in domestic and foreign currency, of reporting banks (billion $US; June 1985)

	OPEC	Non-OPEC Developing Countries	Latin America	Of Which Middle East	Africa	Asia	Total	Of which vis-a-vis Non-banks
Assets	104.4	332.5	211.8	15.6	19.1	86.0	2234.0	689.2
Liabilities	148.8	168.6	67.8	19.9	10.8	70.1	2203.0	502.2

Source: *International Banking and Financial Market Developments*, October 1985 (Bank for International Settlements)

borrower pledge the sales revenues of a specific project, such as an oil well. In the context of corporate financing it means that the company is not allowed to take on future debt which is senior to any existing secured debt. (The enterprise can take on further unsecured debt, though, as this would not prejudice the security of existing secured creditors. The exception is if an existing debenture agreement contains a negative covenant restricting the company from taking on additional debt, for example, without the agreement of the debenture holders.)

The negative pledge sometimes annoys sovereign borrowers as it clearly places a restraint on their future loan agreements. However, lending banks generally consider it to be a necessary provision to safeguard their future interests. A negative pledge does not act as a negative covenant, as it does not place any restrictions on the volume of future borrowing.

The cross-default clause states that a lender will consider a borrower to be in default on his loan if the borrower defaults on another loan. Thus, in the case of a sovereign borrower failing to meet a debt service payment on one loan, all the other outstanding loans will immediately be in technical default, if they carry cross-default clauses. The effect is to prevent a borrower picking out individual loans to default on; on the other hand, it may thereby give undue protection to a lender who does not honour his obligations, and from whom the borrower would be justified in withholding payments. The device has probably been most usefully employed in co-financing arrangements (see below). In this type of arrangement a multilateral agency, for example the World Bank, would finance a project alongside a commercial lender. The latter would feel well protected with a cross-default clause, for if the borrower defaulted on the commercial loan the World Bank would be obliged immediately to call a default on its loan. Developing country governments appear most reluctant to default on World Bank loans.

(f) Portfolio Investment

Bond Issues

As Annex 7.2 shows, developing countries have raised only relatively small amounts through bond issues. Bonds would in principle be a more desirable way of raising funds than syndicated Eurocurrency loans, having, usually, fixed interest rates and longer maturities.[6] Moreover, the interest rates are generally finer in the bond market.[7] However, developing country borrowers have only been able to obtain limited access to individual country bond markets, such as the USA or the UK (issues on individual markets are classed as 'foreign bonds'). The Eurobond market ('international bond' issues) has also been difficult for developing countries to tap.

The main reason for their lack of success is that the markets tend to regard developing country issues as being of low quality. This is particularly true of the Eurobond market, on which western governments, government-backed organizations, and 'blue-chip' corporations issue what is regarded as top-quality paper, with little or no risk of default. The final investor (perhaps an elusive figure) is caricatured as 'the Belgian dentist', who likes to invest in what he regards as top-quality paper giving a secure return. He is not interested in what he regards as riskier issues, even if the return in principle compensates for the extra risk. If offered, say, Malaysian government bonds, he may be inclined to ask 'where is Malaysia?', and 'why should I buy Malaysian government bonds rather than Norwegian government, Shell or World Bank bonds, all of which I *know* are safe?'. Institutional investors tend to think similarly. The Eurobond market is notably conservative.

The same caution may also prevail on national bond markets, but institutional barriers also restrict developing country borrowers. Foreign bonds are negotiable instruments, usually traded on stock exchanges, and therefore need to satisfy the requirements for stock exchange listings. In most major markets, bond issues are subject to queuing and many large institutional investors may be restricted by their articles of association or by law from investing more than a small proportion of their assets in foreign securities. Exchange controls may, of course, present insuperable barriers to foreign borrowers.

Although developing country bond issues are not impossible, they have been limited in recent years to the NICs such as Mexico and Malaysia. Moreover, the limited possibilities are likely to remain, although the growing bond markets in the Middle East may offer slightly wider opportunities to developing country bond issues. However, the lack of access afforded to individual countries may be compensated to some extent by the welcome offered to the bonds of multilateral agencies such as the World Bank, the regional development banks, and the European Investment Bank.[8] These development banks effectively have the backing of nearly all the major western governments, and therefore enjoy the highest possible credit rating. Although the banks add a margin to the interest rate, it is generally the case that developing countries get longer maturities and finer interest rates by tapping the bond markets through the intermediation of multilateral financial institutions/(MFIs) than most could possibly hope for by borrowing directly. Of course, in addition to acting as intermediaries the multilateral banks impose their own lending constraints, which means that the ultimate developing country borrowers do not have freedom of use of the funds, which some may regard as drawback to this form of access to bank markets. By way of compensation, the MFIs do transform maturities by making very long loans to borrowing countries.

Equity Investment

The purchase of shares on third world stock markets by industrialized country investors as a means of risk reduction through international diversification was discussed in Chapter 2. Although statistical evidence is scarce, the volume of such financial flows is clearly small, and limited to a few countries in Latin America and East Asia. Direct investments are generally restricted to unit trusts and investment trusts, since pension funds and life insurance companies are limited by caution, their articles of association or, in some countries, by law from undertaking such investments. Active attempts by third world countries to market their equities are few in number, but the Mexico Fund provides an interesting exception. This is a closed-ended fund, quoted on the London and New York stock exchanges, which invests in Mexican equities. A similar Korean Fund has also been launched.

A further alternative is to obtain listings for developing country companies' shares on industrialized country stock markets. Of course, the firms concerned have to meet the fairly demanding standards and disclosure requirements of the market regulators, which may be a substantial obstacle. However a few Mexican and Philippino firms have market quotations in New York, and Malaysia's Telekom is likely to apply for Singapore and London listings as part of its privatization process, if only because the domestic market in Malaysia is too small to absorb it.

An interesting concept in equity investment is what has become known as venture banking. It involves a foreign commercial bank (or venture capital company) taking an equity stake in a third world company, often alongside a contribution of loan capital. This may be done by
— direct equity participation;
— the conversion of existing debt to equity, usually when companies are in difficulties;
— indirectly supplying funds (equity or debt) to an intermediary such as a development bank or holding company, which then takes an equity stake in the target firm;
— the bank acting as a broker, and finding a firm to put in equity alongside the bank's credit.
The idea of such portfolio investment may appeal to some banks, notably European universal banks or industrial country DFCs, both of which have experience of equity investment, and which may want to avoid further straight debt exposure to a country (or company). The use of convertible loan stocks would offer a halfway house between debt and equity. Little information is available about the few schemes of venture banking which have been implemented. Wellons (1983), however, has chronicled the case of Grupo Pliana in Mexico, in which the Bank of America took a shareholding. Until 1981 the scheme was very successful, but the subsequent collapse of the Mexican economy left the company in considerable difficulties, and its shareholders with substantial paper losses.

(g) Other Sources of Private Sector Finance

Leasing

This is a relatively recent development in providing capital equipment for projects. As with countertrade arrangements, it is a substitute for long-term finance rather than finance itself. However, it can provide a useful alternative to a country whose debt service ratio is uncomfortably high, and which would have difficulty in raising conventional commercial finance; international leasing obligations do not appear in the debt service ratio. Likewise it may provide companies with a source of off-balance sheet finance, if accounting regulations permit leasing to be treated in that way. It may also be attractive for both international and domestic commercial banks to lease imported equipment through their leasing subsidies rather than provide a conventional loan. They remain the owners of the equipment, and if payments fail they can, in principle, claim the equipment. Leasing provides them with direct security. Islamic financial institutions also use leasing rather than lending so as to avoid charging interest. The Islamic Development Bank, for example, has for some years provided international leasing facilities, whereby it purchases the capital goods for a project, and then leases them to a project.

Co-financing

In the true sense of the term, co-financing involves two or more financing agencies combining to produce a package which results in an improvement in the volume, cost, or maturity of the financing of a project. (It should not be confused with joint financing, which simply means that two or more organizations provide finance for a project.) The World Bank has taken the lead in co-financing. It sets out to attract commercial finance alongside its own, with a view to increasing the volume of commercial finance, and improving its terms. Co-financing has operated for a number of years with the World Bank supplying its own funds alongside commercial bank funds. The latter would be attracted by the arrangement of, for example, cross-default clauses which means the commercial banks enjoy similar protection from default as the World Bank. The programme was stepped up in 1983 by three new approaches to co-financing.

— The Bank would participate in a commercial loan, perhaps to the extent of 15–20% of the total amount. The Bank would accept the later repayments, thereby effectively extending the maturity of the loan.
— The Bank would guarantee the later maturities of a commercial bank loan, instead of participating directly. Again, the effect would be to extend the maturities.
— The Bank would offer contingent participation in the later maturities of a commercial loan. Under this arrangement the bank would guarantee a fixed ceiling on debt service. If interest rates rise, then the maturity of the loan would be extended beyond its original time schedule. The Bank would then pick up any payments beyond the original termination date.

Some successful examples of the use of these techniques are given in the World Bank's 1984 Annual Report. (The new methods of co-financing are referred to as 'B-loans'.) Co-financing enables the World Bank to use its reputation, especially in the field of project appraisal, to attract increased commercial flows on improved overall terms. Its own finances are spread more thinly, enabling it to finance an increased number of projects. The commercial banks enjoy reduced risk as a result of co-financing.

(h) Concluding Remarks

The predominance of debt in the external financing of developing countries has increased steadily since 1970, and the costs of the debt have tended to increase. Debt carries risk for the borrower which non-debt finance does not. However, the balance of risk is not entirely weighted in favour of the lender, as was thought a few years ago. The commercial banks involved in third world lending have discovered that their balance sheets are exposed to the risk that borrowers cannot, or will not, service their debts on schedule. The next chapter will examine the growth and incidence of third world debt, but it is important to realize that the bulk of the risk remains with the borrowers. In spite of rescheduling they still have regular interest payments to meet, and the principal is still outstanding. The final chapter will consider, among other things, some proposals to reduce and to redistribute the risk in the external financing of developing countries.

NOTES

1. Poyais is the well-known mythical country. A Scot, Gregor MacGregor, set himself up as the 'Cazique of Poyais', a Kingdom he claimed was on the mosquito coast of Central America, and raised £160,000 on the strength of it. Of course, bond-holders lost their money, as they did with most of the other loans raised by Latin American countries over 1822–25. In a recent witty reconstruction we have the following conversation.

   'So what was so different about Poyais?'
   'It was not there. It never had existed. Investment protection committees, deputations of bond-holders, went out to look for it, only to land on the Caribbean coast, where the Mosquito Indians ate them. MacGregor was on good terms with the Mosquitos. In many ways, the ideal sovereign risk.'
   'But if the real borrowers never paid, either, why did it matter that Poyais was imaginary?'
   'I supposed it did not matter, except that it seemed to hurt more, at the time.'

   Christopher Fieldes, 'The Moorgate Saga', Euromoney, January 1983, p. 144.
2. The contractural and financial arrangements for countertrade deals are complex. The interested reader is referred to Outters-Jaeger (1979); 'North/South countertrade' (Economist Intelligence Unit, 1984) or to the countertrade supplement in The Financial Times of 6 February 1985.
3. Walsh (1983) lists numerous examples of governmental intercessions in countertrade arrangements. Among these are:

   Argentina (auto parts), Ecuador (imports of alcoholic beverages to be paid for with bananas), Indonesia (government and Pertamina imports to be matched by counterpurchases), Korea (auto component imports to be paid for with auto exports), Uruguay (imports of autos must be matched by exports of autos to 105% of import value). Pakistan, Algeria, Iran, Libya, and Nigeria require that certain products, notably oil exports, are subject to counterpurchase arrangements, while Bangladesh, India, and New Zeland have import entitlement regimes for their manufacturers who export. Brazil and Israel operate informal schemes. France, Germany, and Japan are three industrialized countries mentioned as being involved in buy-back deals.

Further information is contained in OECD (1985b).

4. A recent study of debt management by the IMF, reported in World Bank (1985), found that only four countries out of 20 studied managed their debt systematically. The same source gives details of debt management in The Philippines, where debt service in 1 year must not exceed 20% of foreign exchange receipts (including capital inflows) in the previous year. Thailand, too, is introducing the comprehensive vetting of public sector borrowing. However, even in countries where public sector borrowing is vetted by governments, private sector borrowing is not subject to the same scrutiny; only in 1982, for example, did Mexico require that private foreign debt be registered, but by then the damage had been done.

5. It is interesting to note the magnitude of the deposits of $122 billion made by non-OPEC developing countries with the international banks. The net debt to the banking system at the end of June 1984 was $143.2 billion for the non-OPEC developing countries. The deposits in many cases represent a use of reserves. As the detailed BIS statistics show, few countries are lenders or borrowers only; most countries both lend and borrow in parallel. The deposits of non-OPEC developing countries appear to be ignored by some debt statistics, thus exaggerating the net indebtedness.

6. Industrial country borrowers have tended to replace syndicated Eurocurrency loans with floating rate notes (FRNs) recently. FRNs have some of the characteristics of bonds, being negotiable instruments, but, as the name suggests, carry the variable interest rates usually associated with loans. They are available to top-quality third world borrowers. For example, early in 1985 the Korean Development Bank issues $100 million 15-year FRN at $\frac{3}{8}$% over LIBOR. Thailand, and the Electricity and Petroleum Authorities of Thailand, all issued 20-year FRNs at $\frac{1}{8}$% over 6-month LIBOR. The Syndicated Note Insurance Facility (which carries the unappealing acronym SNIF) has also replaced the syndicated loan for top quality borrowers. SNIFs involve the continuous issuance (and refinancing) of short-term negotiable paper and are cheaper than syndicated credits. SNIFs have spread to the corporate market, and now also to sovereign borrowers such as Portugal or Turkey. The traditional syndicated loan may before long become an instrument used by medium-rated developing country borrowers only.

7. For example, early in 1985 the Korean Exchange Bank launched a $600 million 9-year credit at $\frac{3}{8}$% over LIBOR for the first 3 years and $\frac{3}{4}$% thereafter. This is markedly more expensive than the Korean Development Bank's FRN mentioned in Note 3.

8. Some bilateral agencies also tap the market. For example, the Caisse Centrale de Coopération Economique, the French government-owned development bank, raised $200 million early in 1985 through a 20-year floating rate note, at $\frac{1}{8}$% spread above the mean of London interbank bid and offer rates, known as Limean.

Chapter 9

Debt, Adjustment, and the IMF

1. CURRENT ACCOUNTS AND CAPITAL ACCOUNTS

In discussing economic instability it is usual to distinguish between external disequilibrium, which generally means a balance of payments deficit, and internal disequilibrium, which generally refers to price inflation, but which may also embrace other variables such as excesses or deficiences in aggregate demand, or rising unemployment. Frequently a number of symptoms of disequilibrium will be encountered simultaneously. This chapter will be concerned mainly with external disequilibrium, external debt, debt rescheduling, and the role of the IMF in implementing stabilization policies.

External disequilibrium arises initially from a deficit on the current account. The current account is given by

Current account = Exports − Imports − Net factor payments abroad.

A fall in the current account of the balance of payments may arise from a fall in exports, a rise in imports, or a rise in factor payments. The latter are largely interest payments on outstanding external debt, and also dividends. A deficit on the current account must, by definition, be balanced by a surplus on the capital account, which is given by

Capital account = Reduction in reserves + Grants + New borrowing + Other capital inflows − Repayment of principal on debt − Other capital outflows.

Typically a current account deficit will be balanced by a fall in reserves and/or by an increase in net new borrowing. Other capital inflows are receipts of direct investment, repatriated earnings, and portfolio investment inflows, while other capital outflows consist of debt repayment, portfolio investment abroad, and direct investment abroad. In the last chapter we discussed in detail the principal elements of capital inflows to developing countries. However, the heavy dependence on borrowing since 1973, and the increasing proportion of debt on market terms, with its higher interest charges, has given rise to a substantial growth in external debt. The aggregate figures for external debt of developing countries are given in Annexes 9.1–9.4.

2. THE GROWTH OF DEBT

(a) Statistical Analysis of Debt

Annexes 9.1–9.4 need little further elaboration. They illustrate conclusively the rapid increase in debt, especially debt arising from commercial bank loans; the corresponding build-up in debt service (which fell in 1983 only because some debtor countries were unable to meet their obligations); the rising interest cost on debt, especially floating rate debt, whose interest rates rose from 8.4% in 1978 to 12.7% in 1983; and finally the net long- and short-term indebtedness of developing countries, which is still very substantial ($410 billion) even after allowing for their offsetting external assets ($153 billion). The OECD figures given may be underestimates. The World Bank (1985) pulled together the various sources of data on debt, and estimated that by 1984 gross debt of developing countries reached $895 billion, of which $717 billion was long-term, compared with long-term debt of $658 billion in 1983. (The OECD figure for gross long-term debt at the end of 1983 was $606 billion.)

However, the distribution of the debt is highly skewed. At the end of 1983 the four largest debtors, Brazil ($80.6 billion), Mexico ($70 billion), Argentina ($29.5 billion), and South Korea ($22 billion, end 1982) accounted for over one-third of total developing country gross long-term debt of $606 billion. The problems of Brazil, Mexico, and Argentina, and the attempts to resolve them, have received wide publicity; it is interesting to note that South Korea appears to have managed its debt successfully, as Table 9.1 shows.

Table 9.1 Total gross interest payments as percentages of total exports of goods and services

	1978	1981	1982	1983	(1984)[a]
Non-OPEC, non-OECD developing countries	8	13	17	15	14
Four largest debtors					
Brazil	24	39	50	39	40
Mexico	20	26	31	31	35
Argentina	11	34	52	42	44
South Korea	6	14	14	14	13
All others	6	8	10	9	8

[a] 1984 figures are conjectural, and make no allowance for possible payment of substantial interest arrears outstanding.
Source: OECD (1984b)

In addition these four countries had gross short-term debt of a further $51 billion outstanding at the end of 1983. They are the countries most exposed to commercial lending at floating interest rates, and with substantial short-term debt. However, concentration on a few larger debtor countries should not obscure the fact that many smaller debtor countries also face extreme difficulties. Debt statistics for developing countries, collectively and individually, have been thoroughly analysed elsewhere (OECD, 1984b; Commonwealth Secretariat, 1984; World Bank, 1985) so we will concentrate here on explanations, consequences, and solutions. However, it must be pointed out that the countries whose debt problems have received most publicity are not always the most intractable cases. Table 9.2 shows that the burden of debt is much greater in many smaller countries, notably several in Africa. Although the absolute debt ratios vary depending on the data sources and exchange rates used the relative positions will stay the same. At the end of 1982 the debt service ratio (i.e. debt service/exports) in several countries was rather higher than in Argentina, Brazil, or Mexico, as was the ratio of debt/GNP, perhaps the better indicator of likely future difficulties. Moreover, Argentina, Brazil, and Mexico probably have better prospects of growth and exports than many of the other countries. However, the potential threat that the large debtors posed to the commercial banking system meant that their problems received rather more publicity than the smaller debtors. The latter, though, are often heavily indebted to the IMF, and the possibility of defaults to the IMF is growing. The IMF is not permitted to reschedule its loans, so other ways of helping defaulters would be needed, such as extending more bilateral aid, or World Bank structural adjustment loans.

(b) Explanations of the Debt Problem

It is facile to say that the debt problem has arisen because countries borrowed unwisely and lenders lent unwisely during the 1970s, and that the problems which arose were purely the result of the 'unwise' borrowing and lending. Both borrowers and lenders usually made projections of the economic growth and trade of borrowing countries and saw that the expected debt service ratios looked tenable. What they did not take into account was the risks faced by developing country borrowers, and the impact that risk would have on their economic performance and financial position. I will examine in turn the systematic risk, specific risk, interest rate risk, exchange rate risk, and terms of trade risk which the borrowers faced.

Systematic (or Market) Risk

Table 9.3 shows changes in GDP, export volume, and terms of trade for the more important groups of developing countries. From 1978 growth in GDP started falling, taking all developing countries together, and over 1981–83 growth rates averaged less than 2% per year. As population growth was

Table 9.2 Debt ratios of selected countries (percentages)

	External debt/GDP (end 1982)	External debt service/Exports (1982)
Argentina	42	38
Brazil	29	39
Korea	32	21
Mexico	35	54
Bolivia	38[a]	37
Chile	56	53
Costa Rica	103	18
Egypt	63	81
Israel	44	29
Ivory Coast	69	54
Jamaica	56	35
Kenya	47	28
Mauritania	157	21
Morocco	66	74
Nicaragua	90	74
Peru	39	49
Philippines	30	37
Senegal	35	54
Sudan	52	20
Tanzania	44	27
Togo	101	20
Tunisia	53	27
Yugoslavia	21	35
Zaire	78	27
Zambia	69	18

[a] 1981 GDP.

Note: Short-term debt is excluded, as is military debt financed by official credits, and debt to the IMF.

Sources: Debt and debt service: OECD, *External Debt of Developing Countries* (1984); GDP: World Bank, *World Development Report* (1984); Exports: IMF, *International Financial Statistics*, December 1984.

somewhat larger, real incomes per head fell in these years. The decline was most noticeable in fuel-exporting countries, but the capital surplus oil-exporters, generally speaking, had adequate reserves and little debt, and were able to absorb the shock. Others, such as Nigeria and Venezuela, faced substantial problems with debt service. The decline in these countries came about as a result of declining oil export values from 1982 onwards, as can be seen from part (b) of Table 9.3

By region, declines in output growth were most conspicuous in the western hemisphere, which as a whole experienced absolute declines in output in 1982 and 1983, following only insignificant growth in 1981. By contrast Asian countries managed to maintain steady and considerable growth throughout

Table 9.3 Indicators of systematic risk: changes from preceding years (percentages)

Developing countries	Average 1967–76[b]	1977	1978	1979	1980	1981	1982	1983	1984
Growth in Real GDP[a]									
All developing countries	6.0	5.8	5.3	4.5	3.4	2.4	1.6	1.5	3.7
Fuel-exporters	8.1	5.7	2.9	3.7	1.0	1.2	-0.2	-0.8	2.0
Non-fuel-exporters	5.3	5.9	6.3	4.8	4.3	3.0	2.5	2.7	4.4
Africa	5.0	4.3	1.4	4.2	3.7	0.9	0.1	-0.2	2.2
Asia	5.2	7.2	9.4	4.8	4.7	5.8	5.1	7.1	6.4
Middle East	9.3	6.9	1.9	1.8	-1.8	-0.7	0.3	0.6	2.3
Western hemisphere	5.9	5.3	4.1	6.1	5.3	1.0	-1.0	-3.1	2.4
Countries with recent debt service difficulties	5.5	5.4	3.7	5.3	3.9	1.1	-0.1	-1.9	2.0
Export volume									
All developing countries	6.0	2.5	3.9	5.4	-2.6	-4.0	-7.2	0.9	8.0
Fuel-exporters	5.3	1.0	-1.9	2.0	-10.9	-12.6	-15.1	-5.7	2.5
Non-fuel-exporters	6.8	4.0	9.4	9.0	9.0	7.0	1.0	6.2	12.0
Terms of trade									
All developing countries	4.1	3.7	-6.7	10.8	15.2	1.2	-1.7	-2.1	0.3
Fuel-exporters	11.4	1.0	-9.7	26.9	40.4	8.5	-1.1	-7.5	0.1
Non-fuel-exporters	-0.6	6.2	-4.1	-1.6	-5.7	-5.5	-2.2	2.4	0.6
Industrial countries									
Change in real GNP[c]	3.7	4.0	4.1	3.5	1.3	1.6	-0.2	2.6	4.9
Export volume	8.0	5.1	5.7	7.1	3.7	3.4	-2.2	2.4	9.9
Terms of trade	-0.9	-1.4	3.0	-3.0	-6.8	-2.1	1.8	2.0	-0.2

[a] Arithmetic average of country growth rates weighted by the average US dollar value of GDPs over the preceding 3 years.
[b] Compound annual rates of change. Excludes China.
[c] Composites for the country groups are averages of percentage changes for individual countries weighted by the average US dollar value of their respective GNPs over the preceding 3 years.
For country groups definitions, see Note 1 to Chapter 7.
Source: Derived from IMF Annual Report 1985.

the recession, although African countries experienced low growth rates. The export volume of non-fuel-exporters fell heavily in 1982, and their terms of trade fell in each year from 1978 to 1982.

The fuel-exporting countries experienced sharp falls in export volumes following the high increases in oil prices over 1979–81. Since 1982, though, their export earnings were reduced by oil price falls.

In the industrialized countries, growth in GNP was lower over 1980–83 than it had been in earlier years, being about one-third of the earlier growth rates. The impact of the recession was greater, though, in the developing countries, where growth rates were about one-quarter of the growth rates of earlier years. Moreover, the recession in the developing countries probably lagged about a year behind that in the industrialized countries, and growth in 1984 was slower in the former. The conclusion is that developing countries suffered declining growth and export earnings to a more marked extent than did the industrialized countries. In capital market theory terms the developing economies are more volatile than the industrialized economies, in other words they have a higher 'β value' relative to the world economy than do the industrialized countries.

The downturn in growth and exports undoubtedly affected their ability to service debts, just as a downturn in earnings affects the ability of a highly geared company to service its debts. High debt would merely have the effect of increasing the β value of a country. Taken as a whole, developing countries were adversely affected by systematic risk over 1980–84. By contrast in earlier years, they had benefited from it, experiencing rather higher growth rates in output than had the industrialized countries.

It is likely that those involved in lending and borrowing failed to take systematic risk into account. Their projections of future debt service ability were probably based on a continuation of the relatively high historic rates of growth that many developing countries had enjoyed throughout the 1960s and most of the 1970s, although the impact of the first oil price increases of 1972–73 should have indicated the high systematic risk to which developing countries were exposed. It is of course a matter for conjecture what growth rates were predicted by borrowers and lenders for individual countries. The growth rates incorporated in national plans may give a guide, but from the borrowers' point of view use of such growth rates in such an important practice as external borrowing would come dangerously close to believing one's own propaganda.

Specific Risk

The volatility of GDP in developing countries generally, leading to high systematic risk, is exacerbated in some countries by high specific risk. This usually arises with undiversified economies which depend on exports of a narrow range of commodities. The world prices of many commodities are extremely volatile, and changes in industrial production, agricultural production, or protective legislation in consuming countries, or an expansion of production of the commodity in other countries, can have a severe effect on an exporter's foreign exchange earnings, and therefore on its debt service capacity. The impact of specific risk may coincide with the cyclical impact of systematic risk; indeed, the response to economic recession in industrialized countries may result in increased protection. Alternatively, specific risk may result from the long-run secular decline in the real price of the commodities on world markets, and therefore may be experienced even in times of rapid world economic growth. Specific risk is readily identifiable; it arises in countries dominated by one or two major activities, and which therefore have not diversified away their specific risk. The risk should be obvious to external lenders such as commercial banks, and exists, however promising the commodity on which a country depends. For example, oil- and gold-producers have experienced substantial price falls in recent years in dollar terms. In discussions of the adjustment process some writers emphasize the need to take into account the long-run structural changes which economies face (e.g. W. A. Lewis, 1978). A structural deterioration in a country's economy is the same thing as suffering adversely from specific risk. Unfortunately the remedy of diversification, which is available to stock market investors and to some countries, is simply not available to other countries in the foreseeable future.

A further cause of specific risk lies in the quality of the economic management of the countries; this is a factor which is currently emphasized by the IMF, the World Bank, and increasingly by bilateral aid agencies in their negotiations with developing country governments. Two different types of problem of economic management can be identified. The first is incompetent management brought about through inexperience, lack of understanding, lack of information, and inability to take and implement decisions on the part of politicians and civil servants; at the extreme it becomes dishonest economic management. The second can be broadly described as the use of inappropriate policies. What is 'inappropriate', of course, depends on one's political, economic, and social objectives. In the view of the financial institutions and aid donors of the North, they are usually taken to mean direct controls on trade and production, and controls on prices, interest rates, and exchange rates which 'distort' economies, and lead to mis-allocation of resources and depressed economic activity. At the extreme they mean extensive state involvement in the economy at the expense of the private sector.

Clearly any country is likely to be exposed to both systematic and specific risk. The former clearly is a consequence of external factors, namely economic growth in the rest of the world and particularly in the industrialized countries. With the occasional exception, developing countries can have no influence on this. Specific risk may also be exogenously determined or brought about through internal factors. The ability of a country to adjust to the consequences of specific risk will depend upon the source of the risk, and in general the mix of causes of external disequilibrium is different in each country.

Interest Rate Risk

Annex 9.4 shows the nominal interest cost of debt to developing countries over the period 1972–83. The highest interest rates, and the most volatile, have been those on floating interest debt, typically commercial bank credits. This debt is denominated in a variety of currencies but about 55% is in US dollars. Table 9.4 compares the nominal cost of debt with the US inflation rate and arrives at an estimate of the real cost of debt, for that part which is in US dollars. The cost of floating interest debt has been calculated taking annual interest payments and other charges (including fees) as a percentage of disbursed debt at the beginning of the year.[1] The steady increase in real interest costs to 1982 represented a substantial real increase in interest payments to developing countries, and a real transfer of resources from borrower to lender. The real interest cost became substantially greater than the real growth rates in national income, which tended to decline in the

Table 9.4   Nominal and real interest costs to developing countries, 1972–83

	1972 /73	1974 /76	1977 /78	1979	1980	1981	1982	1983
Cost of floating interest debt[a]	8.3	9.9	8.4	12.3	15.5	17.4	17.1	12.7
US GNP deflator[b]	5.7[c]	7.7	6.6	8.7	9.2	9.4	6.0	4.2
Real cost of floating interest debt[d]	2.5	2.0	1.7	3.3	5.8	7.3	10.5	8.5

[a] *Source*: Annex 9.3
[b] *Source*: IMF Annual Reports, 1980 and 1984.
[c] 1973.
[d] Real interest rate $= (1+i)/(1+r)-1$, where i = nominal interest rate and r = inflation rate.

1980s. This real increase in interest rates to very high historical levels is clearly a factor which borrowing countries cannot influence; nor can they be held in any way responsible for it. They are exposed to a risk which is quite beyond their control. Even prudent borrowers, who borrow little relative to export earnings because of their awareness of the risks of gearing and adverse interest rate and exchange rate fluctuations, would have received an unpleasant shock from the magnitude of the real interest rate increases.

Exchange Rate Risk

A debtor country is exposed to the risk that the currencies in which its debt is denominated may strengthen relative to its own currency, or relative to the currencies in which its major exports are traded. The impact will be to make both the interest and principal more difficult to repay. The exposure to exchange rate risk is well illustrated by the estimates of OECD (1984b) that over 1981–83 about 55% of developing country long-term debt was denominated in US dollars, and that 70–80% of short-term debt may be in US dollars. The strong rise in the US dollar over 1981–84 is estimated by the same source to have resulted in a repression of the figures of outstanding long-term debt of about $84 billion. If exchange rates had remained constant since 1980 the reported outstanding long-term debt at the end of 1983 would have been $690 billion rather than $606 billion, the non-dollar debt having been reduced in dollar terms. The difference represents an understatement of the true repayment problem faced by debtor countries, in that they have to export more to earn the same number of dollars than before the appreciation of the dollar. (The only exceptions to this rule are countries whose exports are priced in dollars and whose currency is tied to the dollar; Liberia and Panama have probably suffered least from exchange rate risk.)

Terms of Trade Risk

Generally speaking, developing countries are still exporters of commodities and importers of manufactured goods. Should the unit price of developing country imports increase relative to their exports, then for a given volume of trade their balance of trade will deteriorate, resulting in a smaller surplus with which to meet debt servicing payments, or an increased deficit which requires additional borrowing to finance it. An adverse movement in the terms of trade may occur independently of any shift in exchange rates; it is quite a separate problem. Of course, shifts in relative prices of imports and exports will also affect the volume of trade. The magnitude of the effects will depend on the price elasticities of demand for imports and exports, and, given the right elasticities, a fall in export prices relative to import prices may lead to an improvement in the balance of trade. Table 9.3 shows changes in the terms of trade in recent years.

If changes in the terms of trade of all developing countries are compared with those of the industrialized countries, the developing countries have tended to enjoy shifts in their favour. However, sharp increases in oil prices, notably in 1979 and 1980, distort the underlying picture, as the industrialized countries on balance import oil from the developing countries. Non-fuel-exporters also import oil, and this group of countries have experienced deteriorating terms of trade in most years.

The impact of the terms of trade on the balance of trade is likely to have been adverse for most developing countries. In many cases they are unable to expand the volume of exports sufficiently in response to any relative fall in prices. Indeed, if the worsening terms of trade represents a weak world market, exports may fall in volume as well as in unit price. Conversely, imports may in many cases be 'essential', and it may be difficult to reduce their volume in response to a relative price increase. As the former prime minister of Jamaica, Michael Manley, was fond of saying, a deterioration in the terms of trade means that developing countries must export more bananas than before in order to buy one tractor.

Summary of Effects of Risk

It is clearly difficult to quantify the impact of the different risks to which developing countries have been exposed. An attempt to estimate some of the effects has been made by Cline (1984), as shown in Table 9.5. Using Cline's definitions, debt of non-oil developing countries increased by $482 billion over 1973–82, so in his calculations the above external factors could be held responsible for over 80% of the increase in indebtedness. The calculations are on an ex-ante basis, and so are not strictly comparable with the ex-post debt figures, as governments did to some extent pursue adjustment measures to reduce balance of payments deficits, and debt, from what they otherwise would have been. Therefore Cline's figures may exaggerate the contribution of external factors to total debt build-up. Indeed, it could be argued that it was the *failure* of governments to respond appropriately to external shocks that led to the increase in debt. However, Cline's estimates do indicate the magnitude of the shocks which developing countries experienced.

The possibility alluded to in the previous paragraph, that developing country governments contributed to the debt build-up by their failure to adjust to increasing external problems, cannot readily be dismissed. The debt problem has been building up since the early 1970s, but really became a major problem following the second round of oil price increases in 1979–

Table 9.5 Impact of exogenous shocks on external debt of non-oil developing countries

Effect	Amount (billion $s)
Oil price increase in excess of US inflation, 1974–82 cumulative[a]	260
Real interest rate in excess of 1961–80 average: 1981 and 1982	41
Terms of trade loss, 1981–82	72
Export volume loss caused by world recession, 1981–82	21
Total	401

[a] Net oil importers only
Source: Cline (1984), p. 13.

80 and the subsequent global recession. The coincident change in policies in several industrialized countries which restricted monetary growth with the object of controlling inflation led to high real interest rates, a strong dollar, and a further deepening of the recession. The adverse impact of these measures on developing countries has been outlined above. How did they react to the adverse external circumstances?

There was, of course, a surge in borrowing, especially from commercial banks, in 1981 and early 1982. Commercial borrowing had enabled developing country governments to overcome the difficulties brought about by the first round of oil price increases, so why should it not work again? Why go to the IMF, and be faced with its unpopular conditions, except as a last resort? The difference was that this time all the external risks were simultaneously acting adversely on developing countries, which had not been the case earlier. In particular the low real interest rates in the mid-1970s had made debt easy to service. Moreover, in the 1980s the recession in the North was deeper than previously, which, through systematic risk, affected growth and export earnings from developing countries more seriously than before. Developing countries and the lending banks may have lacked the foresight to see the consequences of further borrowing, but they were not alone in this. Moreover, the alternative of adjustment through restricting imports would have led to a contraction of their economies, a further deepening of the world recession, and the consequent severe social problems which of course were encountered subsequently in many countries when effective adjustment finally was made. However, it is not true that debtor countries did not attempt to adjust in 1980 and 1981. Cline (1984) chronicles the (generally unwise) efforts made by Brazil and Argentina in 1981. The other two major debtors, Mexico and Venezuela, had of course benefited from oil price increases and it was not until after the decline in oil prices in 1982 that their problems were exposed. Balassa (1984) has pointed out that outward-oriented economies, which used output-increasing policies of export promotion and import substitution to offset external shocks, fared better than inward-oriented economies. The latter tended to rely on increased foreign borrowing, but were eventually forced to take deflationary measures as their increased indebtedness restricted further borrowing. That some adjustment attempts were unwise and unsuccessful was unfortunate; however, developing countries do not have a monopoly of ill-advised macroeconomic management.

(c)   The Impact of Debt on the Commercial Banks

In order to appreciate fully the subsequent steps advocated and taken to neutralize the debt crisis, it is necessary to examine the impact of developing country (and East European) debt on the commercial banks which had lent heavily. Following the major oil price increases in 1973–74 and 1979–80, the commercial banks had carried out the bulk of the recycling of oil surpluses, which had maintained the continuity of international liquidity and trade. Some banks had, as a result, built up substantial loan exposure to a number of developing and Eastern European countries. By the end of 1982 the exposure of the nine largest US banks to non-oil developing countries amounted to 221% of their capital, compared with 163% in 1977. The equivalent figures for Eastern Europe were 14% and 25%. In 1982 exposure to Brazil and Mexico combined amounted to 90% of the capital of the nine banks, compared with 75% in 1977. The loans, though high in relation to bank capital, still represented only 14% of the total assets (i.e. loans) of the nine banks (data from Cline, 1984).

Although this last figure sounds more reassuring, certain banks were heavily exposed to certain countries and groups of countries which were considered to be high default risks. Manufacturers Hanover, for example, had an exposure to Argentina, Brazil, Mexico, Venezuela, and Chile which represented 263% of its capital. The ill-starred Crocker National Bank had an exposure of 196% to the same countries, and Citibank 175%. Continental Illinois, subsequently the subject of a rescue package, had a relatively modest exposure to these countries of 107% of total capital. The exposure to high-risk developing countries[2] was compounded by the shakiness of a substantial part of the banks' domestic loan portfolio. Oil, real estate, and, later, agricultural loans, were the main sectors which had difficulty in meeting loan repayments, and whose asset values (and, therefore, banks' security) were declining sharply. European banks were also exposed to developing country risk, but not usually to the same extent as the US banks, whose 'traditional' developing country lending area of Latin America contained most of the high-debt, high-risk countries. However, some European banks, especially the German banks, had substantial exposure to Poland and other East European countries.

The fear in the industrialized countries was that inability or unwillingness to service debts on the part of developing country borrowers would lead to a lack of liquidity and collapse of confidence in one or more major banks, leading in turn to a run on the banks' deposits. If one major bank failed, then a domino effect would lead to the collapse of other banks, and with them a collapse of international financial mechanisms and world trade. Governments of the major industrialized countries, and the international financial institutions, were much concerned to prevent such an occurrence. It was generally understood in the UK that the Bank of England would not permit the collapse of one of the big four clearing banks, and following the rescue of Continental Illinois in June 1984 the US Federal Reserve announced that it would not allow the collapse of a major money centre bank. Nonetheless, in 1983, 48 US banks did fail, the highest annual figure since the 1930s depression, but which in turn was exceeded by 79 failures in 1984. The reasons for most of these failures, including Continental Illinois, were mainly domestic in origin, but they serve to underline the fragility of the US banking system. They also raise doubts about the overall quality of bank management in the USA.

By August 1982 Mexico could no longer meet its principal repayments. By the end of 1982 it had become clear that other major debtor countries, notably Brazil and Argentina, were having great difficulty even in meeting interest payments on their debt. The industrialized country governments, notably the US government, and the IMF were by then involved in organizing new loan packages, not for capital investment but merely to enable these countries to meet interest payments on outstanding debt.[3] In January 1983 Brazil, Rumania, and Cuba had all announced to the banks and to the world at large that they were halting repayments of principal on medium- and long-term loans which were about to fall due. The object now became one of rescheduling existing debt, and ensuring that debtor countries had adequate liquidity to meet interest payments, so that the loans did not become 'non-performing' in US law, which would require banks to write off the loans in their accounts, thereby weakening their balance sheets and depositor confidence.

3. DEBT RESCHEDULING

Although attention has been concentrated so far on commercial bank debt, it represents only one leg of developing country debt, if perhaps the largest and most expensive form of debt. The other two legs are ODA and official debt (non-concessional government and multilateral lending, and official export credits.) All three contribute to the debt service problems of developing countries, and all three have been subject to rescheduling in order to alleviate the burden of interest repayments; also to reduce the risk of widespread default, and the consequent threat to the stability of the international financial system. The mechanisms of debt rescheduling are quite different for the three forms of debt. The figures in Table 9.6 give orders of magnitude for debt rescheduling for the three types of debt. It is clear that commercial bank debt rescheduling has far outweighed the other two categories. Moreover, the final figure for rescheduling in 1984 will probably be greater than the $56 billion for 1983. I will now examine the three debt rescheduling mechanisms in turn.

(a) Bank Debt

By late 1983 the first major rescue packages had been organized for Mexico, Argentina, Brazil, and Yugoslavia. The US government took the lead in the cases of Mexico and Brazil, the Swiss government in the case of Yugoslavia. Industrialized country governments, often through the Bank for International Settlements, were essentially involved in arranging short-term bridging finance to buy time for the IMF and the commercial banks to work out a long-

Table 9.6   Debt rescheduling, 1978–1984

	Period	Amount rescheduled (billion $)
1. Commercial bank debt	1978–81	1.5
	1982	5.0
	1983	56.0
2. Official debt	1981–Feb. 1984	15.8
3. ODA	To end 1983	5.7 (of which 3.3 represents cancellation)

Source: Derived from Commonwealth Secretariat (1984).

term rescheduling agreement and macroeconomic adjustment package with the debtor countries. The reluctance of some banks, notably smaller ones, to agree to commit further funds to some individual countries initially threatened to undermine debt rescheduling packages. As a consequence the IMF found itself playing a more active role than it had been accustomed to. Instead of relying on a stand-by lending programme to act as a 'seal of approval' to a debtor country, which would encourage the renewal of commercial bank lending, the IMF now had to put pressure on some commercial banks. Essentially the IMF took the position that it would not become involved *unless* the private banks agreed to provide new lending which was at least pro-rata with their existing lending, and to reschedule existing loans which were falling due for repayment. The IMF had suddenly shifted from its late 1970s position of an institution with apparently little role to play in the world. Its lending has always been small in volume terms, it had been virtually eliminated from assisting industrialized countries by their agreement of mutual assistance through the Bank for International Settlements, and in 1977 and 1978 it had been a net recipient of funds from developing countries — see Annex 7.2. Now it was orchestrating the reaction to the greatest international financial crisis for at least 50 years.

Debt rescheduling soon spread to other debtor nations. By April 1984, 30 countries had had their private bank debts rescheduled.[4] The IMF was involved in almost every case.

Essentially no formal mechanism exists for rescheduling bank debt. Each country has been treated on a case-by-case basis, and the elements of each arrangement have been worked out on an ad-hoc basis by the parties involved. Some negotiations have gone smoothly; others have been characterized by public wrangling and brinkmanship. It is worth commenting, though, that the commercial banks have generally shown the same degree of flexibility and responsiveness (even if under duress) as they did when initially recycling the surpluses of OPEC. The attitudes displayed by the IMF have not always received such accolades, but I will examine this subject below, and the adjustment packages associated with rescheduling.

The terms of bank debt rescheduling varied, of course, but typically the amounts rescheduled were given a maturity of 6–10 years, with a grace period on the repayment of principal of 3–5 years. Spreads were around 2% over LIBOR or US prime rate, with a new medium-term loan provided to assist with interest and new maturing debt. More controversially, commercial banks charged rescheduling fees, in addition to the generally increased spreads they negotiated. The realization that rescheduling, intended in part by industrialized country governments and the IMF to bail out the banks, was merely enabling the banks to increase the profitability of their lending, rankled in some quarters, and the practice of charging rescheduling fees declined.

(b) Non-Concessional Official Debt Rescheduling

The 'Paris Club' is the institutional arrangement established in 1956 for the rescheduling of official debt (non-concessional loans and export credits) between a developing country on the one hand and the members of OECD's Development Assistance Committee on the other. It is essentially a means for ensuring that creditor nations all receive the same terms in any rescheduling agreement. Although it has no formal constitution, it has evolved a set of procedures over the years, the main features of which are:

— It is a precondition of the IMF that the debtor country has an 'upper credit tranche' agreement with the IMF, and any agreement with the Paris Club is dependent on the debtor nation maintaining a satisfactory relationship with the IMF.
— Rescheduling is restricted to bilateral official debt, debt to multilateral institutions being excluded.
— Rescheduling agreements are limited to 85% of the principal due on official debt. Interest and arrears may also be included. In 1983 an exception was made in the case of Sudan, when 100% of the principal due, plus interest and arrears, was rescheduled. Rescheduling is restricted to a 'consolidation period' which is usually 1 year.
— As a matter of principle, interest rates on rescheduled loans are at commercial rates, and interest payments cannot be capitalized.
— A new maturity period of between 6 and 10 years is usually agreed, with a grace period of 3–5 years. Low-income countries are sometimes given longer maturities and grace periods.

The official debts of 22 countries[5] were rescheduled (for some countries, more than once) through the Paris Club between 1981 and February 1984. Although the Paris Club was involved in rescheduling official export credits to Mexico and Brazil, it is generally concerned with aid loans to the poorer developing countries, most of whom have little or no outstanding commercial bank debt. As a precondition, the IMF is involved in all Paris Club reschedulings.

(c) ODA Rescheduling

Since the Pearson Commission Report (1969) debt relief has been viewed as a legitimate form of aid, and debt cancellation has frequently been called for by developing countries. The DAC has treated ODA debt rescheduling rather differently from official debt rescheduling. With ODA, cancellation of debt is permitted, as is retroactive adjustment of the terms (since UNCTAD Resolution 165 of 1978). Moreover, involvement of the IMF is not a precondition. ODA rescheduling has often been done through 'Aid Consortia' established for individual countries — India and Pakistan, for example. Bilateral arrangements have also been used and several least developed countries have had substantial or significant portions of their aid debt (which accounts for most of their debt) cancelled. Several other least developed countries have received little or no benefit from aid cancellation though, and in some cases aid cancellation has been subtracted from aid budgets rather than treated as additional aid.

(d) Review of Debt Rescheduling Procedures

There can be little doubt that the procedures which have evolved over the past 20 years for rescheduling developing country debt represent a great improvement on what occurred in the previous major debt crises of the early 1930s, the early 1880s, and the 1830s. The possibilities of default and repudiation, and their legal consequences and market stigmas, have been all but avoided. This has been made possible largely by the flexibility which major creditors, notably the commercial banks, have shown (and indeed, have been forced to show). The flexibility has been made possible to some extent by the nature of the debt. Bank loans, which are concentrated in relatively few hands, are easier to renegotiate than bond debt, which is widely dissipated among a large number of institutional and individual holders, although councils of foreign bond holders have had some successes in the past. Moreover, the rigidity of redemption dates on bonds means that rescheduling is impossible. As before, the debt remains outstanding and prospects of the principal being repaid are, in many cases, remote. Many developing countries have built up an external national debt, most of which is held by the banks in a non-negotiable form.[6] Debt rescheduling has been on a case-by-case basis, which has led to some concern, and promoted a number of radical proposals for handling the debt problem on a global basis. Some of these proposals are outlined in Chapter 11. However, at the time of writing the present procedures have managed to avoid the worst fears of a global financial collapse, at least for the time being. Nonetheless the feeling persists in some quarters that the world's financial institutions and governments could do better than muddling through, on a year-by-year, and case-by-case basis, with its repeated traumas. For some countries at least, the heavy borrowing appears to have created a permanent external national debt, as permanent as the internal national debt of the industrialized countries. The sooner this is recognized and accepted, the better.

Commercial banks have been criticized for adopting a short-term view (1 year) in negotiations, and for opportunism in charging higher spreads and rescheduling fees. However, to the Commonwealth Secretariat (1984), the deficiencies in Paris Club negotiations as they affect low-income countries are, if anything, more serious than those of rescheduling bank loans, and have been less exposed to public scrutiny. Official creditors, according to the Commonwealth Secretariat, are less sensitive than private creditors to the implications of their negotiations for new financial flows. Export credit agencies have sometimes withdrawn insurance cover, and hardened the terms of export credits. Terms of other debt have also hardened, and there is a reluctance to tailor the repayment terms to the projected external position of creditor countries. The distinction between official debt and aid reschedulings seems arbitrary and unhelpful. Finally the insistence on IMF programmes, usually of a short-term duration, together with their conditionality, is not always felt to be appropriate to the needs of the debtor countries. It is without doubt the role of the IMF in debt negotiation, whether in association with bank or official debt, which has caused most concern in the developing countries, and it is to the IMF which we now turn.

4. THE ROLES OF THE IMF

The IMF commenced operations in 1947, a few months later than the IBRD, as a result of the Bretton Woods negotiations in 1944. Its principal functions are first to provide an international code of conduct concerning mainly international payments and excange rates, and secondly to provide additional liquidity to its members in the form of foreign exchange. Most of its attentions have been concentrated on balance of payments difficulties. It was never intended to be an aid agency or a development agency; these functions were to be carried out by the IBRD or, since its establishment in 1956, the IDA. The main objectives of the Fund are set out in Article 1 of its constitution and included as Annex 9.5. The fund has become a complex organization with several different financial facilities. This complexity is compounded by the specialized terminology which the Fund has developed concerning its operations. (For example, a member country does not borrow and repay a loan; it purchases facilities which the Fund repurchases.) On 30 April 1984 the Fund had 146 members, which included most of the important countries of the world, with the notable exceptions of the Eastern European bloc (although Rumania and Hungary are members) and Switzerland.

Since 1977 the IMF has become, *de facto*, an organization almost exclusively concerned with the developing countries. Since borrowings by Italy and the UK in 1975 and 1976 the major industrialized countries have generally obtained additional liquidity through the BIS, which had been formed in 1930, well before the IMF, but which had been almost dormant between 1931 and 1956. The BIS arranged several rescue packages during the 1960s and 1970s for the industrialized countries (Tew, 1982).

In the second half of the 1970s the IMF looked for a time to be in danger of becoming a redundant organization. The industrialized countries had their own 'club' and the developing countries made net repayments to the Fund in 1977 and 1978. Furthermore, as a financial institution its resources were small and becoming increasingly dwarfed by the expanding commercial bank lending. Countries with a foreign exchange constraint found that they could borrow easily from commercial banks, in large amounts and on longer maturities than the IMF could offer, and without the IMF's conditionality. The IMF became an institution to which members turned only as a very last resort. It was the debt crisis, and the consequent reluctance of commercial banks to offer further credits, which once again gave the IMF a substantial role to play in international finance, and in the economic stabilization of countries which turned to it.

(a) The Theoretical Framework of Stabilization

Outline of the Theory

The main theoretical work underlying the conventional stabilization package (credit restraint, devaluation, reduction in government borrowing) is the Polak model (Polak, 1957). Briefly this states:

Income   = Money supply × Velocity of circulation (from quantity theory of money);
Money supply = Domestic credit expansion + International reserves.

If velocity is constant, money supply will grow at the same rate as income, in equilibrium. If domestic credit grows at a faster rate than income, then international reserves must fall, which means the balance of payments is in deficit. Therefore if domestic credit grows faster than national income a balance of payments deficit will occur. The solution is to restrain domestic credit. This explains in part why all IMF programmes set limits to domestic credit expansion. The other explanation is that such limits reduce the risk that the impact of devaluation on relative prices may be eroded by inflation.

The devaluation component of the package is intended to correct a trade deficit by encouraging exports and discouraging imports. Following devaluation, exports are cheaper to buyers, or more valuable to sellers in local currency than before. Imports become more expensive to buyers. The third element, reduction in government borrowing, is justified as follows. If government borrows then from national accounts:

$$M - X = I - S + G - T$$

where M = imports; X = exports; I = investment; S = saving; G = government expenditure; T = taxes, and

$$G - T = \text{government borrowing.}$$

If excess government expenditure is causing the trade deficit, $M - X$, then the solution is to reduce G, or increase T, or both. The net result is a reduction in government borrowing.

Criticism of the theory

The initial criticisms came from the structuralist school in the 1960s. They maintained that inflation was caused not by monetary expansion but by structural rigidities in the economy, such as agricultural ouput being unresponsive to price changes. Monetary expansion was seen as an accommodating consequence of structural inflation rather than as a cause of inflation. More recently, the argument has been widened by the neo-structuralists, along two broad lines.

— Devaluation may not have the desired impact on exports and imports, because the price elasticity of supply of exports may be too low, and the price elasticity of demand for imports too low (in other words the Marshall–Lerner condition may not hold). The consequence may be a worsening of the balance of payments. For example, take the case:

$$P_{0x} X_0 - P_{0m} M_0 = -100$$

where P_{0x} and P_{0m} = initial rupee price of exports and imports and X_0 and M_0 = initial quantity of exports and imports.

Then a devaluation which doubles P_{0x} and P_{0m}, but leaves the traded quantities X_0 and M_0 unchanged (zero price elasticities) would merely double the trade deficit so that

$$2P_{0x} X_0 - 2P_{0m}M_0 = -200$$

The argument is presented in detail in Ahluwalia and Lysy (1981), but it ignores the fact that the pessimism on price elasticities is not supported by empirical findings (Donovan, 1981; G. Bird, 1982a).

— The second main theoretical criticism is that tight money caused by credit ceilings produces higher interest rates. Alternatively higher interest rates may be an explicit part of an adjustment package, perhaps arising as a result of liberalization of financial markets. These higher interest rates will increase producers' costs, which will lead to increased selling prices, thereby producing increased inflation, exactly the opposite of what was intended. The argument is elaborated in detail in Taylor (1981). Clearly the argument has some appeal, at least in the short term. It is well known that increased inflation results from higher interest rates in the industrialized countries, if only for the technical reason that mortgage costs are a significant component of the retail price index. The argument is criticized because it does not take into account the long-run impact of monetary restraint on inflation, and it seems to be outweighed by the empirical evidence, quoted by Cline (1983), on the long-run relationship between monetary growth and inflation.

This brief account of a major theoretical debate cannot do full justice to the arguments on each side. Cline (1983), on which I have drawn, presents a much fuller discussion. Nonetheless controversy remains, and while the orthodoxy may retain the upper hand, at least in practice, there remains much concern about the suitability of IMF policy packages, especially in the developing countries which nowadays are the recipients of the packages.

(b) The Fund's Resources

The main source of finance for the IMF is the contributions made by its members. Each member is alloted a quota, which it contributes to the Fund. The quota contribution may consist of up to 75% in a member's domestic currency, with at least 25% in SDRs, gold or convertible currencies. During the Fund's financial year ending 30 April 1984 total quotas were increased from SDR 61.1 billion to SDR 89.2 billion. A substantial part of the Fund's resources from quotas is in the form of non-convertible currencies, and these cannot usefully be used for lending to members with balance of payments difficulties. It is generally thought that about half the quota contributions are of this type.

The second type of resource available to the Fund is certain borrowing facilities. These are:

— *The general arrangements to borrow* (GAB) which first became effective in 1962, allow the Fund to borrow from the Group of Ten countries and Switzerland.[7] Until 1983 any funds so borrowed were available only to the 11 participants, but in 1983 the rules were amended, making resources under the GAB available for the following 5 years to other members of the Fund. The limit of the GAB was raised from SDR 6.4 billion to SDR 17 billion in 1983/84.

An arrangement with Saudi Arabia was agreed in 1983/84 and operates in parallel to the GAB. Under this arrangement Saudi Arabia agreed to lend up to SDR 1.5 billion to the Fund.

— *The supplementary financing facility* (SFF) was agreed in 1977 with 13 member countries and the National Bank of Switzerland. SDR 7.8 billion were available under the facility. The last drawings of SDR 1.1 billion in 1983/84 brought the total of borrowings used under this facility to SDR 7.2 billion over the period of 5 years since the scheme became operational.

The borrowing arrangement ended in February 1984, and the repayments of the facility are due by 1991.

— *Borrowing to finance enlarged access to resources* (EAR) was established at the end of 1981, as a replacement for the SFF. The Fund arranged a SDR 8 billion medium-term credit with the Saudi Arabian Monetary Agency, SAMA, with the possibility of a further SDR 4 billion. A further SDR 1.3 billion line of short-term credit was arranged with 18 other members. By 30 April 1985 the Fund had borrowed SDR 6.6 billion from SAMA and had utilized all the SDR 1.3 billion credits. Given the oil price weakness in recent years, SAMA's ability to contribute the full SDR 12 billion may be open to question. In 1984 the Fund concluded four new short-term borrowing arrangements under the enlarged access policy for a total of SDR 6 billion with SAMA, the BIS, Japan, and the National Bank of Belgium. By 30 April 1984 the total available to the Fund under the enlarged access policy was SDR 15.3 billion, on maturities ranging from 6 months to 7 years.

It will have become apparent that the Fund enlarged its resources considerably in 1983/84. This was in response to the pressing needs of the debt crisis in its developing member countries. The arrangements were not without controversy, however. Developing member countries wanted to see quotas expanded from SDR 61 billion to SDR 120 billion, whereas the USA wanted to restrict expansion to SDR 85 billion. The compromise of expansion to SDR 89.2 billion was not to the liking of the developing countries. Likewise, a hope that the GAB would be expanded to SDR 20 billion was not fulfilled. Hopes that the Fund may borrow on the international markets have never been realized. Although the Fund is empowered to do so, neither its management nor its dominant members seem keen to use this method of enlarging the Fund's resources. It appears that the Fund prefers to increase quotas rather than to borrow.

Special Drawing Rights

In 1969 the members of the Fund agreed to create a new artificial reserve currency called the special drawing right (SDR). The SDRs were to be allocated to member countries pro-rata with their quotas. Each SDR was worth US$1 but since the SDR consists of a package of currencies, its value fluctuates against the dollar as exchange rates vary. Currently the SDR is a mix of five currencies, as shown in Table 9.7. The object of creating SDRs was to increase international liquidity at a time when it was felt to be inadequate. Three allocations were made in the years 1971, 1972, and 1973, totalling SDR 9.3 billion. Three further allocations were made in 1979, 1980, and 1981, totalling 12.1 billion, giving an overall total of SDR 21.4 billion. Member countries holding SDRs can use them in transactions among themselves, or in transactions with the Fund. As a result the Fund holds certain SDRs which it has acquired in transactions with member countries. The

Table 9.7 Composition of the SDR

Currency	Amount
US dollar	0.54
Deutsche mark	0.46
French franc	0.74
Japanese yen	34.00
Pound sterling	0.071

Fund receives interest on these SDRs, which is calculated as a weighted average of the yield on short-term securities in the capital markets of the five countries whose currencies are used in the SDR. The Fund also uses the SDR as a unit of account in all its transactions and in its internal accounting (Table 9.8). The facilities shown in Table 9.8 have not been fully utilized by the Fund. At 30 April 1985 total borrowings drawn down totalled SDR 14.2 billion, giving the following liabilities and reserves (SDR billion).

Quotas	89.3
Borrowings	14.2
Accounts payable	0.9
Reserves	1.0
	105.4

Unutilized facilities therefore amounted to about SDR 25 billion, much of which may be in non-convertible currencies.

Table 9.8 Financial resources available to the IMF (SDR billion, at 30 April)

	1982/83	1983/84	1984/85
Quotas	61.1	89.2	89.3
Borrowing facilities			
General arrangements to borrow	6.4	17.0	17.0
GAB–associated loan from Saudi Arabia	—	1.5	1.5
Supplementary financing facility	7.8	7.8	7.8
Enlarged access	9.3	15.3	15.3
Total	84.6	130.8	130.9
Memo item			
Developing country debt	552 (end 1982)	606 (end 1983)	

Source: Figures on IMF resources derived from IMF Annual Reports, 1984 and 1985.

(c) Fund Lending

For lending purposes the Fund is divided into a number of financial facilities. Different rules govern the access of member countries to each facility. All that is given here is an outline. More detailed information is available from IMF (1982), IMF Annual Reports, or specialist works such as Chandavarkar (1984), G. Bird (1982b), or Killick (1984a). The facilities, access to them and normal repayment periods are, briefly, as shown in Table 9.9.

Fund lending ('purchases') over 1970–85 are shown in Table 9.10, broken down by category of lending and showing also repayments ('repurchases') by members. Also shown in Table 9.10 are the borrowings made by non-developing countries by calendar year. It is evident that developing country lending has accounted for the bulk of total lending since 1979, but over 1974–78 purchases by industrialized countries accounted for a substantial proportion of total Fund lending. It is also apparent that since 1978 the bulk of Fund lending has been within the 'conditional' credit tranche and extended fund facilities. These are the facilities which require the agreement of borrowing countries to adjustment programmes, and the meeting of certain performance criteria specificied in the programmes. In 1984/85 new borrowing fell from the high levels of 1983 and 1984. The explanation for the fall is that the improvement in current accounts of developing countries resulted in lower demand for new borrowing. However, outstanding Fund credit rose from SDR 31.8 billion at 30 April 1984 to SDR 35 billion at 30 April 1985.

The Importance of Fund Lending

The volume of Fund lending is small in relation to total financial flows, but rather larger relative to the balance of payments deficits, the problem it is intended to solve. Comparison of Fund lending with non-oil developing country current account deficits in Annex 7.1 shows that Fund lending has grown faster than current account deficits since 1979, and in 1983 covered 20% of them. Moreover, with the tendency to regard the Fund as the last resort in financing current account deficits, the relevant figure to examine is the additional finance it provides to countries which turn to it. Killick (1984a) cites the cases of Peru, Jamaica, Burma, and Sri Lanka, whose drawings in 1978 covered over 40% of their trade deficits in that year. The increase in quotas in 1983 may allow the Fund to finance even higher proportions of external deficits of individual countries. IMF finance is likely to be of greater importance to the least developed countries which do not have significant access to international capital markets than to those countries which do.[8]

This raises the question of the importance of the Fund's 'seal of approval' in encouraging commercial banks to renew their lending programmes to countries which have agreed an adjustment programme with the Fund. In some cases a small amount of Fund lending may act as a catalyst stimulating

Table 9.9 IMF facilities

Facility (date established)	Amount available (percentage of quota)		Access	Normal repayment period
Reserve tranche (1947)	Quotas less Fund's holding of members' currency (usually a maximum of 25% of quota).		On demand	None
Use of Fund credit (a) Ordinary resources Credit Tranches				
1		25%	Semi-automatic; low conditionality.	Usually 1–2 years
2		25%	Increasing conditionality from 2–4—see text	Exceptionally up to 7 years
3		25%		
4		25%		
Compensatory financing facility (CFF) (1963)	83% of export shortfalls, 83% of cereal import excesses. Maximum 105% under borrowing for both purposes.		Dependent upon sudden short-term adverse movements in exports or cereal imports. Conditionality linked to Credit Tranches.	Up to 5 years, normally less
Buffer stock financing facility (BSFF) (1969)	45%		To assist members to contribute to international commodity buffer stock arrangements. Borrower must co-operate with Fund in solving balance of payments problems.	Up to 5 years
Extended fund facility (EFF) (1974)	140%. Purchases under credit tranches and EFF financed with ordinary resources subject to a		For long-term balance of payments difficulties. Subject to upper credit tranche conditionality.	$4\frac{1}{2}$–10 years

(b) The following facility is used to provide additional financing under Credit Tranche and extended fund facilities:

Enlarged access to resources (EAR) (1981)	102% or 120% in 1 year; 308% or 375% over 3 years; 408% or 500% cumulatively.	For substantial, long-term problems; subject to high conditionality	$3\frac{1}{2}$–7 years

(c) The following special facilities are now terminated:

Oil facility (1974–76)	Now terminated.	To assist with large increases in oil import bills.	
Trust fund (TF) (1976–81)	Now terminated. (But see note 14)	For least developed countries only; at least first credit tranche conditionality.	6–10 years
Supplementary financing facility (SFF) (1979–84)	102% or 120% in one year; 308% or 375% over three years; 408% or 500% cumulatively. Now terminated.	For substantial, long term problems; subject to high conditionality.	$3\frac{1}{2}$–7 years

Sources: IMF Annual Reports. *International Financial Statistics,* January 1985 (IMF); *International Financial Statistics.* Supplement on Fund Accounts, 1982 (IMF).

Notes:
(a) The SFF and EAR are used to provide supplementary financing for the Credit tranches and the EFF.
(b) The terms of each facility are modified by the Fund from time to time. The above details were correct towards the end of 1984.
(c) Apart from the reserve tranche, access to any facility and terms of access are subject to Fund discretion, and should not be considered as rights of member countries.
(d) The Fund acts as trustee to the trust fund, whose lending ceased in 1981 and is now confined to the receipt of repayments, and to the SFF subsidy account. The latter was established in 1980 to reduce the cost of using the SFF for low-income developing country members. It is financed by repayments of, and interest on, trust fund loans, donations, and low-interest loans from the wealthier members. The trust fund was originally financed by sale of IMF gold holdings. The oil facility was also subsidised by an oil facility subsidy account, financed by a group of members for which the Fund acted as trustee.
(e) Facilities are often made available under a stand-by arrangement for a specified period (usually up to 3 years). This operates as a line of credit which a country can tap by agreement.

Table 9.10 Annual purchases and repurchases of Fund resources (SDR million)

Year ending 30 April	Within reserve tranche	Within credit tranches[a]	Of which SFF[b]	Of which EAR	Extended fund facility	Of which SFF[b]	Of which EAR	Compensatory financing facility	Buffer stock facility	Oil facility[b]	Total purchases	Total repurchases	Purchases by industrialized countries[c]
1970	689	2,297						9			2,995	1,671	983
1971	811	354						3	20		1,168	1,657	1,362
1972	1,577	265						167	5		2,029	3,122	784
1973	641	323						206			1,176	540	322
1974	608	239						212	—		1,059	672	2,113
1975	982	1,604						18	—	2,499	5,103	518	2,044
1976	1,324	461			8			828	5	3,966	6,592	960	3,175
1977	161	2,370			190			1,753	—	437	4,911	868	2,389
1978	136	1,937			109			322	—		2,504	4,485	2,474
1979	2,480	485	485	—	242			465	48		3,720	4,859	73
1980	223	1,106	384	—	216	119	—	863	26		2,434	3,776	—
1981	474	2,682	1,127	308	920	389	—	784	—		4,860	2,853	—
1982	1,080	2,748	1,508	941	2,578	548	781	1,635	352		8,041	2,010	342
1983	1,134	3,703	957	2,227	2,463	1,002	241	3,740	102		11,392	1,555	87
1984	1,354	4,164	469	1,537	4,717	614	1,808	1,180	—		11,517	2,018	—
1985	229	2,767	—		2,044	—	1,024	1,248	—		6,288	2,730	28

[a] Lending from ordinary resources, unless otherwise stated.
[b] New lending from these facilities has now terminated.
[c] Calendar years, not IMF financial years.

Source: IMF Annual Reports: *International Financial Statistics* (January 1985) and *Supplement on Fund Accounts* (1982) (both IMF)

much larger flows of finance from commercial banks or bilateral government lending. Evidence on this point, though, is ambivalent. Friedman (1981) expressed what is often thought to be the banks' view by stating 'The IMF's presence is valued by the banks because it increases confidence in the quality of the program and enhances the likelihood of its implementation.' But he went on to point out that 'Banks obviously are uneasy when their criteria of stabilization needs in any country differ from the IMF's criteria', a point we return to below. In the debt crises of late 1982–84 anecdotal evidence suggests that some banks were not at all happy to follow where the IMF 'led,' and that it was coercion by others, and the threat of default to their balance sheets and even an international banking collapse, which led them reluctantly to reschedule existing credits and in some cases to provide new money. Proposals to establish closer relationships between the IMF and the commercial banks will be discussed in the final chapter.

The Cost of Fund Lending

On the subject of lending, little emphasis in discussions of the IMF is given to the interest rates ('periodic charges') on IMF loans. These are as shown in Table 9.11. In spite of the increase in 1984, interest rates charged on

Table 9.11 Schedule of Fund charges (percentage per annum[a] payable on holdings for the periods stated)

	1 May 1982 through 30 April 1984	From 1 May 1984	From 1 November 1985
Purchases in the credit tranches and under the compensatory financing, buffer stock financing, and extended fund facilities			
Service charge	0.5	0.5	0.5
Periodic charge	6.6	7.0	7.87
Supplementary financing facility			
Service charge	0.5	0.5	0.5
Periodic charge			
Up to 3½ years	Rate of interest paid by the Fund plus 0.2%		
Over 3½ years	Rate of interest paid by the Fund plus 0.325%		
Enlarged access policy			
Service charge	0.5	0.5	0.5
Periodic charge	Net cost of borrowing by the Fund plus 0.2%		

[a] Except for service charge, which is payable once per transaction and is stated as a percentage of the amount of the transaction.
Source: IMF Annual Report 1985.

credit tranche borrowings, the CFF, the BSFF and the EFF remain comfortably below market rates. During March 1985, for example SDR-linked time deposits earned about 9% in London, although the rate was down to 8% by November 1985, when the fund raised its rate on ordinary resources to 7.87%. By April 1986, rates on SDR-linked deposits were below 7%. The average rates of interest per annum paid on outstanding Fund borrowings for the year ending 30 April 1985 were:

General agreements to borrow	4%	(all repaid)
Oil facility	7.25%	(all repaid)
SFF	11.85%	
Enlarged access to resources	10.48%	

Source: IMF Annual Report 1985

The level of interest rates has on occasion caused consternation to borrowers. Killick (1984b) reports that the Kenya government considered the Fund's interest rates to be too high. On the other hand the US Treasury has pressed[9] for a further increase in Fund lending rates in order to provide increased remuneration to the creditor countries as well as to build up the Fund's reserves through increased profits. The US Treasury sees no reason why creditor countries in the Fund should continue to subsidize debtors. But borrower countries still pay lower interest rates to the Fund than they would on commercial credits, even supposing that they could get them.

The Financial Position of the Fund

The consolidated balance sheets (Table 9.12) conveniently summarize the financial position of the Fund at the end of financial years 1983, 1984, and 1985.

(d) IMF Conditionality

It is beyond dispute that the Fund is required by its Articles of Agreement to safeguard its loans. Irrespective of its Articles, few would disagree that the Fund should take steps to ensure that its loans should be used for the intended purpose (balance of payments adjustment), that they should be repaid and, given the limited resources of the Fund, that repayment should be 'reasonably' quick, so that the Fund can make the resources available to other needy borrowers. Another point to bear in mind is that the Fund is not a 'development' agency and is not, therefore, concerned with concessional, long-term lending. Any discussion of IMF conditionality is circumscribed by the confidentiality of the agreements between the Fund and borrowing countries, which makes it difficult to arrive at any firm conclusions. However, lack of information about Fund programmes should not necessarily protect it from outside criticisms. Analysts must make judgements on what information is available.

IMF discussions with a potential borrower are formalized in a Letter of Intent, which sets out the policies which it is agreed the government should

Table 9.12   IMF consolidated balance sheet, at 30 April (billion SDR)

	1983		1984		1985	
Assets						
Currencies and securities arising from:						
Members' quotas	61.1		89.2		89.3	
Less members' reserve tranche positions	−20.6		−27.4		−28.3	
Members' use of fund credit[a]	23.6		31.8		35.0	
		64.1	64.1	93.6	93.6	96.0	96.0
SDR holdings[b].		4.3		6.4		4.6
Gold holdings		3.6		3.6		3.6
Borrowed resources held in suspense		1.8		0.6		0.2
Charges receivable and accrued		0.5		0.8		0.9
Accrued interest on SDR holdings		—		0.2		0.1
Total assets		74.3		105.2		105.4
Quotas, reserves and liabilities						
Quotas: subscriptions of members		61.1		89.2		89.3
Borrowings						
Supplementary financing facility		6.0		6.9		6.2
Enlarged access to resources		4.1		6.9		8.0
General arrangements to borrow		0.8		—		—
Remuneration payable		1.0		0.7		0.4
Accrued interest payable and other liabilities		0.3		0.4		0.5
Reserves		1.0		1.1		1.0
		74.3		105.2		105.4

Notes

a. *Members' use of Fund credit*	*1983*	*1984*	*1985*
Regular facilities	4.7	5.2	5.5
Compensatory financing facility	6.8	7.3	7.5
Buffer stock financing facility	0.3	0.4	0.3
Extended fund facility	3.3	5.6	6.5
Supplementary financing facility	6.1	6.9	6.3
Enlarged access to resources	2.4	6.4	8.9
	23.6	31.8	35.0

b. SDRs acquired by the Fund in settlement of financial obligations, and which may be used by the Fund in transactions with its members. The Fund earns interest on its SDRs.

Source: IMF Annual Reports, 1984 and 1985.

follow, together with certain targets to be adjusted, usually the balance of payments and the inflation rate. Policies would range from direct action on the balance of payments such as exchange rate policy (devaluation is sometimes a precondition, and one which is contentious), and export incentives, to overall macroeconomic fiscal and monetary policy. In some instances the Letter of Intent may go further and specify action to be taken on public sector pricing policy, agricultural price reform, wages policy, and public sector expenditure, employment and borrowing. Certain performance criteria are specified numerically, with tight definitions to avoid ambiguity, and precise dates by which they should be met. Performance criteria invariably seem to include a ceiling on domestic credit, a minimum level of foreign exchange reserves, a target for reducing arears of debt service, and ceilings for government debt, both domestic and foreign, are chosen on the grounds that they can be readily defined and measured and that the instruments lie within government control.

Published examples of Letters of Intent include those for Jamaica (in Killick, 1984b) and Italy (in Williamson, 1983). However, most are not published. The contents of the Letters of Intent refer mainly to the 'high conditionality' facilities, that is credit tranches 2–4, and the extended fund facility. The compensatory financing facility and the buffer stock financing facility do not attract high conditionality unless used in conjunction with a facility which does. However, as Table 9.10 shows, the CFF and BSFF provide rather less than do the high conditionality facilities.

The available evidence on IMF preconditions and performance criteria has been compiled by Killick (1984a) based on unpublished IMF surveys. Over 1978/79, 13 of 23 programmes included preconditions, some containing more than one. The frequency of the preconditions was:

Exchange rate actions	9
Pricing policies	5
Interest rate policies	8
Tax measures	3
Liberalization of trade and payments	1
Reduction of specified public sector expenditures	1

For performance criteria a study of 10 agreements in each of three periods produced the results shown in Table 9.13. The incidence of ceilings on credit expansion seemed to increase in the 1970s. This is borne out by reference to Reichmann and Stillson (1978), who found that only 40 out of 79 upper tranche programmes implemented between 1963 and 1972 contained ceilings on credit expansion. By contrast, Reichmann (1978) analysed 21 programmes implemented between 1973 and 1975, finding that all contained credit ceilings, and that 15 called for a reduction in credit expansion. Killick (1984a) went on to analyse all cases of higher tranche credits between 1973 and 1981. Out of 186 cases exactly half were accompanied by devaluation within 6

Table 9.13 Selected performance criteria—upper tranche stand-by arrangements

	1964–69	1970–73	1974–79
1. Credit ceilings			
(a) Total domestic credit	3	10	9
(b) Credit to government/public sector	7	5	7
(c) Credit to private sector	5	—	1
2. Devaluation	3	—	—
3. Reduction in current payment arrears	—	1	2
4. Minimum levels for foreign exchange reserves	1	1	4
5. Restrictions on new external debt	3	7	5

Source: Killick (1984a) based on IMF Special Survey, conducted in 1981.

months prior or 6 months after a credit arrangement. The figure may be an underestimate, though, as it does not allow for countries which did not use credits, and includes some francophone African countries whose exchange rate is tied to the French franc. Nevertheless, devaluation may not be as frequent as is sometimes supposed.

(e) The Debate on Fund Programmes

Criticisms

The most vociferous critics of the IMF tend to come from the developing countries and from the 'development lobby', especially its left wing. In general they consider the Fund to be insensitive and uncaring towards the problems and needs of the developing countries, and to insist on conditions which are unduly harsh. The main specific criticisms are:

— The Fund is inflexible, in that it insists on a similar package of conditions for all borrowers, regardless of the underlying causes of the problems. In some cases the package amounts to an 'overkill' (Diaz-Alejandro, 1981; Dell, 1982).
— The Fund is asymmetrical, in that it can only exert pressure to adjust on countries with persistent current account deficits, while it can do nothing about the problems created by countries which run persistent current account surpluses.
— Developing country deficits are frequently caused by external factors beyond the control of governments, rather than internal mismanagement. IMF stabilization programmes fail to take exogenously determined deficits into account (Dell and Lawrence, 1980). This point does appear to be supported by the estimates of Cline (1984) quoted earlier.
— The Fund is 'monetarist' in that it invariably insists on credit ceilings as a measure of performance, and anti-development in that its prescriptions

are deflationary, causing much hardship. There is a trade-off between monetary restriction and development.

— Fund programmes take no account of the 'structural' causes of current account deficits, and their stabilization programmes are too short-term to permit the structural changes necessary to correct the imbalance to take place. In fact, structuralists argue that monetary restriction will slow down growth, and therefore delay the necessary structural changes (Taylor, 1981; Schydlowsky, 1982).

— Devaluation is often not a useful part of the package, as the Marshall-Lerner conditions do not hold in many developing countries. If exports cannot be increased because of adequate expansion of supply or overseas demand, devaluation will merely be inflationary. Discretionary import controls (or multiple exchange rates) may be better, but the Fund generally insists on liberalizing trade and payments (Dell, 1982; Taylor, 1981; Schydlowsky, 1982).

— The liberalization of trade and payments necessitates domestic demand deflation to limit the demand for foreign exchange, which is 'anti-growth'. Why should unilateral liberalization of trade be followed in the South when the North is becoming increasingly protectionist? Liberalization is likely to damage import substitution industries.

— Current account deficits in many cases are only temporary, so there is no need for stabilization programmes and high conditionality.

— The Fund imposes capitalist, free-market solutions which may not be politically acceptable to some borrowers. It is dominated by the industrialized countries and is anti-socialist (Payer, 1974).

From a different point of view the Fund has been criticized for sustaining incompetent economic management in developing countries and protecting the rulers from the consequences of their past actions by providing funds which puts off the necessary adjustments. It has also been criticized for rescuing the commercial banks from the full consequences of their unwise lending. These criticisms have come from the right of the political spectrum, mainly in the USA. Friedman (1981) points out that some policies which private banks would favour do not appear in IMF agreements. Banks are likely to emphasize policies which would reduce government involvement in markets, reduce restrictions on foreign enterprises, and, particularly, introduce policies to attract foreign equity investment.

The Reply to Criticisms

Defenders of the IMF (who now include the Fund itself; see Nowzad, 1981) point out that the Fund helps member countries through the provision of finance and advice. It has shown its flexibility over the years by introducing the CFF to help with exogenously caused balance of payments difficulties, and the EFF to allow a longer period for adjustment to disequilibrium caused by structural problems. The Fund's stabilization policies have a broad theoretical underpinning (the Polak model). It tries to be flexible by using only a small number of performance criteria, and chooses those which the government can control, and which are measurable. Can the critics suggest any better measures?

Empiral studies of the effects of devaluation show that it generally has the desired effect on imports and exports (G. Bird, 1982a). Supporters point out that the Fund is not anti-development; in fact it encourages development to the extent that balance of payments constraints permit. However, it does have the task of correcting earlier mistakes of governments, which is often difficult, and which are not of the Fund's making. The problems are usually made more acute because governments approach the Fund too late. There is a limit to what the Fund can achieve in difficult circumstances, and too much may be expected of it.

A major plank in the argument of Fund supporters is that the cause of the balance of payments deficit is secondary. The main consideration is whether it is expected to be transitory or not. If it is transitory it will be self-correcting, and low conditionality finance is appropriate, hence the low conditionality attached to the CFF and BSFF. If a deficit is expected to be persistent than a stabilization programme is needed, and conditionality is necessary to encourage and to monitor progress in adjustment.

The Evidence from the IMF Programmes

There are major methodological obstacles to the evaluation of Fund programmes, as there are with any economic policies. The easiest method is to compare the state of an economy (specifically balance of payments and the inflation rate) after a Fund programme with the state beforehand. We then need to make various *ceteris paribus* assumptions, which in fact are unlikely to hold. Improvements or deteriorations in the balance of payments may have occurred anyway, even without IMF intervention. Under these circumstances it would be wrong to attribute either the successes or the failures to the IMF. A theoretical alternative would be to compare the economy after the programme with what it would have been in the absence of the programme; the practical difficulty is to forecast what *would* have happened. A third, rather narrower, approach is to compare the outcome with the balance of payments and inflation targets and the performance criteria, established in the Letter of Intent. Such an approach, though, depends on the targets set as much as the economic outcome. If the targets were unrealistically optimistic the performance may unjustifiably appear poor. Finally, the relationships between policy instruments and targets are at best loose, and time lags between action and reaction make the effects difficult to identify and to measure.

Nonetheless, some serious efforts have been made to try to assess the impact of Fund programmes. They fall into two categories: first the generalized studies, notably by Reichmann and Stillson (1978), Reichmann (1978),

Connors (1979), Donovan (1982), and, finally, Killick (1984a,b) which review all the earlier studies as well as producing some new evidence. Killick (1984a) found that Fund programmes probably have limited effectiveness and that most tests conducted produced results which were of low statistical significance. Among the results of the analysis of Fund programmes are:

— Modest short-term improvements resulted in the current account of the balance of payments, and greater improvements in the overall balance.
— There are indications that Fund programmes result in modest additional inflows of capital from other sources.
— Programmes have not generally had strong deflationary effects on the growth rate.
— Programmes probably result in a net short-term increase in the inflation rate.
— Programmes are likely to have rather complex, but not systematic, effects on income distribution. A large proportion probably had no significant effect on inequality.
— Both stand-by and EFF programmes are subject to fairly frequent breakdowns, especially the latter. However, there is little evidence that results with the EFF have been weaker than with stand-bys.

The second category of research is the study of the effect of IMF programmes on individual countries.[10] It is beyond the scope of this book to discuss them in detail, but some of the findings may cast further light on the discusion of the role of the IMF. For references, see Note 10.

Three studies (Indonesia, Jamaica, Peru) which investigated the causes of instability found that domestic rather than external factors were responsible. Credit ceilings were found to be inappropriate in Indonesia, where the major objectives of the programme were achieved despite failure to keep within prescribed credit ceilings. In Argentina, Brazil, and Chile there seemed at times to be an inverse relationship between inflation and compliance with credit ceilings, in that inflation fell when ceilings were not complied with, and vice-versa. In Kenya, in 1979/80, credit ceilings were unworkably tight. An IMF programme was widely found to be catalytic in securing new funds from other sources, although in the cases of Indonesia, Portugal, and Turkey bilateral government finance played a much more important role than commercial bank credits, and in the case of Peru rescheduling of both private and Paris Club debt was important. The catalytic role of the Fund was of significance also in the Southern Cone countries.

There was widespread evidence that programmes needed to have strong commitment from the government to succeed. The necessary commitment was present in Portugal, Turkey (1980), and Indonesia, but not in Jamaica up till 1980, where the government was unwilling to accept high conditionality, and where there was no noted improvement in the economy (in some years there was a marked deterioration). Moreover, there was evidence that the policies need to be sustained for a long period. Failure to maintain policies was thought to have contributed to failures in Southern Cone countries, Peru before 1978 and Turkey 1978–79. The Kenya government was reported to have been reluctant to grasp the nettle of uncomfortable decisions. Reports of the effect of the IMF programmes on growth were limited, but in Argentina and Uruguay the programmes may have had some brief and moderate negative effects, while in Chile and possibly Peru the effects were more severe. In the case of Kenya the Kenyans considered that the Fund took too short a view, but there was also in place a World Bank structural adjustment loan programme, which 'took care of the long term', and is reported to have worked well.[11] In Mexico the Fund 1977–78 programme was not considered to be too short-term, as it was in a 3-year time frame.

(f) Assessment of IMF Lending

It is difficult to come to any general conclusions on the limited evidence available, but even given full disclosure of information by the Fund, there might still be no general conclusions to be drawn. The circumstances of each borrowing country are different, and the economic and political framework of policy-making makes stabilization programmes more of an art than a science. It is not, therefore, surprising that every experience is different, with some being less satisfactory than others.

The IMF can be seen as playing two distinct roles. First, with countries which usually have access to commercial bank borrowing, Fund programmes serve primarily as a catalyst in mobilizing further commercial credits, or, to a lesser extent, bilateral credits. In these cases the volume of Fund money is less relevant than the confidence the programme builds. In countries without access to commercial credits (generally the least developed countries), however, the volume of Fund money becomes important, as does its maturity, in that it might need to provide the 5–10 year credits which more advanced countries can obtain from the market. Both these points raise the question of the adequacy of Fund resources, which will be discussed further in the final chapter. The Fund's normal role is seen as a lender of last resort. However, in her study of the Indian Fund programme in 1981, Gwin (1983) highlights the role the Fund played as a lender of first resort. India, finding growth restricted by a balance of payments constraint, obtained an IMF loan at an unusually early stage, indeed at a time when it could have easily raised (more expensive) commercial bank loans. The Indian EFF loan was considered by the United States to be wrong in principle, in that it could threaten the Fund's liquidity and restrict its ability to help others. However, it does seem that the Fund acted within its Articles of Agreement, and the agreement with India appears to have worked unusually smoothly.

The Fund's supporters make the point that countries in difficulty usually approach the Fund too late, and when all else has failed. This results in the Fund being faced with exceptionally severe problems, which generally require severe measures to restore the health of the economy. On the other hand, one can question why countries approach the Fund only when all else has failed. It is clear that much of the third world regards the Fund with suspicion and dislike, and as an organization which acts in the interests of its dominant industrialized country members rather than in the interests of third world countries. The Fund at least has a credibility gap to bridge.[12]

The Fund has clearly played an important role in the widespread debt crisis of the early 1980s. It is as yet too early to evaluate the success of the measures taken, but the hasty, almost panic reaction to the crisis has led to proposals for a 'global' approach to debt problems rather than the present case-by-case approach. I will examine the alternatives proposed and some of the ideas put forward for reforming the IMF in the final chapter. However, the question that critics of the Fund have to answer is 'Can you propose alternatives to Fund packages which result in adjustment at lower economic cost?' It is not clear that the critics have a satisfactory answer to this question.[13] One alternative is currently being tried by Nigeria, which is following a policy of countertrade to maintain an external balance, rather than accepting an IMF package of devaluation and internal economic reforms (*The Financial Times*, 5 June 1985). Trade controls tend merely to repress the symptoms of disequilibrium, and cannot be removed without the problems reappearing. It remains to be seen whether the Nigerian government can gain sufficient breathing space to enable it to undertake reform measures itself.

To sum up, the main shortcoming of the IMF's lending in response to the debtor crisis is that the problems in many countries are too deep-seated to be solved by the normal 1–3-year time horizon which the Fund takes in its programmes. Although the Fund has the possibility of providing longer-term credits, its need to revolve its funds so that it can assist others limit this possibility. In order that this restriction should be relaxed, the Fund would need increased resources or, alternatively, might act in concert with World Bank structural adjustment loans, which would provide the longer maturities. The likelihood that structural adjustment loans will in future account for rather more than the present 10% of World Bank lending gives credence to the feasibility of the sister organizations acting increasingly in concert.[14]

Annex 9.1: Total Disbursed Long-term Debt of Developing Countries at Year-end 1971–83, by Source and Terms of Lending ($ billion)

Sources and terms of lending	1971	1975	1976	1977	1978	1979	1980	1981	1982	1983
1. DAC countries and capital markets	68	131	160	200	255	301	342	381	414	455
ODA	24	34	36	41	49	53	57	57	59	61
Total export credits	26	40	49	64	82	98	110	117	121	127
Total private	18	57	74	95	124	151	175	207	234	267
of which: bank loans[a]	10	46	59	75	98	123	145	175	200	234
bonds	4	5	6	9	13	13	15	16	16	15
others	3	6	9	11	13	14	15	17	18	18
2. Multilateral	9	21	26	32	39	46	55	64	75	84
of which: concessional	6	10	12	14	17	20	24	27	30	33
3. CMEA countries	6	9	9	11	12	15	15	16	17	18
of which: concessional	5	8	8	9	10	11	12	13	13	14
4. OPEC countries	..	6	8	11	13	15	18	20	21	23
of which: concessional	..	5	6	8	9	11	12	14	15	16
5. Other LDCs	2	3	3	4	5	6	7	7	7	8
of which: concessional	1	2	2	2	3	3	3	3	3	3
6. Other and adjustments	1	3	5	5	7	8	8	13	18	18
Total debt	86	173	211	262	331	391	445	501	552	606
of which: concessional	33	59	65	76	89	99	109	114	121	130
non-concessional	53	114	146	186	243	292	336	387	431	476

[a] Bank loans other than export credits.   .. = negligible.

Reproduced with permission from OECD (1984b)

Annex 9.2: Total Annual Long-term Debt Service of Developing Countries during 1971–83, by Source and Terms of Lending ($ billion)

Source and terms of lending	1971	1975	1976	1977	1978	1979	1980	1981	1982	1983
1. DAC countries and capital markets	8.8	21.4	26.4	34.6	48.5	62.7	72.4	87.8	94.3	82.7
ODA	1.3	1.7	1.9	2.0	2.3	2.6	2.8	2.8	2.7	2.7
Total export credits	4.9	10.4	11.9	15.8	19.6	23.9	28.1	32.4	31.3	30.0
Total private	2.6	9.3	12.6	16.7	26.5	36.2	41.5	52.5	60.4	50.0
of which: bank loans[a]	1.9	7.8	10.2	13.6	22.5	31.3	36.3	46.8	53.4	44.4
bonds	0.4	0.7	0.5	0.8	1.3	1.9	1.6	2.1	3.0	2.6
other	0.4	0.9	1.8	2.4	2.8	3.1	3.6	3.7	3.9	3.0
2. Multilateral	0.9	1.6	2.0	2.5	3.2	3.7	4.6	5.6	6.5	7.4
of which: concessional	0.2	0.6	0.6	0.7	0.8	0.7	0.8	0.9	1.2	1.4
3. CMEA countries	0.6	0.8	0.9	1.1	1.3	1.6	1.8	1.9	1.9	1.8
of which: concessional	0.5	0.7	0.7	0.9	0.9	1.0	1.4	1.4	1.4	1.4
4. OPEC countries	..	0.2	0.2	0.6	0.9	1.2	1.3	1.8	1.9	1.8
of which: concessional	..	0.1	0.1	0.4	0.4	0.5	0.6	0.8	0.9	0.9
5. Other LDCs	0.1	0.3	0.4	0.4	0.4	0.6	0.7	0.9	1.0	0.9
of which: concessional	..	..	..	..	..	0.1	0.1	0.1	0.1	0.1
6. Other and adjustments	0.2	0.7	1.0	0.9	1.0	1.3	1.5	1.7	1.9	1.5
Total debt service	10.5	25.1	30.9	40.1	55.3	71.2	82.3	99.7	107.6	96.1
of which: interest	3.2	8.8	10.2	12.7	17.4	25.5	35.2	43.2	50.3	48.1
amortization	7.3	16.3	20.6	27.4	37.9	45.7	47.1	56.5	57.3	48.0
Total debt service										
of which: concessional	1.7	3.2	3.4	4.1	4.5	4.9	5.7	6.0	6.2	6.5
non-concessional	8.9	21.9	27.5	36.0	50.8	66.3	76.6	93.7	101.4	89.6

[a] Bank loans other than export credits.   .. = negligible

Reproduced with permission from OECD (1984b)

Annex 9.3: Interest Cost to Developing Countries during 1972–83, by Type of Long-term Credit Disbursed and Income Group (percentages)

Interest cost on disbursed debt[a]	1972/73	1974/76	1977/78	1979	1980	1981	1982	1983
1. Fixed-interest debt	4.4	4.9	5.5	5.8	6.0	6.0	6.3	6.7
DAC ODA loans	2.5	2.4	2.3	2.2	2.3	2.2	2.1	2.2
DAC export credits	6.3	7.0	7.6	7.8	8.2	7.9	8.1	9.0
Bonds	5.2	4.9	6.1	7.0	7.5	7.6	8.1	8.1
Other private credits	8.4	8.5	8.5	9.2	11.5	13.4	13.1	12.6
Multilateral loans: concessional	3.5	3.2	2.8	2.2	1.9	1.9	1.9	1.9
non-concessional	8.9	9.0	9.8	10.0	9.6	8.6	8.9	9.5
Non-DAC total bilateral loans	2.2	2.3	3.4	3.2	3.6	3.6	4.5	4.5
2. Floating-interest debt	8.3	9.9	8.4	12.3	15.5	17.4	17.1	12.7
3. Total LDC debt	5.0	6.0	6.3	7.7	9.0	9.7	10.0	8.7
of which:								
LICs	2.9	3.2	3.4	3.8	3.8	3.8	4.0	3.7
LMICs	4.6	5.0	5.2	7.3	8.7	9.0	9.8	8.3
UMICs	6.4	7.6	7.8	9.3	11.0	12.1	12.2	10.6
Total non-OPEC, non-OECD debt	4.5	5.4	6.0	7.1	8.8	9.5	9.6	8.4

[a] Annual interest payments and other charges (including spreads and fees on floating-interest debt) as a percentage of disbursed debt at the beginning of the year.

Reproduced with permission from OECD (1984b)

Annex 9.4: Estimated Total Long- and Short-term External Assets and Liabilities of non-OPEC, non-OECD Developing Countries, year-end 1980–83[a] ($ billion)

Type of liabilities and assets	Liabilities				Assets				Balance			
	1980	1981	1982	1983	1980	1981	1982	1983	1980	1981	1982	1983
1. Long-term	−321	−374	−418	−460	28	36	45	51	−292	−338	−373	−409
Fixed-interest[b]	−204	−232	−250	−265	25	31	38	41	−179	−201	−212	−224
Floating-interest[c]	−116	−142	−168	−195	3	5	7	10	−113	−137	−161	−185
2. Short-term[d]	−89	−111	−113	−103	105	103	99	102	16	−8	−14	−1
of which: foreign exchange reserves[e]	—	—	—	—	(79)	(80)	(70)	(73)	—	—	—	—
3. Total	−409	−485	−531	−563	133	139	144	153	−276	−346	−387	−410
Fixed interest	−204	−232	−250	−265	25	31	38	41	−179	−201	−212	−224
Floating interest	−205	−253	−281	−298	108	108	106	112	−97	−145	−175	−186
of which: 4 countries[f]	−117	−153	−171	−179	30	26	26	27	−87	−127	−145	−152
LICs	−17	−20	−21	−24	20	18	18	20	3	−2	−3	−4

[a] Excluding direct foreign investment, gold, and IMF transactions, as well as interest payable and receivable.
[b] The bulk of which is *not* denominated in US dollars.
[c] The bulk of which is denominated in US dollars.
[d] Liabilities include arrears; assets exclude capital flight to foreign countries. All short-term transactions are assumed to be on floating interest, although a significant part of trade credits (for both imports and exports) and of arrears are assumed to be invested in short-term instruments.
[e] All foreign exchange reserves are assumed to be invested in short-term instruments.
[f] Argentina, Brazil, South Korea, and Mexico.

Reproduced with permission from OECD (1984b)

ANNEX 9.5: ARTICLE I OF THE IMF'S CONSTITUTION

Article I   The Purposes of the International Monetary Fund are:

(i) To promote international monetary cooperation through a permanent institution which provides the machinery for consultation and collaboration on international monetary problems.

(ii) To facilitate the expansion and balanced growth of international trade, and to contribute thereby to the promotion and maintenance of high levels of employment and real income and to the development of the productive resources of all members as primary objectives of economic policy.

(iii) To promote exchange stability, to maintain orderly exchange arrangements among members, and to avoid competitive exchange depreciation.

(iv) To assist in the establishment of a multilateral system of payments in respect of current transactions between members and in the elimination of foreign exchange restrictions which hamper the growth of world trade.

(v) To give confidence to members by making the general resources of the Fund temporarily available to them under adequate safeguards, thus providing them with opportunity to correct maladjustments in their balance of payments without resorting to measures destructive of national or international prosperity.

(vi) In accordance with the above, to shorten the duration and lessen the degree of disequilibrium in the international balances of payments of members.

The Fund shall be guided in all its policies and decisions by the purposes set forth in this Article.

NOTES

1. An alternative measure of interest costs is to measure the burden of interest payments in terms of export earnings and to deflate nominal interest rates by the export prices obtained by all developing countries. Using this deflator the World Bank (1984) estimated that real interest rates moved from −10% in 1980 to 19.4% in 1982. This measure reflects increases in nominal rates and falls in developing country export prices. It is particularly influenced by the falls in oil prices over 1980–82. Using middle-income oil-importers' export prices as the deflator, real interest rates still increased from −0.2% in 1980 to 20.4% in 1982.

2. Exposure to developing countries was not without its returns and banks usually charged higher interest rates to these borrowers than to others. Over 1971–76 profits of 10 leading US banks from international operations rose from 23% of total profits to over 50% of total profits. In 1977 foreign profits accounted for 82% of Citibank's total profits and 79% of Bankers Trusts profits (estimates by Salomon Brothers reported in *Die Welt* of 28 April 1978 and in *The Financial Times* of 6 June 1978). Therefore by the time the second oil price rise came round the banks had reason to view further developing country lending with some eagerness.

3. *The Economist* of 11 December 1982 wrote 'The I.M.F. wants the world's banks to stuff yet more dollars into the stocking of Latin America's debt. The banks have little choice but to concede. They know as they do it, however, that the money will probably not be seen again; indeed, they will be lucky even to get paid the interest.'

4. The countries were Argentina, Bolivia, Brazil, Chile, Costa Rica, Cuba, Dominican Republic, Ecuador, Guyana, Honduras, Ivory Coast, Jamaica, Liberia,

Madagascar, Malawi, Mexico, Morocco, Nicaragua, Nigeria, Panama, Peru, Philippines, Poland, Romania, Senegal, Sudan, Togo, Uruguay, Yugoslavia, and Zambia. For further details of all these cases, see Commonwealth Secretariat (1984).

5. The countries were Brazil, Central African Republic, Costa Rica, Cuba, Ecuador, Liberia, Madagascar, Malawi, Mexico, Morocco, Niger, Pakistan, Peru, Poland, Romania, Senegal, Sierra Leone, Sudan, Togo, Uganda, Zaire, and Zambia. For further details see Commonwealth Secretariat (1984).

6. A small secondary market in loans to developing countries has recently arisen, with banks prepared to trade debt among themselves in order to diversify country or currency exposure. This is, as yet, a very small market, and does not offer the possibilities of my proposal (Kitchen, 1985) to convert bank debt into negotiable bond debt, outlined in Chapter 11.

7. The Group of Ten consists of Belgium, Canada, France, Italy, Japan, Netherlands, Sweden, United Kingdom, United States of America, and West Germany.

8. Increased lending by the IMF, especially to least developed countries in Africa, has raised doubts about the ability of some borrowers to repay the loans on schedule (*The Economist*, 8 June 1985, p. 63). As the IMF is prevented by its rules from rescheduling loan repayments, it remains to be seen what would happen if a borrower defaults.

9. *The Financial Times*, 27 March 1985.

10. Many such studies have been published, including the following, some of which are referred to in the text. Cline and Weintraub (1984) contains studies of the Southern Cone Countries (Diaz-Alejandro); Mexico from 1977 to 1979 (Weintraub); Peru, 1975–78 (Cline); and Tanzania in the 1970s (Weaver and Anderson), although this programme included only low conditionality facilities. Williamson (1983) includes studies of Peru 1977–80 (Diz); Argentina, Brazil and Chile (Marshall, Mardones and Marshall); Brazil (Bacha); Tanzania 1974–81 (Green); the UK (Crawford); Italy (Spaventa); Portugal, 1978 (Lopes); India (Gwin); and Turkey, 1978–82 (Okyar). Killick (1984b) contains studies on Indonesia 1966–70 (Sutton); Jamaica, 1972–80 (Sharpley); and Kenya 1975–81 (Killick). Other studies are Portugal, Turkey, and Peru (Bogdanowicz-Bindert, 1983) and Egypt and Turkey (Radke and Taske, 1983).

11. There is yet little systematic evidence available about the results of the World Bank structural adjustment loan programmes, but two World Bank programme loans were made to Tanzania in 1975 and 1977, when IMF conditionality was unacceptable to the government. The World Bank loans were longer term and lower interest than an IMF loan would have been, and appear to have had some measure of success, at least for a time (see Weaver and Anderson in Cline and Weintraub, 1981). For an account of World Bank structural adjustment loans by a staff member, see Stern (1983), and for some lessons, and assessments of structural adjustment loans to Turkey, Malawi, and Philippines, see Yagci, Kamin, and Rosenbaum (1985).

12. In some countries politicans may use the Fund as a scapegoat to avoid being blamed for unpopular decisions. On the other hand the silent masses may, on occasion, welcome the Fund as an organization which might take economic management out of the hands of local politicians. The point is highlighted by a conversation between a journalist and a member of the IMF mission to the UK in 1976.

UK journalist:	Does this mean that the IMF will take over the management of our economy?
Fund staff member:	Sorry. There's no such easy way out for you.

13. A recent suggestion by Spraos (1984) is that the Fund should concentrate on the balance of payments as a target, and that the current account of the balance of payments should be the main performance criterion. This suggestion may go some way towards satisfying developing country consternation about using credit ceilings as the main performance criterion, without fully appeasing the more extreme neo-structuralist critics.

14. The announcement at the end of March 1986, of a new IMF structural adjustment facility came too late to be included in the main text. The facility will provide SDR 2.7 billion for the world's 60 poorest countries (although China and India have agreed not to use it) over the next 6 years in 10 years loans, including a 5 year grace period, with interest of 0.5%. The facility will be administered jointly by the IMF and the World Bank, and is the first component of the Baker plan to materialize. The facility will be financed by repayments of loans to the IMF trust fund, which was originally financed by sales of IMF gold in the mid-1970's. To some extent, therefore, the new facility is in effect a mechanism for rescheduling some existing IMF debt. Nonetheless, it appears to be a step in the right direction.

Chapter 10

The Financing of Capital Investments

1. INTRODUCTION

I will now shift the discussion towards micro-finance again. This chapter will be concerned with the financing of capital investments in the third world. Compared with the industrialized countries, the developing countries are faced with a greater shortage of financial resources, and narrower and less perfect capital markets. The public sector, whether of the socialist or state capitalist variety, tends to be more dominant than in the industrialized countries. A fourth difference, which is perhaps a symptom of the three earlier differences, is that equity capital tends to be scarce. Although these differences are matters of degree rather than principle, they do result in some attitudes to investment financing in developing countries which differ from those in industrialized countries. These differences may become less apparent over time, as economies, financial institutions and capital markets develop, and enable practices to approach those in the industrialized countries.

The investment decision cannot be divorced from the financing decision. For the firm, the net present value of an investment depends upon the risk-adjusted discount rate used. This in turn depends upon the sources of finance, and the risk perceived by the financiers. A firm will invest so long as the cost of additional capital investment is less than the price at which it can sell a package of debt and equity claims on that capital. For public sector projects, the relationship between investment and financing decisions may be more distant, given the fungibility of finance in the government budget. Nevertheless, a government is still faced with the cost of borrowing, its usual marginal supply of capital. For many third world governments, foreign borrowing represents the marginal supply of capital, and the cost of foreign borrowing acts as a floor to any social discount rate which may be used in its investment analysis.

The main distinction to be made is that between projects which are financed 100% from the public sector, and those which are private sector or joint ventures between the public and private sectors. It will be helpful to subdivide public sector projects as follows.

'Non-corporate' projects
— 'Social' projects whose output is not sold commercially (These include health, education, roads, and some housing and infrastructure projects).
— Infrastructure projects whose output is sold commercially, or, at least, with an object of achieving a target rate of return.

'Corporate' projects
— public corporations, which are expected to operate commercially. This group would generally include industrial and agricultural and some services (for example, insurance and banking).

From a financing point of view the chief distinction between a public sector undertaking and a private sector (or joint) undertaking is that in the public sector one cannot go bankrupt. In the event of financial distress it is almost universally assumed that the government will cover the losses, and in the event of liquidation the government will be expected, if not strictly required, to meet the proven claims of all creditors. In the case of private sector projects there is no such financier of last resort. Perceptions of risk and, therefore, capital structures, are very different in the two cases.

In addition to project financing, described here, the identification, preparation, appraisal, implementation, and management of capital investments are of great importance in developing countries, where investment finance is often scarce. It is vital to make the best use of the available resources. Also important is the financial management of enterprises, notably through management accounting systems, liquidity control, and working capital management. These subjects together would fill a separate book, and their exclusion here is only to keep this book within reasonable bounds rather than lack of appreciation of their importance.

2. PRIVATE SECTOR INVESTMENTS

Most physical investments in both industrialized and developing countries are undertaken by existing companies,[1] or by subsidiaries of existing companies. These companies already possess an array of assets and liabilities, and of debt and equity financing instruments. Therefore the financing of any new investment, unless truly marginal to the enterprise, must be arranged in the light of the existing capital structure of the parent company. Only in cases of pure project finance, described below, can a new investment be divorced from the financing of the parent company. In the case of investments made by new companies without any existing assets or liabilities, the financing of the project and the financing of the company become one and the same thing. The same principles apply, though, to the financing of a project by an existing enterprise, so we concentrate our discussion on the latter.

A general principle of financing is to match the maturity of assets and liabilities. Thus it is desirable to finance long-term assets with long-term financing, whether it be long-term debt or equity (which in principle is indefinite). The return to long-term assets is usually spread over a number of years; therefore they cannot be expected to earn sufficiently quickly to enable them to repay debt in under 12 months, or 2 years, or in some cases in under 5 or even 10 years. The financing should be arranged so that the enterprise can service the debt, and pay the expected dividends comfortably out of its cash flow. The corollary of the general principle is that short-term assets (current assets, or working capital) can, and generally should, be financed with short-term funds.

The above principle may be difficult to meet. The company may be unable to raise long-term finance, whether of debt or equity. For example, its existing capital structure may be such that borrowers may be unwilling to provide further long-term funds, and either its record or the state of the capital market may make it difficult to raise any further equity capital. In developing countries a much more widespread problem is the general reluctance of banks to provide long-term debt finance. Hard evidence is patchy, and experience varies from country to country, but a few writers have assembled some evidence. Brodersohn (1981) has produced figures for the mid-1970s for corporate financing (see Table 10.1). Of course interpretation

Table 10.1 Corporate financing in Argentina, Uruguay and Ecuador.

(percentages of total financing)	Argentina[a]	Uruguay[b]	Ecuador[c]
Short-term debt	36.8	55.4	37.7
Long-term debt	6.5	13.4	21.5
Shareholders' funds	56.7	31.2	40.8

[a] 1977; [b] 1976; [c] average 1974–76.

of the figures is ambiguous; the need for more long-term debt depends upon the ratio of long-term to short-term assets in company balance sheets. However, Brodersohn considers that the high degree of short-term financing in Latin America does pose a problem. The practice of financing long-term assets with short-term debt does require that short-term debt will be renewed when it falls due. The risk to the enterprise is that it will not be renewed. The prevalence[2] of short-term debt over long-term debt could go some way to explaining the general preference in many developing countries for trading activities rather than investment in agriculture or manufacturing. The UNIDO's Secretariat, in its Foreword to the series of four studies of domestic financing of manufacturing enterprises in developing countries, concludes that 'In most of the countries surveyed the shortage of long-term capital is greater than that of short-term capital. There is thus a case for encouraging maturity transformation.' Dorrance (1981) found that in some African countries banking legislation restricted banks to excessively short-term assets, and that the Anglo-American concept of banking would be beneficially modified by the introduction of German–Japanese concepts such as universal banking. We saw in Chapter 4 how the reluctance of commercial banks to provide long-term credit had created the need to establish development banks. Further, the absence of a secondary market in company loan stock (debentures) further limits the ability of firms to raise long-term debt in a number of countries. The available evidence tends to support the view that corporate financing in developing countries is hampered by a shortage of long-term debt.

(a) Capital Structures

The key question when discussing capital structures is always to ask 'What if the enterprise fails?' While this may appear an unduly pessimistic note to sound at a time of arranging finance for a new project which sponsors are obviously optimistic about, it is nonetheless an important consideration which will determine the provision of finance.

In Chapter 1, under the heading financial risk, I listed the order of pay-out in cases where companies fail. I now need to expand the discussion of financial risk by presenting an overview of corporate financing, and the different instruments used. Essentially I am interested in two different types of instrument, equity and debt. The main instruments, in descending order of risk, are:

Equity	{ Ordinary shares Preference shares
Equity/Debt	Convertible loan stock
Debt	{ Secured loans 　long-term loan stock (debentures) 　long-term loans 　short-term loans Unsecured loans 　unsecured loan stock 　long-term loans 　commercial paper and short term loans

Shares and loan stock (or corporate bonds) are, in principle, negotiable instruments, as in short-term commercial paper. Loans from financial institutions such as banks are not negotiable. The only instrument which requires further explanation is convertible loan stock. As its name implies, this is a negotiable debt instrument which is convertible into ordinary shares at some prescribed time in the future, and on some prescribed terms. An attractive convertible will enable a company to raise funds at lower cost than a straight loan stock. It also gives the holder an effective stake in the equity while retaining some of the usually higher yield associated with a debenture. An analyst would count it as debt in a debt/shareholders' funds ratio, but he would count it as equity in estimating future earnings/share, as conversion would dilute existing equity.[3]

The key to company financing lies in the ratio of debt/equity, or more precisely, debt/shareholders' funds, as retained earnings belong to shareholders, and are also a very common method of financing new investments. For convenience we will use the former term, and assume the inclusion of retained earnings. Consider a new company set up to undertake a new project involving a total investment of £1 million. Assume an expected trading profit of £150,000 a year, and that no tax is payable. Some different combinations of debt/equity and different actual pre-tax profits are shown in Table 10.2, together with the return to equity which results in each case. With 50% debt at 10% interest, the return to equity is

$$\frac{150,000 - 50,000 \text{ (interest)}}{500,000} = 20\%$$

Table 10.2 shows that the effect of gearing is to boost the return to equity when the rate of return on total capital employed is above the rate of interest (10%), but to reduce the return to equity when the return on total capital is below 10%.[4] In the former case the shareholders receive the benefit of gearing; in the latter case they experience the cost of gearing. The two cases show the risk of gearing to the shareholders where annual profits fall to £20,000; they are insufficient to cover even the interest charges, let alone any principal. The lender too now experiences the risk of gearing.

Traditionally it was generally believed that the value of a firm depended on its capital structure. The three diagrams in Figure 10.1 illustrate the different positions which have been held from time to time. The first shows the value of the firm increasing as gearing increases. The second suggests

Table 10.2

| | Actual trading profit (£) | | | |
	150,000	200,000	100,000	20,000
Return on total capital (£1 million)	15%	20%	10%	2%
Debt/equity ratio				
(a) 100% equity	15%	20%	10%	2%
(b) 50% equity/50% debt (10% interest per annum)	20%	30%	10%	−6%

For £150,000 pre-tax profit, the return to 100% equity financing is

$$\frac{150,000}{1,000,000} \times 100 = 15\%$$

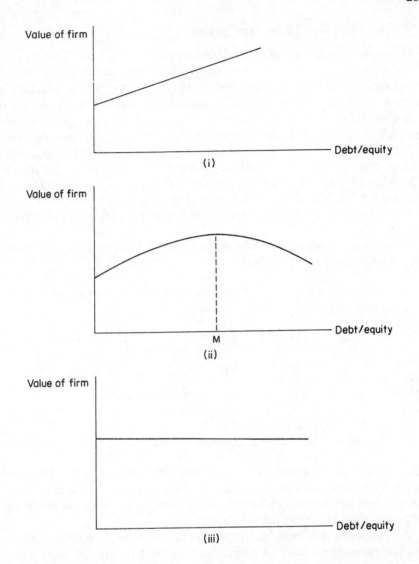

Figure 10.1 Alternative theories of the value of the firm. (i) Value of firm increases with D/E ratio; (ii) the optimum capital structure (M); (iii) value of firm is independent of D/E (Modigliani and Miller, Proposition 1)

that the value increases at low levels of gearing, but tends to fall at higher levels of gearing, as the risk of debt makes itself felt; therefore at some point there exists an optimum level of gearing, M, which maximizes the value of the firm. The third figure shows the value to be independent of the gearing. This is the representation of Modigliani and Miller's Proposition 1.

(b) The Modigliani–Miller Propositions

The central debate on capital structures centres on what are known as the Modigliani and Miller (MM) propositions. These were first presented in 1958 and amplified in three further articles (1959, 1963 and 1966), and look at capital structures, and the cost of equity capital from the point of view of the firm. MM's proposition 1 states that, with a perfect capital market and no taxation, the market value of a firm is independent of its capital structure. In other words, a firm cannot change its value to its shareholders by increasing or decreasing its debt. Intuitively, this can be explained by stating that the value of a firm is determined by its real assets, not by the method of financing them. The choice of debt or equity, ordinary or preference shares, convertible loan stock, long-term or short-term debt all have no effect on the firm.[5]

MM's proposition 2 states that the expected rate of return on the equity of a geared company is given by:

Return to total capital = Proportion of Equity × Return to equity + Proportion of debt × return to debt

or

$$R_A = \frac{E}{D+E} \times R_E + \frac{D}{D+E} \times R_D$$

or

$$R_E = R_A + \frac{D}{E}(R_A - R_D)$$

where R_E = the return to (or cost of) equity capital;
R_A = the return to total capital;
D/E = debt/equity ratio;
R_D = the return to (or cost of) debt.

This is the relationship illustrated in the numerical example above. Of course, $R_E = R_A$ in companies with no debt. The rate of return shareholders expect increases as the debt/equity ratio increases, unless $R_D > R_A$, when the rate of return decreases with the debt/equity ratio.

Although this may make gearing sound attractive to shareholders, we did start by pointing out the risk in the numerical example. In fact we will show that gearing is neither attractive nor unattractive; it is neutral. The higher expected returns as a result of gearing do no more than compensate for the increased risk. In the example we saw that a fall in trading profit from £200,000 to £100,000 (50%) reduced the rate of return from 20% to 10% (or by 10%) in the case of 100% equity, but from 30% to 10% (or by 20%) in the case of 50% debt finance. We can now recall β from Chapter 2 as the measure of riskiness of the shares. Whatever the β of equity before debt, it is twice as high with debt.

In the same way as the expected return on a firm's assets is a weighted average of the expected return on the individual securities, so the β value of the firm's assets is a weighted average of the β of the individual securities.

β of assets = (Proportion of debt × β of debt) + (Proportion of equity × β of equity)

$$\beta_A = \frac{D}{D+E} \times \beta_D + \frac{E}{D+E} \times \beta_E$$

or
$$\beta_E = \beta_A + \frac{D}{E}(\beta_A - \beta_D)$$

The increased risk to equity as a result of taking on debt rises as the debt/equity ratio rises, in just the same way as required return rises as the debt/equity ratio rises. Therefore the increase in the required return merely compensates for the additional risk of taking on debt. The relationship is illustrated in Figure 10.2, assuming that debt is risk-free (i.e. $\beta_D = 0$, so $\beta_E = \beta_A (1 + [D/E])$. We have taken the case of profit of £200,000 in our example, and $D/E = 1$, so $\beta_E = 2\beta_A$.

So far we have assumed that the firm can borrow as much as it wishes, and that its bonds are risk-free and carry the risk-free rate of interest. But the increase in debt does increase the riskiness of debt. The higher the debt, the higher the risk that a downturn in profits will mean that the firm cannot meet the interest payments on the debt. Therefore as the firm borrows more the risk of default increases and so lenders will demand higher returns to compensate for the higher risk. Figure 10.3 illustrates the position.

Up to the dotted line, lenders consider the debt to be risk-free. As the D/E ratio increases beyond the dotted line, lenders perceive that debt

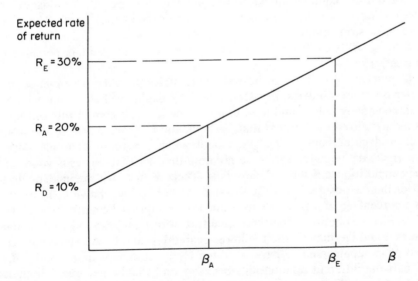

Figure 10.2 Relationship between expected return and risk for ungeared and geared equity (expected trading profit = £200,000)

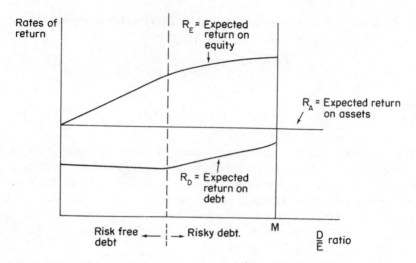

Figure 10.3 MM Proposition 2: rates of return and the debt : equity ratio

becomes increasingly risky, and the cost of debt increases gradually. The effect on R_E is that it no longer increases in a straight line as debt increases, but flattens out. This is because the suppliers of risky debt are increasingly taking over the firm's business risk. There is a maximum debt/equity ratio, M, beyond which lenders are no longer prepared to lend. This can be illustrated by taking the *reductio ad absurdum* case of 100% debt. At this level the firm's equity is valueless, and it is therefore by definition bankrupt. The creditors own the firm, and their debt becomes the equity. Therefore debt must stop somewhere short of 100%. The position of the dotted line and of M will vary from firm to firm, depending how lenders perceive its business risk.

In practice M is likely to be well short of 100%, although practice may differ between countries. Lenders, especially banks, will ask 'what happens if the company fails?', and look to their security. A common rule of thumb in industrialized countries is that, in liquidation, a forced sale of the assets will produce perhaps 50% of their book value. Therefore cautious lenders prefer the debt/equity ratio to be no more than 1 : 1. If it goes beyond 1 : 1 they stand to lose if the company fails. Their security will be inadequate to cover their exposure. The OECD found the borrowings shown in Table 10.3 as a percentage of total assets for some major industrial countries. The main difference lies between the three countries with high gearing ratios (Japan, France, and Germany), and the lower-geared UK and USA. These patterns, except in Japan, tend to have persisted for a century or more, and reflect in part the different relationships between banks and companies, discussed in Chapter 3. However, in the reconstruction following the Second World War, high debt ratios were encouraged in Japan and Germany so that the shortage of equity would not restrain growth. There was a perceived trade-

Table 10.3   Balance sheets of non-financial enterprises

	1970	1982
France	65	73
Germany	63	59
Japan	84	83
United Kingdom	52	53
United States	44	37

Source: OECD, Non-Financial Enterprises Financial Statements.
Financial Statistics Part 3 (various issues).

off between growth (high debt/equity) and robust balance sheets (low debt-/equity). The model has been considered relevant for developing countries, where the pursuit of growth is often considered to be worth the risk of increased instability.

White (1984), in discussing the above ratios, concludes that variations between countries in gearing ratios calculated from reported company balance sheets are significantly greater than the true effective gearing. A realistic estimate of Japanese gearing ratios may be 60–70%, and the US nearer to 30%. Nonetheless, the differences are still considerable. The usual explanation is that Japan, France, and Germany have relatively underdeveloped equity markets, and the agency costs of raising equity capital are rather higher than in the USA and the UK. By contrast, the relationship between firms and their bankers is much closer in Japan, France, and Germany than in the USA and the UK, which may mean that agency costs of debt are relatively low, and shareholders may benefit from company gearing. Nonetheless White (1984) concludes by emphasizing that 'the cost of gearing in terms of more volatile earnings to shareholders and the risk of insolvency has stimulated much of the well-documented encouragement that is currently being given in France, Germany and Japan for a greater use of equity finance by companies in these countries'.

To return to the MM propositions, it must be explained that MM should not be interpreted to mean that the debt/equity ratio does not matter. Rather, it suggests that under certain assumptions there is no reason for a company to prefer debt to equity. A high proportion of debt, though, produces a fragile capital structure, leaving a firm vulnerable to external shocks, which can readily lead to financial distress. In an economy where high gearing is widespread, an unfavourable external shock can lead to widespread distress, and the knock-on effects can threaten other firms and major banks and lending institutions.

(c)   A Review of the MM Propositions

In deriving their two propositions described above, MM made the following major assumptions.

(a) The capital market is highly competitive.
(b) Shareholders can borrow on the same terms as companies.
(c) There are no taxes.
(d) There is no risk of bankruptcy, and shareholders can sell short.

Bromwich (1976) has a full discussion of the assumptions and the debate surrounding the MM propositions. The theory was clearly designed for countries with large and efficient stock markets, and for companies with stock market quotations. Under these circumstances the market will recognize the increase in risk when a company borrows at a rate below the cost of equity, and will not increase the value of the shares as a result of the borrowing. By and large a case can be made that stock markets in industrialized countries are sufficiently efficient generally to fulfil the MM propositions.

The assumption that shareholders can borrow on the same terms as companies is necessary, so that one can argue that shareholders are just as well off

(a) by buying geared company equity; or
(b) by buying ungeared company equity and obtaining the gearing by borrowing directly themselves.

The individual, it is argued, can arrange his own gearing, and does not need a company to do it for him. There has been substantial debate on this point. It has been argued that the individual borrower cannot enjoy the same conditions as the company borrower, because the latter enjoys limited liability whereas the former does not. Therefore by borrowing to buy equity the individual stands the risk of losing not only his investment but his loan as well. He might therefore prefer the company to borrow on his behalf. It is also argued that individuals cannot borrow as cheaply as companies, although academics are divided on this point. Individuals can often raise subsidized debt (for example, for housing finance).

A major qualification arises when corporation taxes are introduced. Now the borrowing company can offset its interest costs against its profits before taxes are calculated, thereby reducing its after-tax cost of borrowing. In many countries individual shareholders cannot set the interest charges against their tax bill (or only for specific borrowing such as for house purchase), and therefore the shareholders are better off if the company borrows on their behalf than if they borrow directly.[6] The benefit which accrues to the shareholder from company borrowings depends upon the mechanics of the corporation tax system.

The deductibility of interest for tax purposes is clearly one reason for corporate borrowing, but if MM, as seems to be the case, is a reasonably robust theory, what other explanations are available to explain the popularity of corporate borrowing? One possibility is that it is cheaper and often quicker to arrange bank debt than to issue fresh equity, either via a rights issue or via a placing. Moreover, the discount which it is necessary to offer shareholders and underwriters may increase the cost of equity capital, especially at times when the market is reluctant to accept rights issues. Private or unquoted public companies may not be able to obtain more capital from existing shareholders, and may be unwilling to dilute ownership and control by offering shares to outsiders. Moreover, shares in unqoted companies tend to have much lower ratings than shares in quoted companies, making the cost of equity capital relatively expensive for unquoted companies. Under these circumstances debt may be more attractive to existing owners than issuing further equity. A further possible explanation is that managers, and their shareholders, believe that they can earn extraordinary returns from additional capital, and that the market does not fully recognize this ability. In this case they believe that shareholders really will obtain benefits from debt.

A more substantial reason for firms to take on debt may be its fairly easy availability. This comes about because investors prefer to hold some of their financial assets as money in the form of bank deposits. As banks in many countries prefer to lend rather than take equity, this money is available to firms only in the form of debt. There is an institutional division, therefore, between the markets for debt and the markets for equity. But whatever the explanation for firms' debt/equity ratios, it is not to be found in MM, and more research may be needed on the subject.

A word is necessary about the impact of inflation on debt, and whether or not inflation increases the attractiveness of debt. Managers expecting negative real rates of interest may feel justified in borrowing on shareholders' behalf. However, shareholders still have the possibility of borrowing for themselves. Moreover, in efficient money markets an expectation of rising inflation will be met by rising money rates of interest, as holders of money demand higher returns in compensation. Only if borrowing is made at fixed rates can a borrower have the possibility of benefiting from inflation in an efficient market. He also has the risk of losing, should interest rates decline.

(d) MM and the Developing Countries

If one accepts that MM holds up reasonably in industrialized countries, it is far from clear that it can be exported readily to the majority of third world countries. Its weakness lies in the assumptions made. Although these may hold by and large in industrialized countries, they may be unrealistic in the bulk of developing countries. The major weakness lies in the assumption of highly competitive capital markets.

As shown in Chapter 6, most developing countries do not have stock markets. Of those which do, many have narrow markets which are far from efficient, and which tend to have only a handful of quoted companies. Under these circumstances market valuations of shares may vary with the gearing of the company, and managers may perceive some benefits in borrowing. Even companies with stock market quotations may find that the narrow markets and limited underwriting facilities make it difficult to raise further equity capital as an alternative to borrowing. Unquoted companies will find they have even less room for manoeuvre. Repression in money markets may mean that the cost of debt does not reflect the risk of debt, and that debt may be available very cheaply, perhaps at substantially negative real rates of interest, to some corporate borrowers. On the other hand the rationing of debt, which is the consequence of financial repression, may mean that some borrowers have their access to debt restricted. Company managers may find that they have difficulty in raising additional capital, even for attractive projects, and that they have limited control over the level of the debt/equity ratio. The ability of shareholders to borrow, and at terms similar to those enjoyed by the firms, are both questionable assumptions in repressed money markets. Finally, the qualification to MM concerning tax applies equally in developing and industrialized countries.

To summarize, it appears in developing countries that firms may at times be able to benefit their shareholders by borrowing, but that they will generally be more constrained in their access to new finance, either equity or debt, than their equivalent is in industrialized countries which face large and competitive capital markets. As a generalization, it seems that MM is of questionable relevance to firms in developing countries, who generally must finance any new investment in whatever way they can. Only a few large firms, operating in the few developing countries with reasonably competitive capital markets, may be exceptions to this rule.

(e) Is there a Shortage of Equity in Developing Countries?

Chapter 3 discussed the prevalence of financial repression in developing countries, the impact it had on the intermediation process, and the consequent bottleneck in the supply of loanable funds. The conclusion was that debt finance is in shorter supply, and/or is higher cost than it would be in a competitive market, and that the availability of debt finance to a firm is restricted. By contrast, it is sometimes suggested that it is the shortage of equity capital which acts as a constraint on investment, as lending institutions set limits on the debt/equity ratios of borrowers, which means that there is a point beyond which debt will no longer be forthcoming without a proportionate increase in equity. This is a constraint which the debt-intermediation theory of financial repression, discussed in Chapter 3, does not recognize.

Lenders, of course, in some instances take a very relaxed view of the debt/equity ratio of firms, allowing it, almost by default, to reach and maintain very high levels. In these cases the shortage of equity capital does not act as a constraint on investment. Firms can pay out a high percentage of profit in dividends, yet continue to invest by using debt. Debtors might not attempt to restraint dividends, which, if they did, would lead to an increase in retained earnings, and a fall in the debt/shareholders' funds ratio.

Although the shortage of equity may not constrain investment, it will lead to fragile balance sheets, which are extremely vulnerable to business risk, interest rate risk, and, if foreign currency debt is included, exchange rate risk.

Shortages of equity could arise for the following reasons:

— The level of private savings held by individuals may be too low to enable them to put up share capital.

— Although private savings may be plentiful there may be a reluctance among individuals to accept the risk of domestic equity investment, for reasons of low risk preference, social or religious constraints or lack of opportunity, understanding, or confidence in equity investment. Some savers may prefer to invest abroad.

— Among existing enterprises the level of profits or the level of retained earnings may be inadequate to finance new capital investment. This may be brought about by shareholders expecting high dividend yields.

— Government regulations may discourage the supply of equity capital. Some sectors of the economy may be restricted to the government only; in others the bureaucratic process which has to be gone through to obtain permission to invest may discourage investors (the processes are usually installed by government in the name of economic planning); taxation may be considered too high; regulations and attitudes may discourage private investment from abroad. Finally the financial markets and institutions may be controlled and repressed in ways which discourage portfolio or physical investment. Egypt, from 1952 to the late 1970s, exhibited most of these factors which discourage equity investment.

— Family business may be reluctant to expand if it implies admitting some outside equity, which may result in a loss of financial privacy or control, or both.

The scarcity of equity capital in developing countries relative to industrialized countries is best illustrated by reference to Annex 4.2. Here the dominance of the commercial banking system over other financial institutions in mobilizing savings showed that institutional equity investment is likely to be very low in most developing countries. Commercial banks, as a rule, do not provide equity capital, whereas other financial institutions generally do. The provision of personal portfolio equity capital in most countries is similarly restricted by the small size, or absence, of stock markets. Therefore for most firms, equity capital can only come from the proprietor's own sources or from retained earnings. Comprehensive studies of the financing of business in developing countries are scarce, or not well publicized. I quoted earlier some figures of debt and shareholders' funds for three Latin American countries. The ratios obtained for debt to shareholders' funds are shown in Table 10.4. An analysis of combined balance sheets of Indian companies gives the ratios shown in Table 10.5. Rao is of the opinion that even the low debt ratios shown in Table 10.5 over-state the true magnitude of debt. In India the guidelines issued by the Controller of Capital Issues limit the debt/equity to

Table 10.4   Capital structures in Argentina, Uruguay and Ecuador

	Long-term debt: shareholders' funds	Total debt: shareholders' funds
Argentina	0.11:1	0.75:1
Uruguay	0.43:1	2.23:1
Ecuador	0.53:1	1.44:1

As short-term debt is used widely in Latin America to finance long-term debt, it may be more appropriate to compare total debt, rather than long-term debt, to shareholders' funds.

2 : 1, even for new companies, and only in exceptional circumstances is a higher level of debt permitted, for example for large fertilizer or paper projects. Only the total debt ratio of the small private limited companies exceed the 2 : 1 ratio. In aggregate it appears that companies in India have adequate equity and the 2 : 1 maximum permitted ratio is rather lower than that pertaining in many developing countries.

Information in other countries is less comprehensive, if available at all. Shetty (1982) estimated that for 'pioneer' companies in Malaysia the ratio of paid-up capital to total capital investment varied between 42% and 82% for the years 1975–79. Shetty thought that as pioneer companies have par-

Table 10.5   Capital structures in India

	Long-term debt: shareholders' funds	Total debt (excluding trade debt): shareholders' funds
396 Large public limited companies (1977/78)	0.35:1	0.74:1
957 Medium-sized public limited companies (1977/78)	0.54:1	1.8 :1
678 Small public limited companies (1977/78)	0.18:1	0.97:1
114 Government companies (1976/77)	0.62:1	0.92:1
1125 Small private limited companies (1975/76)	0.38:1	2.2 :1
New projects of 129 new public limited companies	2:1	2:1

Source: Derived from Rao (1981), based on Reserve Bank of India data.

ticular appeal they may have attracted a relatively large paid-up component. Nonetheless, the proportion of equity looks at least adequate and in some years, very substantial. The same study embraced also Bangladesh, Indonesia, Sri-Lanka, and Thailand, but was not able to find any further representative data on capital structures.

Drake (1983) reports an unpublished World Bank Study on the financial sector in Korea, which found a ratio of outside liabilities to equities of 82 : 18, or 4.56 : 1, for Korean corporations. Drake comments that Korean companies are still largely family concerns whose owners resist the reduction of control which would result from admitting outside equity. Also Korean shareholders expect a return on equity similar to that available on risk-free bank deposits. Therefore equity can be difficult to service. Moreover, the availability of concessional credit from a highly directed system, and the deductibility of interest for tax purposes, makes debt attractive relative to equity. A Securities and Exchange Control regulation requiring new shares to be issued at par inhibits their issue if they stand above par in the secondary market. Much the same conditions are found in some other countries, notably Indonesia and the Philippines, where high debt ratios are common. Debt of up to 85% of shareholders' funds has been reported from the Philippines. The corporate sector experienced considerable financial distress in the early 1980s; subsequently the Developing Bank of the Philippines started to insist on a maximum debt ratio of 75%, because of unhappy default experiences with more highly geared companies. In recent years the debt/shareholder's funds ratio in Indonesia has been restricted to 2 : 1, and permission from Bank Indonesia (the central bank) is required if this ratio is to be exceeded.

The patchy information which is available can lead to no general conclusion. Moreover, the data are open to different interpretations. High debt ratios may suggest that equity is scarce, but equally they can be interpreted to mean that debt is plentiful. Likewise, low debt ratios may suggest that equity is used extensively because long-term debt is scarce. A knowledge of the financial markets in individual countries is needed before conclusions can be reached on the relative availability of debt and equity.

(f) Financing Small-scale Enterprises (SSEs)

It is a widely held belief that SSEs are potentially fast-growing enterprises, and significant creators of employment. It is equally frequently alleged that their growth is restricted because of lack of access to external capital. The discussion of the financial problems of SSEs is usually couched in terms of lack of access to credit, but it seems that lack of access to outside equity may be just as important in some cases. The problems, and the measures proposed to counter them, are encountered in industrialized countries just as much as in developing countries. The definition of an SSE will vary considerably from country to country; in some cases it may refer to a single proprietor with a handful of employees; in others it may refer to much larger enterprises, with a number of shareholders, fairly substantial assets, and perhaps 100 or more employees. For our purposes we will define them as enterprises which have little access to formal sources of finance, whether debt or equity.

SSEs are generally considered to be high-risk enterprises to lend to. Although their growth rate may in some instances be spectacular, their failure rate is also rather higher than larger, better-established concerns. A bank or other formal financial institution, when approached for credit from an SSE, may raise a number of the following objections to lending.

— The proprietor/manager has little experience, and the enterprise has little or no history of past performance.

— Financial records (book-keeping) may be in a poor state, or non-existent, with the result that the lender cannot form an accurate view of the trading performance of the enterprise.

— The value of the assets, as collateral for a loan, may be negligible or difficult to assess.

— The costs of administering loans to such an enterprise may be greater that the profit from the loan. (For example, a bank which lends £1000 with a 5% margin between its borrowing and lending rates will earn only £50/year. This is less than the cost of one man-day of professional employee's time, yet has to cover the cost and time of visits, and the cost and time of record-keeping, even assuming that no difficulties arise with the loan.)

— Banks may be constrained by government in the interest rates they charge, which means that they cannot charge higher rates to compensate for the higher risk involved in SSE lending.

The degree of risk, as measured by the default rate in small enterprises lending programmes, varies considerably. Anderson (1982) speaks of variations from 10% to 60% or more; Bottomley (1975) found similar variations in the default rate on agricultural credit. In cases where the perceived risk is high, lenders need to charge high rates to compensate for high risk. This the informal credit market does; formal credit institutions find it more difficult to do it, with the result that all SSE borrowers pay high rates. The low-risk borrowers suffer because of the high-risk borrowers.

The conventional approach to the problem of financing SSEs is to recognize their need for funds at interest rates below those charged by the informal sector, and for governments to institute some form of subsidy scheme, usually by providing guarantees to commercial banks on SSE lending, or by offering rediscounting facilities through the central bank (e.g. World Bank, 1978). For example, in India the Deposit Insurance and Credit Guarantee Corporation guarantees loans to SSEs of up to 90% of the amount in default. According to Rao (1981), 'the flow of credit to the small borrowers has been considerably facilitated by the small loan guarantee scheme'. In the Gambia the UN Capital Development Fund guarantees 75% of bank loans to SSEs which are made in cooperation with the Indigenous Business Advisory Service.

The author observed that the scheme was working quite well, although heavily dependent on expatriate expertise. The UK government also operates a scheme which guarantees 75% of credit advances by commercial banks to small businesses.

The problem with guarantee schemes is that they bring with them moral hazards. Lenders may lend carelessly, and borrowers may not give as much attention as they might to prompt debt service. Nevertheless, they do appear to assist the flow of credit to SSEs. What they cannot do is to help SSEs raise outside equity. There comes a time in the life of many SSEs when their expansion is restricted by the inability of shareholders to contribute adequate new equity, and their existing debt/equity ratio makes further borrowing unwise or impossible. In the USA and the UK in recent years, some SSEs have been able to raise new equity from venture capital enterprises, who, roughly speaking, take the view that the gains from backing one 'winner' more than offset the losses from four 'losers'. Larger SSEs have been able to raise equity on the over-the-counter stock markets, especially in the USA, while the advent of the Unlisted Securities Market in the UK and the Second Marché in France have provided access to new equity for companies which would not qualify for a full stock exchange listing.

For many developing countries we see considerable potential in the venture capital approach to SSE financing. The provision of equity, rather than loan, capital conforms to the principle that the higher the risk, the lower the debt to equity ratio should be. More important, it also enables suppliers of funds to share in the growth of the successful companies which will offset the losses subsequent on financing the companies which fail. Schemes which provide only credit have the worst of both worlds; they face the high risks associated with SSEs, but do not have the opportunity to share in the rewards of success. The establishment of SSE financing programmes or vehicles which offer the benefits as well as the costs of high-risk investment should obviate the need for the subsidies or guarantees which are needed in pure credit programmes.

Venture capital companies could be established by merchant banks, commercial banks and development banks, pension funds, and life insurance companies, either as wholly owned subsidiaries or with a number of shareholders. (Investors in Industry in the UK, which provides both equity and loan capital for small and medium enterprises, is owned jointly by the clearing banks and the Bank of England.) If stock markets exist, financial institutions can float venture capital firms on the market, thereby bringing in outside equity. The firms would be regarded as specialized investment trusts (closed-ended funds) or as financial companies. Individuals or groups could establish venture capital firms financed by their own resources and/or by borrowing from commercial banks. The possibilities are considerable, but the details depend on the financial infrastructure of individual countries. Venture finance is essentially risk capital; equity is the obvious form, but it may also be provided in the form of convertible loan stock and non-collateralized debt (perhaps with options), such as pure project finance. The pay-off for a venture capital firm generally comes when it sells a shareholding in a successful company at a profit. Ideally this is done by arranging a stock market quotation for a company, which implies the existence of an active stock market. Alternatively the shares could be sold on an active over-the-counter market. The latter can (and should) be developed by financial institutions acting as market makers in developing countries where stock markets do not exist. The idea of venture capital enterprises for developing countries is recent, although not new. Since 1978 the IFC has invested in venture capital firms in Spain, Brazil, and the Philippines. The Development Bank of Malaysia also has a venture capital fund. Brazil, Malaysia, and the Philippines are, significantly, developing countries with active stock markets. However, the potential for venture capital appears to be considerable, and the important role that it can play underlines the need to encourage the development of securities' markets. The tax position of venture capital firms needs careful consideration, and it is of interest that the USA and French governments provide special tax concessions.

(g) Pure Project Financing (Non-recourse Financing)

The definition of pure project financing is the provision of debt in which the lender has recourse only to the assets of the project for his security and to the cash flow of the project for amortization of his loan. Although it is used mainly in private sector projects, it is applicable to public sector investments also. The intention of pure project financing is to separate the financing of the project from the other activities of its sponsors. Pure project finance, therefore, does not depend upon a guarantee of a parent company or government which owns the project in question. For a company, pure project finance may be attractive if the debt incurred can legitimately be kept off the balance sheet. For a government it may be attractive if the debt can be kept out of the government's foreign debt statistics. It may be attractive to lenders if the project appears an attractive risk, while at the same time the sponsor's existing balance sheet could not comfortably take in more debt. Likewise, a lender may prefer pure project financing to a government guarantee if he feels that the government is already over-borrowed. Pure project financing would enable the lender to keep clear of any debt rescheduling which may occur, negative pledge clauses permitting.

The incidence of absolutely pure project financing may be relatively rare. Lenders do like to have some security outside the project, especially during the construction period. During this time the value of the fixed assets as security is generally very little. If the lender has to take possession of, for example, a half-built refinery, then he is likely to receive very little for it in a forced sale. A guarantee may be provided by the sponsor for the construction period, or, if the liability is to be kept completely off balance sheet, then a guarantee may be provided by a third party such as the sponsor's bank, or a party with a strong interest in the project such as the contractor or an important supplier. After start-up the lender may find his security in some arrangement like a throughput agreement rather than from the sponsor. Throughput agreements have been used in oil refinery financing when the refinery will be used by third parties. The third parties enter into processing agreements with the sponsor for, say, 3 or 5 years, and arrange to pay a portion or all of the processing fees to the lender. The lender's security is derived from the throughput agreement rather than from the sponsor. The lender will still keep a first charge over the assets. In spite of such agreements, project finance is generally higher-risk debt than conventional lending.

The extent to which a company can legally use pure project financing depends on the nature of the company laws and tax regulations under which it operates. Exactly the same qualification applies to leasing rather than buying assets; the law will determine whether or not a company can keep such arrangements off balance sheet, or whether or not there are tax advantages to be obtained. The subject of structuring such loans is discussed in much greater detail by Nevitt (1980), particularly in the context of US law. Pure project finance has been used principally for large projects, mainly in the oil, mining, forest products, utilities, and transportation fields, and two illustrations will help to show how it works.

Project financing with a throughput agreement was arranged for a proposed processing refinery in Sicily in the mid-1970s. At the time the sponsor's balance sheet could stand only a limited increase in debt, and it was not in a good position to raise further equity capital. Debt finance was sought and the potential clients requested to enter into throughput agreements, under which they agreed to process a minimum quantity of crude oil for 4 years, and to pay the fees for the minimum quantities direct to the lending banks. The banks were in effect guaranteed their repayments for 4 years by the users. In the event the arrangement collapsed because of the expected decline in demand for oil products and the appearance of surplus refining capacity in Europe. The banks decided that the agreements were not adequate security. They foresaw that the users of the refinery may attempt to release themselves from the contracts, and may not even be able to afford to honour them. Furthermore, a first claim over the assets would not be worth very much if considerable excess capacity did arise in Europe. With the benefit of hindsight, the banks were wise to pull out of the arrangement.

A further case which was successful is that of project financing for BP's Forties field in the North Sea. Brealey and Myers (1981) given an account of the arrangements (pp. 491–3). Essentially the syndicate of banks made the loan to a company called Norex, which was controlled by the banks. Norex paid the money over to BP Development, not as a loan, but as an advanced payment for oil, to be produced by the Forties field. They further arranged for BP Trading (another subsidiary) to repurchase the oil from the Norex at a prescribed price. The banks stood the risk that the reserves would be inadequate to service the loan; they had no further claim against BP's other assets. The huge loan of $945 million did not appear in BP's balance sheet — it would have upset it considerably. All that appeared in the accounts was a deferred liability of BP Development to supply oil to Norex and of BP Trading to repurchase it.

3. PUBLIC SECTOR PROJECTS

The government budget is the key to financing of government-owned projects. In any year the amount available for capital expenditure is given by

Tax revenue + Net borrowing + Foreign aid + Earnings (−Losses) of state enterprises − Current expenditure.

For a country with a foreign exchange constraint, the budget should be separated into domestic currency and foreign currency components.

With the exception of certain foreign finance, government funds from specific sources are not earmarked for specific projects. Even bonds issued with names such as Energy 1995 or Transport 2000 are not used to raise revenue for Energy or Transport projects. The proceeds merely go into the overall government budget. In many cases such bonds may be used simply to retire existing debt. Government finance is fungible. Therefore given the estimates of what is available for capital expenditure, government has to divide the amount among the various sectors according to its priorities, and according to the available projects which have been prepared and which have passed its various economic tests. It is necessary, though, to take account of the future annual requirements of the projects in terms of current expenditures or expected operating losses. Any project which does not have a positive cash flow will require future funding, and add to the government's current expenditure.

The use of foreign financing for projects is less clear-cut. Project aid is clearly earmarked for individual projects, agreed by the recipient and donor. Export credits are just as clearly tied to individual projects, ex-post, unless they come in the form of a line of export credit when the recipient can allocate the credit to projects ex-ante.[7] Eurocurrency loans, though, are not usually tied to specific projects, except in cases of pure project financing, discussed above. The difficulty with foreign currency debt is that it has to be serviced in foreign currency. Except in cases of pure project financing the debt service will be met from the government's foreign exchange availability, which will come largely from the country's export earnings rather than from the foreign exchange earnings of the project.

This may be taken to imply that the foreign exchange earning potential of an individual project is irrelevant to a decision to use foreign debt finance for that project. Government should not look to an individual project to earn sufficient foreign exchange to meet the foreign exchange debt service arising from the project. While this analysis may be correct for an individual project, its weakness is exposed when many government-financed projects do not earn sufficient foreign exchange to cover their foreign exchange debt service. The implicit assumption when one such project was being considered was that the economy would somehow generate sufficient additional foreign exchange to meet the additional (and relatively small) debt service obligation. What may be an acceptable assumption for one project no longer holds when a substantial number of such projects are undertaken, since the economy is now required to generate a non-marginal amount of additional foreign exchange to meet the total additional debt service requirement. The government should now consider the country's forecast foreign exchange earnings, and their riskiness,[8] and its forecast foreign exchange obligations, again taking into account the risk of interest rate and exchange rate movements, before accepting foreign exchange debt to finance projects which are not expected to service their own foreign exchange debt. In practice, one of the reasons for the third world debt problem is the practice of widespread use of foreign exchange to finance infrastructure and social service projects which do not generate foreign exchange. Any downturn (or shortfall in forecast growth) in foreign exchange earnings then leaves the country unable to meet its external debt service obligations. Project financing with external debt carries greater risks than financing with a country's own resources, or with non-debt external finance, such as grants or direct foreign investment. As a general rule it is prudent to use external debt finance only for projects which are expected to serve the foreign debt out of their foreign exchange earnings, but for most countries, such an ideal is not practicable. A country with adequate foreign exchange can afford to take a more relaxed attitude, but then it probably does not need foreign debt anyway.

(a) 'Non-corporate' Projects

We include under this heading social services projects, educational and health projects such as schools and hospitals, and infrastructure projects which do not generate income. The chief characteristic of non-corporate projects is that they are not intended to produce any revenue, or perhaps only a small amount which may be generated from prescription charges or token school fees. These projects fall into areas where the government intends to provide services to the population which are free or heavily subsidized.

The lack of any significant income from these projects suggests immediately that debt finance is unsuitable for them, and that they should be financed either by a grant from the government or from overseas grant aid. Moreover, in an ideal world a grant from the government should be financed from tax revenues, rather than from government borrowing, as the projects do not yield income which can be used for servicing the debt. Such a counsel of perfection can rarely be followed. However, the fungibility of government income (tax revenues and borrowings all go into the same pool) means that government expenditure does not carry a tab saying 'from tax income' or 'from borrowing'. Secondly, the tendency of governments to borrow more to retire existing debt, thereby gradually increasing the national debt, means that they are less concerned about the means of financing non-corporate projects than they might be. The only likely constraints are those which might be applied to the overall government budget, such as a fixed ratio between tax revenue and borrowing, or an annual ceiling or public sector borrowing.

The remarks made earlier about taking on foreign debt apply with particular force if it is to be used to finance the non-corporate type of project. The projects do not even produce local currency to use for debt service. A country which embarks on a programme of financing its schools, hospitals, or road-building programme using foreign debt is exposing the whole economy to considerable future risk. The risk is lower with low-interest, long-maturity aid than with commercial Eurocurrency loans, but it is there nonetheless. As a general rule non-corporate projects should be financed with domestic currency. Of course this is not always possible. Donors will from time to time offer concessional loans to finance schools, hospitals, or roads. However, before these offers are accepted, government should be confident that domestic currency is being invested which will earn sufficient foreign exchange to cover the debt service of the aid, whether the domestic currency investment is made by the public or the private sector. Such a conservative financing policy may slow down the rate of investment a little, but so too does an external debt crisis. Any cost in investment forgone is more than offset by the benefits of avoiding a possible external debt crisis, and the disruption it causes by reducing essential imports such as raw materials and spare parts for factories. Governments must try to ensure that their, and the country's, foreign exchange obligations do not exceed their resources.

(b) 'Corporate' Investments

Public sector investments in utilities such as electricity, gas, water, communications, and public transport are usually made by public corporations,[9] as are government investments in industry and agriculture. The public corporation has six possible sources of investment capital.
— government equity
— government grant
— government loan
— domestic borrowing (non-government)
— foreign borrowing
— retained earnings.
The essential difference between analysing capital structures for state and private sector corporations is that there exists no body of theory which is applicable to state corporations. First, the private shareholder can be attri-

buted a straightforward motive, to maximize his returns, whereas the government as shareholder usually has a mixture of motives. Secondly, the state corporation is not always expected to operate in a way which maximizes the shareholder's return. Third, and perhaps most critical, is the absence of the risk of financial failure in the state sector. The government will usually be relied upon to finance any losses which arise, thereby nullifying the risk which may arise from the gearing in the capital structure. If all the finance comes from the government, the capital structure is unimportant; all government finance ranks equally and the cost of different types of capital to the government is the same. The capital structure becomes important only when outside debt comes in, from domestic bank, foreign bank, or aid loans, and ranks above government debt. The lack of theory for the financing of state corporations means that for practical purposes no guidelines exist; therefore practice varies enormously from country to country and even within countries.

Government Finance

First in many countries it is not clear whether the finance which government contributes is equity, a grant, or a subsidized loan. (A grant is really an extreme case of a subsidy; one that clearly does not give rise to any claims.) In most public corporations it is not clear that government expects to receive any dividend. Gillis, Jenkins and Lessard (1982) quote Indonesia, Pakistan, and Sri Lanka as three countries where state corporations have an obligation to transfer a portion of after-tax income to the government, but such a clear obligation is exceptional. In many state corporations, of course, the question of dividend obligations is academic, as profits are negligible or negative. In some enterprises losses are financed by further injections of government funds which may enter the balance sheet as debt or equity, depending on established practice. The distinctions between debt, grant, and equity hardly matters; in the absence of the risk of failure, capital structures are unimportant.

In some countries government funds may be classed as loans in order to place the enterprise under an obligation to service the debt. The title 'loan' may be used in order to impose some discipline on the state corporation. Another reason is that loans may not be classified as government expenditures whereas equity or grant would be. A further circumstance under which loans are provided is when the government is the formal recipient of aid from another government or international agency which is intended for a state corporation. The money would then be on-lent with, usually, a comfortable mark-up added to the interest rate by the government to accompany it. The ultimate obligation to repay the foreign debt rests, of course, with the government rather than the state corporation. Even if an injection of finance to an enterprise is nominally a loan, it certainly cannot be assumed that the principal will be repaid, or even that the interest will be paid. Even in industrialized countries, such as the UK, it has been common practice to finance losses of state corporations with loans, which are eventually written off or converted into equity. In the absence of dividends and the possibility of sale of equity, these amount to the same thing; the government will not get its money back.

Domestic Borrowing (Non-government)

The access of state corporations to non-government credit varies from country to country. At one extreme is the case where borrowing is permitted only exceptionally. In the UK, for example, borrowing by state corporations needs the prior consent of parliament. In other countries, borrowing by state corporations is widespread and substantial. Gillis, Jenkins, and Lessard (1982) consider that state corporations frequently have preferential access to credit from state-owned financial institutions such as commercial banks and development banks. In countries where interest rate ceilings are in force, the effect may be to allow state corporations to pre-empt the limited amount of domestic credit which is available, at concessional interest rates. Moreover, the general reluctance of governments to allow state corporations to fail removes the risk of bankruptcy to private sector financial institutions. This gives them preferential access to credit, and on the finest terms when the lenders have discretion in setting lending rates.

Government loans, though, will almost certainly be subordinate to non-government loans, which means that the gearing effect will increase the risk of the return to the government as a shareholder. In many countries, though, governments may prefer state corporations to raise loans outside the government. Such borrowing may not appear in the public accounts as central government debt, whereas a loan provided by the government would imply a commensurate increase in government borrowing.

Lending by the non-government financial institutions will clearly be granted on the basis of the perceived creditworthiness of the government rather than the borrowing corporation. The lender will usually be even less concerned about the use to which the loan will be put. Therefore state corporations which have access to non-government borrowing may not have their investment projects thoroughly checked by outsiders; the government ministry to which they are responsible may not have the capacity, except for large investments, and the lenders have no incentive to examine the projects.

Foreign Borrowing

Foreign debt may be raised by state corporations in two ways, either by borrowing directly itself with an explicit or implicit government guarantee, or by government borrowing which is then on-lent to the corporation. In the case of borrowing (or grants) from foreign governments or multilateral agencies such as the World Bank group, the latter channel is always used.

The risks of foreign borrowing for public sector investments have already been explained at some length. Suffice it to add that it is desirable that foreign borrowing should be carefully held within a country's debt service capacity, and, ideally, used on projects which will earn or save foreign exchange which are generally in the industrial and agricultural sectors. The dictum cannot be applied to utilities, however, as they do not generate foreign income, but they do need foreign exchange to pay for the capital equipment which most developing countries still need to import.

As export credits and foreign bank loans to state corporations are explicitly or implicitly guaranteed by the state, such lenders need take little interest in the risk, expected return, or capital structure of the project, or of the enterprise undertaking it, except in cases of pure project finance. Aid finance is similarly guaranteed, but suppliers take great pains to plan and appraise projects, and may make the aid conditional on changes in capital structure or organizational structure of the corporation. They may feel especially uneasy with enterprises which continue to pile up debt. Ultimately, though, all suppliers of external debt to the government or state corporations are exposed to country risk rather than project risk. What is more, their claims in most cases must rank equally with existing claims.[10] Therefore new projects requiring external finance are usually judged for creditworthiness not on their own merits but on the perceived creditworthiness of the entire country.

The extent to which state corporations have freedom of action in foreign borrowing is worth examining. In the early 1970s Pertamina, the Indonesian government-owned oil corporation, borrowed heavily on the Eurocurrency market to finance a wide range of projects without formal government guarantees, and without even complying with its government's regulations on foreign borrowing. The government at the time was generally unwilling to guarantee the borrowings of any state corporation. Pertamina's foreign debt mushroomed, and its debt service capacity did not grow apace. In March 1975 the government was forced to intervene, and take over responsibility for all Pertamina's debt. The banks' risk-taking paid off; and they had higher interest rates than they would have done for loans backed by a state guarantee. Yet ultimately their loans were rescued by government intervention. Wellons (1977) discusses the case in detail. He found (p. 83) that although a number of governments which are opposed to state guarantees in principle nonetheless are not prepared to allow a parastatal borrower to default if they can support it. Wellons also found that the parastatals accounted for most Eurocredits to developing countries, and that few of the public sector projects financed by these loans were foreign exchange earners. Some were for import substitute projects, but the bulk of project loans appeared to be for infrastructure or service projects.

Retained Earnings

As a source of finance, retained earnings are perhaps as near to pure equity as many state corporations get. The use of retained earnings generally entails no further obligation to government (apart from permission to retain them), nor does it entail the risk involved in debt finance. Gillis (1980) reports that retained earnings have been an important source of investment finance in several countries where the state corporations generated over 10% of total national savings (Korea, 1961–72; Brazil, 1966–75; Uruguay, 1975–76; India, 1970–72; Taiwan, 1960–74; and Sri Lanka, no dates). Trebat (1980) found that some 40 of the largest state enterprises in Brazil financed between 40% and 60% of their gross investment from retained earnings. However, in many countries the opposite holds, and many state corporations, because of their losses, act as a drain on government revenue, and by increasing current expenditure inhibit the use of government resources for investment purposes. Further evidence was given in Chapter 4.

NOTES

1. Investments may also be undertaken by other forms of organization, such as partnerships, cooperatives, or sole traders. For ease of explanation we will limit the discussion to companies, but by and large the same principles apply to other forms of organization.
2. Of course, not all countries suffer from a shortage of long-term debt. (Rao (1981) found that in India 'Long-term borrowings were of the order of 42.5% of net fixed assets', a not unhealthy ratio.) Indian financial institutions which provide long-term debt often take an option to convert a part of their loan, generally about 20%, into equity. This may encourage the supply of long-term debt, but may discourage some borrowers who fear dilution of ownership and control.
3. For the sake of completion we should mention warrants, which are an option to buy ordinary shares at a specified price before a specified date. A combination of a straight corporate bond with warrants is similar to a convertible. In financial theory, all company securities can be analysed in terms of options, but that is beyond the scope of this book. See, for example, Brealey and Myers (1981), Chapter 20.
4. The formula for calculating the rate of return to equity (or, from the firm's point of view, the cost of equity capital) is:

$$R_E = R_A + \frac{D}{E}(R_A - R_D)$$

where
R_E = rate of return to equity
R_A = rate of return to total capital
D/E = debt/equity ratio
R_D = cost of borrowing (debt)

This is Modigliani and Miller's Proposition 2.
5. A number of formal proofs of Proposition 1 exist, apart from MM (1958). Brealey and Myers (1981) give one based on the capital asset pricing model.
6. It is sometimes argued that individuals can get around this problem by buying shares in investment trusts, which can offset borrowing for share purchases against tax, and that given a good range of investment trusts, individual firms still do not need to borrow. This assumes, though, that there are investment trusts available which match the investors' requirements.
7. Developing country governments are rarely advised to accept lines of credit. If they then feel obliged to use them, they are in effect tying procurement to the

country which offers a line of credit. It is better for buyers of equipment to go to competitive bidding, and decide which equipment they prefer on specification, price, and export credit terms offered. Credit terms can even be negotiated after the bids have been evaluated; they will still be available. The author has experience of Pakistan buying equipment unsatisfactorily from Bulgaria as a result of tying itself unnecessarily to a line of export credit. The availability of Bulgarian equipment was even allowed to determine which projects were selected.

8. The riskiness of foreign exchange earnings may be measured by their past volatility, or variance. The riskiness of individual exports may also be measured in the same way in cases where a country is dependent upon one or two key export commodities.

9. Fundamentally there is no reason why utilities and transport should not be in the private sector, as many of them are in some industrialized countries, and in a few developing countries. If they are natural (or *de facto*) monopolies, then they must be regulated. Perhaps the best (non-ideological) reason for them to be in the state sector is that the capital investment required is not available in the domestic private sector, and foreign investment may not be acceptable if it is felt that national control and security may be eroded.

10. The '*pari passu*' clause common in loan agreements ensures that new sovereign debt cannot claim priority over existing debt. An interesting case arose in 1981 when Wells Fargo Bank, in negotiating a new loan to Turkey, at that time heavily in debt, attempted to stake a prior claim on the proceeds of the country's hazelnut exports for the servicing of its loan. Existing creditors protested, and the scheme was dropped.

The question of whether or not bonds rank as superior debt to bank loans arose in the case of Costa Rica, which in 1982 tried to include a SF20 million sovereign bond, issued in 1980, alongside its bank borrowings in a rescheduling exercise. Conventional wisdom held that bonds, unlike bank loans, could not be rescheduled. The case was taken to a Swiss court by a plaintiff (Dow Chemical Bank) wanting to have Costa Rica declared in default on the bonds. The case went against the plaintiff, thereby allowing Costa Rica to reschedule its bond, but on the technicality that the plaintiff was not the true beneficiary (*The Economist*, 26 February 1983).

Chapter 11

Recent Proposals to Improve the Quantity and Quality of Development Finance

The object of this final chapter is to describe some of the recent proposals which have been made with a view to increasing the quantity and improving the quality of developing country financing. Some of the proposals are already being introduced; others are ideas which may or may not lead to changes in the future. Moreover, these proposals and changes are by no means all recent ideas; some have been discussed, perhaps in different guise, for many years. In order to avoid the discussion being merely a rag-bag collection of ideas I will group the proposals under thematic headings. The emphasis is on international finance, as this is the area where most of the proposals have been made, but first I briefly examine some ideas to improve domestic financial arrangements.

1. DOMESTIC FINANCE

For many developing countries the improvement of domestic financial markets offers greater prospects of improving the quantity and quality of finance than changes in foreign financing. Indeed, in the long run it is to be expected that domestic financial institutions, instruments, and mechanisms will increasingly take over the functions now provided by external financing. This trend has already been evident in the NICs where the role of concessional foreign aid has been steadily reduced. To some extent aid has been replaced by commercial capital flows, but dependence on these sources too should diminish as countries develop. The process of financial development, though, is likely to be slow, and the least developed countries seem likely to be heavily dependent on foreign aid indefinitely. Even in some NICs, too, the level of accumulated foreign debt is certain to ensure that an external national debt persists for many years, and may in some cases grow over time, rather than diminish.

Most developing countries offer considerable scope for improvements in the debt markets, equity markets, and in the taxation and tax-gathering systems. The main proposals concerning the development of financial markets centre on the growth of the financial sector, and the liberalization of financial markets, discussed in Chapter 3. The main policy implication is that interest rates should be freed, leading to increased mobilization of funds and thus increased resources and improved efficiency in the allocation of debt. Given a freer market in debt, opportunities would arise for the development of further debt instruments such as corporate bonds.

Secondly, many developing countries have scope to improve their markets in corporate equity. This would provide an alternative to using debt capital, and therefore offer some competition to debt markets. At the same time it would offer firms the possibility of deepening their equity base and improving their ratio of debt/shareholder's funds. To the extent that this ratio acts as a constraint on new investment, access to new equity capital would alleviate the constraint.

Clearly the obvious way to expand equity markets is through the growth and development of formal stock markets. In some countries, though, this may hardly be practicable as the number of securities which are potentially tradeable, and which would meet the listing requirements of the stock exchange authorities, may be low. Alternatives are the development of over-the-counter trading, with financial institutions such as development banks acting as market makers, or the development of 'second tier' stock markets such as Britain's Unlisted Securities Market, or Japan's Second Section or France's Second Marché. Non-bank financial institutions also have an important role to play in developing equity markets. For SSEs financing I favour the development of venture capital funds, as discussed in Chapter 10.

There is currently a fairly widespread view that government ownership of state enterprises has not been very successful. Privatization of state enterprises is being widely discussed, and put into practice in countries such as Morocco, Bangladesh, the UK, and Japan. In countries with active stock markets the potential for sale of shares in state enterprises exists. An alternative, especially in countries without active stock markets, is to sell state enterprises to private sector companies, or to bring in private sector shareholders such as financial institutions, trading and manufacturing concerns. Privatization may be partial, with government maintaining a shareholding, and perhaps acting as a regulating authority in cases where the enterprise has a monopoly. However, it is essential that the privatized enterprise should be run on commercial lines, free from government interference. Moreover, the shares must be attractive to private investors, which in most cases means that the enterprise must be operating profitably prior to privatization. In many cases this implies that the state enterprise must be turned around from loss-making to profitability as a first step.

In domestic financing, therefore, current thought is inclined to give more emphasis to developing financial markets and placing heavier emphasis on the role of private capital in development. In view of the disillusionment with the record of state investment, this seems to be a worthwhile change of emphasis, especially in view of the success of these countries, notably in the far east, which have pursued a capitalist path to development. A similar emphasis on the importance of the private sector is now growing in international financing, too.

2.   FOREIGN FINANCE: WHAT IS AN 'IMPROVEMENT'?

The objectives of the many proposals which have been made in the field of foreign finance are to increase the volume of the flows, ('additionality') and/or to improve the terms. Some proposals for new mechanisms for financial flows run the risk that they might merely divert flows from other mechanisms, without any additionality or improvement in terms. Figure 11.1 provides a framework for analysing additionality and terms of foreign finance.

Capital flows from North to South may be analysed in terms of capital market theory. Capital will flow only if the combination of risk and return is acceptable to the supplier of capital. Investments must therefore lie on or above the international capital market line. In imperfect markets they may lie above the line, C, giving the investor (a term which includes lenders) an element of rent in his return. If the risk/return combination lies below the line, then, compared with alternative investments, the investor is offered either

— a lower return for a given risk (investment A), or
— a higher risk for a given return (investment B).

Investments A and B are not attractive to private capital. Therefore, if capital is to flow to them some subsidy is needed. The subsidy can only be

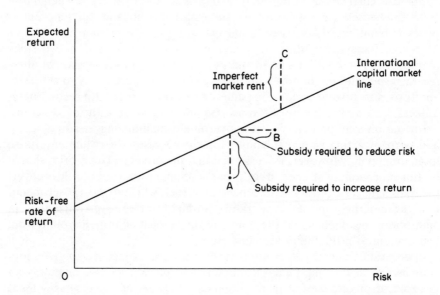

Figure 11.1 International capital flows: risk, return, and subsidies

provided by ODA through a grant element, private aid, or host country incentives. Investments A and B can be financed by aid flows. Alternatively they could be financed by private capital, but require incentives which raise the expected return to private capital, or subsidies (such as guarantees) which reduce the risk to private capital. Therefore to increase the volume of financial flows in a static framework, a new mechanism needs to improve the combination of risk and return, or to increase subsidies to developing countries. Alternatively to reduce the cost of financial flows to developing countries it is necessary to reduce the risk to the suppliers of private capital, or to reduce interest rates. Any new proposal, therefore, should be assessed on the basis of its impact on risk, on expected return, or on the level of subsidies, especially interest rate subsidies.

I will discuss the proposals concerning public sector flows first, and then move on to private sector flows. However, rigid demarcation between the public and the private sector is not always possible, as some proposals encompass both.

3. PROPOSALS PREDOMINANTLY RELATING TO PUBLIC SECTOR FOREIGN FINANCE

(a) The Brandt Commission: First Edition

Perhaps the most comprehensive package of proposals in recent years relating to financial flows has come from the Brandt Commission. The main proposals in its first report (1980) relating to finance were:
— There should be a substantial increase in the transfer of resources to developing countries to finance projects and programmes to alleviate poverty, expand food production and commodity processing, increase exploration and development of energy and mineral resources, and to stabilize commodity prices and earnings.
— ODA should be increased to 0.7% of GNP of industrial countries by 1985, and to 1% before the end of the century. It should be augmented by 'an international system of universal revenue mobilization' (an international tax on all countries, based on income), and taxes on international trade and travel, arms production and trade, and sea-bed minerals.
— Lending through international financial institutions should be stepped up through increased borrowing by the World Bank and regional development banks, to be made possible by increasing their borrowing to capital ratios, from 1 : 1 to 2 : 1 in the case of the World Bank. An increasing share of development finance should be channelled through regional institutions. Programme lending should be increased, and further IMF gold sales should be made to help to finance development. Borrowing countries should have an increased role in decision-making in international institutions.

— A new international financial institution — a World Development Fund — might be created, with universal membership, mainly to increase programme lending, and to administer the funds raised by the new international taxes suggested in the second item above. Borrowers would have more say in decision-making than they have in the existing institutions. A new facility for mineral and energy exploration and development is also required.

— Private sector bank lending should be increased, with extended maturities, and increased access for poorer developing countries. This should be facilitated where necessary by co-financing and the provision of guarantees by the World Bank and other international financial institutions. Measures should be taken to increase the access of developing countries to international bond markets.

— An SDR–aid link should be established (see below).

These (and other) proposals for substantial increases in development aid ('massive transfers') have been argued largely on the basis of the mutual interdependence of the North and the South. Increased aid, it was argued, would result in increased orders for the capital goods industries of the North, which would help to pull the North (and the rest of the world) out of the then prevailing recession. This Keynesian argument is not acceptable to monetarists, who see it as either a transfer which is met by printing money (which is merely inflationary) or, if the money stock is held constant, a transfer of resources which could only be met initially by a reduction in economic activity in the donor country.

In any event, only limited attempts have been made to implement these proposals. The resulting Cancun summit meeting produced no tangible results, although programme lending has increased, and serious discussion has taken place on increasing the World Bank's borrowing to capital ratio, and to setting up an Energy Affiliate of the World Bank. Since 1980 the political climate on overseas aid has turned against the Brandt Commission. Disillusion with aid has increased in many donor countries, notably the USA, and even in some recipient countries. It is widely thought that after some 30 years of development aid the impact has been negligible or even negative. Disillusion with multilateral institutions is also rife in the industrialized countries, and the possibility of establishing new institutions, or even expanding existing ones, is remote for the foreseeable future. Moreover, it became recognized that massive transfers of finance were unlikely to be successful without parallel massive transfers of complementary factors such as management and technology.

(b) The Brandt Commission: Second Edition

By the time the Brandt Commission produced its second report, early in 1983, the recommendations had been modified to recognize the changes in the political and economic climate. It called on governments and world leaders to take the following immediate action (1983 report, pp. 13–15).

— Increase the resources of the IMF through a major new allocation of special drawing rights, to be distributed in a way which would help those developing countries in deficit. IMF quotas should be at least doubled, and the IMF should borrow more from central banks, and should start to borrow on capital markets. The funds available from the IMF's low conditionality tranches, and from the compensatory financing facility should be increased.

—Enable the Bank for International Settlements and the central banks of industrialized countries to extend bridging finance to cover the time gap between an approach to the IMF and disbursement of IMF resources.

— Increase the World Bank's project and programme lending, and raise the limit on its structural adjustment lending from 10% to 30% of its total lending. Increase the IDA's resources in real terms in its seventh replenishment.

— Increase aid to least developed countries by providing '0.15% of GNP or a doubling of aid to these countries by 1985'. Waive all official debt of least developed countries.

— Increase informal coordination between official lenders in commercial banks in debt rescheduling negotiations 'to ensure adequate provision of resources through the support of all lenders'.

It is worth noting that many of the second, less radical, package of proposals are being partially implemented. The resources of the IMF have been increased, if not in the way required; the BIS has provided bridging finance; discussion is in progress about increasing the World Bank's resources; and informal coordination among the IMF, World Bank, other official lenders, and commercial banks in negotiations on debt rescheduling has improved. However, prospects of increases in ODA, apart from efforts such as the recently announced funds for Africa (USA, World Bank, and France) remain slight.

(c) The UNIDO Proposals

At about the same time as the first Brandt Commission report, UNIDO (1979) made several proposals, mainly with a view to stimulating industrial development in the South. The UNIDO proposals in the main called for the establishment of new international institutions, namely an International Industrial Finance Agency which would operate as an international industrial development bank, with membership restricted to developing countries and financed by them (in effect, mainly by the capital surplus oil-exporting countries). Funds would be recycled through this new agency, rather than through the commercial banks of the North. The Agency would be expected to establish a market in developing country financial instruments. UNIDO's second proposal was to establish a Global Fund for the Stimulation of

Industry, a modern version of the Marshall Plan for developing countries. Industrialized and developing countries would provide the capital, only a proportion of which would be paid up. The fund would then be able to borrow on international capital markets (as the World Bank and regional development banks do). The resources of the fund would be used for programme rather than project lending to the South, and would be used to purchase industrial goods from the North. Loans to least developed countries would carry an interest rate subsidy to be financed by the contributions of the industrialized countries. The proposal was rooted in the concept of international Keynesianism; it was seen as a form of North–South cooperation which would stimulate the international economy at a time of recession and considerable surplus industrial capacity in the North.

As well as the above proposals UNIDO has for some years been discussing the establishment of an International Bank for Industrial Development (IBID), modelled substantially on the International Fund for Agricultural Development, affiliated to the FAO. The IBID would be within the UN system, with all UN members eligible for membership. It would start with an initial paid-up capital of $10 billion, rising to $50 billion, would be able to borrow on international financial markets, and would provide mainly project lending with subsidized interest rates. Unlike, say, the World Bank, voting in the IBID would be based on one country one vote, as in the rest of the UN system. Incidentally, IFAD, on which the IBID proposal is based, cannot borrow, and is dependent on member governments for financing (60% industrialized countries, and 40% OPEC). Over 1982–84, IFAD lent $1.5 billion, but its financing is now under pressure, as OPEC members say they cannot afford to contribute their share. *The Economist* (9 March 1985, p. 68) proposed that IFAD should be allowed to raise money on capital markets, 'With its reputation for good housekeeping and successful investments, it might be a popular borrower.' To return to the IBID proposal, it is unlikely to make any headway as the industrialized countries (the B Group in the UN system) are opposed to the establishment of any new international institution, and generally take the view that industry should be financed on market terms, without subsidies.

UNIDO (1979) contained some interesting proposals which were not dependent on establishing a new institution. One was that co-financing should be taken up by bilateral aid agencies, but so far it has met with a cool response. The object would be to spread scarce aid funds over a greater number of projects, and to extend access to commercial bank finance to countries which are not normally considered creditworthy. Specific methods of co-financing might include:

— The provision of repayment guarantees to the banks.
— The provision of funds to stabilize interest rates or repayment schedules at an agreed level.
— The provision of funds to protect borrowers against the effects of appreciation of the loan currency against the borrower's currency.
— The acceptance by the aid agency of the later maturities of the loan.

Any such schemes would need to be implemented so that the commercial banks are left with a significant proportion of the risk; the object is to increase available funds to borrowers, while at the same time protecting them from some of the risks inherent in commercial bank loans. Anecdotal information suggests that banks would be interested in such schemes, particularly in arrangements where the bilateral agencies would pick up the later maturities in co-financing packages. Aid agencies would need to enter into co-financing arrangements with discretion. Clearly, any large-scale guaranteeing of commercial bank loans in the past might have left the agencies with substantial contingent liabilities in view of the inability of some borrowers to service their debts. Co-financing may be appropriate if done on a modest scale, for project lending, rather than for programme lending, and perhaps restricted to borrowers who do not normally have access to commercial bank credits.

(d) Other Proposals

In addition to the Brandt Commission and UNIDO proposals, a number of other individual proposals have been made with a view to transferring substantial amounts through the public sector. Briefly, these were:–

The Venezuelan Proposal (1977)

A fund of $16–20 billion would operate as a special trust fund of the World Bank and/or regional development banks. It would be financed to the extent of 20–25% from developed country aid budgets, and 75–80% from the sale of long-term (12–20 year) OPEC Development Bonds. OPEC would buy 20–25% of these bonds, and guarantee the remainder. The fund would be used to finance projects on long-term maturities with concessional terms to the least developed countries. As with all proposals based on OPEC surpluses, this has become a non-starter since the OPEC's surpluses started to decline.

The Mexican Proposal (1978)

This scheme was similar to the Venezuelan proposal, in that it was to be a fund administered by the World Bank to provide long-term project finance for the purchase of capital goods from industrialized countries. The fund would issue 15–year bonds, guaranteed by industrialized countries and capital surplus developing countries. Industrialized countries would have to guarantee or buy the bonds in order to be eligible to supply capital goods under the scheme.

The Commonwealth Secretariat Proposal, 1979

This proposal was similar in many ways to the above except that it was intended to provide programme finance for balance of payments support and structural adjustment loans, which would contain a subsidy element.

The Arusha Proposal of the Group of 77 (1978)

This proposal was not thought out in much detail, but called for an additional transfer of $35–40 billion, to be drawn from international capital markets under the 'collective guarantee of the international community'. It would provide both project and programme lending, with an element of subsidy, and on terms and conditions consistent with the debt servicing capacity over the longer term. As with other schemes, it was rooted in international Keynesianism, and intended to provide stimulation to the global economy.

A Multinational Trust Fund for Industrial Development (Inter-American Development Bank, 1979)

The IDB proposed the establishment of a fund, to be financed by member governments and by borrowings on international capital markets. The fund would make equity investments in small and medium-scale industrial enterprises in IDB member countries. Besides providing equity capital it would help to strengthen recipient securities markets. The fund was designed on a much more modest scale than most of other proposals at the time, with a target of the order of $30–50 million.

An Energy Affiliate of the World Bank (1980)

This scheme was intended to finance energy projects in developing countries. Starting with $12 billion, it was intended to grow to $25 billion, and would be financed by World Bank members supplemented by co-financing from OPEC countries. Unlike most of the schemes discussed above the proposal still has some life in it, although the emphasis now being placed on private sector finance for such development means that it is unlikely to win the support of OECD countries.

All such proposals for large-scale transfers of resources were overtaken by the shift to more conservative policies in the North, and a parallel scepticism of the value of aid and international institutions. They were overshadowed, too, in 1982 and 1983 by the growing world debt crisis, which concentrated the mind of international economists on much more immediate problems. The debt crisis itself sparked off a wave of new proposals, this time aimed at 'solving' the debt crisis rather than providing a massive transfer of resources. The atmosphere in development finance in 1985 was very different from that in 1979 and 1980. I will examine proposals for the debt crisis under the section on private sector finance, as it is more concerned with the private than the public sector, although a number of the proposals require public sector involvement, some on a substantial scale.

The Development Committee proposals

Before the debt crisis broke, the Development Committee of the IMF and the World Bank (1982) considered measures to improve non-concessional flows to developing countries. Its principal recommendations were directed at the World Bank and the regional development banks (multilateral development institutions, or MDIs), so I include them under public sector finance, even though the recommendations related to private sector flows as well. However, the Development Committee appears to have restricted its work to debt, rather than equity flows. The principal recommendations were:

— There should be an increase in the capacity of the MDIs. Steps have subsequently been taken towards a major increase in the financial resources of the World Bank, but, embarrassingly, it managed to commit only about $11 billion in 1984/85, rather than the $13 billion expected. The African Development Bank has considerably increased its resources as a result of admitting industrialized country members.

— The co-financing arrangements between MDIs and commercial lenders should be widened. Again, the World Bank has accepted this recommendation with the establishment of its 'B–loan' procedures, described in Chapter 7, but more could probably still be done. Commercial banks welcome project co-financing as it reduces their risk, compared with straight balance of payments loans.

— MDIs should sell portfolio participations to commercial banks. This can be done either by 'participation' sales, defined as loan sales by an MDI to private lenders after the terms of the loan have been agreed, but before any disbursement to the borrower, or by 'portfolio' sales from loans on which disbursements have been completed. The World Bank did make 'portfolio' sales until 1977, but then discontinued the practice. In either case the sale is made on a basis of no recourse to the MDI. There are a number of potential difficulties, notably concerning interest rates, but these are no greater than the established swap procedures involving fixed and variable rate loans, and loans of different currencies. It is necessary, though, that the borrower should agree to the loan sale.

— The MDIs should consider the issue of partially guaranteed loan pass-through certificates. This scheme involves the MDI packaging certain loans, and selling shares in the interest and principal repayments as a bond, with a view to attracting non-bank finance. The MDI would guarantee a portion of the risk (e.g. 75%). A secondary market in the certificate might be organized. The attraction of such bonds to buyers must be very uncertain. Moreover, the additionality provided is limited, as MDIs have a contingent liability of the guaranteed portion of the bond, and their articles of agreement would probably require that this contingent liability should be counted as lending.

— The report of the Task Force to the Development Committee discussed a proposal for a multilateral partial guarantee framework (MPGF), whereby MDIs would guarantee a portion of commercial bank loans to 'threshold' developing countries, that is those countries which were on the borderline of commercial creditworthiness. Any such scheme might consider the guarantee (perhaps full) of later stages of loan maturities, and operate on a case-by-case basis, rather than defining 'threshold' countries. Again, additionality would be limited to the non-guaranteed portion if the MDI had to treat the guarantees as lending under its articles of agreement.

Although overshadowed by the debt crises, and subsequent proposals, some of these schemes have much to recommend them, notably the first three. However, as with most proposals to increase financial flows, the true additionality of these schemes is uncertain. Emphasis is currently being placed on the role of MDIs in assisting private sector development. The Asian Development Bank is planning to lend to private sector borrowers without obtaining government guarantees, and the IFC has been given a large increase in resources. The United States government in particular is putting pressure on MDIs to switch lending from the public sector towards the private sector. The World Bank is also pursuing the creation of a new affiliate, to be known as the Multilateral Investment Guarantee Agency, to provide political risk insurance to foreign investors and lenders. However, some developing countries are concerned that it might increase pressure on them to accept increased direct foreign investment on terms which they may not like.

The Lessard and Williamson Proposals

In a study of longer-term approaches to the debt problem, Lessard and Williamson (1985) recommended a package of proposals including the following:

— An increase of \$40 billion in the capital of the World Bank.
— Prompt ratification of the Multilateral Investment Guarantee Agency.
— Improved debt management to be a major focus of World Bank operations.
— An agreement by industrial countries to resume the supply of official export credits as soon as a debtor nation adopts a realistic adjustment programme.
— The creation of mutual funds designed to facilitate the repatriation of flight capital to debtor countries.
— Efforts by developing countries to attract more direct foreign investment, and generally to induce new flows of private capital to developing countries.

Among the steps to encourage private capital flows, they recommend:
— Investment by non-bank financial institutions in developing country equities.
— Pure project finance lending by foreign banks with the earnings of the project placed in escrow accounts to meet the debt service of the project.
— The issue of long-term, indexed bonds issued by consortia of developing countries, with partial guarantees initially funded by industrialized countries.
— The issue by developing countries of commodity-linked bonds, described under portfolio investment, below.

— Direct foreign investment in joint ventures, in which the traditional return to equity is replaced by 'quasi-equity' arrangements for the sharing of production, revenue, or profits.

— The use by developing country governments of options markets to hedge interest rate risk, and of swap arrangements to ensure that the currencies of debts are matched by the currencies of export earnings. This would help to hedge exchange rate risks.

Many of these proposals have been under discussion for some time, but certainly stand repeating. The risk with wide-ranging packages of proposals, though, is that the package is seen as over-ambitious in its entirety, and consequently several worthy individual elements are lost sight of. The above proposals, though, are worthy of serious attention.

Proposals for Reform of the IMF

Proposals vary from the conservative 'do nothing' to modest reform policies of increasing the Fund's resources and lending while relaxing its conditionality, to radical restructuring of the Bretton Woods agreement and the institutions which arose from it.

The conservative view is opposed to the growth of public sector multilateral institutions, and dislikes attempts to increase the resources of the IMF. The clearest expression of this view has come from sections of the US Congress, notably during the negotiations to increase IMF resources in 1983. Proponents of this view would regard the creation of SDRs as printing money which will fuel world inflation, and would deplore the use of taxpayers' money to bail out over-lent private banks and over-borrowed developing countries through the IMF, or in any other way, as throwing good money after bad.

Reformers, on the other hand, generally consider that the IMF plays a valuable role, and needs additional resources to maintain its role. Proposals to increase its resources include higher quotas (which apparently the Fund prefers), ad-hoc borrowing, as, for example, the borrowing from Saudi Arabia, borrowing on capital markets through the issue of medium- and long-term bonds, further gold sales, and the creation of new SDRs. The proposals for increases in quotas, sale of gold, and SDR creation would increase the Fund's 'equity capital' and would allow it to provide interest rate subsidies to borrowers. Borrowing from governments or on markets would be on commercial terms, and the Fund would need to charge near commercial interest rates to borrowing countries. Its borrowings would, however, be on the finest terms, and would therefore be cheaper to borrowing countries than if they borrowed directly. One's view of these proposals depends on whether one believes that there should be a transfer of real resources from the North to South, and whether the Fund is an appropriate vehicle for effecting such a transfer. While we support a real transfer, it is questionable whether the IMF is an appropriate vehicle, as it may give the impression that the reward for economic mismanagement is access to subsidized resources. Moreover, the Fund may understandably find it difficult to act simultaneously as a corrective institution and one that provides subsidies. While we support the availability of subsidized long-term programme lending to developing countries, it may be preferable for such transfers to be made through bilateral agencies, the IDA or the World Bank's structural adjustment lending programme, in parallel with a Fund programme.

Proposals to modify conditionality also abound. The main theme is for the IMF to devote more thought to designing tailor-made programmes for individual countries, a point emphasized by Killick (1984). Others, for example Keller (1980), have suggested that ceilings on domestic credit expansion may unnecessarily restrict production for exports and for import substitution. Many commentators have suggested that IMF loans are of too short maturity to allow countries to make the necessary structural adjustments to their economies. It was in response to this criticism that the extended fund facility was introduced, but it is likely that it is insufficient. If the Fund were to offer longer-term facilities it would need an increase in its resources. In our view this is the strongest argument for an increase in Fund resources. Killick (1984) presents a substantial statement of the reformist position, with a well-reasoned package of proposals. Spraos (1984) has argued that IMF conditionality should be switched from credit control targets to balance of payments targets, and specifically to the current account. This would switch the emphasis to the variable which the Fund programme is aiming to adjust, rather than emphasizing policy instruments. Aiming conditions at policy instruments has achieved only limited success, and there is never an unambiguous one-to-one relationship between policy instruments and targets.

The radical position would like to see major reforms in the control and the attitude of the IMF, or even abolishing it and starting again. Certainly the present voting structure, which ensures that effective control is vested in a handful of developed countries, is a bone of contention with the developing countries who nowadays provide the Fund with all its business. The other main argument is that the Fund should be transformed from a hard-line, corrective organization to a development institution, lending long-term at low interest and easy conditions, dropping particularly the emphasis on devaluation and domestic credit expansion ceilings and price reform. The major weakness of the radical position is that it has failed to come up with a plausible alternative to the IMF. The alternatives seem to be to neglect the causes of the disequilibrium, which is likely to lead to an even greater crisis subsequently or de-linking from the North-based IMF. The author (Kitchen, 1981) has suggested the development of a Third World Monetary Fund to be created by amalgamating existing credit arrangements among developing countries.[1] Since then the magnitude of the external problems of the third world would mean that a Third World Monetary Fund could only make a small contribution to the problem: however, the idea of South–South balance of payments support did receive further discussion at the Caracas and Jamaica meetings of the Group 77, discussed under proposals for a South Bank.

Perhaps the most far-reaching proposal is to convert the IMF into a World Central Bank, which would act as a lender of last resort. Implementation of this idea would imply a massive increase in the IMFs resources and authority, and probably a dilution of the authority of national central banks. It is difficult to see this idea being acceptable to many industrialized or developing countries in the foreseeable future.

The SDR–aid Link

This is a proposal for increasing development aid through the creation and distribution of new SDRs by the IMF. Essentially it amounts to increasing international liquidity (or printing money, to its detractors), and lending it to developing countries. The proposal was much in vogue in the 1970s and has earlier antecedents, notably Stamp (1958), but as increased liquidity and increased aid are both now out of fashion with the dominant members of the IMF, little is now heard of it. However, a full discussion of the variations of the SDR–aid link is given by G. Bird, (1982b). The attractions of the scheme may now be less than they were a few years ago, as interest rates on SDRs have risen to nearer commercial lending rates, thereby reducing the grant element in the scheme. The additionality, too, may be restricted to providing funds to countries which do not have access to commercial bank credit, although since the debt crisis the accessibility of commercial credit has certainly shrunk.

4. PROPOSALS PREDOMINANTLY RELATING TO PRIVATE SECTOR FLOWS

This section will examine bank lending, mainly under proposals to ease the international debt crisis, export credits (which also appear to some extent among the debt proposals), DFI, and portfolio investment. In some cases, notably the debt crisis proposals, there is considerable overlap between public and private finance. This seems to be a general trend, as mixed credits and co-financing already blur the distinction between public and private financial flows.

Many of the proposals discussed below concentrate on the problem of commercial bank debt, rather than official or officially guaranteed debt. Commercial bank debt is crucial because the debt crisis threatens the stability of the major banks, and thus the stability of the international financial system, and the international economy. In discussing solutions to the debt crisis, several issues arise. The main issues concern the incidence of losses. Should the banks lose, or should they be subsidized? Should borrowing countries be subsidized? If subsidies are to be given, who should bear them? Should a global approach be sought to what some see as a global problem, or should the problem of debt be dealt with on an individual country basis? I will return to these questions subsequently, after outlining the main proposals which have been made.[2]

(a) Proposals for the Transfer of Commercial Bank Assets

The Rohatyn Proposal[3]

Mr. Rohatyn proposed the establishment of a new agency, modelled on the Municipal Assistance Corporation (established for the financial rescue of New York City), which might be a subsidiary of the IMF or the World Bank. The agency would have the objectives of:
— stretching out the maturities of debt;
— providing interest rate subsidies to developing countries;
—transferring risk from the banks, in exchange for banks taking some losses.
The agency would acquire part of developing countries' debt from banks in exchange for its own low-coupon long-term bonds. A secondary market would subsequently be established in the bonds. The agency would reschedule debts over 15–20 years, at 6% interest. The agency (or its shareholder governments) and the banks would lose, while the debtor countries would receive subsidies, saving interest of perhaps $15–20 billion annually. Banks' assets would still be frozen until a secondary market is established.

The Kenan Proposal[4]

Professor Kenan proposed a new International Debt Discount Corporation which would exchange its bonds for debt held by banks at, say, a 10% discount. It would then reschedule developing country debt, and the discount would be used to reduce interest rates. The banks have their risk reduced in exchange for losses, but the new agency would not lose. Essentially, this is a more modest form of the Rohatyn proposal.

The Morgan Grenfell Proposal

This scheme is similar in principle to the Rohatyn and Kenan schemes, with a new agency (perhaps IMF-backed) buying bank loans in exchange for its non-interest-bearing bonds, which could be sold in the secondary market. Again, the banks would stand all the losses in exchange for reduced risks.

The Gutentag and Herring Proposal[5]

An agency (new, or the IMF or World Bank) would buy loans from banks at 'market prices', and reschedule debts. Countries with serious debt difficulties can convert debt to 'Consols' (undated bonds) at market interest rates. The losses would again be borne by the banks.

The above schemes envisage the establishment of a new agency, which currently would be unacceptable to the main western governments, and for the moment can be considered non-starters. The following schemes envisaged using existing agencies, including central banks and the IMF/World Bank.

The Barclays Bank (Leslie) Proposal[6]

Central banks would buy bank loans at a discount. The cash obtained by the banks would be used to finance exports to worthy developing country borrowers, guaranteed by the lenders' national export credit agencies. OECD governments might be attracted by increased exports, and in the event that the loans are not repaid, the losses would revert to the commercial banks.

The Lever Scheme[7]

This scheme proposes that central banks discount commercial banks' developing country loans on condition that banks increase their loan loss provisions. Banks again stand the losses, but buy time. As a second proposal Lord Lever suggested that existing export credit guarantee agencies should insure new commercial bank lending, or support a new international agency which would perform the function, under IMF guidance.

The Bailey Proposal[8]

Central banks would issue exchange participation notes (EPNs) to the private banks in exchange for developing country loans. Debtor countries would then repay interest as before, but principal repayments would be an agreed percentage of a country's foreign exchange earnings. Banks may stand losses on sale of EPNs on a secondary market.

The Weinert Proposal[9]

The World Bank would be the key agency, accepting banks' loans in exchange for its own low-interest bonds, the interest rate depending on a country's ability to pay, but being high enough for the bank to remain sound. Any gap would be met by the World Bank, which would then reschedule debts at a lower interest rate. Losses would be borne by the banks, and to some extent by the World Bank, while the developing countries would receive an interest rate subsidy.

The Lindbeck Proposal[10]

Existing debt would be converted into long-term bonds or Consols which would be marketable. Central banks in creditor countries would offer to buy part of the bond issue. New debt would be raised by countries issuing priority bonds, approved by the IMF, which would have priority over old bonds. The banks would lose, as might their central banks, but the debtor countries would not receive a subsidy. This has much in common with my own proposal (Kitchen, 1985) whereby existing debt is converted into bonds, which banks then sell or place on the secondary market, but without any involvement of central banks or the IMF.

(b) Insurance and Guarantee Proposals

As an alternative to asset transfer proposals, a number of schemes have been put forward to guarantee bank lending, aimed at encouraging the flow of new lending to developing countries. The main proposals are as set out below, but there is always present the moral hazard of any insurance scheme.

Wallich's Insurance Scheme[11]

The IMF, World Bank, commercial banks, and existing insurance organizations would insure banks' loan portfolios (rather than individual loans). Given the historical rate of banking losses of under 1% of loans, the insurance premium can be of modest size, e.g. about 2% of banks' portfolios. Banks themselves would contribute, governments would contribute through existing agencies in the form of cash or guarantees, and borrowers would contribute through a surcharge or increased spread in the loan.

Deposit Insurance Proposals[12]

This type of proposal envisages the creation of an International Deposit Insurance Corporation, which insures bank deposits not covered by existing national arrangements. Although the proposal is not specific to the developing country debt problem, it is relevant in that it aims to maintain confidence in the banking system. The insurance would be partial (80–90%) and premiums would depend on risk.

The Soros Proposal

This scheme envisages the establishment of a new International Lending Agency (ILA) with capital contributed by present bank lenders, a contingent SDR allocation and debtors (in an escrow account) which would form an insurance fund. Existing debt would be converted into long-term fixed-interest bonds (say 25 years at 11%). It would graduate from debt crisis management to a self-sustaining, long-term lending agency which would smooth out interest rate fluctuations. The ILA would be guaranteed by member governments. Both banks and debtors may stand to lose.

The Witteveen Proposal[13]

With a view to insuring new lending to ensure additional net flows of finance, Dr. Witteveen proposed the establishment of an International Credit Guarantee Fund backed by the IMF, or as an IMF facility, which would provide insurance against political risk. Lenders would pay premiums to insure up to 75% of their loans. Insurance would be conditional on debtors complying with IMF programme performance criteria. The scheme might help banks to lend more, but political risk insurance is available to some extent (for example on export credits). The proposal would certainly extend the authority of the IMF, and would require an increase in its resources. A similar scheme is in fact under discussion in the World Bank, and referred to in the previous section.

The Bolin and Canto Proposal[14]

Bolin and Canto proposed a new agency, an Export Development Fund, which would make (and/or guarantee) new loans of 8–15 years maturity to support industrial countries' capital goods exports. The agency would be backed by the World Bank and national export credit agencies, and would raise funds by issuing 8–14-year floating rate notes on international capital markets. The scheme would extend the maturities of export credits, and has much in common with the Mexican proposal, described above.

The Zombanakis Proposal[15]

Debtor countries would reschedule bank loans to 13-year maturities, in conjunction with an agreed IMF programme. If after 10 years countries still could not meet debt service obligations in spite of adherence to IMF programmes, then payments for the final 3 years would be guaranteed by the IMF. The IMF would establish a new loan guarantee fund to perform this function. Such a scheme would be difficult to monitor, as 'adherence to IMF programmes' is virtually impossible to define unambiguously.

The Journal World Financial Markets[16]

This journal proposed two alternative insurance/guarantee schemes. The first is the establishment of an insurance pool for new loans to developing countries, backed by the IMF. The borrowers would pay the premiums, but the IMF guarantee would enable them to borrow at lower interest rate spreads. The alternative proposal would be a link between World Bank lending and commercial bank lending, presumably as an extension of existing co-financing arrangements. The first scheme would place a substantial contingent liability on the IMF, requiring an increase in its resources. The second would have a marginal impact, as World Bank lending is only of the order of $10 billion per year.

The Mahbub ul Haq Proposal[17]

This scheme envisages the establishment of a new IMF debt refinancing subsidiary which would provide resources for extending maturities, reducing interest payments to a declining ceiling of export earnings, and would guarantee new loans. New resources would be created by an SDR issue and the banks may take some losses. It would encourage new lending under IMF auspices, which would ensure sound economic management of debtor countries.

(c) Proposals Affecting Interest Charges

A number of proposals have been made with a view to easing the problem which borrowers face as a result of high and fluctuating interest rates. The two main proposals are:

The Solomon Proposal[18]

This scheme suggests that banks consider interest rate capping, not with a view to providing an element of concessionality to borrowers but in order to ease debt service difficulties. Interest above a certain level (the 'cap') would be added to the principal, thereby extending the maturity of the loan. Under this scheme banks would not lose, nor would borrowers be subsidized. The scheme recognizes the inevitable need to extend maturities of debt.

The Economist *scheme*[19]

The Economist has proposed that the interest rate problem should be met by establishing a new compensatory facility to cover interest rates above a certain level, probably within the IMF. The parallel compensatory financing facility for fluctuations in commodity prices already exists. As with some other schemes this would require an agreement to increase IMF resources, which may be difficult politically. *The Economist* would like to see the IMF borrowing in the markets to finance the new facility. The scheme seems workable, but it does imply a degree of subsidy if the IMF lends at below market rates.

Support for both the Solomon and *The Economist* proposals came in early 1985 from the Washington-based Institute for International Economics, which also supported the proposal that the World Bank should be more generous in guaranteeing loans and in arranging co-financing schemes with commercial banks (*The Economist*, 20 April 1985).

(d) Proposals to Convert Debt into Equity

A number of commentators have suggested that debtor countries should offer equity in national enterprises in exchange for debt. Such a scheme would certainly reduce the annual debt service costs faced by countries, as no principal would be repaid and dividends would probably be below interest rates. Any governments proposing to do this are likely to encounter domestic oppostion on the grounds that they are 'giving away national assets to foreigners'. However, the principle that risk capital should be in the form of equity rather than debt seems sound, given the problems which have arisen with debt.

(e) Proposed Debt Repudiation

The best-publicised proposal for a united repudiation of external debt came from President Castro of Cuba, in a meeting in Havana in July 1985. There has been other support for debt repudiation, but no country, not even Cuba, has attempted it. The consequences for any country (or group of countries) which do attempt it are imponderable but probably far-reaching. They would include a complete halt of any external financial flows, including bank debt, export credits, and probably aid and direct foreign investment. Most important would be the lack of any trade credit, which would mean that external trade would be seriously disrupted, and may only be able to continue on a barter basis, as the repudiating country presumably has virtually no foreign exchange anyway. The disruption to the economy is likely to be far greater than anything yet caused by the crisis. It is notable that the Consensus of Cartagena,[20] the group of Latin American countries which meets periodically to discuss proposals to alleviate the debt problem, has tended to shy away from suggestions of repudiation.

(f) Concluding Remarks on Debt

Discussions of third world debt frequently avoid recognition of the inevitable — that the external indebtedness of many borrowers will, under existing circumstances, remain *in perpetuity*. It has become a form of national debt, just as permanent as the national debt of any developed country, but with the difference that it is external, and denominated in foreign currencies. It is also in the form of loans, rather than negotiable securities. Once the permanence of debt is recognized, the first problem is for developing countries to be able to pay the interest on the debt. This depends upon their ability to maintain a trade surplus. The second problem is to ensure the liquidity of lending banks, and to ensure their stability. It is almost certain that the banks will never recover the principal outstanding, but it may be desirable for them to get some of it off their balance sheets.

Of the schemes discussed, it seems reasonable that a conversion of loans into bonds of long maturity, to be sold on secondary markets, supported by an interest rate stabilization scheme, but without a new financial institution, may be workable and fairly widely acceptable. *A priori*, there seem to be few grounds for either the banks (unwise lenders) or the debtor countries (unwise borrowers) to be subsidized, either by the taxpayers of industrialized countries, or by a transfer of aid from the least developed countries to middle-income debtor countries. Under such a scheme the banks would take a once-and-for-all loss equal to the difference of the par value of the bond, and the price at which it is sold on the market. The one possible case for a subsidy seems to be on the high level of interest rates which borrowers face, and which have risen because of the economic policies and excessive borrowing of the industrialized countries, but through no fault of the developing country borrowers. Some mechanism for interest rate subsidies, for example an IMF compensating facility, should therefore be widely acceptable.

A further possibility which has been little discussed is to permit debtor countries to repay part of their loans or interest in local currency, or even locally produced goods. This would involve creditors in marketing non-convertible currencies, and third world goods. Facilities already exist for handling goods received in barter deals, and the marketing of currently non-convertible currencies would lead to a degree of convertibility, which would probably be beneficial. Governments paying in their own currencies would have to permit the purchase of its exports with its own currency, and would have to agree to limit increases in their money supplies, so that the value of debt service payments in local currency is not rapidly eroded by inflation.

However, the schemes which are more likely to be politically acceptable generally involve an increase in debt. Unless new debt is highly concessional, with very long maturities or extremely low interest rates, there is a grave danger that the 'solution' will merely fuel an even greater debt crisis at the next cyclical downturn in the world economy. The proposals introduced by the US government at the 1985 IMF/World Bank annual meeting (the Baker plan) seem merely to be schemes to increase debt with a minimum of concessional content. If the debt problem is to be reduced this does not seem to be the way to do it. Moreover, the amount proposed of $29 billion is small relative to the overall debt.

(f) Portfolio Investment

One proposal to encourage equity flows in the form of portfolio investment is being examined by the IFC. This would involve the IFC creating an international investment trust (closed-ended fund) to invest in equities of developing country companies.[21] The fund would start with an initial capital of $25 million, but may increase to perhaps $500 million. Developing country governments may thereby be encouraged to make their stock markets more accessible to foreign investors. A sum of $500 million may provide a considerable stimulus, especially to some of the smaller stock markets. Moreover, independent capital may flow in once access to stock markets is easier. The IFC believes that the sum of $500 million can easily be raised from institutional investors wanting to diversify internationally, and to invest in some of the faster-growing companies in the developing countries. $500 million represents a small fraction of 1% of the $2000 billion funds which institutions world-wide manage. A further proposal is for the IFC to set up a World Stock Market, but this can only be regarded as a long-run possibility. However, any form of equity capital adds to the non-bank money flowing to developing countries, and thereby eases the debt problem, which is likely to persist for many years. Developing country equity could be made more attractive to investors in industrialized countries if they are offered a tax concession (possibly as part of a government's aid programme) on such investments. It has been suggested that this form of contribution by taxpayers may be more acceptable than other forms of contributions to the debt crises, such as bailing out banks or increasing direct aid (*AMEX Bank Review*, 19 June 1984).

Further proposals in UNIDO (1979) were concerned with shifting the risk-bearing element of private sector financing. One proposal was for the promotion of equity instruments with limited voting rights so that equity finance could be raised overseas without loss of control by the developing country. A second suggestion to spread risk was for the issue of commodity-indexed or trade-indexed bonds. With commodity-linked bonds the value of the bond, and the interest paid on it, is determined by the international price of the commodity in question. At times when the commodity price is weak, the country's debt service liability falls. When the commodity's price is strong the country's debt service liability rises, but then it can afford it. The proposal is suitable for use in connection with commodities for which there is an organized world market, and a world price which cannot be rigged. It is suitable for countries whose exports or GNP are heavily dependent on one or two such commodities; for example, Zambia might consider issuing copper-indexed bonds. The trade-indexed bond would similarly be linked to a country's export performance. Commodity-linked bonds particularly may find willing buyers on international capital markets. They would offer a more straightforward way of speculating on commodity price movements than commodity futures markets. The idea of commodity-indexed bonds is not new; France has issued domestic bonds tied to the prices of gold, electricity, and steel price/production volume. Michelin bonds were tied to sales volume and rubber price. Mexico has issued Petrobonds tied to the crude oil price, and Israel has issued bonds tied to the price of cement. Pichler (1982) has recorded details of these, and other, index-linked bonds. The subject has been discussed in more detail in Lessard and Wellons (1979).

(h) Direct Foreign Investment (DFI)

Although some industrialized country governments have recently emphasized the increased role which DFI should play in financing development, few proposals have been made to make it more attractive, either to firms or to the host countries. The US government's Caribbean Basin Initiative, for example, was not a great success among private companies and was regarded with widespread suspicion in the Caribbean countries. Proposals for a code

326

of conduct governing the behaviour of TNCs do not seem likely to stimulate further flows. The provision of incentives by developing countries are likely merely to increase competition between them to attract a limited pool of available foreign investment, which if anything will benefit the foreign investors rather than the third world as a whole. Moreover, anecdotal evidence suggests that companies are not influenced by investment incentives, preferring to assess an investment without incentives and regarding incentives as a pleasant and perhaps ephemeral bonus. It does seem, though, that export processing zones have increased the total amount of DFI in the third world. One possible arrangement to make DFI more acceptable to third world governments may be to increase the involvement of bilateral development banks which are government-owned (such as CDC, KfW, and CCCE) alongside private firms. These institutions are unlikely to tolerate the worst abuses which developing countries fear, and may therefore make DFI more acceptable. The bilateral development banks would need additional resources, but this could be arranged through direct government support, for example from the aid budget, or by allowing them to raise debt or equity finance on their domestic or international capital markets.

(i) Export Credits

A further set of proposals have arisen with a view to helping developing countries to raise funds with which to provide export credits on terms competitive with those provided by the industrialized countries. Through the 1970s and early 1980s UNCTAD developed a scheme for a multilateral export credit guarantee facility (ECGF). The object of the scheme was to enable developing countries to obtain export credits. It called for subscribed capital of $800 million, of which $160 million would be paid up. It would be an independent facility with the participation of developing and developed countries and the World Bank group, supplemented by borrowing on capital markets.

The scheme proposed that the importer would issue promissory notes to the exporter (or his government), who then passes them on to the new ECGF, which then adds its guarantee and has them discounted at the finest rates on the world's financial markets. The promissory notes would carry the guarantees of the exporting and importing countries' governments, and the ECGF. The ECGF, it was proposed, should be backed by member governments and the World Bank, either with finance or guarantees, so that the money markets should have confidence in its paper, although there have been variants of this proposal. Essentially the proposal calls for the establishment of multilateral financial agency, backed by the world's governments, to accept the risk of developing country export credits, and to provide medium-term credit.

The proposal suffered from the shortcoming that the credit would be provided at market terms, and would not be competitive with export credits from industrialized countries (which at the time were heavily subsidized). A variant was proposed by Kitchen (1979b), for a multilateral export credit fund, which would be financed initially by capital grants or long-term loans from ODA. It would then be authorized to supplement its funds by borrowing on the world's financial markets. As it would be guaranteed by its member governments it would be able to borrow at the finest terms. Developing country governments would then be able to draw upon the fund to an agreed amount, and would pass on the funds to re-finance its exporters. Use of the fund would be conditional on the presentation of a promissory note from the importer (or his government), with an insurance policy taken out by the exporter. The fund would make a service charge to cover its costs, and an interest charge to cover its weighted average cost of capital. However, the revolving of the initial capital would enable the fund to charge an interest rate well below its cost of borrowing, thus providing an interest rate subsidy. The subsidy should be the same as the subsidy provided by developed country export credits.

None of the multilateral schemes for providing export credits for developing countries went any further than the discusssion stage, largely because of the opposition of the industrialized nations, who did not want to meet any of the cost, and who were also opposed to the proliferation of international institutions. (However, it is worth noting that their usual argument, that such types of financing should be left to the market, sounds rather hollow in the light of interest rate subsidies, government insurance and guarantees, and mixed credits provided by the industrial countries to support their exports.)

A further market-based approach to financing export credit was proposed by Haschek (1980), the President of the Österreichische Kontrollbank, Austria's export credit finance institution. Haschek took the view that developing country export financing institutions could appear as attractive new borrowers to international banks. The latter were becoming concerned that general balance of payments lending was becoming too hazardous (a view which proved correct in the event), and they were unwilling to become heavily involved in project financing which required long-term funds. Export financing institutions would require short- to medium-term credits, which would fill a convenient gap in the banks' lending portfolios; moreover, the assets of the export financing institutions would be repayable export credits, well diversified internationally, mostly with reliable industrialized countries, and insured on the insurance market or guaranteed by government. Export financing organizations from several industrial countries (Norway, Denmark, Sweden, Finland, Canada, and Austria) have borrowed on the Eurocurrency markets, and there is surely scope for developing countries to follow this pattern. However, this mechanism in itself would not provide any interest rate subsidy; that would have to be provided by the government of the borrowing export financing organization.

(j) Proposals for Increased South–South Financial Flows

The two ideas behind South-based initiatives are those of collective self-reliance, and economic cooperation among developing countries. Over 1981–83 meetings of the Group of 77 in Caracas, Jamaica, Buenos Aires, Ljubljana, and Tunis on South–South financial cooperation culminated in a proposal for a new South Bank. During the course of the meetings a number of gaps in financing were revealed. They are described in Avramovic (1983) and are outlined below.

South–South Joint Ventures

Essentially, this would involve the surplus developing countries investing in commercial activities in deficit countries. Such investment may be direct, through equity and debt, or indirect, through portfolio investment. The scheme as proposed would involve establishing a publicly owned and run holding company, which would have some of the features of a South-based IFC. Support is provided by the success of the IFC, which has earned a rate of return on its equity portfolio which at various times has compared favourably with the rates of return earned on the main Wall Street indices.

Financing of Energy Investment

A South-based energy financing institution was suggested, which would be financed largely by OPEC members, and open to developed countries, who would help to provide the technology. In the meantime, though, it seems that the major world oil companies have provided a great deal of energy exploration and investment in developing countries.

Export Credit, Financing, Guarantee, and Insurance

Although the Jamaica meeting acknowledged the need for increased financial support of developing country exports, it was the earlier Caracas meeting which had proposed the establishment of regional and inter-regional export development banks, modelled to some extent on BLADEX in Latin America. Some other proposals are discussed elsewhere in this chapter.

Commodity Finance

The need for UNCTAD's common fund to stabilize commodity prices was recognized, but further commodity price support was considered desirable.

Balance of Payments Support Arrangements

The five existing regional arrangements were seen to require additional support, by creating a common stabilization fund, which would be guaranteed by its participants, and which would borrow on world markets. This would reinforce the embryo stabilization arrangements of the existing groups.

Payments Arrangements for Oil Imports

A special facility could be established whereby part-payment of a developing country's oil imports could be made in local currency, and subsequently used for development finance purposes or for OPEC equity investments in joint ventures.

The South Bank Proposal

In order to fill the above gaps, a South Bank was proposed. Although still under discussion, the more optimistic proponents in the Group 77 and UNCTAD envisage the bank having a total capital of around $38 billion, of which $5 billion would be paid-in, and the remainder callable. Much of the paid-in capital would be in local currencies, only about $1.5 billion being in convertible currencies. Capital would come mainly from governments, but a certain amount of private sector capital would be welcomed. The South Bank would be self-sustaining and commercially viable. It is hoped that the participation of the forty leading developing countries, who account for over 90% of the aggregate GNP and reserves of the third world, would provide the South Bank with sufficient creditworthiness to enable it to borrow on capital markets. The debt : capital ratio would be 1 : 1. Developed countries may be invited to participate to a limited extent.

Although a well-intentioned proposal, the auspices for the South Bank do not appear particularly good. Some key developing countries, notably Saudi Arabia, Kuwait, Qatar, and Nigeria, have expressed strong reservations, questioning the need for a new organization. Although proponents of the South Bank have attempted to reduce the dependence of the scheme on contributions from the surplus OPEC members, these will obviously be of some importance. Following the weakness of the world oil market, however, the surpluses are not what they were. Moreover, OPEC members have shown little inclination to support schemes for the direct financing of developing countries, preferring instead the lower-risk route of recyling via the North-based institutions and instruments. The exceptions are where the Gulf States have set up their own institutions, such as the OPEC Fund for International Development and the Gulf Investment Corporation (which started with paid-up capital of $3 billion). The Gulf States feel that they control these institutions, but fear that in a South Bank effective control would be vested in the large number of borrower countries rather than the smaller number of large contributors. The establishment of a new South Bank may eclipse organizations such as the OPEC Fund and the Gulf Investment Corporation, and certainly the role of the South Bank *vis-à-vis* these, and the existing regional and sub-regional development banks, is not at all clear. Some countries, notably India, have attempted to modify the proposal by suggesting a rather smaller bank to start with, which could have fewer functions to perform. Moreover, the additionality arising from the proposal may be limited. The main financial benefit would probably arise from facilitating export credits and payments arrangements between developing countries. Suggestions of a novel approach to conditionality attached to balance of payments lending still remain unclarified. The development finance offered by the South Bank would probably be on harder terms than that offered by MDIs, as its standing in capital markets would not be so high, resulting in higher borrowing costs. However, the major problem with this initiative, as with earlier proposals for South-based financial institutions, is that there appears to be insufficient will among third world governments to establish a new institution, and to stump up the cash.[22]

The Private South Bank Proposal

In 1983 Mr Agha Hasan Abedi, the President of the Bank of Credit and Commerce International, one of the larger developing country based commercial banks, proposed the establishment of a new commercial Bank of the Third World. The bank would be owned by existing commercial banks, who would pay an initial capital of $500 million. The bank would raise wholesale deposits and issue bonds to augment its initial capital. The functions of the bank would be as follows.[23]

— To finance trade, countertrade, and barter between member countries.
— To provide short-term (up to 12 months) balance of payments support against assigned foreign exchange earnings.
— To provide bridging finance against firm arrangements with approved international financial agencies such as the IMF and the World Bank.
— To provide short-term finance for essential imports.
— To provide short-term pre-export financing of principal exports.

Central to the trade financing activities of the bank would be the creation of a 'third world dollar', which would be a common unit of account for all transactions.[24] No concrete steps have yet been taken to implement this proposal, though.

(k) Concluding Remarks

The theme of new proposals has shifted from an emphasis on public sector transfers of aid to greater dependency on private sector financing, both in domestic capital mobilization and international capital flows. Experience with debt has led to greater emphasis on equity capital investments. However, fashions change quite rapidly in this field, and earlier proposals which are currently under a shadow may be revived in the future. Of the many proposals described few are likely to be implemented, and then perhaps only partially. However, the abundant variety of the proposals is in itself a healthy sign, and indicative of the thought and concern which is going into the problem of financing the developing countries. Given the disappointing results of conventional public sector development aid, radical proposals to stimulate private sector flows, and to encourage the growth of the private sector in developing countries are encouraging. Those sceptical of new proposals should be reminded that the conventional pillars of international finance, the IMF and the World Bank, were once themselves radical proposals.

In spite of the myriad proposals on international flows, the prospects for increased flows do not look very great. The trend is to cut back on aid in real terms rather than to increase it; the volume of bank debt is such that future flows are likely to be restricted; export credits will no doubt continue to be available, but they are strictly project finance rather than programme finance; and DFI, even with changes in attitude by both investors and host countries, is unlikely to provide much increase in volume. In recent years it has provided only about 10% of total capital flows, so it is difficult to see DFI filling the wide void left by bank lending, and to a lesser extent, aid. However, declining dependence on foreign finance may, in the long run, be beneficial to developing countries.

Likewise none of the proposals, even if adopted, is likely to make much more than a marginal impact on developing country debt. A number of countries can now be regarded as having a permanent, external national debt, and difficulties with debt servicing are likely to re-occur as their current account balances fluctuate. Creditors will have to learn to live with the problem. The main hope for alleviating the debt crisis is for sustained world economic growth, and improved access for debtor country exports to international markets. Growth rate figures necessary to stave off further crises are difficult to estimate, but suggestions of at least 3% per year (World Bank) and 3–4% (Commonwealth Secretariat) for growth in industrialized countries are probably not far wide of the mark. Meanwhile, ad-hoc arrangements to handle periodic debt crises are likely to continue.

The need, then, is for the major industrialized countries to adopt and maintain macroeconomic policies which are conducive to their own growth, and the growth of the rest of the world's economies. Only in this way can recurrent debt crises be avoided, together with the attendant hardship among the populations of the debtor countries.

NOTES

1. These were the Arab Monetary Fund, established in 1977 with 20 members: the Andean Reserve Fund, established in 1976 with five members; the Central American Monetary Stabilization Fund, established in 1974 with five members, and the Latin American Free Trade Association's Financial Assistance Agreement, established in 1969 with 12 members.

2. In this section I have drawn on the Commonwealth Secretariat (1984) and the *Amex Bank Review* (Vol. 11, No. 5), 19 June 1984, as well as some of the original sources quoted.
3. Testimony before the US Senate Committee on Foreign Relations, 17 January 1983 and *Business Week*, 28 February 1983.
4. *New York Times*, 6 March 1983.
5. Testimony before US Congress House Committee on Banking, Finance and Urban Affairs, 26 April 1983.
6. *The Banker*, April 1983.
7. *The Economist*, July 1983.
8. *Business Week*, 10 January 1983.
9. *Foreign Policy*, Spring 1983.
10. Chatham House Lecture, 1984.
11. Insurance of Bank Lending, Group of Thirty, 1984.
12. For a good (if slightly dated) account of. proposals for extending bank deposit insurance schemes, see Baker (1978).
13. 1983 Per Jacobsson lecture.
14. *Foreign Affairs*, Summer 1983.
15. *The Economist*, 30 April 1983.
16. *World Financial Markets*, June 1983.
17. Paper for North–South Round Table on Money and Finance, September 1984.
18. US Senate Banking Committee Hearings, May 1984.
19. *The Economist*, 2 April 1983.
20. The Consensus of Cartagena consists of Argentina, Bolivia, Brazil, Chile, Columbia, the Dominican Republic, Ecuador, Mexico, Peru, Uruguay and Venezuala.
21. The IFC has already sponsored the $60 million Korea Fund, an investment trust which buys shares in South Korean companies. The Korean Fund had a successful launch on the New York Stock Exchange in August 1984.
22. More details of the proposal, and its drawbacks, are given in *South*, July 1983 and November 1983.
23. See *South*, August 1983, for further details.
24. The idea of a third world currency to facilitate inter-third world trade was proposed by Frances Stewart and Michael Stewart (1980). Certainly the widespread lack of convertibility of developing country currencies is a major obstacle to trade and growth, and any steps towards convertibility are to be encouraged.

References

Abe, S., Fry, M. J., Byoung Kyun Min, Pairoj Vongripanond and Teh-Pei Yu (1977) Financial liberalisation and domestic saving in economic development: an empirical test for six countries. *Pakistan Development Review,* **16** (3) 298–308.

Adams, D. W. (1980) Recent performance of rural financial markets. In Howell, J. (ed.) *Borrowers and Lenders: Rural Financial Markets and Institutions in Developing Countries.* Overseas Development Institute, London, pp. 15–34.

Adler, M., and Dumas, B. (1975) The long term financial decisions of the multinational corporations. In Elton, E. J., and Gruber, M. J. (eds.), *International Capital Markets.* North Holland, Amsterdam/Oxford, pp. 360–387.

Agmon, T., and Kindleberger, C. P. (eds.) (1977) *Multinationals from Small Countries.* MIT Press, Cambridge, Mass.

Agmon, T., and Lessard, D. R. (1977) Financial factors and the international expansion of small-country firms. In Agmon, T., and Kindleberger, C. P. (eds.), *Multinationals from Small Countries.* MIT Press, Cambridge, Mass., pp. 197–220.

van Agtmael, A. W. (1981) Stock markets in development countries. IFC, Mimeo.

van Agtmael, A. W. (1984) *Emerging Securities Markets.* Euromoney Publications, London.

van Agtmael, A. W., and Errunza, V. R. (1982) Foreign portfolio investment in emerging securities markets. *Columbia Journal of World Business,* Summer, pp. 58–63.

Ahluwalia, M. S., and Lysy, F. J. (1981) Employment, income distribution and programs to remedy balance-of-payments difficulties. In Cline, W. R., and Weintraub, S. (eds.), *Economic Stabilisation in Developing Countries.* Brookings Institution, Washington, DC, pp. 149–190.

Ahmed, Z., Aqbal, M., and Khan, M. F. (1983) *Money and Banking in Islam.* International Centre for Research in Islamic Economics, Jeddah, and Institute of Policy Studies, Islamabad.

Ajayi, S. I., and Ojo, O. O. (1981) *Money and Banking: Analysis and Policy in the Nigerian Context.* George Allen & Unwin, London.

Anderson, D. (1982) Small industry in developing countries: a discussion of issues. *World Development,* **10** (11), 913–948 (November).

Archer, S. H., and D'Ambrosio, C. A. (eds) (1983) *The Theory of Business Finance: a Book of Readings* (3rd edition). Macmillan, London and New York.

Archer, S. H. and D'Ambrosio, C. A. (1972) *Business Finance Theory and Management,* 2nd edition. Macmillan, New York and London.

Arndt, H. W. (1982) Two kinds of credit rationing. *Banca Nazionale del Lavoro Quarterly Review,* **XXXV** (143), 417–425 (December).

333

Arrow, K. J. (1966) Discounting and public investment criteria. In Kneese, A. V., and Smith, S. C. (eds.) *Water Research*, Johns Hopkins, Baltimore, pp. 13–32.

Atherton, J., and Yap, D. C. L. (1979) Risk reduction by international diversification. *Managerial Finance*, **5** (1), 18–28.

Avramovic, D. (ed.) (1983) *South–South Financial Corporation*, Frances Pinter, London.

Bailey, M. J., and Jensen, M. C. (1972) Risk and discount rate for public investment. In Jensen, M. C. (ed.), *Studies in the Theory of Capital Markets*. Praeger, New York, pp. 269–293.

Baker, J. C. (1978) *International Bank Regulation*. Praeger, New York.

Balassa, B. (1984) Adjustment policies in developing countries: a reassessment. *World Development*, **12** (9) (September) 955–972.

Bauer, P. T. (1976) *Dissent on Development*. Weidenfeld & Nicolson, London.

Bauer, P. T. (1981) *Equality, the Third World and Economic Delusion*. Weidenfeld & Nicolson, London.

Bauer, P. T., and Yamey, B. (1981) The political economy of foreign aid. *Lloyds Bank Review*, No. 142 1–14 (October).

Baumol, W. J. (1963) An expected gain–confidence limit criterion for portfolio selection. *Management Science*, 174–182 (October).

Bavishi, V. (1979) Capital budgeting for US-based multinational corporations: an assessment of theory and practice. Working Paper, University of Connecticut.

Begashaw, G. (1977) The role of traditional saving and credit institutions in Ethiopia. Ohio State University, mimeo.

Begley, C. D. (1978) The savings–aid relationship in Latin America. Ph.D. dissertation, University of Texas at Austin.

Bhatia, R. J., and Khatkhate, D. R. (1975) Financial intermediation, savings mobilisation and entreprenemial development: the African experience. *IMF Staff Papers*, **22** (1) 132–158 (March).

Bierman, H., and Schmidt, S. (1975) *The Capital Budgeting Decision*. Collier-Macmillan, London.

Bird, G. (1982a) Should developing countries use currency depreciation as a tool of balance of payments adjustment? A review of the theory and evidence, and a guide for the policy maker. *Journal of Development Studies*, **19** (4), 461–484 (July).

Bird, G. (1982b) *The International Monetary System and the Less Developed Countries*, 2nd edition. Macmillan, London.

Bird, R. M. (1978) Assessing tax performance in developing countries: a critical review of the literature. In Toye, J. F. J. (ed.), *Taxation and Economic Development*. Frank Cass, London, pp. 33–61.

Black, F., Jensen, M., and Scholes, M. (1972) The capital asset pricing model: some empirical tests. In Jensen, M. (ed.), *Studies in the Theory of Capital Markets*. Praeger, New York, pp. 79–121.

Black, J., and Dunning, J. H. (eds) (1982) *International Capital Movements*. Macmillan, London.

Blask, J. K. (1978) A survey of country evaluation systems in use. In Goodman, S. H. (ed.), *Finance and Risk in Developing Countries*. Praeger, New York, pp. 65–70.

Blume, M. E., and Friend, I. (1973) A new look at the capital asset pricing model. *Journal of Finance*, **28**, 19–33 (March).

Blume, M. E., and Friend, I. (1974) Risk, investment strategy and the long-run rates of return. *Review of Economics and Statistics*, 259–269 (August).

Bodie, Z. (1976) Common stocks as a hedge against inflation. *Journal of Finance* Vol. **31** (2), 459–470 (May).

Bogdanowicz-Bindert, C. A. (1983) Portugal, Turkey and Peru: three successful stabilisation programs under the auspices of the IMF. *World Development,* **11** (1), 65–70 (January).

Bolnick, B. (1982) Concessional credit for small scale enterprise. *Bulletin of Indonesian Economic Studies* **XVIII** (2), 65–85 (July).

Bortolani, S. (1975) *Central Banking in Africa.* Casse di Risparmio delle Provincie Lombarde, Milan.

Bottomley, J. A. (1963) The premium for risk as a determinant of interest rates in underdeveloped rural areas. *Quarterly Journal of Economics,* **LXXVII**, 637–647 (November).

Bottomley, J. A. (1964) Monopoly profit as a determinant of interest rates in underdeveloped rural areas. *Oxford Economic Papers,* **16**, (3) 431–437 (November).

Bottomley, J. A. (1975) Interest rate determinations in underdeveloped rural areas. *American Journal of Agricultural Economics,* **57**, 279–291 (May).

Bowles, T. S. (1978) *Survey of Attitudes Towards Overseas Development.* HMSO, London.

Brandt Commission (1980) *North–South: a Programme for Survival.* Pan Books, London.

Brandt Commission (1983) *Common Crisis North–South: Co-operation for World Recovery.* Pan books, London.

Brealey, R. A., and Dimson, E. (1976) The excess return on UK equities: 1919–1975. London Business School, mimeo.

Brealey, R., and Myers, S. (1981) *Principles of Corporate Finance.* McGraw-Hill, New York/London (2nd edition, 1984).

Brecher, J., and Abbas, S. (1972) *Foreign Aid and Industrial Development in Pakistan.* Cambridge University Press, Cambridge.

Brodersohn, M. S. (1981) *Financing of Industrial Enterprises and Financial Repression in Latin America.* UNIDO, Vienna.

Bromwich, M. (1976) *The Economics of Capital Budgeting.* Penguin, Harmondsworth.

Broyles, J. E., and Cooper, I. A. (1981) Growth opportunities and real investment decisions. In Derkinderen, F. G. J., and Crum, R. L. (eds), *Risk, Capital Costs and Project Financing Decisions.* Martinus Nijhoff, Boston/The Hague/London, pp. 107–118.

Buckley, P. J., and Casson, M. C. (1976) *The Future of the Multinational Enterprise.* Macmillan, London.

Calamanti, A. (1979) The Tunis Stock Exchange. *Savings and Development,* **III** (3), 157–184.

Calamanti, A. (1980a) The Abidjan Stock Exchange: an instrument for savings mobilisation and the indigenisation of economic activity. *Savings and Development,* **IV** (2), 92–122.

Calamanti, A. (1980b) The Stock Exchange and the securities market in Morocco. *Savings and Development,* **IV** (4), 266–302.

   (The above three articles are reprinted in Calamanti, A. (1983) *The Securities Market and Underdevelopment.* Guiffre, Milan.)

Cassen, R., Jolly, R., Sewell, S., and Wood, R. (eds.) (1982) *Rich Country Interests and Third World Development.* Croom Helm, London.

Casson, M. C. (1983) *The Growth of International Business.* George Allen & Unwin, London.

Chandavarkar, A. G. (1984) *The International Monetary Fund. Its Financial Organisation and Activities.* IMF, Washington, DC.

Chenery, H., and Strout, A. (1966) Foreign assistance and economic development. *American Economic Review,* **56** (4), 670–733 (September).

Cheng, P., and Grauer, R. (1980) An alternative test of the capital asset pricing

336

model. *American Economic Review,* **70** (4), 660–671 (September).

Cheng, P., and Grauer, R. (1982) An alternative test of the capital asset pricing model: reply. *American Economic Review,* **72** (5), 1201–1207. (December).

Christian, J. W., and Pagoulatos, E. (1973) Domestic financial markets in developing economies: an econometric analysis. *Kyklos,* **26**, 75–90.

Clapham, J. H. (1936) *Economic Development of France and Germany 1815–1914,* 4th edition. Cambridge University Press, London.

Clements, K., and Sjaastad, L. (1985) *How Protection Taxes Exporters.* Trade Policy Research Centre, London.

Cline, W. R. (1983) Economic stabilisation in developing countries: theory and stylized facts. In Williamson, J. (ed.), *IMF Conditionality.* Institute for International Economics, Washington, DC, 175–208.

Cline, W. R. (1984) *International Debt. Systemic Risk and Policy Response.* Institute for International Economics, Washington, DC.

Cline, W. R., and Weintraub, S. (eds) (1981) *Economic Stabilisation in Developing Countries.* Brookings Institution, Washington, DC.

Cohen, K. J., and Pogue, J. A. (1967) An empirical evaluation of alternative portfolio selection models. *Journal of Business,* 166–190 (April).

Cohen, J. B., Zinbarg, E. D., and Zeikel, A. (1982) *Investment Analysis and Portfolio Management,* 4th edition. Irwin, Homewood, Ill.

Cohn, R. A., and Lessard, D. R. (1981) The effect of inflation on stock prices: international evidence. *Journal of Finance,* **36**, 277–289 (May).

Collyns, C. (1983) Alternatives to the Central Bank in the Developing World. IMF Occasional Paper No. 20, Washington, DC.

Commonwealth Secretariat (1984) *The Debt Crisis and the World Economy.* Commonwealth Secretariat, London.

Conine, J. E. Jr. (1982) On the theoretical relationship between business risk and systematic risk. *Journal of Business Finance and Accounting,* **9** (2), 199–205.

Connors, T. A. (1979) The apparent effects of recent IMF stabilisation programs. International Finance Discussion Paper No. 135. Federal Reserve, Washington, mimeo.

Cottrell, P. L. (1975) *British Overseas Investment in the 19th Century.* Macmillan, London.

Croswell, M. (1981) Growth, poverty alleviation and foreign assistance. AID Discussion Paper No. 39.

Dell, S. (1982) Stabilisation: the political economy of overkill. *World Development,* **10** (8), 597–612 (August).

Dell, S., and Lawrence, R. (1980) *The Balance of Payments Adjustment Process in Developing Countries.* Pergamon Press, New York.

Derkinderen, F. G. J., and Crum, R. L. (1981) *Risk, Capital Costs and Project Financing Decisions.* Martinus Nijhoff, Boston/The Hague/London.

Development Committee of World Bank and the IMF (1982) Non-concessional Flows to Developing Countries. (Report of the Task Force on Non-concessional Flows to the Joint Ministerial Committee of the Board of Governors of the Bank and the Fund on the Transfer of Real Resources to Developing Countries.) Development Committee, Washington, DC.

De Zoete and Bevan (annually) *The Equity-Gilts Study,* London.

Diamond, W. (1957) *Development Banks.* Johns Hopkins Press, Baltimore and London.

Diaz-Alejandro, C. F. (1981) Southern cone stabilisation plans. In Cline, W. R., and Weintraub, S. (eds), *Economic Stabilisation in Developing Countries.* Brookings Institution, Washington, DC, 119–148.

Dickie, R. B. (1981) Development of third world securities markets: an analysis of general principles and a case study of the Indonesian market. *Law and Policy in International Business,* **13**, 177–222.

Dimson, E., and Marsh, P. R. (1982) Calculating the cost of capital. *Long Range Planning*, **15** (2), 112–120.

Donovan, D. J. (1981) Real responses associated with exchange rate action in selection upper credit tranche stabilisation programs. *IMF Staff Papers*, **28** (4), 698–727.

Donovan, D. J. (1982) Macro-economic performance and adjustment under Fund-supported programmes: the experience of the seventies. *IMF Staff Papers*, **25** (2), 171–203 (June).

Dorrance, G. (1981) Financing of Manufacturing in Africa (UNIDO, Vienna).

Dowling, J. M., and Hiemenz, U. (1985) Biases in the allocation of foreign aid: some new evidence. *World Development*, **13** (4), 535–542 (April).

Dowling, J. M. and Hiemenz, U. (1983) Aid, savings and growth in the Asian region. *Developing Economies*, **XXI** (1), 3–13.

Drake, P. J. (1977) Securities markets in less-developed countries. *Journal of Development Studies*, **13** (2), 74–91.

Drake, P. J. (1980) *Money, Finance and Development*. Martin Robertson, Oxford.

Drake P. J. (1983) Increasing the supply of securities: some experience in South East and East Asia. Paper presented to the International Conference on Capital Market Development, Cairo, May.

Economist Intelligence Unit (1984) *North/South Countertrade*. EIU, London.

Edelmen, J. A., and Chenery, H. B. (1977) Aid and income distribution. In Bhagwati, J. (ed.), *New International Economic Order: The North–South Debate*. MIT Press, Cambridge, Mass., pp. 27–49.

Edgren, G. (1984) Conditionality in aid. In Stokke, O. (ed.), *European Development Assistance*, vol. II. European Association of Development Research and Training Institutes, Tilburg/Norwegian Institute of International Affairs, Oslo, pp. 153–162.

Elton, E. J., and Gruber, M. J. (eds.) (1975) *International Capital Markets*. North Holland, Amsterdam.

Emery, R. F. (1970) *The Financial Institutions of Southeast Asia*. Praeger, New York.

Errunza, V. R. (1977) Gains from portfolio diversification into less developed countries' securities. *Journal of International Business*, **8** (2), 83–99.

Faaland, J. (ed.) (1981) *Aid and Influence*. Macmillan, Basingstoke.

Fama, E. F. (1965) The behaviour of stock prices. *Journal of Business*, **38**, 34–105 (January).

Fama, E. F. (1970) Efficient capital markets: a review of theory and empirical work. *Journal of Finance*, **25** (2), 383–417 (May).

Fama, E. F., and MacBeth, J. (1973) Risk, return and equilibrium: empirical tests. *Journal of Political Economy*, **81**, 607–636 (May/June).

Feder, G., and Ross, K. (1982) Risk assessments and risk premiums in the Eurodollar market. *The Journal of Finance*, **27** (3), 679–691 (June).

Fischer, B. (1981) Interest rate ceilings, inflation and economic growth in developing countries. *Economics*, **23**, 75–93.

Fishlow, A. (1961) The Trustee Savings Banks, 1817–1861. *Journal of Economic History*. **21** (1), 27–40 (March).

Franks, J. R., and Broyles, J. E. (1979) *Modern Managerial Finance*. Wiley, London.

Friedman, Irving, S. (1981) Is optimism on developing country debt justified? Paper given at *The Financial Times* World Banking Conference, London, 14 December.

Fry, M. J. (1974) *The Afghan Economy: Money, Finance and the Critical Constraints to Economic Development*. Brill, Leiden.

Fry, M. J. (1978a) Monetary policy and domestic saving in developing ESCAP countries. *Economic bulletin for Asia and the Pacific*, **29** (1), 79–99 (June).

Fry, M. J. (1978b) Money and capital or financial deepening in economic development? *Journal of Money, Credit and Banking*, **10** (4), 464–475 (November).

Fry, M. J. (1980) Saving, investment, growth and the cost of financial repression.

338

World Development, **8** (4), 317–327 (April).

Fry, M. J. (1981a) Interest rates in Asia: an examination of interest rate policies in Burma, India, Indonesia, Korea, Malaysia, Nepal, Pakistan, the Philippines, Singapore, Sri Lanka, Taiwan and Thailand. University of California at Irvine, mimeo.

Fry, M. J. (1981b) Inflation and economic growth in Pacific Basin developing countries. *Federal Reserve Bank of San Francisco Economic Review,* 8–18.

Fry, M. J. (1982) Models of financially repressed developing countries. *World Development,* **10** (9), 731–750 (September).

Furness, E. L. (1975) *Money and Credit in Developing Africa.* Heinemann Educational Books, London/Nairobi.

Galbis, V. (1977) Financial intermediation and economic growth in less developed countries: a theoretical approach. *Journal of Development Studies,* **13** (2), 58–71 (January).

Galbis, V. (1979a) Inflation and interest rate policies in Latin America, 1967–76. *IMF Staff Papers,* **26** (2), 334–366 (June).

Galbis, V. (1979b) Money, investment and growth in Latin America, 1961–1973. *Economic Development and Cultural Change,* **27** (3), 423–443 (April).

Galbis, V. (1981) Interest rate management: the Latin American experience. *Savings and Development,* **V** (1), 5–44.

Galbis, V. (1982) Analytical aspects of interest rate policies in less developed countries. *Savings and Development,* **6** (2), 111–167.

Galbraith, J. K. (1975) *Money. Whence it Came. Where it Went.* André Deutsch, London, 1975; Penguin, Harmondsworth, 1976.

Gandhi, D. K., Saunders, A., and Woodward, R. S. (1980). Thin capital markets: a case study of the Kuwaiti stock market. *Applied Economics,* **12**, 341–9.

Gantt, A., and Dutto, G. (1968) Financial performance of government-owned corporations in less developed countries. *IMF Staff Papers,* **25**, 102–42.

Gerschenkron, A. (1962) *Economic Backwardness in Historical Perspective.* Harvard University Press, Cambridge, Mass.

Gill, D. (1983) Capital markets and financial systems development. Paper presented at the International Conference on Capital Market Development, Cairo, May.

Gillis, M. (1980) The role of public enterprises in economic development. *Social Research,* **47** (2), 248–289.

Gillis, M., Jenkins, G. P., and Lessard, D. R. (1982) Public enterprise finance: towards a synthesis. In Jones, Leroy, P., (ed.), *Public Enterprise in Less-developed Countries.* Cambridge University Press, Cambridge, pp. 257–280.

Giovanni, A. (1983) The interest elasticity of savings in developing countries: the existing evidence. *World Development,* **11** (7), 601–608.

Goldsmith, R. W. (1966) *The Determinants of Financial Structure.* OECD, Paris.

Goldsmith, R. W. (1969) *Financial Structure and Development.* Yale University Press, New Haven.

Goldsmith, R. W. (1971) The development of financial institutions during the postwar period. *Banca Nazionale del Lavoro Quarterly Review,* No. 97 (June).

Goldsmith, R. W. (1973) A century of financial development in Latin America. Yale University Economic Growth Center Paper No. 196.

Goode, R. (1980) Limits to taxation. *Finance and Development,* **17** (1), 11–13 (March).

Goodman, S. H. (1977) How the big US banks really evaluate sovereign risks. *Euromoney,* February, pp. 105–10.

Goodman, S. H. (ed.) (1978) *Financing and Risk in Developing Countries.* Praeger, New York.

Gordon, D. L. (1983) Development finance companies, state and privately owned: a review. World Bank Staff Working Paper No. 578.

Griffith-Jones, S. (1982) The role of financial policies in the transition to socialism. IFDA Dossier 28, March/April, pp. 71–74.

Grubel, H. G. (1968) Internationally diversified portfolios: welfare gains and capital flows. *American Economic Review,* **58** (5), 1299–1314 (December).

Gulati, U. (1978) Effect of capital imports on savings and growth in less developed countries. *Economic Inquiry,* **16** (4), 563–569.

Gupta, K. L. (1975) Foreign capital inflow, dependency burden, and saving rates in developing countries: a simultaneous equation model. *Kylos,* **28** (2), 358–374.

Gupta, K. L. (1984) *Financial and Economic Growth in Developing Countries.* Croom Helm, London.

Gupta, K. L., and Islam, M. A. (1983) *Foreign Capital, Savings and Growth. An International Cross-Section Study.* Reidel, Dordrecht, Holland/Boston, Mass.

Gurley, J. G., and Shaw, E. S. (1955) Financial aspects of economic development. *American Economic Review,* **45** (4), 515–538 (September).

Gurley, J. G., and Shaw, E. S. (1960) *Money in a Theory of Finance.* Brookings Institution, Washington, DC.

Gurley, J. G., and Shaw, E. S. (1967) Financial structure and economic development. *Economic Development and Cultural Change* (April), pp. 257–268.

Gwin, C. (1983) Financing India's structural adjustment: the role of the fund. In Williamson, J. (ed.), *IMF Conditionality.* Institute for International Economics, Washington, DC. pp. 511–532.

Hanson, A. H. (1965) *Public Enterprise and Economic Development,* 2nd edition. Routledge & Kegan Paul, London.

Hanson, J. A. (1980) The Colombian experience with financial repression and incomplete liberalisation: stagnation, growth and instability 1950–1978. Proceedings of the First International Conference on the Financial Development of Latin America and the Caribbean. Inter-American Institute of Capital Markets.

Harvey, C. (1983) *Analysis of Project Finance in Developing Countries.* Heinemann, London.

Haschek, H. (1980) What the LDC's need are export credit schemes *Euromoney.* 8–15 (September).

Hayter, T. (1971) *Aid and Imperialism.* Penguin, London.

Healey, J., and Clift, C. (1980) The developmental rationale for aid re-examined. *ODI Review,* No. 2, 14–34.

Hirschleifer, J. (1965) Investment decision under uncertainty: choice–theoretic approaches. *Quarterly Journal of Economics,* **LXXIX** (4), 509–536 (November).

Hobson, C. K. (1914) *The Export of Capital.* Constable, London; reprinted 1963.

Hooley, R. W. (1963) *Savings in the Philippines.* Institute of Economic Development and Research, University of the Philippines.

Howell, J. (ed.) (1980) *Borrowers and Lenders: Rural Financial Markets and Institutions in Developing Countries.* Overseas Development Institute, London.

Hymer, S. (1976) *International Operations of National Firms: a study of Direct Investment.* Farnborough, Lexington.

Ibbotson, R. G., and Sinquefield, R. A. (1982) *Stocks, Bonds, Bills and Inflation: the Past and the Future.* Financial Analysts Research Foundation.

International Monetary Fund (1982) *International Financial Statistics.* Supplement on Fund Accounts. IMF, Washington, DC.

Isenman, P. (1976) Biases in aid allocation against poorer and larger countries. *World Development,* **4** (8), 631–642 (August).

Islam, N. (1972) Foreign assistance and economic development: the case of Pakistan. *Economic Journal,* **82** (325S), 502–530 (March).

Jackson, T., and Eade, D. (1982) *Against the Grain.* Oxfam, Oxford.

Jacoby, N. (1966) *U.S. Aid to Taiwan: a Study of Foreign Aid, Self-help and Development.* Praeger, New York.

Jaffe, J. F., and Mandelker, G. (1976) The Fisher effect for risky assets: an empirical investigation. *Journal of Finance,* **31** (2) (May) 447–458.

Jao, Y. C. (1976) Financial deepening and economic growth: a cross-section analysis. *Malayan Economic Review*, April, 47–68.

Jenks, L. H. (1927/1963) *The Migration of British Capital to 1875*, 1963 reprint of 1927 edition. Nelson, London. Augustus Kelly, New York.

Jetha, N. (1973) Some aspects of domestic financing of central government expenditure: the case of Kenya. in David, W. L. (ed.), *Public Finance, Planning and Economic Development*, Essays in honour of Ursula Hicks. Macmillan, London, pp. 95–139.

Johnson, H. G. (1967) *Economic Policies Towards Less Developed Countries*. George Allen & Unwin, London.

Johnston, R. B. (1983) *The Economics of the Euro-Market. History, Theory and Policy*. Macmillan, London.

Kane, J. A. (1975) *Development Banking*. Heath, Lexington, Mass.

Keller, P. (1980) Implications of credit policies for output and the balance of payments. *IMF Staff Papers,* **27** (3), 451–477 (September).

Khatkhate, D. R. (1972) Analytical basis of the working of monetary policy in less developed countries. *IMF Staff Papers,* **19** (3), 533–558.

Khatkhate, D. R. (1982a) National and international aspects of financial policies in LDCs: a prologue. *World Development,* **10** (9), 689–694.

Khatkhate, D. R. (1982b) Anatomy of financial retardation in a less developed country: the case of Sri Lanka, 1951–1976. *World Development,* **10** (9), 829–840.

Khatkhate, D. R., and Riechal, K.-W. (1980) Multipurpose banking: its nature, scope and relevance for less developed countries. *IMF Staff Papers,* **27** (3), 478–516 (September).

Killick, T. (ed.) (1982) *Adjustment and Finance in the Developing World: the Role of the IMF*. IMF and ODI, Washington, DC and London.

Killick, T. (1983) The role of the public sector in the industrialisation of African countries. *Industry and Development*, No. 7, UNIDO, 57–88.

Killick, T. (ed.) (1984a) *The Quest for Economic Stabilisation*. Heinemann Educational Books and the Overseas Development Institute, London.

Killick, T. (ed.) (1984b) *The IMF and Stabilisation. Developing Country Experiences*. Heinemann, London.

Kindleberger, C. P. (1969) *American Business Abroad*. Yale University Press, New Haven.

Kindleberger, C. P. (1978) *Manias, Panics and Crashes. A History of Financial Crises*. Basic Books, New York; Macmillan, London.

Kitchen, R. L. (1978) The decision process and lending to small-scale enterprises. OECD/DSE Panel Meeting on Training for Development Bankers, June 1978; ed. Scharf, T. and Traumann, G. DSE/OECD, West Berlin (published 1979), pp. 159–172.

Kitchen, R. L. (1979a) Financial flows: statistical background. In UNIDO, *Industry 2000—New Perspectives*. Collected Background Papers, Vol. 1: *International Financial Flows*. UNIDO, Vienna, pp. 73–112.

Kitchen, R. L. (1979b) The development and expansion of south-based financial arrangements and institutions. In UNIDO, *Industry 2000—New Perspectives*. Collected Background Papers, vol. 1: *International Financial Flows*. UNIDO, Vienna, pp. 112–127.

Kitchen, R. L. (1981) Alternative possibilities for handling balance of payments and debt crises: a Third World Monetary Fund. IFDA Dossier 25, 86–91 (September/October).

Kitchen, R. L. (1985) A market-based approach to the debt. *Latin American Times*, No. 64, 1–3 (March).

Knight, F. H. (1921) *Risk, Uncertainty and Profit*. Houghton Mifflin, Boston.

Kraus, A., and Litzenberger, R. (1976) Skewness preference and the valuation of risk assets. *Journal of Finance*, **31** (4), 1085–1101 (September).

Krueger, A. O. (1978) Foreign trade and economic regimes and economic development: liberalization attempts and consequences. *A Special Conference Series on Foreign Trade Regimes and Economic Development*, Vol. 10. Ballinger, Cambridge, Mass.

Krueger, A. O. (1979) *The Development Role of the Foreign Sector and Aid*. Council on East Asian Studies, Harvard University, Cambridge, Mass.

Lal, S. (1983) *The New Multinationals: The Spread of Third World Enterprises*. John Wiley, Chichester.

Landau, L. (1971) Savings functions for Latin America. In Chenery, H. B. (ed.), *Studies in Development Planning*. Harvard University Press, Cambridge, Mass., 299–321.

Leff, N. H., and Sato, K. S. (1980) Macroeconomic adjustment in developing countries: instability, short-run growth and external dependency. *Review of Economics and Statistics*, **62** (2), 170–179 (May).

Leipziger, D. M. (1983) Lending versus giving: the economics of foreign assistance. *World Development*, **11** (4), 329–336 (April).

Leite, S. P. (1982) Interest rate policies in West Africa. *IMF Staff Papers*, **29** (1) (March) 48–76.

Lessard, D. R. (1971) Multinational portfolio diversification for developing countries. *Stanford Journal of International Studies*, 80–112 (June).

Lessard, D. R. (1975) The structure of returns and gains from international diversification. In Elton, E. J. and Gruber, M. J. (eds), *International Capital Markets*. North Holland/American Elsevier, Amsterdam, 207–220.

Lessard, D. R. (1982) Appropriate non-concessional industrial financing for developing countries. Information paper prepared for the first consultation on industrial financing, UNIDO/PC 48, Vienna.

Lessard, D. R. and Wellons, P. A. (1979) Financing development: innovations and private capital markets. In UNIDO, *Industry 2000—New Perspectives*. Collected Background Papers. UNIDO, Vienna, 127–234.

Lessard, D. R., and Williamson, J. (1985) *Financial Intermediation beyond the Debt Crisis*. Institute for International Economics, Washington, DC.

Levitz, G. D. (1974) Market risk and the management of institutional equity portfolios. *Financial Analysts Journal*, 53–60 (January/February).

Levy, H. (1978) Equilibrium in an imperfect market: a constraint on the number of securities in the portfolio. *American Economic Review*, **68** (4), 643–658 (September).

Levy, H. (1983) The capital asset pricing model: theory and empiricism. *Economic Journal*, **93**, 145–165 (March).

Levy, H., and Sarnat, S. (1970) International diversification of investment portfolios. *American Economic Review*, **60**, 668–675 (September).

Levy, H., and Sarnat, S. (1982) *Capital Investment and Financial Decisions*, 2nd edition. Prentice-Hall, Englewood Cliffs, NJ.

Levy, R. A. (1974) Beta coefficients as predictors of return. *Financial Analysts Journal*. 61–69 (January/February).

Lewis, C. (1938) *America's Stake in International Investments*. Brookings Institution, Washington; reprinted 1976 by Arno Press, New York.

Lewis, S. R. Jr. (1984) *Taxation for Development, Principles and Applications*. Oxford University Press, Oxford.

Lewis, W. A. (1956) *Development Planning*. George Allen & Unwin, London.

Lewis, W. A. (1978) *The Evolution of the International Economic Order*. Princeton University Press, Princeton, NJ.

Lintner, J. (1965) The valuation of risk assets and the selection of risky investments in stock portfolios and capital budgets. *Review of Economics and Statistics,* **47**, 13–37 (February). Reprinted in Archer and d'Ambrosio (1983).

Lloyd, B. (1976) The role of capital markets in developing countries. *Moorgate and Wall Street,* Spring, 45–48.

Lloyd, B. (1977) The efficiency of financial institutions and markets. *Investment Analyst,* No. 47, 5–16 (May).

Long, M. F. (1973) Credit for small farmers: Indonesia, Malaysia and Thailand. US AID, *Spring Review of Small Farmers Credit,* **XV**, (February).

Lumby, S. (1981) *Investment Appraisal and Related Decisions.* Nelson, London.

McDougall, G. D. A. (1960) The benefits and costs of private investment from abroad: a theoretical approach. *Economic Record* **36**, 13–35 (March).

McDonald, D. C. (1982) Debt Capacity and Developing Country Borrowing. *IMF Staff Papers,* **29** (4), 603–646.

McKinnon, R. I. (1973) *Money and Capital in Economic Development.* Brookings Institution, Washington, DC.

Maizels, A., and Nissanke, M. K. (1984) Motivations for aid to development countries. *World Development,* **12** (9), 879–900.

Mandelbrot, B. (1963) The variation of certain speculative prices. *Journal of Business,* 394–419 (October).

Markowitz, H. M. (1952) Portfolio selection. *Journal of Finance,* 77–91 (March).

Markowitz, H. M. (1959/70) *Portfolio Selection: Efficient Diversification of Investments.* Wiley, re-issued by Yale University Press, 1970.

Merrett, A. J., and Sykes, A. (1973) *The Finance and Analysis of Capital Projects,* 2nd edition. Longman, London.

Mikesell, R. F. (1968) *The Economics of Foreign Aid.* Weidenfeld & Nicolson, London.

Miller, M. H., and Modigliani, F. (1966) Some estimates of the cost of capital to the electrical utility industry, 1954–57. *American Economic Review,* **56** (3), 333–391 (June).

Miller, N. C. (1966) *The Great Salad Oil Swindle* Victor Gollancz, London.

Milward, A., and Saul, S. B. (1973) *The Economic Development of Continental Europe, 1780–1870.* George Allen & Unwin, London.

Miracle, M. P., Miracle, D. S., and Cohen, L. (1980) Informal savings mobilisation in Africa. *Economic Development and Cultural Change,* **28** (4), 701–724 (July).

Modigliani, F., and Miller, M. H. (1958) The cost of capital, corporation finance and the theory of investment. *American Economic Review,* **48** (3), 261–297 (June). Reprinted in Archer and d'Ambrosio (1983).

Modigliani, F., and Miller, M. H. (1959) The cost of capital, corporation finance and the theory of investment; a reply. *American Economic Review,* **49**, 655–659. Reprinted in Archer and d'Ambrosio (1983).

Modigliani, F., and Miller, M. H. (1963) Corporate income taxes and the cost of capital: a correction. *American Economic Review,* **53** (4), 433–442 (September). Reprinted in Archer and d'Ambrosio (1983).

Mosley, P. (1980) Aid, savings and growth revisited. *Oxford Bulletin of Economics and Statistics,* **42** (2), 79–96 (May).

Mosley, P. (1982) The quality of overseas aid. *ODI Review,* No. 2. 46–56.

Mossin, J. (1966) Equilibrium in a capital asset market. *Econometrica,* **34**, 768–783 (October).

Nagy, P. (1976) The debt service ratio — how useful a tool? *Banker,* 347–350 (April).

Nelson, C. R. (1976) Inflation and rates of return on common stocks. *Journal of Finance,* **31** (2), 471–483 (May).

Ness, W. L. Jr (1974) Financial markets innovation as a development strategy: initial results from the Brazilian experience. *Economic Development and Cultural Change,* **22** (3), 453–472.

Ness, W. L. Jr (1983) The Capital Market Development Experience of Latin America. (Paper presented to the International Conference on Capital Market Development, Cairo, May).

Nevin, E. (1961) *Capital Funds in Underdeveloped Countries.* Macmillan, London.

Nevitt, P. K. (1980) *Project Financing.* Euromoney Publications, London.

Newlyn, W. T. (ed.) (1977) *The Financing of Economic Development.* Clarendon Press, Oxford.

Newlyn, W. T. (1985) Measuring tax effort in developing countries. *Journal of Development Studies,* **21** (3), 390–405 (April).

North, D. (1962) International capital movements in historical perspective. In Mikesell, R. F. (ed.), *U.S. Private and Government Investment Abroad.* University of Oregon, Eugene.

Nowzad, B. (1981) The IMF and its critics. *Essays in International Finance,* No. 146, Princeton University.

OECD (1969) *Development Assistance Efforts and Policies. 1969 Review,* OECD, Paris.

OECD (1978) *Revenue Statistics of OECD Member Countries, 1965–76.* OECD, Paris.

OECD (1982) *The Export Credit Financing Systems in OECD Member Countries,* revised edition. OECD, Paris.

OECD (1983a) *Development Cooperation. 1983 Review.* OECD, Paris.

OECD (1983b) *Investing in Developing Countries.* OECD, Paris.

OECD (1984a) *Development Cooperation. 1984 Review.* OECD, Paris.

OECD (1984b) *External Debt of Developing Countries: 1983 Survey.* OECD, Paris.

OECD (1985a) *Twenty-five Years of Development Corporation. A Review.* OECD, Paris.

OECD (1985b) *Countertrade. Developing Country Practices.* OECD, Paris.

Osuntogun, A., and Adewunmi, W. (1983) *Rural Banking in Nigeria* (Longman/Nigerian Institute of Bankers, London).

Outters-Jaeger, I. (1979) *The Development Impact of Barter in Developing Countries.* OECD, Paris.

Papanek, G. F. (1973) Aid, foreign private investment, savings and growth in less developed countries. *Journal of Political Economy,* **8** (1), 120–130.

Parkinson, J. M. (1984) The Nairobi Stock Exchange in the context of development of Kenya. *Savings and Development,* **VIII** (4), 363–372.

Patrick, H. T. (1966) Financial development and economic growth in underdeveloped countries. *Economic Development and Cultural Change,* **XIV** (2), 174–189 (January).

Patrick, H. T. (1972) Finance, capital markets and economic growth in Japan. In Sametz, H. W. (ed.), *Financial Development and Economic Growth.* New York University Press, 109–139.

Patrick, H. T. and Rosovsky, H. (eds) (1976) *Asia's New Giant. How the Japanese Economy Works.* Brookings Institution, Washington, DC.

Payer, C. (1974) *The Debt Trap.* Penguin, Harmondsworth.

Pearson, L. B. (1969) *Partners in Development: Report.* Commission on International Development.

Pedse, D. R. (1985) Some reflections on the role of donor agencies in the privatisation process. *National Westminster Bank Quarterly Review,* 2–18 (November).

Pichler, H. (1982) 'Comments' on Systems of Indexation. In Bruck, N. (ed.), *Capital Markets under Inflation.* Praeger, New York, pp. 206–217.

Pischke, J. D., von, and Rouse, J. (1983) Selected successful experiences in agricultural credit and rural finance in Africa. *Savings and Development,* VII (1), 21–44.

Polak, J. J. (1957) Monetary analysis of income formation and payments problems. *IMF Staff Papers,* 6, 1–50 (November).

Porter, R. C. (1966) The promotion of the banking habit and economic development. *Journal of Development Studies,* 2 (4), 346–366 (July).

Pouliquen, L. Y. (1970) Risk analysis in project appraisal. World Bank Staff Occasional Paper No. 11, IBRD, Washington, DC.

Prest, A. R. (1978) The taxable capacity of a country. In Toye, J. F. J. (ed.), *Taxation and Economic Development.* Frank Cass, London, pp. 13–22.

Prindl, A. R. (1976) *Foreign Exchange Risk.* Wiley–Interscience, London.

Radke, D., and Taake, H. H. (1983) Financial crisis management in Egypt and Turkey. *Journal of World Trade Law,* 17 (4), 325–336 (July/August).

Rahman, M. A. (1968) Foreign capital and domestic savings: a test of Haavelmo's hypothesis with cross-country data. *Review of Economics and Statistics,* 50 (1), 137–138 (February).

Randall, R. W. (1972) *Real del Monte: a British mining venture in Mexico.* University of Texas Press for the Institute of Latin American Studies. Latin American Monographs No. 26.

Ranis, G. (1983) Global implications of the 'Mexican disease'. *The Financial Times,* 12 January.

Rao, J. C. (1981) *Financing of Manufacturing Enterprises in India.* UNIDO, Vienna.

Reichmann, T. M. (1978) The Fund's conditional assistance and the problems of adjustment. *Finance and Development,* 15 (4), 38–41 (December).

Reichmann, T. M. and Stillson, R. (1978) Experience with programs of balance of payments adjustment: stand-by arrangements in the higher credit tranches 1963–1972. *IMF Staff Papers,* 25 (2), 293–319.

Rietti, M. (1979) *Money and Banking in Latin America.* Praeger, New York.

Rippy, J. F. *British Investments in Latin America, 1822–1949.* University of Minnesota.

Rischer, G. (1975) The Teheran Stock Exchange. *Euromoney* (supplement), 32–36 (May).

Roll, R. (1972) Interest rates on monetary assets and commodity price index changes. *Journal of Finance,* 27 (2), 251–277 (May).

Roll, R. (1977) A critique of the asset pricing theory's tests: Part I: On past and potential testability of the theory. *Journal of Financial Economics,* 4, 129–176 (March).

Ross, S. A. (1976a) Return, risk and arbitrage. In Friend, I, and Bicksler, J. (eds), *Risk and Return in Finance.* Ballinger, Cambridge, Mass., pp. 189–218.

Ross, S. A. (1976b) The arbitrage theory of capital asset pricing. *Journal of Economic Theory,* 13, 341–360 (December).

Rugman, A. M. (1979) *International Diversification and the Multinational Enterprise.* Farnborough, Lexington.

Samuels, J. M. (1981) Inefficient capital markets and their implications. In Derkinderen, F. G. J., and Crum, R. L. (eds), *Risk, Capital Costs and Project Financing Decisions.* Martinus Nijhoff, Boston/The Hague/London, 129–148.

Samuels, J. M., and Yacout, N. (1981) Stock exchanges in developing countries. *Savings and Development,* V (4), 217–232.

Schydlowsky, D. M. (1982) Alternative approaches to short term economic management in developing countries. In Killick, T. (ed.), *Adjustment and Financing in the Developing World; The Role of the International Monetary Fund.* IMF, Washington, DC/ODI, London, pp. 105–135.

Seers, D. (1981) Inflation: the Latin American experience. Institute of Development Studies Discussion Paper 188, Brighton, England.

Shapiro, A. C. (1982) *Multinational Financial Management*. Allyn and Becan, Boston.

Sharpe, W. F. (1963) A simplified model for portfolio analysis. *Management Science*, **9**, 277–293 (January).

Sharpe, W. F. (1964) Capital asset prices: a theory of market equilibrium under conditions of risk. *Journal of Finance*, **19**, 10–18 (September).

Shaw, E. S. (1973) *Financial Deepening in Economic Development*. Oxford University Press, New York/London.

Shetty, M. C. (1982) *Financing of Manufacturing Enterprises in Bangladesh, Indonesia, Malaysia, Sri Lanka and Thailand*. UNIDO, Vienna.

Spraos, J. (1984) IMF conditionality—a better way. *Banca Nazionale del Lavoro Quarterly Review*, No. 151, 411–422 (December).

Stamp, M. (1958) The Fund and the future. *Lloyds Bank Review*, No. 50, 1–20 (October).

Stern, E. (1983) World Bank financing of structural adjustment. In Williamson, J. (ed.), *IMF Conditionality*. Institute for International Economics, Washington, DC, pp. 87–108.

Stewart, F., and Stewart, M. (1980) A new currency for trade amongst developing countries. *UNCTAD Trade and Development Review*, No. 2, 69–82 (August).

Stiglitz, J. E. (1981) The allocation role of the stock market. Pareto optimality and competition. *Journal of Finance*, **36** (2), 235–251 (May).

Stokke, O. (ed.) (1984) *European Development Assistance* (2 vols). European Association of Development Research and Training Institutes, Tilburg/Norwegian Institutes of International Affairs, Oslo.

Sweeny, R. J. (1982) An alternative test of the capital asset pricing model: comment. *American Economic Review*, **72** (5), 1196–1200 (December).

Tait, A. A., Grätz, W. L. M., and Eichengreen, B. J. (1979) International comparison of taxation for selected developing countries, 1972–76. *IMF Staff Papers*, **26** (1), 123–156 (March).

Taylor, L. (1981) IS/LM in the tropics: diagrammatics of the new structuralist macro critique. In Cline, W. R., and Weintraub, S. (eds), *Economic Stabilisation in Developing Countries*. Brookings Institution, Washington, DC, pp. 465–506.

Tew, B. (1982) *The Evolution of the International Monetary System 1945–81*, 2nd edition. Hutchinson, London.

Thirlwall, A. P. (1976) When is trade more valuable than aid? *Journal of Development Studies*, **12** (5), 35–41.

Thirlwall, A. P. (1983) Confusion over measuring the relative worth of trade and aid. *World Development*, **11** (1), 71–72 (January).

Timberg, T. A., and Aiyar, C. V. (1984) Informal credit markets in India. *Economic Development and Cultural Change*, **33** (1), 43–60 (October).

Toye, J. F. J. ed. (1978) *Taxation and Economic Development*. Frank Cass, London.

Trebat, T. (1980) An Evaluation of the Economic Performance of Large Public Enterprises in Brazil 1965–1975. Technical Papers, Series 24. University of Austin, Texas.

Turnbull, S. M., and Winter, R. A. (1982) An alternative test of the capital asset pricing theory: comment. *American Economic Review*, **72** (5), 1194–1195 (December).

UNCTAD (1974) *Export credits as a means of promoting exports from developing countries* (TD/B/494). UNCTAD, Geneva.

UNCTC (1983a) *Transnational Corporations in World Development: Third Survey*. UN, New York.

UNCTC (1983b) *Issues in Negotiating International Loan Agreements with Transnational Banks*. UN, New York.

UNESCO (1973) *Savings Mobilisation in Developing African Countries*. UNESCO, Paris.

346

UNIDO (1979) *Industry 2000—New Perspectives*. UN, New York.
UNIDO (1979a) *Industry 2000–New Perspectives*. Collected Background Papers Vol I International Financial Flows. UNIDO/IOD324, Vienna.
United Nations (1949) *International Capital Movements during the Inter-war Period*. UN, New York.
United Nations (1956) *Financing of Economic Development: the International Flow of Private Capital, 1953–1955*. UNESCOSOC, New York.
Vernon, R. (1966) International investment and international trade in the product cycle. *Quarterly Journal of Economics*, **80**, 190–207.
Vogel, R. C., and Buser, S. A. (1976) Inflation, financial repression and capital formation in Latin America. In McKinnon, R. I. (ed.), *Money and Finance in Economic Development*. Marcel Dekker, New York, pp. 35–69.
Wai, U. Tun (1957) Interest rates outside the organised money markets of underdeveloped countries. *IMF Staff Papers*, **VI** (1), 80–142 (November).
Wai, U. Tun (1972) *Financial Intermediaries and National Savings in Developing Countries*. Praeger, New York.
Wai, U. Tun (1977) A revisit to interest rates outside the organized money markets of underdeveloped countries. *Banca Nazionale del Lavoro Quarterly Review*, No. 122, 291–312 (September).
Wai, U. Tun, and Patrick, H. T. (1973) Stock and bond issues and capital markets in less developed countries. *IMF Staff Papers*, 253–317 (July); reprinted in Wai, U. Tun. (1980).
(Wai (1957 and 1977), and Wai, U. Tun, and Patrick, H. (1977) are reprinted in Wai, U. Tun (1980) *Economic Essays on Developing Countries*. Sijthoff and Noordhoff, Alphen an den Rijn, Netherlands.)
Walsh, J. I. (1983) Countertrade: not just for East–West any more. *Journal of World Trade Law,* **17** (1), 3–11 (January/February).
Weisskopf, T. E. (1972) The impact of foreign capital inflow on domestic savings in underdeveloped countries. *Journal of International Economics,* **2** (1), 25–38 (February).
Wellons, P. A. (1977) *Borrowing by Developing Countries on the Eurocurrency Market*. OECD, Paris.
Wellons, P. A. (1983) The case of the 'Grupo Pliana' in Mexico. OECD, mimeo, Paris.
Wells, L. T. Jr (1983) *Third World Multinationals. The Rise of Foreign Investment from Developing Countries*. MIT Press, Cambridge, Mass.
White B. (1984) International differences in gearing: how important are they? *National Westminster Bank Quarterly Review*, 14–25 (November).
White, J. (1974) *The Politics of Foreign Aid*. Bodley Head, London.
Van Wijnbergen, S. (1982) Interest rate management in developing countries, theory and simulation results for Korea. World Bank Staff Working Papers, No. 593.
Williamson, J. (ed.) (1983) *IMF Conditionality*. Institute for International Economics, Washington, DC.
Wilson, F. A. (1980) Commercial banks and rural credit. In Howell, J. (ed.), *Borrowers and Lenders: Rural Financial Markets and Institutions in Developing Countries*. Overseas Development Institute, London, 131–140.
Winkler, M. (1933) *Foreign Bonds: An Autopsy*. Swain, Philadelphia.
Witt, S. F. (1978) International portfolio diversification. *Managerial Finance,* **4** (2), 198–203.
Witt, S. F. and Dobbins, R. (eds) (1979) *An Introduction to Portfolio Management*. MCB Publications, Bradford.
Woolmer, K. J. (1977) The financial system and economic development in Nigeria, 1950–1971. In Newlyn, W. T. (ed.), *The Financing of Economic Development*. Clarendon Press, Oxford, pp. 259–286.
World Bank (1968) *Economic Growth, Trade and the Balance of Payments in the*

Developing Countries 1960–65. Economics Department Report No. EC–159. IBRD, Washington, DC.

World Bank (1975) *Agricultural Credit: Sector Policy Paper*. World Bank, Washington, DC.

World Bank (1978) *Employment and Development of Small Enterprises: Sector Policy Paper*. World Bank, Washington, DC.

World Bank (1979) State Intervention in the Industrialisation of Developing Countries: Selected Issues. World Bank Staff Working Paper No. 341.

World Bank (1984) *The World Bank Annual Report 1984*. World Bank, Washington, DC.

World Bank (1985) *World Development Report 1985*. Oxford University Press, Oxford.

Yagci, F., Jamin, S., and Rosenbaum, V. (1985) Structural adjustment lending. An evaluation of program design. World Bank Staff Working Papers, No. 735.

Yassin, I. H. (1982) When is Trade More Valuable than Aid? Revisited. *World Development,* **10** (2), 161–166 (February).

Author Index

348

350

Subject Index